The Longest War

Sex Differences in Perspective

SECOND EDITION

The Longest War

Sex Differences in Perspective

SECOND EDITION

Carol Tavris

Carole Wade

San Diego Mesa College

Under the Series Editorship of Irving L. Janis, Yale University

HARCOURT BRACE JOVANOVICH, PUBLISHERS
San Diego New York Chicago Washington, D.C. Atlanta
London Sydney Toronto

With love to my mother,
who taught me to want to become something,
and to the memory of my father,
who believed I could become anything I wanted.

Carol Tavris

To my children, Jessica and Jason,
whose generation is a step closer to the truce.

Carole Wade

ISBN: 0-15-551186-6
Library of Congress Catalog Card Number: 83-82510
Printed in the United States of America

Cover and interior art by Saul Bass/Herb Yager and Associates.

Copyrights and Acknowledgments and Illustration Credits appear on pages
401–02, which constitute a continuation of the copyright page.

At any rate, when a subject is highly controversial—and any question about sex is that—one cannot hope to tell the truth. One can only show how one came to hold the opinion one does hold. One can only give one's audience the chance of drawing their own conclusions as they observe the limitations, the prejudices, the idiosyncrasies of the speaker.

—Virginia Woolf, *A Room of One's Own*

Preface

The battle of the sexes is not only the longest war but the oldest mystery. There are many puzzles in the relationship of the sexes: Why isn't "man's best friend" woman? Why has male supremacy rather than status equality been the norm? Why is men's work everywhere more valued than women's work? Why have women not achieved as much as men have in science, business, politics, the arts? Why, when so many men and women love each other, is there so much distrust and animosity between them as well? Why are people inclined to emphasize the sexual differences between men and women, instead of their human similarities?

When we began working on the first edition of this book, in the early 1970s, these questions had just erupted into national debate and scholarly research. Unfortunately, those who were seeking thoughtful answers to them were in the position Alfred Kinsey, the ground-breaking sex researcher, was when he set out to teach human sexuality in the late 1930s: ignorant. Much of the existing evidence that people were calling on to argue that "women were X" and "men were Y" was outdated, flawed, or biased.

But in the remarkably short time of a decade, studies of women and men have burgeoned: We are learning about women previously lost to history; about men's changing feelings and desires; about the physiology and psychology of sex and gender; about work, love, the family, and how people seek to combine them. In that same decade the political debate has sharpened its teeth: The women's movement has grown and organized, changed focus, provoked a backlash. Meanwhile, quietly, its basic goals—once considered radical and hysterical—have been accepted by the great majority of Americans: equal pay for equal work; protection against rape and sexual harassment; more freedom for men to be nurturant, expressive, paternal; the belief that it is just fine for women to work, that work does not make them "unnatural" or "unwomanly." The old saying "A woman's place is in the home" has, in ten years, shifted to "A woman's place is in the house—and Senate."

The Second Edition of this book includes and reflects both the new scholarship about the sexes and the continuing emotional and political debate about the relationship between the sexes. Throughout, we have tried to distinguish *what is* from what people think *ought to be*; people may try to keep the difference clear, but in everyday conversation and political argument they often forget to do so. The *facts* are that most women now work for pay and will do so for most of their lives; that the sexual double standard is fading; that most women are still victims of economic discrimination. Conservatives and liberals, however, tend to disagree about whether these facts are good or bad, and about what to do about them.

We have kept the basic framework of the book—showing how each of several disciplines approaches the question of sex differences—but in each chapter we have updated the research by adding new studies, deleting those that have not survived the test of time and replication, and adding more about men. The result has proved to be a revision more sweeping than we had expected of virtually every chapter. But we wish to encourage the reader not to get mired in particular, time-bound findings about our society, since these can change with rather astonishing speed; instead keep in mind the *perspective* each chapter offers. When you do that, you notice that the more some things change, the more they remain the same.

We begin with an introductory chapter that describes the historical tendency to see the female sex as the different one, the one to be explained. To fully appreciate the contemporary scene, we believe, a person needs to know how the stage was set. The next two chapters (Part I) explore the gap between stereotype and reality, reporting what research has found about the actual differences between women and men in ability, personality, and sexuality.

To account for the strength of sexual stereotypes and the survival of status differences between men and women, Part II examines sex differences from five perspectives, beginning with the smallest unit of analysis, the individual, and moving outward to larger social units. Each perspective has a different emphasis. The biological perspective (Chapter 4) regards sex differences in behavior and status as a result of hormonal, genetic, and reproductive differences. The psychoanalytic perspective (Chapter 5) emphasizes unconscious processes and the way anatomy influences the feelings and sexual development of women and men. The learning perspective (Chapter 6) considers the ways children acquire the culture's standards of masculinity and femininity. The sociological perspective (Chapter 7) stresses the influence of organizations and social roles on people's attitudes and behavior, particularly through the institutions of work and the family. The anthropological perspective (Chapter 8) looks at the adaptive value of social customs for the survival of societies and explains sex roles in terms of the material needs, ecology, and technology of a culture.

Researchers who study sex differences are like archeologists: each marks an area for excavation and digs independently, hoping to unearth the city that lies beneath them all. Each finds fragments—a tool here, a potsherd there—but the complete city has yet to be revealed. The problem is not that one field is searching in the right way while another is trying to shovel dirt with teaspoons. It is that each discipline raises questions specific to its interests, defines goals and problems in its own way, and uses its particular methods to get answers. For example, in psychology the study of sex differences (and, occasionally, similarities) tends to produce descriptions of how women and men do on various tests, or how they act in certain situations. The nature of psychological inquiry, by definition, focuses on the individual, usually at a specific moment in history. Psychological explanations often overlook cultural relativity and changes over time. On the other hand, sociologists, whose central business is to study groups, organizations, and societies, tend to minimize the role of the brain and the body in explaining human behavior. In the final chapter (9), we attempt to integrate the various perspectives and analyze some twentieth-century efforts to achieve sexual equality.

Because the book focuses on differences between the sexes, we had to sacrifice important questions of class and race differences within each sex. The life of a Roman slave had little in common with that of a wealthy Roman. In our own society, the gap between rich and poor, of whatever sex and race, creates enormous differences in people's attitudes and behavior. Further, the lives of many black women, who endure the double prejudice of color and sex, are not wholly comparable to the lives of many white women. For instance, studies on achievement motivation, socialization, family life, and economic discrimination find differences between black women and white. But to summarize these findings without space to discuss them would be more confusing than helpful, we thought, and would deflect attention from our main topic: the chasm between women and men of all classes, cultures, and races.

The subject of sex and status differences is both personally immediate and politically explosive. Questions about sex and the sexes are not mere intellectual puzzles. They affect real human lives and have consequences for all of us. In this book, we have tried to follow a fine line between the bland neutrality that feigns fairness and the polemical commitment that obscures divergent points of view. In addition to evaluating studies and theories in scientific terms, we discuss their social and political implications, pointing out bias at both ends of the political spectrum. When our search for scientific answers led to data-less dead ends, we occasionally turned to personal experience and hunches, which most scientists publicly discount but privately admit inform their most inspired work. We do not apologize for our anecdotes and hunches. They are clearly labeled and cannot be mistaken for scientific truths. Besides, from little hunches mighty theories grow.

This book can be used as a core text or supplement in courses on women's studies, sex differences, women and men, and gender. It will also fit into broader courses that include a unit on sex differences or male-female relations, such as human development, personality, social psychology, social problems, and marriage and the family. Some instructors in the fields of cultural anthropology, political science, sociology, and biology also deal with male-female issues in enough detail to make the book useful. Finally, it may find a place in interdisciplinary courses, since it demonstrates how various groups of scientists formulate and try to answer the same basic questions. Because the book was written mainly for undergraduates, we have kept technical terminology to a minimum and tried to make underlying concepts explicit. Our goal was for readers of all backgrounds and disciplines to be able to understand and evaluate the material. Most of all, we have tried to retain the sense of humor that keeps human beings sane in the face of serious issues.

Many people helped us finish *The Longest War*. We are grateful to our editors on the first edition, manuscript editor Catherine Caldwell Brown and supervising editor Judith Greissman, who helped us shape the basic concept and style; and to their counterparts on the Second Edition, Nola Healy Lynch and Marcus Boggs, whose commitment to the book and moral support kept us going. In addition we again wish to thank Saul Bass and Art Goodman, of Saul Bass/ Herb Yager and Associates, for the apt and delightful cover illustration and chapter drawings. And our gratitude to designer Nancy Shehorn, chief copy editor Catherine Fauver, and production supervisor Pat Braus of Harcourt Brace Jovanovich for their excellent work.

Our academic reviewers and advisers on both editions did their job superbly, criticizing the hardest way—constructively. We wish especially to thank Karen E. Paige, University of California, Davis; Leonore Tiefer, Beth Israel Medical Center, New York; Phillip Shaver,

University of Denver; Cynthia Fuchs Epstein, Queens College; Michele Wittig, California State University, Northridge; Ruth Doell; Letitia Anne Peplau, University of California, Los Angeles; Anne C. Peterson, University of Chicago; Sandra Scarr, University of Virginia; Irving L. Janis, Yale University; Brian Weiss; Robert Merton, Columbia University; Constance L. Hammen, University of California, Los Angeles; Rebecca Stafford, Bemidji State University; Julia R. Heiman, University of Washington; Rose L. Coser, State University of New York at Stony Brook; and Carol Roberts, San Diego Mesa College. We were also aided enormously by those for whom the book was written, students, whose questions, reactions, and complaints directed us to obscurities in the text and to the issues that most concern them.

Finally, our love to the men who love us, and who help us live through the longest war even as we write about it.

Carol Tavris
Carole Wade (Offir)

Contents

Preface   vii

1 | **Introduction: The longest war**   1

the bitter half: themes of misogyny   5
*controlling female sexuality   keeping women in their
place   justifying female inferiority*
the female paradox: attitudes versus reality   16
cultural consistencies   an American dilemma
perspectives on female "otherness"   31

I | *The sexes: Defining the qualities*

2 | **Sex differences, real and imagined**   37

sex differences in physical attributes   43
physical strength   health   activity level   manual dexterity
sex differences in ability   46
*general intelligence   verbal ability   quantitative ability
spatial-visual ability   creativity   cognitive style
mental sex differences: how impressive?*
sex differences in personality   57
*sociability   empathy   emotionality   dependence
susceptibility to influence   self-esteem and
confidence   nurturance   aggressiveness   why personality
differences are elusive*
connections, values, morality: two voices   75

3 | **Sex and love**   81

the Victorian heritage   83
the scientific study of sex   86

the body sexual: his and hers   89
  the sexual response cycle   the matter of multiples
  the vaginal-clitoral debate
sex in mind and action   98
  sexual fantasies   responses to erotica   masturbation
  premarital and extramarital sex   homosexuality
perceptions of sex and love   110
  sexual motives   the mixed messages of courtship
  romance versus intimacy

II | *The sexes: Explaining the inequalities*

4 | Genes, hormones, and instincts: The biological perspective   123

sociobiology: Darwin with a twist   126
  the data gap   dispensable genes   of biology and baboons
prenatal factors   135
  genes and gender   prenatal sex hormones
sex hormones in adults   143
  menstruation and mood   menopause and
  melancholy   testosterone, temperament, and thought
  the maternal instinct
sex differences: a matter of gray matter?   163
evaluating the biological perspective   168

5 | Freud, fantasy, and the fear of woman: The psychoanalytic perspective   173

the unconscious   176
the psychosexual stages of development   179
  the Oedipus complex   consequences of penis envy
  "anatomy is destiny"
attacks on penis envy   185
  a social metaphor?   men's envy of women   men's fear of women
evaluating psychoanalysis   195
  reality or fantasy? the "seduction theory"   science or art?
  experimental evidence   existential identity and vulnerability

6 Getting the message: The learning perspective 207

socialization theories: two sexes and how they grow 213
 social-learning theory cognitive-developmental
 theory identification
sources of socialization 221
 parents: perceptions and lessons teachers: the hidden
 curriculum sex typing as child's play media messages
 subliminal communication
learning about sex 236
some consequences of socialization 238
 the androgynous alternative beyond androgyny
evaluating the learning perspective 244
 a case in point: the achievement motive personality and power

7 Earning the bread versus baking it: The sociological perspective 251

work: grand or grind? 254
 opportunity power the trouble with tokens the work
 force and the forces on work
marriage: cage or castle? 273
 his and hers marriages why wives wilt and husbands thrive: the
 housewife syndrome the working-wife syndrome of housework
 and husbands the family battleground
evaluating the sociological perspective 291

8 The origins of roles and rituals: The anthropological perspective 297

some customs in social context 304
 social dilemmas and sexual rituals sexuality versus the system
 the puzzle of purdah
subsistence and status: why men matter more 319
 the Marxist model man the hunter, woman the
 life-giver? digression: a fable hunters and gatherers
 versus horticulturalists
evaluating the anthropological perspective 331

9 Conclusion: The age of alliance?   337

experiments in equality   339
*the Soviet Union   the People's Republic of China   the
Scandinavian countries   the Israeli kibbutz   an American
experiment: the dual-career couple   defining equality*
the perspectives in perspective   353
*sex ratios and social life   the denial of disadvantage
the age of alliance*

References   369

Index   403

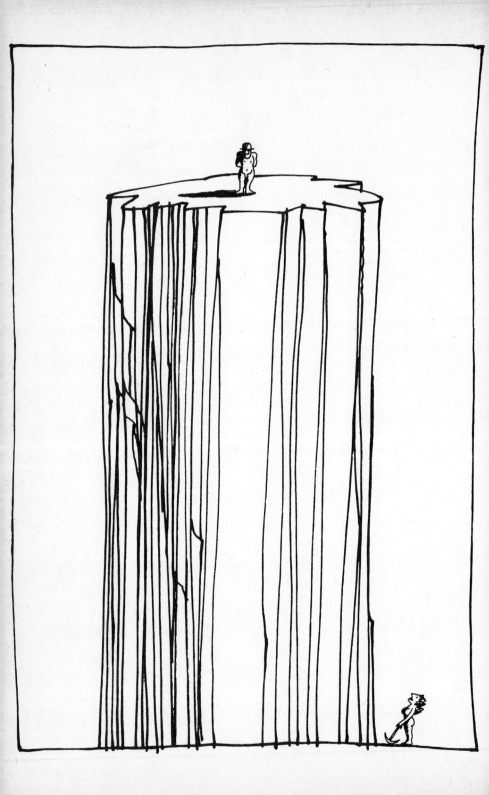

1 | Introduction: The longest war

Men and women are two halves of the same species, so one might expect them to fit together like two sides of a coin. Yet throughout history the sexes have regarded each other less as fellow human beings than as alien and exotic creatures—to be loved, feared, cherished, or confined. In every society, in every century, people have assumed that males and females are different not merely in basic anatomy but in elusive qualities of spirit, soul, and ability. They are not supposed to do the same things, think the same way, or share the same dreams and desires.

Men and women have wooed each other with lustful abandon and ritual restraint, but they have also fought—if not with military weapons, then with psychological, economic, and sexual ones. The battle of the sexes began in the sleepy dawn of prehistory and has continued to the present. There have been countless alliances and dalliances across enemy lines, but the peace treaties never seem to last. It is truly the longest war.

It is also the longest love affair, of course, and the great love stories in history still thrill us: Abélard and Héloïse, Beatrice and Dante, Robert Browning and Elizabeth Barrett, Antony and Cleopatra, the Duke and Duchess of Windsor. But love does not guarantee equal, or even kind, treatment. Periander of Corinth married Melissa of Epidaurus for love, six centuries before Christ, but that didn't keep him from murdering her in a jealous rage—and it was his legal right to do so. The puzzle is why history sometimes records more affinity between man and dog (or horse, or even camel) than between man and woman. Misogyny, the hatred of women, has enjoyed a long and robust tradition, and the enmity on the male side of the sexual barrier has been more openly expressed than that on the female side. Although the Greeks wrote of the Amazons as a "man-hating, man-killing" group, there are few accounts of women who were fervently antimale, and we have no common word for a woman's hatred of men. The word for man-hating, misandry, appears in only a few unabridged dictionaries and rarely in everyday language. Woman-hating is an established custom, with articulate and eminent spokesmen (and, sadly, spokeswomen).

Nonsense, some readers will say, most men *love* women, and vice versa. It is not fair to pick out a few surly males and label the whole lot misogynists. Woman has been esteemed, worshipped, and protected as often as she has been loathed, ignored, and reviled. True. We call these apparently opposite attitudes the pedestal-gutter syndrome. Woman is goddess and devil, virgin and whore, sweet madonna and malevolent mom; she can bring a man up to salvation or drag him down with her to hell. On the face of it, the pedestal-gutter syndrome appears to reflect views that are diametrically opposed: woman is good, woman is bad. But in fact these views represent a single attitude: woman is different. After all, whether you are looking up to women or stooping down to them, you don't have to look them in the eye.

Differences by themselves need not cause animosity. It is only when one group considers the other to be immoral, deficient, or dangerous that conflict arises. In the relationship between the sexes, women have been regarded as deficient men, insatiable sexpots, and incarnations of evil. They are the second sex, the weaker sex, the inferior sex, the sex to be explained. The "woman problem" has proved such an obsession to men that we emerged from our reading with a new sense of appreciation for ourselves. Our sex has been the object of a 10,000-year worry.

Man's concern about woman is marked by passion and paradox. As long as man sees woman as the opposite sex, the mysterious one, he can never explain her satisfactorily. She will shift and change as he does, like a reflection in a pool. The poet Semonides of Amorgos summarized male ambivalence in the seventh century B.C.: "For Zeus designed [woman] as the greatest of all evils—and bound us to it in unbreakable fetters." The fetters are need and desire, but in spite of (or perhaps because of) these powerful motivations, men and women have never faced each other as equals. No culture anywhere has said, "OK, women, who have wombs, will bear the children. Men, who are strong, will fight the wars. Now we can divvy up control of the gods, the arts, the politics, and the McDonald's franchises." Men and women have never shared power, privilege, and status on an equal basis.

Instead, every society has distinguished men's work from women's work and created barriers between the sexes. Sometimes men and women have had so little to do with one another that one wonders how the population explosion ever managed to take place. Sarah Pomeroy (1975), a historian, reported that in classical Athens, which people usually regard as a highly civilized city, the segregation of the sexes was so complete that husbands had to be directed by law to consort with their wives three times a month. That was more than enough, the law supposed, to produce the required number of heirs and, added Plutarch, to reduce marital tensions. Even today, men and women in some cultures work, sleep, and eat apart from each other, getting together on only a few critical occasions for the sake of the species.

The basic questions this book tries to answer are: Why are the sexes so alien to each other? Why are lovers not more often friends? Why has an equal society never existed on this planet? In the first part of this chapter we review three prominent and recurrent themes that seem to characterize men's reflections on women: how to control women's sexuality, assure their obedience, and justify their inferior status. We chose these themes in order to illustrate how attitudes can legitimize inequality, not in an effort to argue that a male conspiracy has caused it. These pervasive male concerns about women provide a background for later chapters, for the themes change in shape but never in substance across the centuries.

And what have women thought about men? In general, until fairly recently, we haven't known as much about women's attitudes toward men as we have about men's attitudes toward women. "In the war of the sexes, as in other wars," wrote Morton Hunt (1967), "history is written by the victors." But persistent historians are now discovering some of the forgotten voices of history. Occasionally, a female voice has lamented inequity and hypocrisy between the sexes: At the turn of the fourteenth century Christine de Pizan wrote numerous poems and essays on women's roles in France. She emphasized the importance for women of education, economic security, and civil rights; these would, she thought, make relations between men and women stronger and more honest. Indeed, Marcia Guttentag and Paul Secord (1983) have observed:

> Christine de Pizan's themes sound amazingly modern: a call to women to prepare themselves for the exigencies of independence, a realistic appraisal of their need to be socially pliant because of their dependence on men and families when they are without civil rights, and a cynical view of men's avowals of love in relationships with women that are sexual and transient. (p. 67)

But many women (such as the eleventh-century historian Anna Comnena or the second-century writer Lady Pan Chao) have accepted the prevailing male view that even the best women are lesser men. And in other societies women have disliked men as much as men have disliked women: In Morocco, for example, men think men are mature, responsible, and self-controlled, but women think men are uncontrolled, self-indulgent, and irresponsible (Mernissi 1975; Dwyer 1978).

Even today in the United States, where both sexes seem to agree on the general superiority of men, we can find many books by women that treat men as if they were childish, silly, weak, and helpless (such as *The Total Woman, The Fulfilled Woman, The Power of the Positive Woman*). Writer Mary Kay Blakely (1983) has noted that under the "saccharin surface of unconditional love" that these authors recommend women give their men, "disgust is audible." The real man-haters, according to Blakely, are women who believe men are stupid and vain enough to be manipulated—not the feminists, who are hopeful of relationships between equals:

> Phyllis Schlafly advises, "A Positive Woman cannot defeat a man in a wrestling or boxing match, but she can motivate him, inspire him, encourage him, teach him, restrain him, reward him, and have power over him that he can never achieve over her with all his muscle." Notice how like a Doberman pinscher the Positive Woman's man is? (p. 136)

What men and women say about each other, however, frequently bears little resemblance to what the sexes actually *do*, and this discrepancy is itself fascinating. Thus in the second part of this chapter we contrast what men think about women with the realities of how they act. Finally, we describe the organization of the rest of the book, which examines the riddle of female "otherness" from various perspectives.

the bitter half: themes of misogyny

controlling female sexuality

Woman is a pitfall—a pitfall, a hole, a ditch,
Woman is a sharp iron dagger that cuts a man's throat.

—Babylonian poet

Woman as a treacherous, seductive manipulator of sexual wiles appears in the earliest recorded literature. In the Gilgamesh epic, a Babylonian classic, the gods create Enkidu from clay to fight Gilgamesh and save the city of Erech. Gilgamesh sends a harlot to distract Enkidu. She does.

She put aside her robe and he lay upon her.
She used on him, the savage, a woman's wiles.
His passion responded to her.

For six days and seven nights Enkidu approached and coupled with the
    prostitute.
After he was sated with her charms,
He set his face toward his game.

(Quoted in Bullough 1973, p. 28)

Enkidu, innocence lost, is now in trouble: his knees wobble, he
weakens, he loses speed. He has learned what Samson will learn
from Delilah, Marc Antony from Cleopatra, and a generation—a past
one, we hope—of football players from their coaches: Sex saps your
strength. (Just for the record, it doesn't.)

Every great religion and almost all regional ones warn men about
women's seductiveness. The Manu code of India, a set of laws dating
from about A.D. 100, explains that "it is in the nature of women to
seduce men [and] for that reason the wise are never unguarded [in
the company of] females. For women are able to lead astray in this
world not only a fool, but even a learned man, and to make him a
slave of desire and anger."

In the Judeo-Christian tradition, the story of Adam and Eve warns
of the tragedy that awaits the man who yields to the temptation of
woman: He must lose paradise. Actually, according to the ancient
Hebrews, God tried three times to make a suitable partner for the first
man. The first woman, Lilith, was made of "filth and sediment"
instead of Adam's pure dust, and she behaved accordingly. She even
had the gall to say, "Why must I lie beneath you? I also was made
from dust, and am therefore your equal" (quoted in Figes 1970).
Naturally Adam was offended and tried to force her into obedience.
Lilith, furious, took off and populated the world with evil demons.
God then tried a second time to give Adam a mate he could tolerate,
but this attempt also failed. Finally God came up with Eve, and we all
know what she did.

The story of Lilith associates the sexual mysteries of women with
reproductive ones. Men have thought of women as not only seductive but unclean. For example, throughout history men have reacted
to menstruation with a mixture of awe, pity, disgust, and fear. The
early Siberians made menstruating women sit in a special hut and
wear a special hat so they would not contaminate the heavens, much
less the men. Segregated menstrual huts are still common in many

parts of the world. The Australian aborigines feared the menstrual flow so much that a man who found his menstruating wife on his blanket might be moved to kill her. The Roman writer Pliny published a long list of the "virulent effects" of the menstrual discharge. He warned that menstruating women could cause bees to abandon their hives, pregnant mares to miscarry, and fruit to fall from the tree. Further, they could blunt the edge of a good razor, sour new wine, and make green grass wither. Religions have reinforced such fears. The Old Testament forbade men to touch a menstruating woman lest they too become "unclean," and Orthodox Jewish women today must still take a ritual bath, the mikvah, following their periods. Hindu law decreed that a menstruating woman should not look at anyone, even her own children. Zoroaster wrote that a menstruating woman was the work of the devil, and during her "periodical illness" she was not to gaze upon the sacred fire, behold the sun, or talk to a man. The Koran, the holy book of Islam, calls the menstruating woman a "pollution." Women themselves accepted the belief in menstrual uncleanliness and transmitted it to their daughters and sons.

Many cultures warned men about the horrible things that could happen to those who yield to female sexual mysteries and lures: they might turn weak, they might die, their penises might fall off, they might lose magic powers. Because sex was so powerful and mysterious, it was taboo on many occasions—before going to war, or hunting, or playing sports, or engaging in serious business.

The harder men tried to suppress their own sexuality, the more anxious their descriptions of female sexuality became. The most intense reaction probably occurred in that heyday of celibacy, the Middle Ages. Monks and priests, striving to adhere to the Christian ideal of sexual abstinence in thought as well as deed, found an outlet in eloquent name calling. Salimbene, a thirteenth-century Franciscan monk, collected some of his colleagues' thoughts on the matter:

> Wouldst thou define or know what a woman is? She is glittering mud, a stinking rose, sweet poison, ever leaning toward that which is forbidden her.

> Woman is adamant, pitch, buckthorn, a rough thistle, a clinging burr, a stinging wasp, a burning nettle.

> Lo, woman is the head of sin, a weapon of the devil, expulsion from paradise, mother of guilt, corruption of the ancient law.

> (Quoted in Bullough 1973, p. 173)

Male anxiety is also revealed in an inflammatory book written by two Dominican theologians in the fifteenth century, Heinrich Kramer and Jacob Sprenger. They issued the *Malleus Maleficarum* (Witches' Hammer), a sort of introductory textbook about the black arts. The two monks had been appointed by Pope Innocent VII as inquisitors and told to wipe out witchcraft in Germany. Their book explained, among other things, why there were fewer male than female witches. Women, they concluded, are more superstitious than men, weaker in mind and body, and insatiable in their sexuality—vices that make them particularly susceptible to the devil. Men, themselves tainted by original sin, had better be on guard lest these voluptuous vessels of lust entice them to the devil's work (van Vuuren 1973).

Few male writers in any age have considered the possibility that a man might stray because *he* is weak or sexually insatiable. The blame has always gone to the woman. (This still happens today, as when rapists protest that they didn't do anything wrong—the victim provoked them by looking seductive.) A fourteenth-century English preacher warned his congregation about the startling power of a provocative woman:

> In the woman wantonly adorned to capture souls, the garland upon her head is as a single coal or firebrand of Hell to kindle men with that fire. . . . In a single day, she inflames with the fire of her lust perhaps twenty of those who behold her, damning the souls God has created and redeemed at such a cost. (Quoted in Hunt 1967, p. 147)

If a simple garland on the head could so inflame a man, drastic action was called for. Throughout history, regulations have appeared on the proper dress for women, specifying what part of the anatomy might (or might not) be revealed, how much makeup a woman could wear without being thought a hussy, whether perfume was allowed, and so on. For instance, an old Athenian treatise advised that the ideal woman would not "cover herself with gold, nor braid her hair with artful device, nor anoint herself with Arabian perfume, nor will she put white makeup on her face or rouge her cheeks or darken her brows and lashes or artfully dye her graying hair; nor will she bathe a lot" (quoted in Pomeroy 1975). (Obviously, that Greek writer knew exactly what aroused him.) In contrast, the ideal Islamic woman "is always elegantly attired. . . . She perfumes herself with scents, uses antimony for her toilets, and cleans her teeth with *souak* [the bark of the walnut tree]." But she must never "surrender herself to anybody but her husband, even if abstinence would kill her" (quoted in Bullough 1973).

Some cultures have adopted both a positive and a negative attitude toward female sexuality. Hindu ideology, for example, regards the female as being either fertile and benevolent or aggressive and malevolent. The woman who controls her own sexuality is considered destructive and cruel; the woman whose sexuality is controlled by men is kind and constructive. Classical Hindu laws, therefore, emphasize women's submission to men and allow women to participate in only the lesser rites (Wadley 1977).

Of course, female *and* male sexual behavior is subject to rituals, rules, and taboos that define what is seductive and sexy, who may make love with whom and how often, and even "proper" activities during lovemaking. Indeed, standards of sexual attractiveness and performance vary from era to era and culture to culture: for women, bodies from Renaissance plump to Virginia slim, clothing from total cover-ups that reveal only the eyes to a G-string minimum that reveals the whole body; for men, bodies from romantically gaunt to macho muscular, clothing from the effete style of Louis XIV to the rough-and-tough style of the urban cowboy. But the point is that regardless of a culture's general attitude about sex, women's sexuality and reproductive ability are always under tighter control than men's. For many centuries men and women have quarreled about who "owns" female fertility, disagreeing about contraception, abortion, and even the very desirability of children (Shorter 1982). It is a fundamental issue between the sexes, not the idiosyncratic gripes and maunderings of a few fanatics.

keeping women in their place

How bitter it is to be a woman. Nothing on earth is held so cheap.

—*Fu Hsuan*

Women and people of lowly station are difficult to deal with. If one is too friendly with them they become obstreperous, and if one keeps them at a distance, they become resentful.

—*Confucius*

Over the centuries the task for men has been to keep women in that middle course between obstreperousness and resentment. This has not always been easy. Any two groups that are unequal in resources, opportunities, and access to the political process—whether by virtue of age, class, race, education, or sex—confront each other from different positions of power. In the case of women, the difference in power has had a specific economic function; they have served as a currency of exchange and negotiation. Often, like slaves, they have been regarded as men's property, to be bought and sold, punished and raped, traded or married off in political allegiances. The thirteenth-century Franks knew exactly what their property was worth. If a man killed a mature woman, he had to pay 500 solidi to her owner; but if he killed a young, unskilled girl, he had to pay only 200 solidi. The law said that any man could beat his wife, but being an advanced law it added, "provided death does not ensue" (Hunt 1967).

Susan Brownmiller argued in *Against Our Will* (1975) that rape, which has been and still is astonishingly prevalent, is much less a sexual act than an act of power and dominance, an assertion of man's control over his property—or his neighbor's property. Even the rules of chivalry during the era of courtly love, when rich women were virtually worshipped, permitted rape now and then. The woman, however adored by her knight, was little more than a pawn in an elaborate chess game, a prize for the best player. Brownmiller quotes an explanation of chivalric rules by Chrétien de Troyes:

> If a knight found a damsel or wench alone, he would, if he wished to preserve his good name, sooner think of cutting his own throat than of offering her dishonor; if he forced her against her will, he would have been scorned in every court. But, on the other hand, if the damsel were accompanied by another knight, and if it pleased him to give combat to that knight and win the lady by arms, then he might do his will with her just as he pleased, and no shame or blame whatsoever would be held to attach to him. (Quoted in Brownmiller 1975, p. 291)

Obviously, if women were to be used as objects of barter and liaison, as tests of courage and symbols of conquest, they had to learn to be obedient. "The courage of a man is shown in commanding, of a woman in obeying," wrote Aristotle, who thought that men were superior to women in all ways, and even that they had more teeth. Throughout history, women's duties were carefully spelled out by anyone who could spell (usually a man). The basic rule, as the Roman historian Livy noted, was that "women's servitude is never terminated while their males survive." The Manu code of India and China's principle of the "three dependencies" stated that a woman was first subject to her father, then to her husband, and finally to her sons. (In most American wedding ceremonies, the father still "gives away" the bride, though the expression is no longer taken as literally as it once was.) The Book of Proverbs tells us precisely how the perfect wife should behave, and it's no wonder that her price is above rubies, because she works constantly with nary a moment's rest. "She riseth also while it is yet night. . . . Her candle goeth not out by night [and] she eateth not the bread of idleness."

Such pronouncements clearly express male fantasies about the perfect woman, but they also raise the question: Why have there been so few fantasies of an intellectual partner, an equal, a friend? Women who stepped out of line, or who tried to step up, were generally greeted by emotional outbursts. As an early Chinese poet said: "Clever men build cities / Clever women topple them." Juvenal, a famous misogynist who wrote in the second century A.D., held a special grudge against women who fancied themselves intellectually equal to men. "I hate a woman who observes all the rules and laws of language," he muttered, "who quotes verses I never heard of."

Scholarly debate from Plato to the eighteenth-century French *philosophes* has pondered the problem of female education. One didn't want them to become too smart, for then they might get out of hand, but one didn't want wives who were mentally feeble, either. The question was how to educate them to the point where they would be knowledgeable but not disobedient. A French Catholic archbishop and writer of the seventeenth century, Fénelon, offered one approach:

> A woman's intellect is normally more feeble and her curiosity greater than those of a man; also it is undesirable to set her to studies which may turn her head. Women should not govern the state or make war or enter the sacred ministry. Thus they can dispense with some of the more difficult branches of knowledge which deal with politics, the military art, jurisprudence, philosophy, and theology. (Quoted in Bullough 1973, p. 272)

What is left, you ask? Fénelon recommended that women learn a little arithmetic for purposes of household economics, reading, writing, and a dash of reasoning to make them less susceptible to flattery.

After the French Revolution even the *philosophes*, who had hoped that education would cure women's defects, were reluctant to advocate full political equality for women. Eva Figes (1970) analyzed this inconsistency in the philosophy of Jean Jacques Rousseau, whose ringing call for freedom—"Man is born free, and everywhere he is in chains"—inspired a generation. The trouble is, wrote Figes, that Rousseau literally meant man, not woman; in *The Social Contract* Rousseau described an exclusively male bond. Females, he said, "must be trained to bear the yoke from the first, so that they may not feel it, to master their own caprices and to submit themselves to the will of others." In *Emile* Rousseau explained in more detail how this training was to be accomplished. A woman must learn to be passive and docile, modest and chaste, "to submit to injustice and to suffer the wrongs inflicted on her by her husband without complaint." Suffer injustice in silence—strange advice from one who wrote so passionately of *man's* right to overthrow tyranny. When it came to women, Rousseau the modern emancipator was no different from the ancient Greek male who admonished wives to endure their husbands' "temper, stinginess, complaining, jealousy, abuse, and anything else peculiar to [their] nature" (quoted in Pomeroy 1975).

Probably the first recorded protest on the part of women (Lilith's was an individual resistance) occurred in 195 B.C., when Roman women gathered to demand repeal of the Oppian Law, which had confiscated much of their wealth and forbade them to display the remainder in dress or carriage. The women won, but certain senators issued dire warnings about the consequences of giving in to women. Livy reported one such speech, attributed to Cato:

> Give loose rein to their uncontrollable nature and to this untainted creature and [you cannot] expect that they will themselves set bounds to their license. . . . It is complete liberty or, rather, complete license they desire. If they win in this, what will they not attempt? . . . The moment they begin to be your equals, they will be your superiors."

It's the old foot-in-the-door theory: Give 'em the vote and they'll run for Congress, give 'em a book and they'll want college, give 'em a job and they'll want yours. Two thousand years after Cato, men were still chastising women who stepped out of line, as in this nineteenth-century reaction to the fledgling feminist movement: "There is no deformity of human character from which we turn with deeper loathing than from a woman forgetful of her nature, and clamourous for the vocation and rights of men" (quoted in Myrdal 1944). Again we must ask what prompted such a worried reaction; why loathing instead of loving?

The reaction is not altogether universal. Some men have been strong allies of women, especially during the last hundred years, when women themselves began to speak up in organized efforts for equality. John Stuart Mill, who wrote "The Subjection of Women" in 1861, was an ardent feminist who believed that marriage conferred excessive power on the husband, that women were conditioned to roles that made them servants of men, and that no biological destiny fitted women to be subordinates. George Bernard Shaw skewered antiwoman mores in his plays and essays, coming out strongly in favor of the independent woman who refused to obliterate herself in the service of the family. "If we have come to think that the nursery and the kitchen are the natural sphere of a woman," he wrote in an 1891 essay on the role of women, "we have done so exactly as English children come to think that a cage is the natural sphere of a parrot—because they have never seen one anywhere else."[1] And sex researcher Havelock Ellis, battling Victorian waves of sexual repression, wrote that women were sexual beings, too, and entitled to full sexual pleasure. It is an interesting question in itself, however, why male feminists—and female feminists, for that matter—should arrive so late on the historical scene, and why movements for sexual equality have figured so insignificantly in human history. (We take this question up again in Chapters 8 and 9.)

justifying female inferiority

What inspires respect for woman, and often enough even fear, is her *nature*, which is more "natural" than man's, the genuine, cunning suppleness of a beast of prey, the tiger's claw under the glove, the naiveté of her egoism, her uneducability and inner wildness, the incomprehensibility, scope, and movement of her desires and virtues.

—*Friedrich Nietzsche*

Historically, men's perception that women were easily overcome by lust, vanity, and greed fit their general view that females were animal-like by nature. Men, who after all had been created in the image and likeness of God, were more noble and intellectual. Plato, when forced to the philosophic wall, stated that "the gifts of nature are alike diffused in both [sexes]; all the pursuits of men are the pursuits of women also"—but then he couldn't help adding, "but in all of them a woman is inferior to a man." The problem for women, according to Plato, is that they are governed by their wombs, not their brains:

---

[1] "No doubt," Shaw continued, "there are Philistine parrots who agree with their owners that it is better to be in a cage than out, so long as there is plenty of hempseed and Indian corn there. There may even be idealist parrots who persuade themselves that the mission of a parrot is to minister to the happiness of a private family by whistling and saying 'Pretty Polly.' . . . Still, the only parrot a free-souled person can sympathize with is the one that insists on being let out as the first condition of its making itself agreeable."

The womb is an animal which longs to generate children. When it remains barren too long after puberty, it is distressed and sorely disturbed, and straying about the body and cutting off the passages of the breath, it impedes respiration and brings the sufferer into extreme anguish and provokes all manner of diseases, besides.

Plato's cure for the "wandering uterus" syndrome was for the woman to get pregnant immediately. He never suggested, however, that any male ills occur because the prostate gland detaches itself and floats up to chat with the lungs.

Some writers, in their effort to show that women were more like animals than human beings, got carried away. Think about the slang words that refer to women and you will have enough animals to populate a small zoo: bitch, bird, cow, pig, cat, dog, hen, chick, mule, filly. But your list will be nothing compared to the catalog that Semonides detailed in the seventh century B.C.:

From the beginning God made the mind of woman
A thing apart. One he made from the long-haired sow;
While she wallows in the mud and rolls about on the ground,
Everything at home lies in a mess.
The god made another from the evil fox,
A woman crafty in all matters—she doesn't miss a thing. . . .
The next one was made from a dog, nimble, a bitch like its mother,
And she wants to be in on everything that's said or done.
Another woman is from the stumbling and obstinate donkey. . . .
[She will] welcome any male friend
Who comes around with sex on his mind.

(Quoted in Pomeroy 1975, pp. 49–50)

Semonides compared women to all manner of beasts, concluding that the only woman who is worth anything at all is like the bee: She bustles about busily and serves her husband, and she "does not take pleasure in sitting among the women when they are discussing sex."

Although the Greeks made the first effort to explain women's inferiority on an empirical basis, it was not until the eighteenth and nineteenth centuries—the Age of Enlightenment—that science took from theology the responsibility for explaining the deficiencies of women. To the rational mind Eve's fall could no longer be used to explain female frailty, but physiology could. Science did not dispel the prevailing concept of female inferiority; instead, the conviction of inferiority directed much of the research. The conclusions that scientists reached about women were similar to those they drew about blacks: Women and Negroes, the white men agreed, had smaller brains and larger instincts, which accounted for and justified their subordinate position in society.

Thus, when the infant science of psychology took up the matter of sex differences in the late nineteenth century, it sought to identify the precise deficiency in the female brain that accounted for her weak intellect and strong emotions. As Stephanie Shields (1975) reported in her review of early psychological research on women, much effort was expended to show that men had larger heads and larger brains and were therefore more intelligent. But this explanation did not hold up, because the males' greater height and weight offset their brain-size advantage. Undaunted, some researchers pointed out that the ratio of brain surface to body surface favors men, but others found that the ratio of brain weight to body weight favored women. Eventually, this general line of reasoning was dropped.[2]

Another attack tried to identify which sections of the brain were different enough in men and women to account for male superiority. When scientists discovered that the frontal lobes were responsible for intellectual ability, several neuroanatomists reported that women's frontal lobes were less ample than men's, while female parietal lobes were larger. Then, at the turn of the century, some scientists argued that the parietal lobes, not the frontal lobes, were responsible for intellect. This change in the concept of brain functions, Shields wryly observed, "involved a bit of revisionism." Neuroanatomists hastened to their laboratories and discovered that parietal lobes were actually smaller in women and the frontal lobes larger. This scientific about-face, along with findings of other supposed anatomical deficiencies in females, required a remarkable lack of objectivity. It didn't help that in many studies the researchers knew the sex of the brain they were dissecting; they saw whatever differences they wanted and expected to see.

Other scientists accounted for the "woman problem" by studying women's bodies rather than their brains. Like Plato, they concluded that it was the female reproductive system that made women so irrational. Because women are built to bear children, their drives and desires are biologically determined, controlled by their fluctuating hormones and the maternal instinct. In 1890 P. Geddes and J. A.

---

[2]But not by everyone. Bkaktivedanta Swami Prabhupada, founder of the International Society of Krishna Consciousness, explained the shortage of women in his movement as follows: "Woman is not equal in intelligence to man. Man's brain weighs sixty-four ounces. Woman's weighs thirty-six ounces. It is just a fact. . . . Women are meant to assist man and that is all" (*Arizona Daily Star*, July 27, 1975).

Thomson explained that the sexes have fundamentally different metabolisms: Men are active, creative, and "catabolic," while women are passive, conservative, and "anabolic." Physically, intellectually, and emotionally, the sexes are complementary, not equal: "Man thinks more, woman feels more. He discovers more but remembers less; she is more receptive and less forgetful" (quoted in Shields 1975).

Efforts to find sex differences in the brain and the body continue today, evoking passion and protest. We will discuss this issue in Chapter 4, but for the moment the reader should keep in mind that no research is conducted in a value-free vacuum. We may ask: What is the reason that one line of research is suddenly favored over another? Why do efforts continue to document sex differences, instead of similarities? How will certain findings be used in our personal lives and in public policy?

the female paradox: attitudes versus reality

To judge from the writings of men, women have never been able to do anything right. They are supposed to be sexy and seductive, but then men complain that they are insatiable and immodest. Women are excluded from direct participation in the political machinery of society, but then men complain that they are sneaky, manipulative, and indirect in getting what they want. Women are often deprived of education and professional training, but then men complain that they are dumb. Women are disparaged as inferior, weak, and passive, yet when women have sought equality in a strong and active manner, men have resisted vehemently.

Some people argue that the traditional male views of women simply mirror the truth: Men have higher status and better qualities because they have always done the "important" productive work while women have handled the menial chores. This theory derives from the assumption that men, by virtue of their greater strength, took on the more strenuous tasks in the course of evolution, while women, weakened by the physiological burdens of pregnancy and nursing, did the simpler tasks.

Many anthropologists today are challenging this assumption. Women may not have held the power, but they have always participated fully in the economic and cultural lives of their societies. Joel Aronoff and William D. Crano (1975), for example, studied a sample of 862 societies from around the world. They found that the supposed universal division of family labor—men handle the economy, women handle the children—was simply not so. Women add significantly to the subsistence economy of their societies, contributing, over the whole sample, 44 percent of the food. In most hunting-and-gathering societies, women, the gatherers, provide fully two-thirds of the tribe's food. Men, the hunters, get the necessary but sporadically available protein. Males, in short, are not the only sex that brings home the bread.[3]

Nor are women a weak sex, even if, on the average, they lack the upper-body strength of men. On the contrary, they often work harder and longer than men. Among one tribe of the Kalahari Desert in Africa, women provide two-thirds of the food for their camps. The men spend a few hours a day hunting, and the women gather vegetables, carrying loads of fifteen to thirty-three pounds back to camp along with small children and water (Friedl 1975). It's rarely been children *or* work for women; more commonly they have done both.

Nor are women the incompetent sex. When countries are at war and the men go off to fight, women customarily manage the economy. They have directed the household, run the shop, superintended the farming, collected taxes for the castle, staffed the factories. Blanche of Castile, for example, was regent of France from 1226 to 1234, after the death of her husband and before her son Louis IX reached adulthood, and again when Louis went on a Crusade to Egypt in 1252 (Herlihy 1978). Numerous women have governed countries that were otherwise entirely partriarchal in structure and philosophy: Hatshepsut and Cleopatra in Egypt, Nee Lu in China, the queens of England and France, Indira Gandhi in India, Golda Meir in Israel. When women had the leisure of court or convent, many became artists and poets: In the eleventh century a Japanese court woman, Murasaki Shikibu, wrote the world's first novel, *The Tale of Genji.* Indeed, the first recorded writer *in history* was a woman—Enheduanna (ca. 2300 B.C.), a Sumerian moon priestess whose poetic incantations still impress her modern readers (Barnstone and Barnstone 1980).

[3]In 1979 Helvi Sipila, Assistant Secretary General for Social Development and Humanitarian Affairs for the United Nations, reported that although women and girls make up one-half of the world's population and one-third of its official labor force, they account for nearly *two-thirds* of the work hours (*Los Angeles Times*, December 2, 1979). Although they work more, they earn only one-tenth of the world's income and own, according to Sipila, only one one-hundredth of the world's property.

Nor have women always been the obedient sex. Many have learned ways to *appear* obedient while behaving independently. (Margaret Mitchell's *Gone With the Wind* presents a classic example, for Scarlett O'Hara behaves one way for men and another way for herself.) Men have tended to call this reaction "two-faced," or "sneaky," or "manipulative," criticizing women for their "feminine wiles." But wiles are what any group uses to get along with a more powerful group: blacks in relation to whites, lower-status men to upper-status men, Untouchables to Brahmins (see Chapter 7).

The voices of rebellious or unconventional women, their individual stories and their collective ones, have often been drowned out by the chorus of traditional historians. Thus you probably haven't heard of the Beguines, groups of independent and heretical women that first appeared in the twelfth century and flourished for several hundred years. Indeed, in the late Middle Ages a "women's movement" (what scholars have called *Die Frauenbewegung*) emerged. "Like modern-day feminists, the female saints and other religious leaders were independent and antiestablishment—but unlike today, the main social establishment was the Church," write Guttentag and Secord (1983). "Women appear prominently in the history of heresy during this time as in no earlier era."

Likewise, you are probably unfamiliar with the courageous women who more recently fought for the simple dignities that now seem trivial. Adeline T. Muhlenberg, who died in 1977 at the age of eighty-nine, protested in 1909 for the right of women swimmers to wear one-piece bathing suits. (Muhlenberg was arrested once for removing her stockings for a swim, and she was censured by the board of education for wearing her one-piece suit in a twenty-four-mile race down the Hudson River—a race in which she defeated the twenty-four male swimmers.) Camilla Urso (1842–1902), one of the great violin virtuosos of the nineteenth century, was not satisfied with her own success but worked for what was then a heretical notion: the right of women not only to be allowed to join symphony orchestras, but also to be paid equally with men. She did not live to see her goal, but the Women's String Orchestra, under its male conductor, played at her funeral in 1902 (Kagan 1977).

And you probably have heard little about the role of American women in the labor movement. But women did not supinely adapt to their inferior position in society, and as more and more of them joined the nation's labor force they organized to assert their strength and improve their condition. Philip Foner (1979) cited a newspaper account of the 1877 Chicago railroad strike: "Women with babes in arms joined the enraged female rioters. The streets were fluttering with calico of all shades and shapes." Women supported the strikes for their men's sakes as well as their own, but the men typically failed to return the favor, refusing to let women join their unions.

So there are some curious discrepencies between man's vision of woman and the reality, between her participation in society and her subordinate status, between beliefs and behavior. Why?

It would be easy to suppose that men's attitudes toward women are somehow the cause of male supremacy: "Most Athenians in ancient Greece hated women, so they shut them up in solitude and took away their rights." But attitudes do not spring forth randomly like wildflowers; they reflect and perpetuate the social order. It is just as possible to argue that misogynistic attitudes were the *result* of a system of male supremacy rather than the cause: "Because women in Athens were walled up and isolated from men, men learned that they were supposed to hate women."

If female inferiority were obvious to everyone, if there were in fact basic personality differences between the sexes that insured the higher status of one sex, controls on female behavior would not be necessary. No law needs to state that dogs and four-year-olds may not run for public office; when we find such laws against women, who some men *say* have the mental capacity of dogs and four-year-olds, we must ask what they accomplish. Human beings erect rules when they are faced with temptations and alternative possibilities, not when everything is obvious and easy.

We must avoid, therefore, the common tendency to attribute conscious plots to the course of evolution. Primitive men did not gang together one languid afternoon and decide to keep women forever barefoot and pregnant. Nor did primitive women, after a gossipy day down at the river washing clothes, decide that they would rather do the weaving and leave the warfare to men. We cannot explain the tenacity of sex differences by name calling; the double standard has not persisted because men are "male chauvinist pigs" and women are "insatiable dumb broads." When we find a custom that is as widespread as polygyny (one husband with several wives) and one that is as rare as polyandry (one wife with several husbands), we can't simply grumble that men are unfair and greedy. When male adultery is regarded as an amusing pecadillo or a God-given right but female adultery brings society's wrath and sometimes the woman's death, we're better off looking for explanations that go beyond group attitudes. When we find cultural universals, patterns that recur in places as disparate as Egypt and China, India and Indiana, we must seek the powerful historical forces behind them.

cultural consistencies

Anthropologists have identified some of those cultural universals, which are impressive in view of the extraordinary diversity of human ritual and social organization. There are notable consistencies, for example, in the tasks that men and women have done throughout history. If a society's economy includes fishing, hunting large game, farming a long way from home, making weapons, or metalworking, men have always handled these activities. Men have always been primarily responsible for fighting the wars, women for tending the children (D'Andrade 1966). Similarly, there are some consistencies to the personality traits that are supposed to mark each sex. A cross-cultural study of 110 societies found that boys are typically trained to be self-reliant and to achieve, while girls learn to be nurturant, responsible, and, as we saw, obedient (Barry, Bacon, and Child 1957). Another cross-cultural sample of 186 world societies found fourteen activities that men, and men only, have done: These pertain either to hunting and butchering or to the processing of hard raw materials, such as smelting and mining (Murdock and Provost 1973).

Apart from these patterns, most of the personality traits and specific activities that cultures assign to men and women vary widely. But almost everywhere in the world masculinity is considered the opposite of femininity, even when the traits and jobs associated with males in one culture are those associated with females in another. In the United States, for example, people tend to think that women are emotional and irrational compared to men, but in Iran women are considered the cold and logical sex. The Manus, according to Margaret Mead (1935, 1963), are convinced that only men enjoy playing with babies, and a Philippine tribe is certain that it is the men who cannot keep secrets. In some tribes men weave and women do not, and in others women weave and men do not.

Further, men's work is usually regarded as more valuable than women's work, no matter how arbitrary the division of labor. In many cultures, including our own, women do the shopping and marketing, and those activities are considered unintellectual tasks for the unintelligent sex. But in ancient Greece marketing was men's work, because buying and selling were considered complicated financial transactions too difficult for the female mind (Pomeroy 1975). Among the Toda of India, men do the domestic chores; such work is too sacred for a mere female. If the women of a tribe grow sweet potatoes and men grow yams, yams will be the tribe's prestige food, the food distributed at feasts (Rosaldo 1974). And if women take over a formerly all-male occupation, it loses status, as happened to the professions of typing and teaching in the United States, medicine in the Soviet Union, and cultivating cassavas in Nigeria.

Surely, in all the myriad forms of social organization that have existed in this world, somewhere women have ruled? The search for matriarchies began in the mid-nineteenth century, when Johann Jakob Bachofen wrote *Das Mutterrecht* (Mother-right). Drawing on myth, poetic epics, and dubious historical tracts, Bachofen concluded that "mother-right" was the first form of human society, that women originally controlled the family and the state. (In the same year, 1861, Henry Sumner Maine published *Ancient Law*, using scripture and Roman law to argue that patriarchy was the basic human model.) Bachofen's theories won him strong supporters, such as the American anthropologist Lewis Henry Morgan. Morgan in turn influenced Friedrich Engels, who thought that the subordination of women had not begun until the emergence of class hierarchies and private property.

It is true that *myths* of matriarchy have flourished (Webster 1975). In stories and folklore around the world, women are often described as the original creators and rulers of the world; men eventually organized and rebelled, seizing power and banishing women from the men's inner sanctums. But myths cannot be taken as reality. Although a horde of archaeologists and social anthropologists have sought evidence to support Bachofen, they have found not one single undisputed case of matriarchy—not one culture in which women *as a class*, not as exceptions, controlled the resources and the men (Bamberger 1974). In some societies, such as the Iroquois, some women could achieve a measure of power and influence (Brown 1975), but even Iroquois women, who played an important role in village politics and lineage, could not join the Council of Elders, the ruling body.

In most societies, in other words, males have held the most prized offices, controlled the basic resources, and extolled the superiority of their sex. Although women in some places had more advantages and opportunities than women in others, and although "male dominance" has not always meant female suppression, the relative position of the sexes in most cultures has favored men. The women of ancient Egypt had more rights than Mesopotamian women, but Egyptian men believed that a woman's place was in the home, even though both sexes worked in the fields. Spartan women were far better off than Athenian women: The girls of Sparta were as well fed as the boys, got as much exercise, and could wear the Dorian peplos, a predecessor of the miniskirt. In contrast, Athenian women were confined to their houses and wore a cumbersome, voluminous garment called a chiton. But the relatively liberated Spartan women did not have the vote, and Spartan men regarded them as decidedly inferior to themselves. Similarly, the upper-class Roman wife of the late Empire had considerably more rights and choices than her foremothers in Rome or her contemporaries in Greece. She could go to parties, plays, and the temple, and she was even allowed to eat with her husband. But Roman men thought their women were licentious and incompetent, and no Roman female ever got into the Senate.

Do you regard all of these stories as archaic bits of ancient history, long behind us, or do you see parallels to modern America? Certainly our society and many others around the world seem to be on the verge of a genuine revolution in sex roles; certainly American women have come a long way from the days in which they were traded like cows or supervised like sheep. Yet the historically contradictory image of woman lives on in the modern mind.

an American dilemma

A woman, as a woman, simply has no place in the academy. Of course, I have a great deal of admiration for her work. But it is like putting a dove in the rabbit hutch. Adding one inhabitant like that makes the place overpopulated.

> —Jean Guitton, of the prestigious French Academy, on the election in 1980 of Marguerite Yourcenar, its first woman member since the Academy's founding in 1635

In the last fifteen years in the United States, female doves have entered many male rabbit hutches. It has been a time of firsts: the first women miners (1973), the first women food venders in New York City sports stadiums (1977), the first woman on the U.S. Supreme Court

(1981).[4] Sally Ride became the first woman selected as an astronaut (1977) and sent into space (1983). Girls became Explorer Scouts and Senate pages (1971). Female tennis players got equal prize money at the U.S. Open tennis tournament for the first time (1973). Sally Priesand became the first woman rabbi (1972), and women became Episcopal priests (1976).

Hundreds of small but important changes were also made: The phone company allowed dual listings of married couples in its phone books. Hurricanes got men's names as well as the traditional women's names, on an alternating basis. Women began to keep their own last names when they married. Stewardesses (now called flight attendants) were allowed to keep working even if they married and had children. Women sportswriters were allowed to enter locker rooms to interview athletes. For that matter, women broadcasters have become an accepted part of television news, when not so long ago men fretted that viewers would never be able to stand listening to female voices. (Well, women broadcasters who are young and attractive; after the age of forty most of them are fired or demoted.)

Some fields have moved far beyond tokenism. Between 1971 and 1981, women became the *majority* in six previously male-dominated job categories: insurance adjusters, bill collectors, real estate agents, photographic process workers, checkers and inspectors, and production-line assemblers. Women were in 1982 45 percent of all bartenders (Bureau of Labor Statistics *News*, March 1982). They are making appreciable inroads into such traditionally male bastions as law (they are 21 percent of all lawyers and judges, and women make up 25 to 50 percent of the students in the nation's law schools), medicine (22 percent of all physicians, up from 9 percent in only a decade), and business (one-third of all MBA students in 1982). One sociologist found that the number of women working in the top three dozen prestigious Wall Street law firms rose from only 40 in 1970 to 600 in 1980 (Epstein 1980). (Men, it may be noted, are not moving with equal alacrity into the traditionally female professions of child care, nursing, and secretarial work.)

There have been so many firsts that the U.S. Department of Labor's *Dictionary of Occupational Titles* has in its latest edition removed almost all sex-linked terms: A repairman is now a repairer, a stewardess is now a flight attendant, firemen (and women) are

[4]When Justice Sandra Day O'Connor graduated from law school in 1952, several major law firms offered her a job—as a legal secretary (Cocks 1982).

firefighters, salesmen are sales agents or representatives. Even a bat-boy is now a bat handler.[5] The fight for job equality would surely seem to have been won, and Betty Friedan has written confidently that women are through the "first stage," of seeking economic equality, and can now direct their attention to the home and family, the "second stage" (Friedan 1981).

Yet when we look behind the headlines we find that although some women have made great advances, the majority have stayed where they were or have actually lost ground—and a significant minority are sliding precipitously downward in status, income, and opportunity. Consider the following aspects of American life.

occupations   Women are advancing into previously male-only jobs, to be sure, and of the 440 occupations classified by the census, women are represented to some degree in almost all of them. But the majority of employed women work in only twenty of these occupations, and most working women are still clustered in a very few women's jobs—secretarial/clerical, sales, domestic work, hairdressing, and waitressing (Cole-Alexander 1982; Wikler 1982).

salaries   The average woman still earns only 59 percent of what the average man earns, and that's comparing year-round, full-time workers with the same skills, education, and training. The Equal Employment Opportunity Commission reports that women are "systematically underpaid," and that *this underpayment has remained constant for the last twenty years*. Within virtually every job category, even jobs in which women far outnumber men, women earn significantly less than men (Table 1). For example, male lawyers earn a median weekly salary of $574, and female lawyers, $407. Women hold 90.6 percent of all bookkeeping jobs, but they earn $98 a week less than men holding the same job. Women are 82.2 percent of all elementary-school teachers, but they earn $68 a week less than male elementary-school teachers. In the highest paid male occupation, aerospace and astronautical engineering, the median weekly pay is

[5]Linguistic changes are everywhere. In the first edition of this book, we reported the protocol crisis that hit England when Mrs. Elizabeth Lane became their first female High Court Justice. As there was no precedent for a woman, the Lord Chancellor's office decided the new Justice would be called Mr. Justice Lane (My Lord in court) and be awarded a bachelor knighthood. Apparently Mr. Justice Lane set a precedent, however. Today, female justices are called My Lady in court; they are Mrs. or Miss Justice; and their full honorary title is Dame Commander of the Order of the British Empire.

Table 1. Median Weekly Earnings for Men and Women Employed Full Time: Selected Occupations with Total Employment of 50,000 or More

Occupation	Men	Women	Percent female workers
Brick- and stonemasons	$401	—a	0.0
*Aerospace and astronautical engineers	619	—	1.2
Mechanics and repairers	328	$275	2.1
Truck drivers	315	—	2.1
Engineers (all kinds)	547	371	4.7
Telephone line installers and repairers	384	—	5.3
Protective service workers (police, fire, guards)	322	226	7.6
*Chemical engineers	583	—	7.8
Farm workers	180	146	12.1
*Stock and bond sales agents	589	—	17.1
*/**Lawyers	574	407	21.5
**Physicians	495	401	23.2
**Operations and systems researchers and analysts	515	422	24.5
**Computer systems analysts	546	420	25.1
Bakers	264	—	26.3
*Economists	580	—	27.1
**Social scientists	522	391	34.0
Accountants	433	308	39.7
Bartenders	212	179	44.7
Health administrators	545	357	49.0
Checkers and inspectors	348	219	54.1
Real estate agents	390	277	54.1
Sales clerks (retail)	229	154	60.3
Lab technicians	324	286	76.3
Clerical workers	325	222	81.5
Cashiers	180	166	85.1
Waiters	200	144	85.1
Bookkeepers	320	222	90.6
Telephone operators	—	239	92.3
Registered nurses	—	331	95.8
Secretaries	—	229	99.3

*Five highest-paying occupations for men
**Five highest-paying occupations for women
aFewer than 50,000 in occupation

SOURCE: U.S. Department of Labor, Bureau of Labor Statistics, *News*, March 1982.

$619; in the highest-paid job for women, operations and systems research and analysis, the median weekly pay is $422.

politics   Women are running for and winning elective office in appreciably greater numbers: There were 301 female state legislators in 1969 but 966 in 1982, 13 percent of the total (Steinem 1983). There were 5,765 elected female officials in 1975 but 14,225 just four years later (Cocks 1982). This is still a very small percentage of all elected officials, however, and there are in the Ninety-Eighth Congress only twenty-one women in the 435-member House of Representatives and two in the 100-member Senate.

the equal rights debate   "Equality of rights under the law shall not be denied or abridged by the United States or by any State on account of sex." This proposed amendment to the U.S. Constitution (the Equal Rights Amendment, or ERA) was ratified by only thirty-five of the necessary thirty-eight states and was thereby defeated in 1982—although the thirty-five ratifying states represented 72 percent of the American population and although a large majority of Americans continued to favor the amendment's ratification.[6] The amendment was necessary to insure uniform nondiscriminatory treatment of women, since at present the states vary widely in their laws and attitudes. Georgia's legal code, for example, decrees that "the husband is the head of the family and the wife is subject to him; her legal civil existence is merged in the husband" (*Newsweek*, April 30, 1979). Although few people discussed this aspect of the ERA, the amendment was not directed solely to women; it would have protected the equal rights of men in cases that are now coming piecemeal before the courts. (Justice O'Connor wrote for the majority in a ruling that an all-woman nursing school in Mississippi was guilty of sex discrimination. No reason men cannot be nurses, after all. And the Supreme Court also has ruled that widowers have the same rights to Social Security benefits as widows.)

The history of the ERA is the history of women's rights—up, down, up, down. Shortly after women won the right to vote in 1920, Alice Paul, head of the National Women's Party, drafted the first ERA. It took seventy years of continued effort for American women to win the vote; it seems that it will take at least that long for American

[6]The fifteen states that failed to ratify the ERA are Alabama, Arizona, Arkansas, Florida, Georgia, Illinois (which has an ERA in its state constitution), Louisiana, Mississippi, Missouri, Nevada, North Carolina, Oklahoma, South Carolina, Utah, and Virginia.

women to have the legal assurance that all men—and women—are created equal. Alice Paul died in 1977, her dream begun but unfulfilled.

the "feminization of poverty"   The percentage of Americans who live at or below the Census Bureau's poverty line has remained about the same since 1969—12 percent. But the *composition* of the poor has changed. The rising divorce rate, the lower pay women receive in comparison to men, the clustering of women in low-paid occupations, and the lack of child-care services have combined to produce a devastating effect on women. Half of all female-headed households with children live in poverty, and two out of three poor adults are women (Cocks 1982; Wikler 1982). Poor women are less likely to be elderly than they once were; widows today are better off economically, as a group, than single mothers. The "new poor" are chiefly divorced women with children and a second large category of "displaced homemakers"—middle-aged women who have been exiled from their familiar roles as wives and mothers by divorce, separation, or widowhood, and who lack skills and experience to find work.

It is, in short, a myth that a divorced woman's financial status, because of alimony and child support, remains the same as when she was married. Men, the myth goes, are drained and impoverished by the claims of ex-wives. But when sociologist Norma Wikler (1982) reviewed the studies on the financial effects of divorce, she found that, overall, divorce is an economic disaster for women and barely affects the standard of living for men. Consider these points:

1. Nationally, 75 percent of absent fathers pay no child support at all, even if required to by law. In some areas of the country that figure leaps to 90 percent; Michigan has one of the best compliance rates, and that is only 50 percent. In any case, the average yearly child support payment was just $2,110 in 1981.

2. According to the Census Bureau, only 15 percent of all divorced women are awarded alimony, and of those, only 43 percent collect it regularly. The mean alimony payment in 1981 was $3,000, which is after inflation a 25 percent decline from the 1978 figure.

3. In a national representative sample of 5,000 U.S. families followed over a seven-year period, researchers at the University of Michigan traced what happened, among other things, to the income levels of married couples and those who divorced. The real income of the divorced women dropped 29 percent (this figure includes income from all sources—welfare, employment, earnings, alimony and child support); that of divorced men dropped 11 percent. (The incomes of married couples rose 22 percent during those seven years, due often to the combined earnings of both spouses, inflation, raises, and so on.) But then the researchers took another step, to see what that loss of income for divorced people meant in terms of their financial need and actual purchasing power. The ratio of income to needs *improved 30 percent* for divorced men (in spite of their 11 percent decline in income), but declined 7 percent for divorced women. In other words, the average divorced woman has many more expenses for herself and her children than her income can accommodate, whereas divorce liberates men from the cost of providing for others.

physical abuse   In 1977 a Wisconsin judge, Archie Simonton, put on probation a fifteen-year-old boy who had been convicted of raping a teenage girl. The boy, said Simonton, was only responding normally to the current mood of sexual permissiveness and women's provocative clothing (the victim had been wearing blue jeans). Simonton was ousted in a special recall election by an outraged constituency. But in 1982 another Wisconsin judge, William Reinecke, survived a recall election that had been organized when he had called a *five-year-old* rape victim "unusually sexually promiscuous." (It may be noted that judges usually do not exonerate robbers who complain that their victims provoked them by wearing jewelry or living in nice houses.)

Perhaps the saddest evidence yet of a war between the sexes comes from the shocking statistics on rape (of strangers, dating partners, even wives) and family violence. The FBI Uniform Crime Reports cited 81,536 reported forcible rapes in 1981; they estimate that many more go unreported. One researcher, analyzing data from national surveys, offered a *conservative* estimate that "under current conditions, 20–30 percent of girls now twelve years old will suffer a violent sexual attack during the remainder of their lives"—an estimate that excludes attacks on children. "The average American woman," he concluded, "is just as likely to suffer a sexual attack as she is to be diagnosed as having cancer, or to experience a divorce" (Johnson 1980, pp. 145–46; see also Lott, Reilly, and Howard 1982; and Russell and Howell 1983, who found the same likelihood of sexual attack in their random sample of San Francisco women).

The violence continues, in spite of important changes that have occurred in the nation's rape laws. By 1980 almost every state had passed some rape reform legislation: for example, limiting the cross-examination of the victim about her previous sexual history, disallowing the judge's traditional instruction to the jury that rape was an easy charge to make but difficult to prove, redefining rape to acknowledge that males as well as females can be victimized (typically by other men, rarely by women), and including forced anal or oral penetration in the definition.

But many people still endorse a set of rape myths—that women "want to be raped," or "are asking for it" if they lead a man on, or can escape a rapist, and so on. Psychologist Neil Malamuth and his colleagues have found that among college students in several areas of the United States and Canada, about 35 percent of the males said they would indeed try to rape a woman who had rejected them "if they could get away with it." The researchers also found that as many as 60 percent of the males said they might rape or "force sex" on a woman given the right circumstances (Malamuth 1981; Briere, Malamuth, and Ceniti 1981).

The rape laws in the United States still generally include what is commonly called "the marital rape exemption": that is, rape is defined as an "act of sexual intercourse with a female, not one's wife, against her will and consent" (Brownmiller 1975; Russell 1982). This exemption comes from a long legal tradition of regarding a wife as a husband's property, to be treated as he wishes. Since a wife owes her husband her body as part of his conjugal rights, this reasoning goes, it is logically impossible for him to rape her. As California State Senator Bob Wilson said to a group of women in 1979, "If you can't rape your wife, who can you rape?" (The correct answer is: No one.)

By 1981 only five states—New Jersey, Oregon, California, South Dakota, and Nebraska—had completely abolished the marital rape exemption. But thirteen states extended the privilege of rape from husbands to men who are cohabiting with women, and five states legally permit "date rape"—rape of women who had previously had voluntary sexual relations with the rapist (Russell 1982; Offir 1982).

Is marital rape really a problem? In sociologist Diana Russell's survey of a random sample of San Francisco households, 14 percent of the wives—one wife in seven—said they had submitted to their husbands' sexual demands against their will. Some of them had been repeatedly raped and brutalized by their husbands. Many of the wives, like the husbands, thought it was the husband's right. Russell's interviews are painful to read as women describe their experiences: "He would put a pillow over my head when he wanted to have sex and I didn't," said one wife. "He didn't want others to hear me scream" (Russell 1982).

Within the U.S. family, husbands and wives are equally likely to abuse each other verbally and even to resort to physical attack (with the exception of rape). In a national study of 2,143 U.S. families, 12 percent of the husbands and wives had attacked each other violently in the past year (Straus, Gelles, and Steinmetz 1980): In one-half of the families, both spouses had assaulted each other with equal frequency; in one-fourth, only the husband was violent; and in the last one-fourth only the wife was. But wife abuse legitimately commands medical and political attention because wives are more likely to be seriously injured by husbands than vice versa—men use fists, guns, and knives, whereas women slap or throw an object. This kind of family violence crosses all racial and economic lines.

attitudes Stereotypes linger long after the realities have changed. If you doubt this, take a look at television, whose characters bear only a minimal relation to what most Americans do or what they are really like. Yet if you ask people to describe the traits they think are typical of most men and women, you will probably get something like this: women are dependent, talkative, timid, weepy, vain, and bad at numbers; men are strong, self-reliant, courageous, independent, nonverbal, and good at math. Years ago a team of psychologists demonstrated that men and women alike assign positive values to more masculine qualities than to feminine ones (Broverman et al. 1972). For example, some of the "masculine" qualities that people admire in men, but not women, include:

Very aggressive	Acts as a leader
Very independent	Very self-confident
Not at all emotional	Never conceited about appearance
Very objective	
Not easily influenced	Thinks men are superior to women (But women must not think they are superior to men)
Very dominant	
Likes math and science	
Very competitive	Feelings not easily hurt
Never cries	Talks freely about sex
Makes decisions easily	Very skilled in business

This research was replicated throughout the 1970s (Whitley 1979), although some adults no longer admit to stereotypes that have become unfashionable. But children, who don't yet know better, believe that boys are freer, happier, more respected, better loved, and have more opportunities and more fun than girls (see Chapter 6).

Some attitude changes have occurred; for example, both men

and women now take for granted the fact of women's employment outside the home (Herzog and Bachman 1982; Tavris 1982a, 1982b). In Herzog and Bachman's randomly selected sample of 3,000 high-school seniors, only 13 percent of the boys wanted a nonworking wife, and only 4 percent of the girls wanted to be one. Both sexes agreed that couples should share equally in child care and house-work. And sociologist Mirra Komarovsky, having studied the attitudes of students in 1943, 1971, and 1980, found a growing commitment among young women to work and a preference among young men to marry women who are not "just housewives" (Komarovsky 1981).

But beneath the modern rhetoric lurk traditional notions of woman's place. As soon as young people imagine their own families, they maintain that the wife, not the husband, should stay at home with preschool children; that the wife, not the husband, should compromise her career for her family's needs; and that equality for women is fine outside the home, but not for mothers. Most people feel that even when both spouses work at jobs they enjoy, the hus-band should earn more than the wife: A man's masculinity is linked no longer to being the sole support of his wife, but to earning more than she does. Psychologist Carin Rubenstein (1982) reviewed the existing studies of what happens in families where the wife earns more than the husband (which is true in about 10 percent of all working couples) and got a gloomy picture indeed. Such couples run a much higher risk than normal of psychological and physical abuse, diminished feelings of love and sexual desire, divorce, and even health problems among the husbands. None of this implies that women *shouldn't* earn more than their husbands—very few do, anyway; it simply reflects the fact that this unusual circumstance is awkward, uncomfortable, and threatening for certain couples.

For all our awareness and sophistication, then, relations between the sexes are not that different from sexual relationships in the past and elsewhere (Table 2). Men's work has the prestige and brings in more income, even when it is neither intrinsically more demanding nor socially more valuable than women's work. Men and women still think men are the better, smarter sex. Why? Male violence against women has not abated. Why not?

perspectives on female "otherness"

For the sake of argument, let us for the moment draw two opposing hypotheses about the nature of sex differences. The first suggests that

Table 2. Gains and Losses in Women's Status in the Last Decade

Gains	Losses
1. More women "firsts" and in traditionally male jobs . . .	but the great majority still clustered in "women's work."
2. Women entering law, medicine, and business in greater numbers . . .	and still earning less than men in the same fields.
3. More than half of the labor force is now female, with up to 80 percent of all women working at some point in their lives . . .	but women earn, on average, only 59 percent of what men earn.
4. The Equal Credit Opportunity Act ended legal economic discrimination against women (for example, denying credit to married women, cutting off employed women's credit when they divorced, disregarding women's income in deciding eligibility for a bank loan). . . .	but today's credit laws offer little protection for women who worked before the legislation was passed (1975–1977), and who will lose their entire credit history if they get divorced.
5. Divorce is easier, on a no-fault basis; more cases of joint custody are awarded by courts; women are paying husbands alimony in rare cases . . .	and divorce is creating an underclass of poor women and children; these women are not getting alimony and child support.
6. Many more women are now running for public office . . .	but there are only two women in the Senate and twenty-one in the House (98th Congress).
7. The majority of the nation is in favor of the Equal Rights Amendment . . .	but the amendment was defeated.
8. Men no longer regard wives' working as a threat to their masculinity . . .	unless their wives earn more than they do.
9. Rape laws were reformed so that the victim is not on trial; rape crisis centers were set up to help victims . . .	and the incidence of rape is increasing (extramarital rape and marital rape); rape myths are still prevalent.
10. The vast majority of young high-school and college women assume they will work for a large percentage of their lives, and that they will combine work with family . . .	but neither business institutions nor young men plan to make professional accommodations or compromises for child care.

the human condition is such that the bliss and the agony of sexual attraction depend on power and mystery. Perhaps we are dealing with paradoxical but inevitable attraction and antagonism between opposites, a natural polarity in body and mind. When all is said and done, perhaps men will always reserve part of themselves for other men and women will share some things only with other women. Perhaps neither sex can understand the experience of the other; male and female may indeed be like the two sides of a coin, in that the bond between them requires them to face in opposite directions.

Or it might be that sex differences in power and personality are archaic, decaying leftovers from old systems. The mystery of the opposite sex, in this view, is a result of ignorance and is hardly inevitable. As soon as economic and social conditions change to allow women equal participation in politics and work, equality in sexual relationships will follow.

In the following chapters we consider the questions raised in this chapter from a set of widening perspectives, beginning with the biology and psychology of the individual and ending with the evolution and anthropology of societies. The two chapters of Part I deal with the basics: which differences between the sexes are real as far as the research shows, and which are imagined. Chapter 2 takes up differences in abilities and personality, the stuff of stereotypes, and Chapter 3 deals with differences in sexual behavior and attitudes.

Part II describes and evaluates various explanations that have been offered for the prevalence of sex stereotypes and sexual inequalities:

—The biological perspective (Chapter 4) argues that women have been subordinate to men because they are internally programed for their roles as wives and mothers: Their hormones, genes, and reproductive instincts channel and limit their skills and personalities.

—The psychoanalytic perspective (Chapter 5) takes as its starting point the anatomical differences between the sexes as represented in the unconscious mind. It states that each sex regards the other's reproductive and sexual abilities with elements of fear and envy, and that these emotions help account for both the attraction and the animosity between the sexes. Male supremacy and misogyny, in this view, derive either from the anatomical superiority of the male or from the ultimate mystery of motherhood.

—The learning perspective (Chapter 6) argues that sex differences in behavior and personality are learned and socially prescribed. Boys and girls are not "naturally" different, but they are treated differently from childhood and taught to play different roles.

This chapter discusses not only how learning occurs but what is learned—the messages about sex roles that fill our books, media, and minds.

—The sociological perspective (Chapter 7) says that roles themselves determine how people act and feel. Sociologists are less interested in why people with certain personality traits choose certain roles than in the reverse: how roles shape personality. Thus, they regard sex differences as created and perpetuated by institutions, especially work and marriage; by patterns of power and discrimination; and by the economic needs of societies.

—The anthropological perspective (Chapter 8) explores the economic and ecological forces that have supported sexual inequalities and that have produced the apparently irrational attitudes and rituals described in Chapter 1. This view looks for the origins of rules and roles in a culture's subsistence economy, history, and social structure.

Some perspectives will suit you and others you will dislike. It is not easy to separate the strengths and weaknesses of an approach from its subjective appeal. Because the topic of sex differences is immediate and personal, it is hard for women and men to regard themselves as products of time and culture, specks in a system that has come a long way and will go a long way hence. But distance from the problem may make its contours clearer, as it does the forms in an impressionistic painting.

Naturally, the perspectives overlap; there are many ways to illuminate a dark room, and they are not mutually exclusive. Probably no perspective, considered alone, is either completely right or completely wrong. Our intent in presenting the perspectives one at a time is not to minimize the overlap but to clarify each field's contribution.

Finally, in Chapter 9, we consider the prospects for sexual equality in the future, reviewing each perspective's answer to the question so plaintively posed by Henry Higgins: "Why can't a woman be more like a man?"

I | *The sexes: Defining the qualities*

2 | Sex differences, real and imagined

In August Strindberg's play *The Father*, a man says to a woman, "If it's true we are descended from the ape, it must have been from two different species. There is no likeness between us, is there?" Some women agree. Writer Arianna Stassinopoulos (1973) argued that it's "futile to attempt to fit women into a masculine pattern of attitudes, skills and abilities and disastrous to force them to suppress their specifically female characteristics and abilities by keeping up the pretense that there are no differences between the sexes." Even Antoinette Brown Blackwell, a nineteenth-century feminist—whose sister-in-law Elizabeth was the first woman to earn an M.D. degree—wrote that although the sexes are equal, they are different: "Women's thoughts are impelled by their feelings. Hence the sharp-sightedness, the direct instincts, the quick perceptions; hence also their warmer prejudices and more unbalanced judgments."

Are men and women really so unalike? Are the sexes separated by a wide gender gap in abilities and personality? Or was Gloria Steinem (1972) closer to the truth when she asserted that males and females share a common humanity with only "minor differences . . . that apply largely to the act of reproduction"? Everyone can agree that there are sex *stereotypes*; if only there were as much agreement on how accurately those stereotypes reflect reality.

But there is not. In an area as controversial as this, personal beliefs can easily affect research results. In the nineteenth century biased assumptions caused scientists to flip-flop in a suspicious manner when they were looking for sex differences in the brain. Scientists nowadays are more enlightened about how their own expectations can influence their experiments, but it is still difficult to run objective studies. Some years ago Robert Rosenthal and his colleagues demonstrated in a dramatic way how belief can become reality. They asked some student-experimenters to train rats to run a maze. Half of the experimenters believed their rats had been specially bred to learn maze-running rapidly, while the other half thought the rats had been bred for dullness. Although there was no real genetic difference between the two groups of rodents, the supposedly bright rats did, in fact, learn faster. If an experimenter's expectations can influence rats, Rosenthal concluded, they surely can influence human beings, and this he demonstrated in many other studies (Rosenthal 1966, 1968).

The manner in which an experimenter produces a self-fulfilling prophecy is usually nonverbal and, like the abominable snowman, hard to track down. For example, Rosenthal observed that male experimenters gave instructions to the men and women in their studies rather differently. Only 12 percent of the researchers smiled at the men, but 70 percent smiled at the women. "It may be a heartening finding to know that chivalry is not dead," noted Rosenthal (1968), "but as far as methodology is concerned it is a disconcerting finding." It's easy to imagine how an experimenter's facial expression might affect his results. For instance, if his smile made people feel friendly and rewarded and his study happened to concern people's need for affiliation (their desire to be with others), he might find a sex difference that he himself had unwittingly caused.

Another methodological problem arises in studies that rely on self-reports. Suppose you believe that males are more independent than females, and you want to prove it. If you merely ask people how independent or dependent they are, your interviewees may slant their answers toward what they believe is socially desirable: A man may try to sound more self-reliant than he feels; a woman, less so. Or your interviewees may have distorted perceptions of themselves that have little to do with the way they behave in daily life. One solution is to question a second party. Many child psychologists use this method; they ask teachers and parents to describe the children in their care. Here again, though, you risk collecting biases instead of objective observations.

Another approach is for the researcher personally to observe the behavior of children or adults in a natural setting, such as home or school. This method allows you to deal with actual behavior, but you still have the problem of your own implicit assumptions. As a psychologist interested in assertiveness, how would you distinguish "passive" behavior from that which is merely "easygoing"? How would you distinguish submissiveness, which is the opposite of assertiveness, from cooperation, which is not? The danger is that you might label the same bit of behavior differently when a female did it than when a male did. (You know: he is "good at details," she is "picky"; he's a "go-getter," she's "pushy"; he's a "demanding" boss, she's a "bitchy" one.) The tendency to label a male's traits as positive and a female's as negative explains why so many people are sensitive about sex differences and their implications for male supremacy.

In addition to assigning different labels to the same act, an observer may simply fail to notice certain kinds of behavior. Someone who claims that housewives are passive and submissive may be overlooking many situations in which housewives are active. (Caring for children and organizing and maintaining a home require considerable assertiveness and initiative.) Similarly, if someone tells you that men tend to be unemotional and insensitive, it may be because she or he has ignored situations that allow men to be expressive.

As if all this were not bad enough, there is another obstacle that impedes the pursuit of scientific truth. Studies that identify sex differences are much more likely to be published in professional journals than those that do not. Nonfindings don't have much drama and, besides, scientific convention dictates that it is impossible to prove that a difference between groups does *not* exist. All a researcher can say is that there is no evidence a difference does exist, which is pretty dull compared to proclaiming: "Eureka! Men do X and women do Y." For that reason, studies identifying even small sex differences often have exaggerated clout.

There have been some attempts to review the vast scientific literature on sex differences and to come up with some reliable generalizations. The reviewers have tended to give more weight to studies that find differences than to those that don't, and they have tended to accept results uncritically. A good example is a 1968 monograph, "Sex Differences in Mental and Behavioral Traits," by Josef E. Garai and Amram Scheinfeld. The authors cited 474 studies but did not explain how they had selected them, nor did they discuss the quality of the procedures used in the studies. Most of their conclusions conformed to popular stereotypes. For example, they found that females have greater social needs than males and that males are superior to females in abstract reasoning and conceptualizing—which, the authors believed, helps explain "the outstanding achievements of men in science, philosophy, and the construction of theories."

In 1974 Eleanor Maccoby and Carol Jacklin, two Stanford psychologists, published The Psychology of Sex Differences, which quickly became a classic text. In preparing their book, Maccoby and Jacklin carefully examined a larger body of research than any of their predecessors—over 2,000 articles and books, most of them published after 1966. Unlike other reviewers, they made a special effort to locate and include studies that might have found differences but did not. They even reanalyzed data when they thought it was necessary. So that readers could follow their analysis, they included a 233-page annotated bibliography and eighty-three summary tables. Maccoby and Jacklin concluded that many common assumptions about sex differences, including some that Garai and Scheinfeld maintained were proven, were completely unfounded; they were simply myths posing as facts. But they also found that males and females do differ in some interesting ways.

The Maccoby and Jacklin review is not without some serious weaknesses. Although the authors discussed methodological problems at length, when it came to evaluating hypotheses their approach was to tally all the studies pro or con, usually without counting the better research more heavily. Often they reached conclusions mainly on the basis of studies with young children, a serious error because some sex differences do not emerge clearly until adolescence and some are outgrown in adulthood.

In an incisive critique, psychologist Jeanne Block (1976) reanalyzed some of Maccoby and Jacklin's data and included some studies they omitted from their tables. She concluded: "The long, arduous, complicated evaluation process undertaken by [Maccoby and Jacklin] in their effort to impose organization upon a sprawling, unruly body of data is vulnerable to error and reasonable argument at every step along the way." So Maccoby and Jacklin's book, although far and away the most complete and thoughtful summary to date, is not the final word on sex differences.

In the following sections we will review research findings most relevant to the issue of sex roles and status differences (see summary, Table 3). Our discussion draws on Maccoby and Jacklin's information (1974), but we also question some of their conclusions and bring in more recent studies. As you read, keep two things in mind. First, when we speak of differences we mean group differences, or average differences. To say that one sex outdoes the other on some test does not mean that all members of that sex do better than all members of the opposite sex. Men and women overlap in abilities and personality traits, as they overlap in physical attributes. Men on the average are taller than women, but some women are taller than most men. Second, in this chapter we confine ourselves mainly to describing research findings on sex differences in the United States, which must not be taken to imply universality. Nor does the existence of a sex difference (say, in aggressiveness) prove that biology is more important than learning. *The existence of a sex difference tells us nothing about its origins.*

Table 3. Sex Differences and Similarities

Physical Attributes

Strength	Males taller, heavier, more muscular.
Health	Females less vulnerable to illness and disease, live longer.
Activity level	Some evidence that preschool boys more active during play in same-sex groups; sex differences for school-age children are qualitative, not quantitative.
Manual dexterity	Women excel when speed is important; findings hard to interpret.

Abilities

General intelligence	No difference on most tests.
Verbal ability	Some evidence that females acquire language slightly earlier; males more often diagnosed as having reading problems; females excel on various verbal tests after age ten or eleven.[a]
Quantitative ability	Males excel on tests of mathematical reasoning from the start of adolescence.[a]
Spatial-visual ability	Males excel starting in tenth grade, but not on all tests or in all studies.[a]
Creativity	Females excel on verbal creativity tests, but otherwise no difference.
Cognitive style	Males excel on spatial-visual disembedding tests starting at adolescence, but no general differences in cognitive style.

Personality Characteristics

Sociability	No consistent findings on infants' responsiveness to social cues; school-age boys play in larger groups; women fantasize more about affiliation themes, but there is no evidence that one sex wants or needs friends more.
Empathy	Conflicting evidence; probably depends on situation and sex of participants in an interaction.
Emotionality	Self-reports and observations conflict; no convincing evidence that females feel more emotional, but they may express certain emotions more freely.
Dependence	Conflicting findings; dependence appears not to be a unitary concept or stable trait.

Susceptibility to influence	Preschool girls more obedient to parents; boys may be more susceptible to peer pressure; no overall difference in adult susceptibility to persuasion across different settings in laboratory studies.
Self-esteem and confidence	No self-reported differences in self-esteem, but males more confident about task performance; males more likely to take credit for success, less likely to blame selves for failure.
Nurturance	No overall differences in altruism; girls more helpful and responsive to infants, small children; some evidence that fathers as responsive to newborns as mothers are, but issue of maternal versus paternal behavior remains open.
Aggressiveness	Males more aggressive from preschool age on; men more violent, more likely to be aggressive in public, more likely to be physically aggressive in situations not involving anger.
Values and Moral Perceptions	
	Some controversial evidence that males and females approach choice and conflict somewhat differently. Males seem more likely to emphasize abstract standards of justice, fairness, balancing of individual rights. Females seem more likely to emphasize the ethics of care, human attachments, balancing of conflicting responsibilities.

[a]Differences statistically reliable but quite small.

sex differences in physical attributes

physical strength

Her weakness is her strength, and her true art is to cultivate and improve that weakness.

—*George Fitzhugh*

The intention of your being taught needlework, knitting, and such like is not on account of the intrinsic value of all you can do with your hands, which is trifling, but . . . to enable you to fill up in a tolerably agreeable way some of the many solitary hours you must necessarily pass at home.

—*Dr. John Gregory*
(to his daughters)

When people think of physical differences between men and women, they often think of strength. The average man is no Incredible Hulk, nor is the average woman a fragile flower, but an average sex difference in strength does exist. Baby boys are a bit larger and heavier than girls at birth, and they seem to have stronger neck muscles. For example, one study found that male infants were able to raise their chins higher than female infants and had a stronger grasp reflex (Jacklin, Snow, and Maccoby 1981). Differences in size and strength are rather slight during childhood, but after puberty males on the average are stronger, heavier, and taller than females. One reason for the strength difference is the innate difference in skeletal structure and upper-body muscular mass, but another reason is the better athletic training that most boys get. Studies find that girls tend to stop developing athletically by the time they reach adolescence, whereas boys continue to improve for several years; but the recent emphasis on athletic programs for girls is changing this "gym gap."

Thus it now turns out that ordinary women, once thought to be incapable of running a thousand meters (or even around the block), are now running twenty-six-mile marathons, pumping iron, and participating in amateur sports. Female athletes are gaining rapidly on men in several sports, most notably running and swimming. (In fact, the English Channel swimming record is held by a woman.)

The question of strength differences matters because some people use it to explain the greater power and success of men. Garai and Scheinfeld argued that the greater height and weight of males gave them an advantage not only in sports but in "all those occupational and recreational domains which require height, weight, physical strength, and vigorous exertion as prerequisites for success." They did not list those domains, though, and they conveniently overlooked the fact that in most parts of the world women do back-breaking physical labor, carrying heavy baskets on their heads, plows in their hands, and children on their hips—often while those muscular men are sitting in cafés, chatting with their buddies.

health

The "stronger" sex does not start life more sturdy than the "weaker" one. On the contrary, males are more likely to suffer from prenatal problems, birth injuries, and childhood diseases of all types, including pneumonia, influenza, measles, diphtheria, polio, and whooping cough. Throughout life males are more vulnerable to a wide range of disorders and infections, and the death rate for American women is lower than that for men in every decade of life. Some people worry that sex-role equality will cause women's health to decline to male levels, but no such decline has been observed. Ulcers and lung cancer are on the increase among women, but this is largely attributable to the rising numbers of women who smoke, not to the rising numbers who work. And the women who are at risk for heart disease are not those in traditionally male, high-pressure high-status jobs, but rather clerical workers who get low pay and feel trapped by their jobs (Haynes and Feinleib 1980).

activity level

Parents will tell you that Little Ludwig was an active child from the moment of birth, unlike Tiny Tina, who slept as contentedly as a clam. But newborn females do not differ from newborn males in activity level; and one- and two-year-old girls are just as likely as boys of the same age to fuss in the bathtub, fidget while being dressed, or explore strange rooms (Maccoby 1980). Many studies of three-year-olds also find no differences, but a few do report boys to be more active, especially when the children are playing in groups instead of alone. Again, we can't say whether preschool boys are "naturally" more active or whether they are just encouraged more often than girls are to play with toys and physical equipment that foster expansive movement.

Once children are in school, boys and girls do not differ much in activity level—but they may differ *qualitatively* if not *quantitatively*. In one study, researchers observed children playing in groups of three boys or three girls. Girls were nearly as active as boys; they jumped on a trampoline, dribbled a beach ball, and ran around. But they rarely roughhoused or wrestled, and they settled disputes verbally. Boys pushed each other playfully, hit each other with the beach ball, and played noisy tug-of-war (DiPietro 1981).

There aren't many studies at all of adult differences in activity, although studies of how busy people are find that women have to be more "active" than men to juggle job, children, and husband (see Chapter 7).

manual dexterity

Although men are credited with stronger shoulders, women are credited with faster fingers—with a superiority in manual dexterity, or the ability to perform tasks that require fine, quick finger movements.

Among those interested in sex roles, manual dexterity is a controversial, emotionally charged issue. When someone says that women are better than men with their hands, antifeminists cheer while feminists bristle or gaffaw. The reason for these reactions is that the assertion has been used to justify the work that women do: typing, sewing, routine factory assignments. The argument that women's nimble fingers equip them for certain jobs crosses all political borders. When one of us (C.T.) visited a silk factory in the People's Republic of China, her host told her that young women did the spinning and worked the looms because of their superior manual skills.

Studies reviewed by Maccoby and Jacklin do show that women perform better on finger dexterity tasks when speed is important. But it is hard to interpret this finding, because the tasks used to measure dexterity are repetitive and boring and it may be that women are more willing than men to stick to such a task. Even if the difference is real, few people have suggested that it means women are better suited than men to become surgeons and pickpockets. And back in the days when typing was a high-status male occupation, no one protested that the great clumsy paws of men should be kept off the keyboard. Nor does anyone today worry about the ability of men to master a computer keyboard.

sex differences in ability

general intelligence

Women's intuition is the result of millions of years of not thinking.

—*Rupert Hughes*

Women are only children of a larger growth; they have an entertaining tattle, and sometimes wit; but for solid, reasoning good sense, I never in my life knew one that had it.

—*Earl of Chesterfield*

Women, as everyone knows, have not achieved fame in the arts, sciences, and professions as often as men; the Madame Curies and Margaret Meads stand out as exceptions. Part of the problem is that many notable women have been lost to history, unrecognized for their achievements. Regardless, a popular explanation for women's relative lack of public success is that females are not as bright as males. Although girls get better grades in school than boys, it is assumed they lack the genius necessary for outstanding achievement.

Tests of general intelligence do not show differences in the average IQs of males and females. This is not surprising, because the most widely used IQ tests were designed to minimize sex differences. If a question happened to differentiate between males and females, the test maker would throw it out or carefully balance the item favoring one sex with an item favoring the other. So we must turn to tests of specific abilities, not to IQ scores, in the search for sex differences.

verbal ability

If a woman could talk out of the two sides of her mouth at the same time, a great deal would be said on both sides.

—George Prentice

When both husband and wife wear pants it is not difficult to tell them apart—he is the one who is listening.

—Anonymous

Pediatricians, parents, and comedians credit females with having the gift of gab from infancy on. They are not necessarily paying women a compliment, though. As we all know, quantity does not guarantee quality; the politician who gives long, windy speeches and the party goer who tells interminable stories are bores. According to the stereotype, women talk a lot but often have nothing worthwhile to say. So the stereotype has more to do with gossip and chit-chat than with intellectual skill. (The stereotype, by the way, is wrong: Women are no more garrulous or prone to gossip than men. Furthermore, gossip springs up in every group and every culture [see Rosnow and Fine 1976; Haviland 1977; Bok 1983]. Far from being a frivolous waste of time, gossip often provides a sort of social glue and acts as an informal system of information storage and retrieval.)

When psychologists speak of verbal ability, however, they refer to specific abilities measurable in specific ways. These include simple measures of articulation, spelling, punctuation, sentence complexity, vocabulary size, ability to name objects, and fluency, as well as more sophisticated, higher-level measures of reading comprehension, creative writing, and the use of language in logical reasoning. In the last decade evidence has appeared to suggest that on the average girls do start to acquire language a bit earlier than boys do. For example, in one study (Schachter et al. 1978) two-year-old girls produced longer utterances than boys; length of utterance is a reliable index of language development (compare "want car" with "take me ride in car").

From age two to age ten, boys are far more likely than girls to be diagnosed as having reading problems. This could mean that boys are verbally slower than girls; it could mean that for some reason boys resist learning to read; or it could mean that teachers are especially likely to notice boys with reading problems (perhaps because they expect boys to have trouble or because boys with academic difficulties act up in class). It's interesting that in a study of more than 12,000 kindergarten and first-grade children, boys generally scored just as favorably as girls on tests designed to predict reading disabilities (Karlen, Hagin, and Beecher 1981). This finding is consistent with the idea that boys outnumber girls in remedial reading classes at least in part because teachers notice boys' reading problems more than girls'.

Aside from problems with reading, five- and six-year-old boys do not have any special difficulties with language. They score as well as girls do on tests of vocabulary size, length of utterance, and grammatical complexity (Maccoby 1980). Nor do boys lag behind girls during most of grammar school. By the age of ten or eleven, however, girls edge ahead. Though not every study reports a sex difference, those that do find that girls perform better on verbal tasks than boys. Girls maintain this superiority, or even increase it slightly, during high school, even though low-achieving boys drop out of school in larger numbers, leaving a rather select comparison group (Droege 1967).

In their 1968 monograph Garai and Scheinfeld said that girls were better at simple verbal tasks but claimed that they were inferior on the higher-level ones. Perhaps, they speculated, that is the reason men do better in science and engineering. The Maccoby and Jacklin review found no evidence for this distinction. After the age of ten or eleven, girls do better on both "lower" and "higher" measures of verbal skill. Apparently it is not for want of a golden tongue that most girls fail to become scientists and engineers—or courtroom lawyers, political orators, and auctioneers.

quantitive ability

She is like the rest of the women—thinks two and two'll come to make five, if she cries and bothers enough about it.

—George Eliot [Mary Ann Evans]

"Don't worry your pretty little head about it," girls used to hear, especially about facts and numbers. And many girls didn't. As a result, math became what sociologist Lucy Sells (1978, 1980) has called a "critical filter," keeping women from a host of occupations: not only chemistry, physics, engineering, and computer science, but also business and the social sciences, which require an understanding of statistics. A study done by Sells at the University of California at Berkeley in the early 1970s found that 57 percent of the entering male students had had four years of high-school math, whereas only 8 percent of entering females had. The other 92 percent of the women were not prepared to take calculus or intermediate statistics, courses required for fifteen of the twenty majors at the university. The only fields they were prepared for were humanities, music, social work, elementary education, and guidance and counseling (Sells 1978). The figures have changed somewhat in the last decade: In 1970 women accounted for only 6 percent of all Ph.D.'s in math, but by 1980 they were up to 14 percent (Tobias 1982). Still, a wide gap in math enrollments remains.

The sexes do not start out mathematically unequal. Two-year-old girls are as good as two-year-old boys at counting (which is to say, not very), and in the early grades the two sexes are equally able to master numerical operations and concepts. There is one qualification: Large studies with disadvantaged children have found that girls outperform boys.

Around puberty the picture changes. Although most studies of children aged nine to thirteen report no sex differences in math ability, a few show that boys do better than girls. By adolescence, boys usually do better, though the magnitude of the difference is not large. Boys do somewhat better than girls on tests of mathematical reasoning (primarily word problems); but boys and girls score about the same on tests of algebra and basic mathematical knowledge, and girls occasionally do better than boys on computation skills (Eccles 1982). Still, males score higher than females on the math aptitude section of the College Board's Scholastic Aptitude Test (SAT), and the math gap survives into adulthood.

Do boys do better simply because they take more math courses than girls? Maccoby and Jacklin (1974) reported a study in which high-school boys did better than girls even though the two sexes had taken the same number of math classes. But more recently, Elizabeth Fennema and Julia Sherman (1977) found sex differences in only two of the four schools they tested, with the number of classes held constant.

The argument about the origins of math differences flared up anew in 1980, when Johns Hopkins psychologists Camilla Benbow and Julian Stanley reported the results of their study of 9,927 seventh- and eighth-graders. The children, who were all exceptionally gifted in math and who had voluntarily responded to six talent searches in the 1970s, all scored in the top 2 percent or top 5 percent on standardized math achievement tests. But when they took the math SAT, a test normally for high-school seniors, the boys scored at least thirty-two points higher on the average than did the girls. Most of the difference occurred at the upper end of the scores; twice as many boys as girls scored over 500 (out of 800). The gap was even greater for scores over 600, and in each of the six talent searches, the top scorer was a boy.

The Benbow and Stanley study made hundreds of newspapers, as well as *Time* and *Newsweek*. What was so newsworthy? The researchers' interpretation of their study. They argued that since the performance difference on the SAT showed up before the boys had taken more courses than the girls, it must be biologically wired in. Benbow and Stanley did not offer any direct evidence for a genetic link to math ability (as we will see in Chapter 4, there is no such evidence). Essentially, they were saying that the sex difference looked impressive to them, so it must be genetic. Again we remind you that the mere existence of a sex difference says nothing about the origins of that difference.

The hoopla over Benbow and Stanley's report masked some important, though less dramatic, facts. According to one critic, if a few high-scoring boys had been removed from the study, average male and female scores would have been the same (Tooney 1981)! Another critic claimed that when all the talent searches are combined, only 2 or 3 percent of the highest-scoring boys out-performed the highest-scoring girls (Tobias 1982).

Today, many researchers and educators know that all sorts of factors contribute to math performance besides the number of classes you take: childhood experiences, self-confidence, attitudes about math, appreciation for the usefulness of math, and the expectations of parents, teachers, and peers (Eccles 1982). (We consider such factors in Chapter 6.) Perhaps the most important factor is conditioned anxiety. As educator Sheila Tobias (1976) has pointed out, "Once a person has become frightened by math, she or he begins to fear all manner of computations, any quantitative data, and words like 'proportion,' 'percentage,' 'variance,' 'curve,' 'exponential.'" Young women are especially likely to suffer from "mathophobia" and to avoid any course that requires math (Tobias 1976, 1978, 1982). Their math anxiety is two-sided: they worry about not mastering the concepts, and they worry about seeming unfeminine if they do.[1]

spatial-visual ability

Women have a wonderful sense of right and wrong, but little sense of right and left.

—*Don Herold*

What do walking through a fun-house maze, assembling a bookcase, and mentally rearranging your living room furniture have in common? They all draw on your ability to imagine, to visualize, objects in space. If you have ever taken a general IQ test you probably had this spatial-visual skill measured. You may have been shown an arrangement of stacked blocks, then asked to say which one of four other arrangements was like the original viewed from another perspective.

It is commonly believed that males have better spatial-visual ability than females, which is why, it is said, they are superior in geometry, auto mechanics, and tracking an elusive antelope. Maccoby and Jacklin's review concluded that a sex difference does exist here, starting at adolescence; but recent studies find that the difference depends on the particular test used, plus various personal and socioeconomic factors, and does not emerge clearly (if at all) until the tenth grade (Eccles 1982). In a recent study of 1,453 thirteen-year-olds and 1,788 high-school seniors, the younger girls actually scored about 5 percent higher than the boys their age; among the seniors no sex difference appeared (Armstrong 1980).

Spatial-visual ability apparently depends to a considerable degree on culture, experience, and practice. In societies where sex roles are flexible or where women play active roles, the sex difference in spatial-visual ability tends to be minor (Vandenberg and Kuse 1979). Taking math and math-related college courses will boost girls' spatial-visual skills (Burnett and Lane 1980), and so will even short

---

[1]We think this explanation has merit in terms of the average male and female learning math, but we do not know whether it explains the greater frequency of male geniuses in the field. Genius in math appears very early and may have, in either sex, a genetic component.

periods of test practice (Connor, Schackman, and Serbin 1978).[2] And regardless of test scores, almost everyone in our society can muster enough spatial ability to weave through traffic, pack a suitcase, read a map, and find his or her way home.

creativity

Very learned women are to be found in the same manner as female warriors; but they are seldom or never inventors.

—*Voltaire*

Women have more imagination than men. They need it to tell us how wonderful we are.

—*Arnold H. Glasgow*

The stereotype alleges that women are emotionally sensitive, aesthetic, and intuitive. It also creates an enigma: Why do these qualities not assure that women will become leading artists, musicians, novelists, poets, and creative scientists? Garai and Scheinfeld thought the problem lies partly in the different ways the sexes relate to the outer world. The male, they claimed, "has an innate drive to act upon and transform the environment, and consequently to engage in exciting and challenging investigation of the numerous unfamiliar objects, shapes, and machines. Thus, in his search for control over the world of things, the young boy is led toward more challenging, farther removed, and more difficult goals than the more sedentary girls." This claim is without merit. There is no basis for assuming that boys are born with a greater urge to transform the environment than girls; little girls are far from sedentary; and, most important, it is not true that males are more creative than females.

Most psychologists define creativity as the ability to produce unique and novel ideas. Psychologists themselves have been very creative in their attempts to assess creativity in the laboratory. One measure, called the Alternate Uses Test, asks people to list as many uses as they can for various common objects, such as a brick. Some people give obvious answers: "You use a brick when you build a house." Others, more creative, go on listing until forced to stop. (Our favorite response, offered by a colleague, was to use a brick as a bug

---

[2]Experience can also affect a person's sense of direction, which is related to, but not quite the same as, spatial ability. Women who are self-accepting, outgoing, and used to orienting themselves in their environment have a better sense of direction than those who are more passive (Bryant 1982).

hider: "You leave it on the ground for a few days, then pick it up and see all the bugs that have been hiding.") The Alternate Uses Test has the advantage of yielding scores that do not correlate closely with IQ; it is a fairly direct measure of the ability to generate novel ideas. The Remote Associates Test, which yields scores that do correlate with IQ, measures flexible thinking in a different way. A person is given three words and must come up with a fourth word that links the first three. For example, for the triplet *stool, powder,* and *ball,* the answer is *foot*; for *house, village,* and *golf* the answer is *green.* People who are widely acknowledged to be creative in real life tend to score higher on such tests than other people.

The research reviewed by Maccoby and Jacklin shows that on creativity tests like these, which involve a degree of verbal fluency, there is indeed a sex difference among children older than seven: females do better. On nonverbal tests of creativity, neither sex does better than the other. They conclude that girls and women "are at least as able as boys and men to generate a variety of hypotheses and produce unusual ideas." Thus the data do no more than the stereotype to explain why most well-known inventors and artists are men.

cognitive style

The sagacity of women, like the sagacity of saints, or that of donkeys, is something outside all questions of ordinary cleverness and ambition.

—*G. K. Chesterton*

We hear all the time that men and women think differently, although most people would be hard pressed to say exactly how. David Wechsler, who developed the widely used Wechsler intelligence scales for adults and children, concluded that "women seemingly call upon different resources or different degrees of like abilities in exercising whatever it is we call intelligence. . . . Our findings do confirm what poets and novelists have often asserted, and the average layman long believed, namely, that men not only behave but 'think' differently from women" (Wechsler 1958).

Some psychologists have suggested that females are more "global" in the way they perceive and solve problems, whereas males are more "analytic." By this they mean that males find it easier to ignore aspects of a problem that are irrelevant to its solution, to restructure the elements of a problem, and to shut out impulsive, incorrect answers. In 1968 Donald Broverman and his colleagues wrote that this difference between the sexes was well established.

Females, they said, are better than males at tasks that require "simple perceptual-motor associations" and at producing fast, accurate, repetitive responses, as in color naming. Males are better than females at "inhibitory perceptual-restructuring tasks" and at producing solutions to novel tasks or situations. In short, "the behaviors [at which men excel] seem to involve extensive mediation of higher processes as opposed to automatic reflexive stimulus-response connections," while those at which women excel involve "minimal mediation by higher cognitive processes."

Freely translated, what this jargon means is that women are better at dicing celery and men are better at what we think of as thinking. Broverman et al. gave some examples of the tasks at which women supposedly do better—reading fast, writing fast, typing, doing simple calculations, walking—and explained the alleged sex difference in terms of the way sex hormones affect the nervous system.[3] Although they spoke of each sex as "superior" in one mode of cognitive performance, the fact is that our culture does not regard tasks like typing and simple arithmetic as highly as tasks that require more thought. Imagine the implications if this hypothesis about cognitive differences is correct. If the average woman cannot inhibit automatic reactions as well as the average man can, and if she does better at simple rote tasks, then is it any wonder we find her in the outer office busily typing letters while he sits in the inner office busily writing them?

A sex difference in thinking is a legitimate possibility. The strongest evidence for such a difference comes from studies of field independence ("decontextualization"), which measure the ability to respond to a stimulus without being distracted by its context. Much of this work uses drawings like those shown in Figure 1, in which a person must identify figures that are embedded in a larger whole. In order to find the hidden items you must suppress your response to the drawing as a whole (the "global" response) and restructure the parts of the picture. For this reason, the ability to disembed has been equated with general analytic ability.

The rod-and-frame test (Figure 2) is also used to measure field independence. In a typical experiment, you would sit in a darkened room where all that is visible is the illuminated outline of a rectangle

[3]In a critique of this article, Mary Parlee (1972) pointed out that Broverman et al. ignored women's superiority on linguistic tasks, which certainly involve more than simple perceptual-motor associations. See her paper also for a critique of their neurophysiological argument.

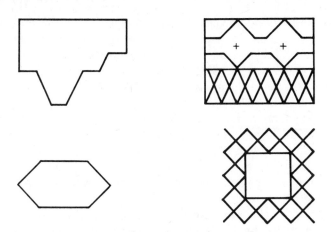

Figure 1. Examples of drawings used in the embedded-figures test. The object is to identify the simple figures in the more complex ones.
SOURCE: Adapted from Ellis.

and, suspended inside the rectangle, a rod. A lever or other device is used to adjust the rod to a true vertical position. The experimenter can make the task difficult by tilting the rectangular frame; in order to judge the position of the rod accurately, you must ignore the frame and attend to subtler cues, such as the angle of your body relative to the floor and the pull of gravity. Again, you must concentrate on the problem and ignore the confusing distractions of its context. Though it is widely believed that males at all ages do better than females on such tasks as embedded figures and the rod-and-frame test, the large body of evidence that Maccoby and Jacklin examined (one table summarizes forty-seven studies) indicates no consistent trend in early childhood. A male advantage emerges at the beginning of adolescence and continues into adulthood. Though many studies find no difference, whenever a difference is found it favors males. Males, then, are said to be field independent and females to be field dependent—even though, as brain researcher Jerre Levy (1981) has observed, it would be just as appropriate to say that females are "context sensitive" and males "context insensitive."

So it seems that men and women analyze problems differently after all. Or do they? Psychologist Julia Sherman (1967) noted that tests of disembedding are usually spatial-visual in nature. That is, they require a person to manipulate objects in space, mentally or physically. Perhaps, said Sherman, the sex difference after puberty is spatial and has nothing to do with analytic ability in general. In other words, people may be misinterpreting what is basically a simple perceptual difference. There are good reasons to think that Sherman is right. First, from adolescence on, males do better at other tasks that involve spatial relations but not disembedding or field dependence—solving mazes, for instance, or playing chess. Second, males do not seem to excel on nonvisual tasks that require disembedding. For example, the sexes do not differ on an embedded figures test that asks them to touch the stimulus instead of looking at it (Witkin et al. 1968), or on a sort of auditory disembedding test that asks them to attend to one voice and block out another (reported in Maccoby and Jacklin 1974).

As for the claim that women are more impulsive when solving problems, Maccoby and Jacklin reviewed many studies in which an impulsive response led to error, and they found no reliable sex difference. When all is said and done, there is little reason to believe that males inhibit impulsive responses while females act on them, or that males use higher mediating processes and women lower ones, or that there is any other simple distinction between the mental styles of the two sexes.

mental sex differences: how impressive?

Let's pause now to consider briefly the significance of the findings we've just reviewed. On the average, females outscore males on verbal tests, whereas males do better on tests of quantitative and spatial-visual ability. Despite the great overlap between the sexes, both professionals and nonprofessionals consider these differences to be well established. And, as psychologist Janet Hyde (1981) pointed out, "well established" typically means "large."

To find out just how large the differences really are, Hyde reanalyzed the verbal, mathematical, and spatial-visual studies reviewed by Maccoby and Jacklin. (This was a bear of a job.) Hyde used statistics that would tell her the magnitude of difference between the sexes, and she got a big surprise. The average male and female scores were quite similar; further, gender accounted for only 1 percent of the variation in scores in verbal ability and quantitative ability and 4 percent of the variation in spatial-visual ability. In other words, the sex differences in mental ability may be consistent, but they are tiny. (You see how valuable it can be to know how to use statistics?)

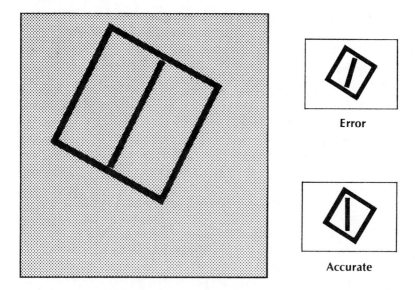

Error

Accurate

Figure 2. The object of the rod/and/frame test is to move the rod into a true vertical position inside the tilted rectangular frame. To do the task accurately, the test taker must ignore the distracting context of the frame.
SOURCE: Adapted from Witkin 1954.

Hyde's work shows that these small sex differences cannot possibly explain why one sex vastly predominates in typing jobs and the other in architecture. It also means that knowing a person's gender is almost useless for predicting that person's ability to do a particular job. As Hyde has pointed out, even if we consider differences in genius rather than average differences, they cannot account for the occupational disparities, or for the small number of women who have won Nobel or Pulitzer prizes. So when we talk about "sex differences," especially in regard to talent or intellectual ability, we must be careful not to create much ado about little.

sex differences in personality

sociability

[Women] no longer engage in spinning and weaving, they do not like any longer to make cap-tassels, they do not make hemp, but they love to gad about on the market place. They neglect the supervision of the kitchen and devote themselves to frivolous pleasures. . . . These ladies indulge in unseemly jokes and pranks.

—*Ko Hung (third century)*

Psychologists have long thought girls to be more sociable than boys. Garai and Scheinfeld's summary is typical: "In psychological development, from earliest infancy on, males exhibit a greater interest in objects and their manipulation, whereas females show a greater interest in people and a greater capacity for the establishment of interpersonal relations." They also claimed that a woman's greater interest in people predestines her to seek satisfaction in life primarily in an intimate relationship "with the man of her choice."

Many studies of sociability begin with babies, who have had little time to be influenced by learning and environment. The psychologist presents a drawing, photograph, or model of a human face (or sometimes a real face) to the infant and measures how much time the child spends looking at it. Sometimes the attention that the infant gives to faces, which in such studies are called social stimuli, is compared to the attention he or she directs to other stimuli, such as geometric forms. According to Sherman (1971), "By the age of six months, girls notice faces more than boys . . . and they are more interested in other people by the age of two." According to Bardwick (1971), "The preference of six-month-old girls for faces . . . is more marked than in boys of the same age and is consistent with findings for older children; this suggests that infant girls have a greater sensitivity to social stimuli."

Maccoby and Jacklin countered the stereotype, arguing that these conclusions were premature. When they reviewed thirty-three studies of visual perception during the first year of life, in most cases they found no sex difference. Ten studies did show a significant sex difference in a baby's attention to visual stimuli, but sometimes the difference favored girls, sometimes boys; the direction of the difference could not be accounted for by whether the stimuli were social or not. Occasionally, male and female infants show a different pattern of preference. For example, Michael Lewis and his colleagues (1966) found that six-month-old girls spent more time gazing at faces than at other objects, while boys distributed their attention fairly evenly. But Bernstein and Jacklin (1973) found no sex differences among infants aged three-and-a-half months in attention to social versus nonsocial stimuli that were equally complex.

Many people believe that little girls are friendlier, or more concerned with having playmates, than boys. This is not true. If anything, boys are more gregarious. A number of studies have shown that boys interact socially with their peers and play with their same-sex age-mates more often than girls do. At certain ages, boys seem to run in packs, while girls prefer to play in pairs or small groups that Maccoby and Jacklin call "chumships."

What about sociability in adults? Psychologists call a concern with liking others and being liked a *need for affiliation*. They measure its strength by analyzing the themes in people's fantasies, such as daydreams or stories made up about ambiguous pictures, and by analyzing answers to questions like "What makes you happy?" College women are more likely than men to fantasize and daydream about love and other affiliation themes (Wagman 1967); women tend to see safety in attachment—whereas men often see threat and danger (Gilligan 1982).

One problem with evaluating affiliation is the eye of the beholder. In *Men in Groups* (1969) Lionel Tiger proposed that men, not women, are the affiliative sex because men form closer relationships with members of their own sex. Women's friendships, he claimed, are superficial shadows of "male bonding," which originated in prehistoric male hunting groups and which shows up today in business, sports, politics, private clubs, and bars. But other men lament the death of "real" male friendships and envy women their apparent ease of close, same-sex attachments (Nichols 1975; Goldberg 1976). We think it is likely that men and women have different kinds of friendship and possibly express their feelings toward their friends differently, but this does not mean that one sex *needs* friends more than the other or has a greater or lesser ability to bond.

empathy

Women are wiser than men because they know less and understand more.

—*James Stephens*

The stereotype says that females are more sensitive than males to other people's feelings and to subtle nuances of behavior. Maccoby and Jacklin concluded that this assumption is incorrect. The two sexes, they said, are equally adept at "understanding the emotional reactions and needs of others," although measures of this ability have been narrow.

Trying to trap empathy in a laboratory is indeed difficult, and we would call the issue undecided. It may be that while women are not "naturally" more empathic than men, empathy in this society is associated with the traditional feminine role and is therefore encouraged in females. Wendy Martyna and Dorothy Ginsberg, working with Sandra Bem, conducted a study in which they asked students to listen to the apparently spontaneous conversation of another person, who was actually a confederate of the experimenters delivering a memorized script. The confederate spoke about some personal problems, and the researchers recorded how often each student listener nodded or made sympathetic comments. It turned out that the most traditionally feminine women reacted with more concern than did men or less traditional women (Bem 1975).

Robert Rosenthal and his colleagues (1974) found that women excel at decoding nonverbal signs of other people's feelings. Rosenthal developed a test called the Profile of Nonverbal Sensitivity (PONS), which measures sensitivity to tones of voice and movements of the face and body. The test consists of a forty-five-minute film of a woman portraying different emotions. Sometimes she makes a definite facial expression; sometimes she speaks a few indistinguishable phrases; sometimes she does both. When you take the test, you look at or listen to a scene and then indicate what emotion the woman is acting out. If the woman appears to be upset, for example, you may have to decide whether she is expressing jealous anger or sadness about her divorce. There is only one correct answer, determined beforehand by the actress herself and a panel of judges who know her. Overall, Rosenthal's group found that people were pretty good at recognizing the emotions being expressed, but females were slightly and reliably better than males from the third grade (the earliest age tested) through adulthood (see also Rosenthal et al. 1979).

But the issue isn't settled yet. In a review of empathy studies done mainly with children, psychologist Martin Hoffman (1977) found that although females do seem slightly more emotionally responsive to other people's feelings, they are no better than males at recognizing or correctly interpreting another person's true emotional state. On the other hand, in a thorough review of seventy-five studies of children and adults, Judith Hall (1978) concluded that females are at least moderately better than males at reading nonverbal signals.

Sensitivity to others probably depends on the sex of the sender and the decoder (you might read your own sex's signals better than those of the opposite sex, or vice versa), as well as the situation you are in; it's too simple to say that one sex is always better than another at reading nonverbal cues (see Mayo and Henley 1981). In fact, the work you do may affect your sensitivity to others: Men who were training for or working in occupations that require nurturance, expressiveness, or artistic skill did as well as women on the PONS test (although it is also possible that unusually sensitive men were drawn to these occupations in the first place). Finally, empathy is related to power: Those who have more of the former may have less of the latter—a less powerful person might learn to read the more powerful person's signals as a matter of self-preservation—whether a child is interacting with a parent, an employee with a boss, a private with a sergeant, or a wife with a husband.

emotionality

Women are timid and 'tis well they are—else there would be no dealing with them.

—*Lawrence Sterne*

According to the *Random House Dictionary of the English Language*, emotion is "an affective state of consciousness in which joy, sorrow, fear, hate, or the like is experienced." But when people complain that women are "so emotional" they usually are not thinking of joy, sorrow, or hate. They mean that women tend to be excitable and easily upset and to overreact in expressing their feelings, and that women therefore are not to be trusted in situations requiring self-control and "maturity." Most studies and casual conversations concerning emotionality use the term in this narrow sense.

The stereotype about female emotionality says in part that females are more timid and anxious than males. Studies based on direct observations of children's behavior do not find that girls are especially fearful, however. Boys and girls react similarly when a parent leaves the room and they cry equally often. They face new experiences, like going to nursery school, or frightening ones, like crossing a narrow plank, with the same degree of courage or resignation. Yet girls and women are more likely than boys and men to report feelings of anxiety or tension on tests of those emotions, and teachers commonly report that girls in their classes are more timid and anxious than boys.

So there is a conflict in the data, with studies of behavior on one side and self-reports and anecdotal observations on the other. Perhaps the discrepancy occurs because females are more willing to admit fear and anxiety than are males, who are under pressure not to be sissies. This raises an important point: *feeling* an emotion and *expressing* it are two different things. Although there is no convincing evidence that women are more emotional than men in terms of feeling, they may more freely express their emotions, at least in certain situations—especially "unmanly" emotions such as fear, sadness, and embarrassment (Cherulnik 1979).

There is one emotion, though, that men supposedly express more often than women: anger. Men supposedly vent their anger openly and directly; women are said to nag, sulk, or suppress their rage. Does anger turn men into the more emotional sex? Not according to recent research (see Tavris 1982 and Averill 1982 for reviews of the literature). Overall, a few sex differences regularly turn up: Women are somewhat more likely than men to cry when they feel angry and to say they withhold some "customary benefit" from the target of their annoyance. Men are more likely than women to express anger in public places, toward strangers; both sexes may feel irritated by the clod who cuts ahead in the supermarket line, but men are more apt to say so to the clod.

However, the similarities between men and women are more striking than the differences, and they illuminate the general question of emotion. That is, both sexes feel angry equally often, and for similar reasons (condescending treatment, insult, and the like). Both sexes report that they have trouble expressing anger to employers, teachers, and parents—to anyone, in short, who has greater power and status than they. Women may restrain anger for fear of losing control and appearing unladylike (especially when their targets are male), but men also restrain anger for fear of losing control and appearing unmanly (especially when their targets are female). And both sexes are especially (and equally) likely to feel and express anger at home, at a "safe" member of the family. The emotion of anger, like other emotions, does not depend on what gender you are, but on the situation you are in and the person you are feeling emotional about.

The lack of difference in anger, however, does not imply a lack of difference in aggressiveness: Anger is an emotion, and aggressiveness is an action; the two can and do occur independently. (We take up aggression on pages 71–73, and another powerful emotion, love, in Chapter 3.)

dependence

Eve would have had no charms had she not recognized Adam as her Lord.

—*Anthony Trollope*

By a girl, by a young woman, or even by an aged one, nothing must be done independently, even in her own house.

—*Manu laws of India*

"Dependence" is as complicated a term as "emotionality" to translate into behavior that can be measured. Those who study dependence in children usually record the amount of touching or eye contact between mother and child, the amount of acting up a child does to attract adult attention, the extent to which a child complies with what others want, or the amount of help a child seeks. Unfortunately, these measures often do not correlate with each other, and many researchers now doubt that dependence can be studied as a unified, coherent trait.

For the moment, let's define dependence as a need for the protection of other people. If a child clings to his mother all day and wants her near at all times, we'll say he's dependent. Psychologists have studied this sort of attachment-dependence by placing a young child in a room with his or her mother and observing the two together. Less frequently, they observe children at home or as they are being left at nursery school. Maccoby and Jacklin went through thirty-two studies in which observers noted the proximity of children to their mothers (or, rarely, their fathers), the amount of touching, and the degree of emotional upset at separation. In some studies girls turned out to be more dependent, in some boys did, and in some there was no sex difference at all.

The older a person gets, the harder it becomes to define dependent behavior. Perhaps that is why there are hardly any studies of adult dependence. Not only that; dependent behavior changes. The teary, clingy child of two may grow into a helpless Hannah or an intrepid Irene. Jerome Kagan (1979) has reported a series of studies that tried to find consistent links between infant personality traits and the same traits in later childhood, and they were unsuccessful. So we cannot expect much consistency from childhood to adulthood.

Still, the notion that women are more dependent than men is alive and well. When writer Colette Dowling published *The Cinderella Complex* in 1981, she touched a nerve. Dowling argued that because of their upbringing, women are psychologically crippled by a pathological need to be taken care of by men. Even when they appear to be happy superwomen, working full time, raising children, baking bread, and caring for husbands, they secretly harbor the hope that some knight in shining armor will come along and rescue them.

It was a beguiling idea, with a big problem: Dowling omitted any discussion of men. Which sex, on its own, gets more physical illnesses, has worse mental health, and can't cook a hot meal? Men. Which sex suffers more at the end of an affair or marriage and remarries sooner (while grumbling about being "trapped")? Men. Which sex is more likely to kill a partner if she threatens to leave him, or does leave? Men. Can we really say that women are more dependent on men than men are on women?

No, say psychotherapists Susie Orbach and Luise Eichenbaum (1983). On the contrary, they argue, men's apparent emotional independence is really a self-confidence born of the knowledge that women will take care of them. Indeed, men's very ability to depend on women to look after their emotional and physical needs *permits* their autonomy. Women appear dependent and fragile, say Orbach and Eichenbaum, but actually they learn in early childhood "that in the most profound sense they must rely on themselves, there is no one to take care of them emotionally."

Again, we must look into the eye of the beholder—and the beholder's idea of what dependency is. We suspect that both sexes occasionally wish to be taken care of, and that both sexes are sometimes intimidated by the responsibilities of adult life. If women dream, now and then, of a Prince Charming whose money and status will make their problems vanish, men dream, now and then, of a Ms. America whose youth and beauty will solve theirs. In exchange for economic security both sexes have been known to forfeit independence—women most typically in marriage, men most typically in a job.

Perhaps men also appear to be more independent than women because they are encouraged to keep their fears and conflicts to themselves; maybe women simply *admit* their emotional dependencies more. Then, too, more women than men bear the brunt of juggling job, children, household, and spouse. When such women try to do it all without much help from employers or husbands, and therefore consider retreating into domesticity, they may be suffering from fear of exhaustion, not fear of independence. In any case, both sexes clearly depend on their loved ones to meet some needs and on their work to meet other needs. The ways in which they balance autonomy and dependence have to do with the practical realities of their lives.

susceptibility to influence

A man must know how to defy opinion; a woman, how to submit to it.

—*Madame de Staël*

If women are not more dependent than men, perhaps they are more wishy-washy? Men, according to the stereotype, wield influence; women succumb to it.

In childhood succumbing means obeying your parents. Maccoby (1980), after examining studies of obedience in very young children, concluded that the old saw about boys being harder to raise than girls may be true. One-year-old boys are more likely than girls to handle forbidden objects, such as ash trays, when they are observed in a waiting room with their fathers (Maccoby and Jacklin 1979). At home boys more often do things forbidden by parents, such as climbing on the furniture or playing with wall sockets (Smith and Daglish 1977); less often obey their mothers' first requests to behave (Minton, Kagan, and Levine 1971); and generally resist parental demands more often than girls do (Hetherington, Cox, and Cox 1976). Boys do get spanked more often than girls—perhaps they are doing something to provoke those spankings! But it is also possible that adults, expecting greater obedience from girls, deliver their demands to daughters with greater authority and assurance, while they are secretly pleased when boys disobey. Children certainly know when a parent means it.

As children begin to play with others, they become susceptible to social pressure from peers—and the stereotype falls apart. Girls are no more likely than boys are to buckle under to peer pressure, according to Maccoby and Jacklin. If anything, boys may be more susceptible to such pressure. In a study by psychologists Edwin Hollander and James Marcia (1970), fifth-grade children filled out a questionnaire in which they had to choose between alternative hypothetical activities. Three items required them to choose between what they wanted to do and what their friends wanted. For instance, they had to decide whether to go to a summer camp featuring activities they particularly enjoyed or one that their friends wanted them to go to. In three other items the problem pitted peers' wishes against those of parents. The boys' answers showed them to be more peer-oriented than girls on both types of choice. Unfortunately, the questionnaire did not have the children choose between their own desires and those of their parents, so we cannot tell whether the girls were less peer-oriented than boys because of greater independence or a greater desire to please grown-ups.

Studies of social influence in adulthood usually focus on how willing people are to be persuaded by the arguments of others or conform to group opinion. Until the mid-seventies most psychology textbooks said that women were the suggestible sex. (This trait was never called "openmindedness," nor was resistence to persuasion ever called "rigidity." In a society that values the ideal of individualism, suggestibility tends to be equated with gullibility.) But a careful survey by psychologist Alice Eagly (1978) found little evidence that females are *consistently* more suggestible across different settings, nor for the belief that men are *consistently* more successful at influencing others. Women seemed to be more easily influenced in small groups, but the male–female difference is very small. Further, *both* sexes are suggestible when they don't know or don't care much about a topic; when the topic matters to them or they are knowledgeable about it, they stick to their guns.

Yet in the world outside the laboratory, women do seem to agree with other people more often than men do. How can this be, given the absence of sex differences in experimental studies? Here's a clue: Suggestibility is related to status. Employers, professors, and doctors have more influence on employees, students, and nurses than the other way around. And in the outside world, women as a group have lower status than men.

self-esteem and confidence

I never yet knew a tolerable woman to be fond of her own sex.

—*Jonathan Swift*

I'm glad I'm not a man, for if I were, I'd be obliged to marry a woman.

—*Madame de Staël*

One of the early goals of the women's movement was to banish the longstanding belief that women don't like themselves or each other very much, that a "real woman" prefers to spend her time with men and gets her self-esteem vicariously, through the man she loves. These efforts, like the "black is beautiful" movement, were aimed at least in part at creating a self-fulfilling prophecy—at encouraging women to like their own sex.

After surveying a slew of self-report studies on self-esteem, Maccoby and Jacklin concluded that females do not really feel any worse about themselves than males do. But we think this conclusion was premature. People do not like to admit dissatisfaction with themselves; they may even insist they are as happy as larks, when they are actually suffering from psychosomatic disorders brought on by stress and anxiety.

Self-esteem is a global quality, difficult to measure. However, when psychologists study people's self-confidence on particular tasks—which can contribute to general self-esteem—a sex difference does emerge, with males usually the more confident sex. For example, when people must predict how well they will do on a crossword puzzle or an anagram test, men and boys are generally more confident than women and girls about their future performance—and they are also more satisfied with themselves after completing the job (Maccoby and Jacklin 1974; Lenney 1977; Parsons 1977). (Exceptions occur with certain kinds of tasks and in situations where clear information is given to individuals about their actual abilities; see Lenney 1977.) Similarly, if you ask students to estimate their grades for the next term, males usually expect to do at least as well as they have in the past, and perhaps better, while females expect to do worse. In one typical study, female college students predicted lower course grades than males did, despite the fact that actually the women's grades turned out to be slightly higher than the men's (Crandall 1969; see also Deaux 1976). Women's self-confidence seems especially vulnerable when their work is to be evaluated by others or when they must compare themselves with others who are highly competent. In one study (Lenney and Gold 1982), people were asked to estimate how they would do compared to others before taking a standardized achievement test on which the sexes ordinarily perform equally well. Not only was the male-female difference in self-confidence greater than in a group that didn't make comparisons, but women's actual performance declined relative to men's.

We do not have here simply a case of feminine modesty and masculine bravado. An important element in differences in self-confidence between the sexes is the way men and women interpret success. Men tend to attribute success to their own ability and effort (they have what psychologists call an *internal locus of control*), whereas women tend to attribute success to the ease of the task, the fickle finger of fate, or blind luck (they have an *external locus of control*) (Frieze 1975; see also Simon and Feather 1973; Deaux 1976).

At a country fair one afternoon, three researchers noticed that women went for games of luck (bingo), while the men liked games of skill (ring tosses). Intrigued, they set up their own fair in the laboratory and found again that 75 percent of the men chose to play a skill game while 65 percent of the women chose a luck game. Why? Expectancy seemed to be the key. Women thought they would do better in a game of luck and men thought they would succeed more often in a game of skill (Deaux, White, and Farris 1975). This is bad news for women. Ability is something you can count on, but luck is not; it's here today, gone tomorrow. If women have learned to attribute their successes to luck, that could explain why their self-confidence is lower and why they feel more insecure than men do about their future performance (Frieze 1975).

Now consider failure, for the same kind of analysis can be applied. When you fail, you might attribute your poor performance to something internal ("I'm a dope"; "I got lazy") or to something external ("The test was tricky"; "I had bad luck"). People who have low self-esteem blame themselves for their failures more often than do people who have high self-esteem (Layden and Ickes 1977); and, you guessed it, more women than men fall into that pattern. Thus, despite the lack of a sex difference in self-reported self-esteem, the evidence on self-confidence and attribution of success and failure suggests that a difference in self-esteem may exist, at least in certain kinds of situations.

It appears that some women are caught in a bind that saps their self-confidence: If they do well, they sacrifice the credit ("It was just luck"), but if they bomb, they shoulder the blame ("It was all my stupid fault"). Such women feel that their lives are externally controlled only when it comes to success; when they fail, they suddenly turn internal. Sooner or later a woman in this situation is bound to decide that if at first she doesn't succeed, she might as well forget it.

nurturance

We must start with the realization that, as much as women want to be good scientists or engineers, they want first and foremost to be womanly companions of men and to be mothers.

—*Bruno Bettelheim*

Among the more positive qualities attributed to women are warmth, cheerfulness, and helpfulness toward others. These are supposed to equip women for certain social roles: wife, mother, nurse, babysitter, charity worker, community volunteer. But research provides mixed evidence on male and female nurturance.

In studies of altruism, or willingness to help others, no overall sex difference has emerged. In a typical study, a confederate of the researchers pretends to be in some sort of trouble: He or she may feign a stroke and collapse in a crowded subway or, less dramatically, drop a bag of groceries. The experimenter watches to see who goes to the victim's aid. Sometimes men are more altruistic, sometimes women, and sometimes they're equally helpful. Whether a Sir Galahad or a Florence Nightingale rushes to the rescue depends on who the victim is and what sort of help is called for.

However, when the person needing help is a small child, girls and women do tend to be more responsive than males. In a cross-cultural survey, little girls were more likely than little boys to be friendly toward infants and offer them help and affection; the boys approached infants and toddlers usually to take something away from them—or to get them to do something (Edwards and Whiting 1977). Helpfulness to small children, though, may be related to the tasks a society assigns to the young. In most cultures, girls babysit and care for their younger siblings more often than boys do; in East African cultures in which boys babysit and have other domestic duties, sex differences in nurturance are relatively small. And in one New England community where girls did very little child care, they were found to be not especially helpful or nurturant (Whiting and Edwards 1973).

When nurturance is defined as being bonkers about babies, almost everyone assumes that women have the lead over men. Harry Harlow, a famous expert on primate behavior, used to tell how he showed a picture of an infant rhesus monkey to groups of undergraduates. He observed, he said, "gasps of ecstasy" from all-female audiences, but singular silence from all-male audiences. Harlow concluded that "nature has not only constructed women to produce babies but has also prepared them from the outset to be mothers" (1971).

It is true that if you watch what people do with an unfamiliar infant while they are sitting in a waiting room, girls are indeed more likely than boys to look at the baby, smile at it, talk to it, or touch it; and boys are more likely than girls to ignore the baby when it makes baby sounds (Feldman, Nash, and Cutrona 1977; Frodi and Lamb 1978). New mothers are more responsive to an unfamiliar baby than other adults—including women who do not have children of their own, pregnant women, and men (Feldman and Nash 1978). Females are more likely to *say* that an infant's crying distresses them, though both sexes show signs of physiological arousal when they listen to an infant's wail (Frodi and Lamb 1978).

The trouble is that because nurturance is supposed to be a feminine quality, men do not always feel free to display it—either to infant monkeys or to infant human beings. Psychologist Phyllis Berman (1975) asked college students to look at pictures of infant and adult monkeys and apes and rate each animal's "immediate emotional appeal" on a five-point scale. She then computed scores that reflected each student's attraction to infants relative to his or her attraction to adults. Some students gave their responses publicly, by voting in view of other participants in the study. Others saw the pictures and made their judgments alone. The men and women differed in their reactions to the infants only when they had to announce their ratings in public. The average score for women who gave group ratings was higher than for women who gave them privately, but for men the opposite was true: Their scores were higher when the ratings were private (Berman 1975). Men, it seems, are quite capable of the "ecstasy response" to small fuzzy animals but suppress it in public.

Fathers, according to stereotype, are supposed to be lumbering oafs in the baby business. But when researchers observed parents of newborns in the hospital, the fathers were as likely as the mothers to hold their babies, rock them, talk to them, smile at them, and look directly at them; and they were just as adept at handling them, too. The fathers continued to be as responsive as the mothers at home (Parke and Sawin 1976). But the researchers also found a few differences: Mothers spent more time than fathers on routine child-care chores (surprise!), and fathers were more playful with the babies (Parke 1978).

If men had more time and opportunity to be with children, we might hear more male gasps of ecstasy than is now the case; if they were more often included in studies of nurturance, we would have more evidence against which to judge the stereotypes. In daily life women and men often behave nurturantly toward each other, as in "How about if you make a fire and pick up a pizza while I put the kids to bed and make us some coffee?" Further, though caring for children, home, and spouse is traditionally the woman's job, protecting them is the man's; he is expected to buy life insurance, investigate night noises in the basement, and go down with the ship if the lifeboats are full. There is no doubt which parent usually spends more time with the children, but we cannot conclude with any confidence at this point that one sex is inherently the more nurturant. (The "maternal instinct" and the possible influence of hormones on maternal behavior are discussed in Chapter 4.)

aggressiveness

[We need men] who love a fight, who when they get up in the morning spit on their hands and ask "Whom will I kill today?"

—Eric Hoffer

Charm is a woman's strength just as strength is a man's charm.

—Havelock Ellis

At last, a clear-cut sex difference! Well, pretty clear cut, anyway. Not every study reports a sex difference in aggressiveness, but of those that do, most find males to be more aggressive. The difference is most obvious in childhood, when boys show more physical aggression, fantasy aggression, verbal aggression, and play aggression than girls do (Maccoby and Jacklin 1974). The difference appears as soon as children begin to play with each other, at the age of two or three.

This does not mean that girls are submissive, by any means. They are no more likely to yield or withdraw under attack than boys are. And they don't have to, because among children the victims of male aggression are usually male. There are several explanations for the finding that both aggressor and victim are likely to be male. First, in our society girls and boys play in highly sex-segregated groups. This reduces the opportunity to fight, or to interact at all, with the opposite sex. Second, many little boys are told in no uncertain terms not to punch little girls. Perhaps girls also learn signals that say, in effect, "You can't hit me—I'm a girl!" Or perhaps, as Maccoby and Jacklin suggest, girls learn ways to inspire affection and sympathy, to make the aggressor feel guilty, and to divert his attention. Third, aggressiveness among children may be related to their efforts to establish dominance, as is the case with nonhuman primates. In general, dominance seems to be a more important issue in male groups than in female.

Some writers have argued that while females are just as aggressive as males, they show it differently. For instance, in a study of first graders, Seymour and Norma Feshbach (1973) found that girls were more unkind and unfriendly toward a newcomer trying to enter a two-member "club" than boys were. The girls would ignore the new child, more away, deny a request for help, or announce directly that the newcomer was not welcome—especially if a boy was trying to join a two-girl club. Boys, on the whole, were nicer. The Feshbachs wrote:

> The quantitative data do not reflect the quality of the children's reactions, especially the disdain that girls expressed toward the new boy and the readiness with which they isolated him and rejected his efforts to play with them. One of the girls even set out to terrorize the newcomer. She spilled out a box of pick-up sticks and, taking one up, began to stalk the new boy around the room. She rolled her eyes and said something about the "strange feeling" that came over her at certain times. (We subsequently removed the sticks from the room.)

However, the girls' hostility was short-lived; after four minutes or so the sex difference disappeared. Perhaps the girls' initial aggression was due to the importance girls place on small, exclusive groups.

Aggressiveness, as we noted earlier, does not have to involve anger. Among children, aggressiveness frequently flares up over issues of dominance, in imitation of television heroes, or simply as a successful strategy for getting their way. Similarly, adults may behave aggressively in response to a bully, as a way of defending their own or someone else's honor, as a way of establishing dominance, or as a way of making someone obey them. A survey of seventy-two studies of anger and aggressiveness in adults found few consistent sex differences except in the category of direct physical aggression without anger—where men clearly took the lead in aggressive action (Frodi, Macaulay, and Thome 1977). Men are publicly more aggressive than women, and more violent, too. They commit more antisocial acts and crimes. They have more automobile accidents, get into more brawls and battles, commit more murders.

The finding that boys are generally more aggressive than girls and that men are more aggressive than women in certain circumstances has stirred up controversy, for in our culture people are ambivalent about aggressiveness and violence. For all the lip service paid to peace and love, many people regard aggressiveness as a good thing and passivity as a bad opposite. They may assume, for instance, that physical aggression in the schoolyard paves the way for psychological aggression in the business world. "Aggressiveness" becomes an umbrella that covers everything from hitting a toy to standing up for one's rights, from striking a playmate to speaking up at a company meeting. So some people worry that the findings on aggressiveness show yet another disadvantage that women have in the world of work, poor passive things that they are.

The problem is largely semantic. Several writers have suggested that we distinguish *aggression*, which is hostile in intent or hurtful in effect, from *assertiveness*, which is the ability to make one's interests and desires known without trampling on other people's rights. Few would argue that hostile, hurtful behavior is desirable. Once we distinguish the two, the male "superiority" in aggressiveness looks more like a liability than an advantage.

why personality differences are elusive

Everybody "knows" that males and females differ, yet scientists searching for sex differences in personality come up empty-handed as often as not. Where have all the differences gone? Is everybody wrong? Following are four possible explanations for the lack of consistent findings:

the instability of personality traits   A psychologist who studies personality traits must keep in mind that people do not behave consistently. They play different roles on different occasions. Suppose you were doing an observational study of timidity, following a young mother through a typical day. At 9:00 A.M. the woman's child injures herself on a jagged rock. Does the mother scream hysterically at the sight of blood? Does she faint dead away? If she is like most mothers of our acquaintance, she scoops up the child, administers first aid, and drives quickly but carefully to the nearest hospital. No fear or timidity there. But that evening the same woman is standing on a chair calling frantically to her husband because a little gray creature with a long tail has appeared. Same woman, different behaviors. Which is she—brave or timid? The same difficulty of attaching one label to a person over many situations applies to men too, of course. A man who is a mouse with his mother may show tremendous courage when battle demands. Which is he—timid or brave?

Again and again we've seen that when sex differences emerge they are always tied to specific situations and conditions. The differences may be real enough, but they do not settle into stable, consistent personality traits. Indeed, the whole concept of a personality trait may be questionable. In an insightful commentary on sex-difference research, Carolyn Wood Sherif (1979) observed that most people do not possess permanent psychological qualities the way they possess money or cars or brown hair:

> The score on a test or the level of task performance is taken as indication that the person *is* intelligent, or aggressive, or submissive, or anxious, or *has* this or that motive. By verbal magic, a specific set of actions in a specific research situation is transformed into the label for something that the person has, is, or possesses as a trait. (p. 115)

But if you think of human beings as people who respond in different ways depending on their expectations, situations, and the requirements of their roles, you will not be surprised by the lack of consistent findings about men and women. As the situation and the times change, so do people.

the significance of status In a laboratory experiment males and females play the same role: that of subject. But in real life, the sexes often play different roles, and these roles are not equal in status or power. High-status people wield more influence than those with less status; the secretary is expected to defer to the boss, not vice versa. But the upper rungs of the status ladder are populated primarily by men; so guess which sex wields more influence? This is a status difference masquerading as a sex difference. When the roles change—he's the secretary, she's the boss—the expected sex difference evaporates (see Eagly and Wood 1982; Eagly 1983).

Likewise, we've noted, lower-status people often learn to decode the nonverbal signals of their superiors. Therefore, status differences help explain certain sex differences in verbal and nonverbal behavior—for example, men's tendency to interrupt women frequently and to touch women in conversation, more often than women interrupt men or touch them (Zimmerman and West 1975) and women's tendency to smile more often and to work harder to keep a conversation flowing (see Mayo and Henley 1981). The status factor explains more about sex differences than sex differences explain about status.

variations in masculinity and femininity What we think of as sex differences may have more to do with psychological gender than with biological sex (Unger 1979). The two are not synonymous. Masculinity and femininity are not opposite ends of a single continuum; not all men are predominantly masculine, nor all women predominantly feminine (Bem 1974). Some people are *androgynous*—having about the same number of traditionally masculine and traditionally feminine qualities—and some are *undifferentiated*, having few traditionally masculine or feminine qualities (Spence and Helmreich 1978).

In studies using these concepts, masculinity, femininity, and androgyny sometimes predict behavior better than the mere possession of a male or female body. For example, in one experiment, traditionally feminine women conformed to a majority opinion more often than men did, but androgynous women did not (Brehony et al. 1977). In another, differences in spatial-visual ability occurred only between adolescent boys and girls who were traditionally masculine or feminine (Nash 1975). And masculine boys and girls scored highest on a test of mechanical reasoning, followed by androgynous, undifferentiated, and feminine individuals (Antill and Cunningham 1982).

Although there are many problems with the concept of androgyny (see Chapter 6), it has taught us that if you just divide up people into males and females, you'll often have trouble finding behavioral differences between the two categories. If you use degree of masculinity and femininity and their combination, however, some differences may turn up.

the difficulty of measuring subtleties Psychological research tends, naturally, to concentrate on the more obvious and easily measured aspects of behavior and personality; it's easier to see an elephant than a bedbug. So researchers miss some of the subtleties of perception and thought that affect the sexes differently.

Yet there are plenty of hints that girls and women see the world through different-colored glasses than boys and men do. They often make different plans, pursue different hobbies, read different books, vote differently, and have different life experiences. What's more, they *think* of themselves as different, which sets the stage for a self-fulfilling prophecy; for when people think they are different, then in some sense they really are. Perhaps expectations, self-images, and especially human values have more to do with the ways that women and men live than do most differences in ability or personality. So we close this chapter with some intriguing research that suggests a subtle yet profound sex difference—one having to do with moral perceptions.

connections, values, morality: two voices

A man named Heinz has a dying wife whose life can be saved by an expensive drug invented by a local druggist. Heinz cannot afford to buy the drug, and the druggist refuses to extend him credit, arguing that he deserves to be compensated for the years he put into the drug's development. Should Heinz steal the drug?

Consider the answers of two eleven-year-old children to this hypothetical situation. Jake responds with a categorical yes. He sees the dilemma as one that pits property against life, and he argues for the logical priority of life:

> "For one thing [says Jake], a human life is worth more than money, and if the druggist only makes $1,000, he is still going to live, but if Heinz doesn't steal the drug, his wife is going to die. *(Why is life worth more than money?)* Because the druggist can get a thousand dollars later from rich people with cancer, but Heinz can't get his wife again. *(Why not?)* Because people are all different and so you couldn't get Heinz's wife again." (Gilligan 1982, p. 26)

In contrast, Amy, who is the same age as Jake, is less certain about whether Heinz should steal:

> "Well, I don't think so. I think there might be other ways besides stealing it, like if he could borrow the money or make a loan or something, but he really shouldn't steal the drug—but his wife shouldn't die either." (Gilligan 1982, p. 28)

Amy's answer is the kind of reply that has caused some psychologists to believe that women's moral development is retarded, deficient, or immature. Psychologist Lawrence Kohlberg (1969, 1976), who has used hypothetical situations like the Heinz dilemma to explore the ways that children and adults make moral choices, constructed a six-stage sequence of "normal" moral development. At the first stage, morality is simply based on fear of punishment or hope of reward; but by the highest stage (which not everyone reaches), morality is a system of universal ethical principles. Moral wisdom, to Kohlberg, involves an increasing appreciation of justice and the importance of individual rights.

Kohlberg's theory is very pretty, but it has a major flaw: It was originally constructed from data *only on males*! Male development was assumed to be the norm, and thus when the moral explanations of girls and women differed from those of boys and men, researchers assumed that females were arrested in their moral thinking.

But *different*, as by now you might agree, does not automatically mean *deficient*. In a brilliant critique of early moral-development research, and adding some research of her own, psychologist Carol Gilligan (1982) has shown that females do resolve moral conflicts and arrive at moral standards, but their thinking and interpretation of the human condition may be somewhat different from those of males. She argues that neither sex has a monopoly on morality and justice, but that the two sexes use different systems of logic and values. Each contributes to a complete human morality.

Thus Jake sees Heinz's moral dilemma as "sort of like a math problem with humans": an equation whose solution can be determined rationally. Lives are worth more than money or an imperfect law; therefore Heinz should steal (and the judge should give him a light sentence). Amy is less concerned with the value of property or with legal issues, and more worried about the effect the theft might have on the relationship between Heinz and his wife:

> "If he stole the drug, he might save his wife then, but if he did, he might have to go to jail, and then his wife might get sicker again, and he couldn't get more of the drug, and it might not be good. So they should really just talk it out and find some other way to make the money." (Gilligan 1982, p. 28)

Of course Amy doesn't want Heinz's wife to die—but she fears that the wife *will* die if Heinz takes the short-run solution of stealing the drug. For Amy, the dilemma is not a math problem but a complex human situation that will continue over a period of time and whose solution depends on the situation. She regards the whole matter as stemming not from the druggist's assertion of his rights, but from his failure to behave responsibly when confronted with the needs of others.

According to Gilligan, male solutions to moral issues, like Jake's answer, generally reflect a concern with abstract standards of justice, fairness, and the balancing of individual rights; they tend to avoid direct negotiation or worry about people's feelings. Female solutions, like Amy's, tend to emphasize the ethics of care, human attachments, the balancing of conflicting responsibilities, and the resolution of conflict through communication and cooperation. As Gilligan notes, in our society the male way has been taken to be the best and most moral, but sometimes it operates at the expense of intimacy and attachment. Luther and Gandhi, for example, whom Kohlberg and others regard as having reached the highest pinnacle of moral development, would not be regarded as such in a scheme of female morality. Both men, Gilligan observes, "are compromised in their capacity for intimacy and live at great personal distance from others. Thus Luther in his devotion to Faith, like Gandhi in his devotion to Truth, ignore the people most closely around them while working instead toward the glory of God." Conversely, a female overemphasis on the needs of others can lead to resentful self-sacrifice, loss of personal integrity, and "situation ethics" in which no moral action is taken.

Gilligan's argument is controversial and the jury is still out on its validity, but we think she may be touching on an important distinction. Men may feel uncomfortable with a female view that seems to them diffuse and inconclusive; women may feel unhappy with a morality of rights that carries with it the potential for neglect and indifference. The male system brings justice, the female system compassion. "While an ethic of justice proceeds from the premise of equality—that everyone should be treated the same—an ethic of care rests on the premise of nonviolence—that no one should be hurt," writes Gilligan. In true moral maturity, both perspectives must converge.

So yes, men and women do differ, but the differences that matter most are not necessarily the ones that capture academic curiosity or the public stereotypes. Differences in physical strength don't mean much. Differences in ability are minor. Differences in personality are elusive. But men and women do have different images of themselves and of how the world works; they seem to have different moral premises; they seem to regard conflict and choice from different directions. Nowhere are these differences more apparent than in the area of love and sexuality, the subject of the next chapter.

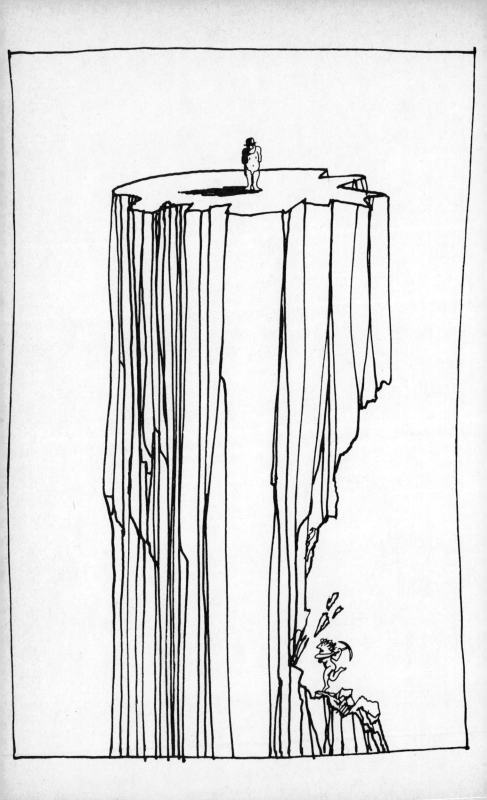

3 | Sex and love

One of the most venerable beliefs about men and women is that they find themselves where they do on the ladder of life because of fundamental, unalterable differences in sexuality and love. In Chapter 1 we pointed out that women are sometimes regarded as oversexed temptresses who need to be tamed so that men can get some work done. But they have also been idealized as asexual angels whose mission is to pacify the passionate nature of man. Vestiges of this view remain in the modern belief that a woman's desire for sex is less urgent than a man's. Sometimes it is also argued that women, who supposedly care more about love than sex, subordinate all other matters of life to their romantic pursuit of love, which is why *they* can't get any work done. The basic difference between the sexes, in this view, is that men want a lover and women want love.

Human sexuality is a many faceted thing; to understand it, we must consider people's physiological responses, attitudes, acts, feelings, and the relationships in which sex occurs. When we do this we find that men and women in our culture are sexually alike in many ways, but different in others. The differences are not merely a matter of one sex having a stronger sex drive than the other; physiologically, male and female responses are remarkably similar. Behaviorally, though, sexual differences do continue to exist, despite the fact that the sexual revolution of the past few decades has shrunk some of them considerably. And when we study what goes on in people's heads rather than in their beds, we find that American men and women often bring different assumptions, goals, and expectations to their intimate relationships. Male versus female ways of perceiving love and sex can create mystery and romance, but they can also lead to misunderstanding and heartache. The peculiar fact is that an activity that brings men and women together for both recreation and procreation can unite them emotionally—and also divide them.

In this chapter we explore the assumed and actual sexual differences between males and females. We consider first the Victorian heritage and the double standard; the rise of the scientific study of sex; sexual physiology; and the "sexual revolution" in sexual behavior. We then turn to the way that men and women regard sex and love, romance and intimacy—and the miscommunication that often results.

the Victorian heritage

Writers on sexual mores usually trace modern concerns about sex to the Victorian era, which spanned roughly the latter two-thirds of the nineteenth century, when Queen Victoria ruled England. According to most accounts, the majority of middle-class Victorians (including Europeans and Americans) considered sex dirty, dangerous, and disgusting. Premarital sex was bad. Sexual fantasies were bad. Masturbation was bad. Coitus in marriage was okay, but only if the partners didn't do it too often, used acceptable positions, and avoided "unnatural" practices. The Victorians were not the first people in history to condemn sexual pleasure as evil and sinful, of course; many cultures, Eastern as well as Western, have done so. Certainly the Judeo-Christian ethic, with which most of us have grown up, consistently discouraged sexual pleasure and promoted a narrow interpretation of normality on religious grounds long before the nineteenth century. The Victorians, however, worried as much about the development of good character, spiritual purity, and physical health as they did about the wrath of God, and the voices of authority that warned them against sex belonged not only to churchmen but to physicians and scientists.

The Victorians divided womankind into two groups, as some people still do today—the good and the sexual. Good women rarely, if ever, desired sexual intercourse. They regarded it as a marital duty, like cooking, sewing, and entertaining guests. The ideal wife was expected to submit stoically and to remain passive and prone. According to an old English joke, when a Victorian girl asked her mother what to do on her wedding night, the mother replied, "Lie still and close your eyes, dear, and think of England." In contrast, men "needed it," and even—the dirty curs—enjoyed it. The most widely quoted sex-advice book in the English-speaking world at the time, Dr. William Acton's *Functions and Disorders of the Reproductive Organs* (1857), instructed readers that "the majority of women (happily for them) are not very much troubled with sexual feelings of any kind. What men are habitually, women are only exceptionally." The "best" mothers and wives, wrote Acton, "know little or nothing of sexual indulgences. Love of home, children, and domestic duties, are the only passions they feel."

Civilized men were expected to recognize that good women were too fragile physically and too sensitive spiritually to engage in frequent intercourse, and thus to exercise their marital privileges with restraint. In a book with the very Victorian title *Amativeness, or Evils and Remedies of Excessive and Perverted Sexuality, Including Warnings and Advice to the Married and Single* (1875), Orson Fowler cautioned that the woman must always be the "final umpire" on the matter of coital frequency: "A husband who tenderly loves a delicate wife will find no difficulty in being continent, because he loves her too well to subject her to what would be injurious." Fowler was wrong; many men did have difficulty complying with the umpire's decision, and they turned in frustration to the second kind of woman. In *The Sex Researchers* (1969), Edward Brecher told how "droves of Victorian males each night saved their wives and sweethearts from pollution by pouring their sexual emissions into London's readily available street women."

Indeed, despite their intention to see no evil, hear no evil, and do no evil, the Victorians saw, heard, and did quite a lot of it. Havelock Ellis, a prodigious documenter of Victorian sexual behavior and one of the first sex researchers to approach his topic with an open mind, filled his seven-volume *Studies in the Psychology of Sex* (1896–1928) with case histories of every kind of sexual experience, from Autoeroticism (masturbation) to Zoophilia (sex with animals). And for all the admonitions to "nice girls," some historians now say that premarital sex was more common during the Victorian period than it had been in previous, supposedly more liberal times (Shorter 1975). In brief, despite all the rules and taboos, people did then all the things they do today, though less frequently and in fewer numbers.

Nor were all Victorian writers as antisexual as Acton was. Historian Carl Degler (1974) reported that some doctors acknowledged that women were sexual beings and boldly advised them to express their sexual impulses without feeling guilty. Degler also discovered a sex survey of forty-five well-educated women, most born before 1870, who were far from the asexual Victorian ideal; they regularly had orgasms, enjoyed intercourse, and thought sex a normal part of life (see Mosher 1980). Thus the traditional picture of Victorian morality is probably overdrawn. People in the Victorian age were not asexual; they were, however, relatively ignorant and prudish about discussing sex. No one knew what anyone else was doing, so everyone worried that only he or she was doing it. This gap between behavior and belief meant that many Victorians paid a large price in guilt and remorse for their sexual pleasures.

During the first half of the twentieth century attitudes toward sex mellowed quite a bit. But despite a proliferation of sex manuals and more open talk about sex, people remained in the dark about what others were doing and uncertain about what was "normal." The growing popularity of psychology, especially Freudian psychoanalysis, made sex a legitimate topic for discussion but at the same time created new insecurities. Those who had abandoned the idea that sex was sinful and caused warts now fretted that their sexual activities might be perverted or immature.

During this period the sexual double standard continued virtually unchallenged. As Joseph LoPiccolo and Julia Heiman (1977) pointed out in a historical review of sexual attitudes, the cultural message shifted from the view that "sex is dangerous to your mortal health and immortal soul" to the idea that "sex is good, but only for men." The double standard was not an unqualified blessing for men, for they were, and still are, under great pressure to pursue and perform. Real men were supposed to have sex frequently—with women who were expected to be only mildly interested. The double standard assured miscommunication between the sexes, with each sex out to prove something different.

Even after World War II, Victorian notions about male and female sexuality lingered. In the absence of information about sexual physiology, many writers, including medical authorities, felt free to peddle prudery as scientific fact. When Diana Scully and Pauline Bart (1973) analyzed gynecology textbooks published between 1943 and 1972, they found that some authors believed women couldn't experience orgasm during intercourse, or at least not very often. Many gynecologists assumed, and some still do, that men have an inherently greater need for sex. One textbook writer observed in 1943 that in women "sexual pleasure is entirely secondary or even absent" and that a common problem the gynecologist faces is "the vast and fundamental difference between the sexes in regard to sexual appetite." The writer added, "Women, with their almost universal relative frigidity, are apt to react to the marital relationship in one of three ways. (A) They submit philosophically to their husbands. . . . (B) They submit rebelliously as a matter of duty. . . . (C) They rebel completely and through refusal try to force the husband to adapt himself to their own scale of sexual appetite" (quoted in Bart 1974). According to this author, attempts to slow a husband down are doomed, because men cannot help being sexual virtuosos: "Biologically for the preservation of the race, the male is created to fertilize as many females as possible and hence has an infinite appetite and capacity for intercourse." Infinite!

The aim of many doctors who treated inorgasmic women was to make life more comfortable for their husbands rather than to increase the women's sexual pleasure. If a woman could not respond with honest enthusiasm, her doctor often counseled her to fake it. In a 1952 text two male physicians wrote:

> Unfortunate marital situations frequently arise because of the husband's resentment at the wife's sexual unresponsiveness. . . . It is good advice to recommend to the women the advantage of innocent simulation of sex responsiveness, and as a matter of fact many women in their desire to please their husbands learned the advantage of such innocent deception. (Quoted in Bart 1974, pp. 6–7)

Notice that the good doctors did not worry about the wife's resentment, nor did they instruct the husband in ways to help the wife be more responsive. Nor did they think *men* should try "innocent simulations" of desire or orgasm—of which they are quite capable.

Today we have a much more realistic picture of female—and male—responsiveness. Yet, incredibly, Victorian myths live on in some gynecology texts. Scully and Bart reported that of the nine books they examined that were published between 1963 and 1972, two still claimed that most women are "frigid."

the scientific study of sex

In 1938 Indiana University selected Alfred C. Kinsey to teach a new course in sex education and marriage. Kinsey was not an obvious choice for the job. He was a biologist who had devoted his career to the study of gall wasps, which reproduce asexually (without insemination of the female by the male). But Kinsey was an extremely conscientious man, so he set out to rectify his lack of knowledge about people by consulting the library. Surprised at the lack of reliable information there, he decided to gather the data himself. Kinsey had spent twenty years collecting and categorizing several million gall wasps; now he applied the same painstaking approach to collecting sexual statistics. For the next eighteen years he spent his mornings, noons, and nights talking to people about their sex lives.

Kinsey was not the first sex researcher, but he was the first to gather extensive sexual histories from men and women from many geographic areas, walks of life, religious backgrounds, marital statuses, and ages, and he was the first to use statistics to analyze his data. Whereas most previous researchers had relied on case histories of patients in therapy or people who came for counseling and advice, Kinsey used a standard personal interview containing hundreds of questions on every aspect of sexual behavior. His results provided the first detailed information on who was doing what and how often.

There were inadequacies in Kinsey's approach, though. For one thing, instead of using randomly selected informants representative of the American population as a whole, Kinsey recruited volunteers, and they may have been sexier than average. Fortunately, Kinsey was so good at appealing to people to contribute their histories for the sake of science that he often succeeded in signing up whole groups of people—PTA groups, business offices, lecture audiences—en masse. Therefore his sample was much broader than those in many subsequent studies, which have relied on informants who have tended to be considerably younger, better educated, more liberal and more affluent than average. Still, in his sample some groups, such as farmers and the poorly educated, were underrepresented, and he interviewed so few blacks that he was unable to include their data in his published reports.

Another common criticism of Kinsey's methods is that the people he and his associates interviewed could have lied, either by omitting sex acts they felt guilty about or bragging about things they did not do. This is a problem with all sex surveys. But after conducting thousands of lengthy interviews, Kinsey and his colleagues developed good noses for sniffing out false answers, and they cross-checked each other or reinterviewed respondents whenever it seemed necessary.

In 1948 Kinsey and his associates published *Sexual Behavior in the Human Male*, based on their interviews with 5,300 American men. This volume was followed in 1953 by *Sexual Behavior in the Human Female* (with Wardell B. Pomeroy, Clyde E. Martin, and Paul H. Gebhard) based on data from 5,940 females. The basic conclusion of the two books was that many of the sexual practices and "perversions" prohibited since Victorian times were actually common, and some were nearly universal.

Since Kinsey's time, scores of smaller surveys have been published, most of them on specific groups, such as college students, homosexuals, or readers of magazines (including *Psychology Today, Redbook, Cosmopolitan, Ladies' Home Journal*, and *Playboy*). The broadest in scope is probably a national study commissioned by the

Playboy Foundation and reported by writer Morton Hunt (1974). (The Hunt survey relied on questionnaires instead of interviews and used different sampling methods from Kinsey's, but it covered all the same topics.) The most controversial are probably two surveys conducted by writer Shere Hite—one on female sexuality (1976) and the other on male (1981). Hite emphasized how people feel about their sexual experiences instead of the numbers that engage in a particular act. And in fact, her data are useless for estimating incidence rates, because of her casual—some would say cavalier—attitude toward methodology (see Offir 1982). Sex is a difficult topic to research, and every survey is flawed in some way—in sample, method, or interpretation. Yet all of them, taken collectively, have demonstrated the enormous emotional and physical variability that exists sexually, for both men and women, and have allowed our knowledge of human sexual behavior to leap forward in just a few decades.

Surveys, however, leave one important area of sexuality unexplored: physiology. As you might imagine, it is usually a waste of time to ask people about the bodily changes they experience during sex. Since many of these changes are internal, one cannot easily observe or report them ("Did my uterus twitch?" "Did my skin flush?"). Besides, people in the throes of passion aren't motivated to make mental notes on physiology. The only reliable way to get such data is to have an uninvolved researcher measure and record responses while sexual activity is in progress.

Enter William Masters and Virginia Johnson. In the mid-1950s Masters and Johnson launched the first major studies of sexual physiology by recruiting volunteers to masturbate and have intercourse in the laboratory. In all, 694 men and women participated. They ranged in age from eighteen to eighty-nine, and their only common characteristic was the ability to have an orgasm. These people were carefully screened for signs of psychopathology, and volunteers who seemed motivated by a desire for sexual kicks were thanked and told to go home. Most volunteers acclimated rather rapidly to the laboratory, and women, supposedly the inhibited sex, did so more easily than men, possibly because the men felt more pressure to perform.

Masters and Johnson charted the sequence of changes that occur during sexual arousal. One of their most useful techniques was to have female volunteers masturbate while inserting a clear plastic artificial penis, containing a light and camera, into the vagina. This device allowed the experimenters to observe the interior of the vagina during sexual excitement and orgasm and to film the responses. During the twelve years of the laboratory research program, Masters and Johnson observed some 10,000 sexual cycles. In 1966 they reported their findings in *Human Sexual Response*. A later volume, *Human Sexual Inadequacy* (1970), dealt with psychological barriers to sexual satisfaction.

Early critics, finding it hard to believe that anyone can respond freely and normally while wired for sight and sound, argued that the sexual responses observed by Masters and Johnson in the laboratory must have been atypical. But the volunteers insisted that their orgasms were indistinguishable from those they had at home. A different problem, related to volunteer bias, is that we cannot infer that because all of Masters and Johnson's subjects were orgasmic, everyone is, or is in precisely the same way; nor can we infer that the physiological patterns Masters and Johnson described actually represent *all* human variation and potential. If you brought into a laboratory a hundred people who could sing on key, you would not conclude that everyone is physiologically capable (even with training) of doing so. A more serious recent criticism is that Masters and Johnson were, and still are, imprecise and careless in reporting their results, and that they do not share their data with scientists who want to replicate their research (see Zilbergeld and Evans 1980; Zilbergeld 1983).

Nevertheless, the physiological work of Masters and Johnson remains the major source of information about bodily responses during sexual arousal and climax, and this research has helped create a more objective attitude toward the topic. As historian Paul Robinson (1976) has pointed out, "High-mindedness and decorum, the usual masks of repression, are overwhelmed by the sheer weight of physiological detail."

the body sexual: his and hers

the sexual response cycle

Which of these descriptions of orgasm (from Vance and Wagner 1977) was written by a woman, and which by a man?

A. "[There is] a build-up of pressure in [the] genitals with involuntary thrusting of hips and twitching of thigh muscles. Also contracting and releasing of the genital muscles. The pressure becomes quite intense—like there is something underneath the skin of the genitals pushing out. Then there is a sudden release of the tension with contraction of genitals with a feeling of release and relaxation." (p. 211)

B. "Orgasm gives me a feeling of unobstructed intensity of satisfaction. Accompanied with the emotional feeling and love one has for another, the reality of the sex drive, and our culturally conditioned [emphasis] on sex, an orgasm is the only experience that sends my whole body and mind into a state of beautiful oblivion." (p. 209)

In this particular case, the answer runs counter to stereotype: A was written by a woman, B by a man. In general, though, when people write descriptions of how orgasm feels to them they say similar things, and most readers are unable to do better than chance at guessing the writer's sex (Vance and Wagner 1977).

Indeed, Masters and Johnson's recordings established that in spite of their obvious anatomical differences, male and female bodies respond in much the same way to sexual stimulation. In both sexes two physiological processes account for specific changes. The first is *vasocongestion* of the genital area: Blood flows into the organs and tissues faster than it flows out, and greatly distends them. The second is *myotonia*, or muscular tension, throughout the body and especially in the genital area. As passion peaks, both sexes become relatively insensitive to pain or noise; the ringing of a telephone or the blare of a radio goes unheeded. During orgasm, the person—whether male or female—is more likely to appear in torment than in ecstasy; the old Hollywood version of orgasm—dreamy, gentle, romantic—just isn't so.

Masters and Johnson refer to the complete sequence of responses during sex with orgasm, from the initial hint of interest to the final sigh of contentment, as the *sexual response cycle*. For ease of description, they divide the cycle into four phases, all of which occur in both sexes.[1] The order and nature of the phases are the same whether a person is masturbating or having intercourse, although different types of stimulation can affect the onset or duration of a particular phase:

1. *Excitement.* In men vasocongestion causes the penis to become erect within the first few seconds of arousal. The skin of the scrotum thickens and tenses and the testes within the scrotum begin to rise and increase in size. In women the first sign of arousal is

[1]It is possible to argue about whether the second stage is actually distinguishable from the first in men (see Robinson 1976).

lubrication of the vagina; droplets of moisture form on the vaginal wall. (The vagina has no sweat glands; the moisture appears to come from congested vessels in tissues behind the semipermeable vaginal wall.) In addition, the clitoris swells, and the cervix and uterus move up and back, which creates a tenting or ballooning of the inner part of the vagina.

2. *Plateau.* In men the penis becomes fully erect. The corona of the glans of the penis increases somewhat in diameter and may deepen in color. The testes continue to increase in size and to rise. In women the outer third of the vagina becomes so congested with blood that the passageway in the lower third of the vagina is narrowed by as much as 50 percent. In contrast, the inner two-thirds of the vagina continue to balloon out. The clitoris, now fully engorged, retracts and seems to disappear, though it remains extremely sensitive to indirect stimulation.

3. *Orgasm.* The male orgasm is marked by rhythmic contractions of several sets of muscles. Three or four vigorous contractions of muscles at the root of the penis cause ejaculation of semen; several less regular and less intense contractions follow. In women the muscles behind the vaginal walls contract, pushing the lower part of the vaginal wall in and out. The first five or six of these muscular contractions are the most intense. The uterus also contracts, but the inner part of the vagina continues to expand.

4. *Resolution.* Muscular tensions subside and all bodily functions return to Start. If an aroused woman fails to reach orgasm, the resolution phase may take longer than usual. The pelvis may stay congested for up to an hour, and the woman may feel tense and uncomfortable. Men have joked for years about the "blue balls" problem—the pain of becoming highly aroused without orgasmic relief—but no one has given a name to the female equivalent. (On the other hand, what goes up *will* come down, and neither sex needs orgasm on every sexual occasion.)

Of course, Masters and Johnson's studies do not tell us how many women versus men regularly experience the entire response cycle, including orgasm; remember, all of their subjects had to be orgasmic to participate. Other sex researchers disagree on this issue. Kinsey (1953) claimed that almost nine women in ten eventually respond with orgasm to sexual stimulation. In his sample, 25 percent of women in their first year of marriage had no orgasms during intercourse, and only 39 percent almost always had them. But by the fifteenth year of marriage, 45 percent of the women in the sample almost always had orgasms during intercourse, and only 12 percent never did. Others, though, think his figures are much too rosy. Some differentiate female orgasm produced by genital contact during intercourse from orgasm produced by manual stimulation (during intercourse or not), arguing that the latter is much easier for women to have (Hite 1976).

Whatever the exact figures, it is clear that far more women than men do not experience orgasm during intercourse. There are all sorts of possible reasons, both psychological and cultural, but this difference does not imply a weaker "sex drive" in women. Often it simply means that a woman is not getting the kind of stimulation she needs. The picture of female sexuality changes with masturbation: Kinsey found that masturbation leads to orgasm for women 95 percent of the time. He also discovered that masturbation brings rapid orgasm: 45 percent of the women who masturbated reached orgasm in one to three minutes; only 12 percent took longer than ten minutes. Kinsey concluded, "There is widespread opinion that the female is slower than the male in her sexual responses, but the masturbatory data do not support that opinion. It is true that the average female responds more slowly than the average male in coitus but this seems to be due to the ineffectiveness of usual coital techniques."

Many sex researchers believe that women climax so rapidly during masturbation because they provide themselves with continuous, effective stimulation of the clitoris. The clitoris is the most sensitive part of a woman's sexual anatomy, and although it is tiny compared to the penis, it may contain as many nerve endings. (Structurally, the clitoris and penis are very similar, since they both develop from the same bit of embryonic tissue.) For many women, clitoral stimulation is less consistent and less effective during coitus than during masturbation.

To some extent, too, female orgasm may be related to the duration of intercourse. If the man has a climax too quickly, sex will be over for the woman before it's begun. Paul Gebhard, of Indiana's Institute for Sex Research, reported that interviews with over a thousand married women showed that penile intromission of less than a minute was insufficient to produce regular orgasm in most women. When intromission lasted one to eleven minutes, half of the wives had orgasms almost all the time. And when intromission lasted sixteen minutes or longer, two-thirds of the women reached orgasm almost all the time (Gebhard 1966). As Leo Durocher once said in a different context, "Nice guys finish last."

But lengthy intercourse alone does not guarantee female orgasm. There is enormous variation in the rhythms, movements, and positions that work for individuals during intercourse, which implies that a certain experimental approach is called for—and a degree of honesty in communication that many couples find difficult to achieve.

the matter of multiples

Masters and Johnson confirmed an observation made earlier by Kinsey: that some women can have several consecutive orgasms.[2] After ejaculation, said Masters and Johnson, males have a *refractory period* during which they cannot have another erection no matter how much they are stimulated. Sometimes the period is brief (one young man in the laboratory had three orgasms in ten minutes), but more often it lasts many minutes or even hours, and as a man ages it tends to become longer. Women, according to Masters and Johnson, do not have a refractory period. If a woman is regularly orgasmic, and if she is stimulated further after her first orgasm, she can continue to climax: The clitoris retracts again; the veins in the genital area refill with blood; the muscles contract. Some women in the laboratory oscillated between the plateau (preorgasmic) phase of sexual arousal and orgasm for a considerable length of time. Masters and Johnson reported that these multiple orgasms were physiologically identical to, and subjectively often more intense than, the first one. During masturbation, especially with an electric vibrator, some women can have as many as fifty consecutive orgasms.

The existence of multiple orgasms in women deals a stunning blow to the old stereotype of female sexuality as emotional rather than physical. However, no one is sure how many women actually experience multiples. (Kinsey estimated 14 percent; others put the number higher.) Furthermore, in recording the physiology of multiple orgasm, Masters and Johnson were describing potential, not prescribing a standard. They did not suggest or imply that there is some ideal number of orgasms that women should strive for, or that a single orgasm is somehow inferior to a hundred consecutive ones. They intended only to report that multiorgasmic women are neither rare

[2]Kinsey's finding, reported in 1953, was too much for some people. Two psychiatrists, Edmund Bergler and William Kroger, rushed into print with *Kinsey's Myth of Female Sexuality* (1954). Bergler and Kroger maintained that Kinsey had been taken in by "vaginally frigid" women, "nymphomaniacs" who were counting near hits as bullseyes. Despite the fact that multiple orgasms had been reported in several studies before Kinsey's, Bergler and Kroger insisted that they were a physical impossibility.

nor unusual. But because individual variations are so great, people keep wondering whether their own experiences are typical or normal, and they are inclined to translate researchers' observations into unrealistic expectations. It's important to realize that no two women are exactly alike. Some women may indeed go from orgasm to plateau to orgasm as long as stimulation lasts. Others say they eventually have a "knockout" orgasm that brings them down to prearousal levels and leaves them insensitive to further stimulation. Still others are totally satisfied by a single, comparatively mild orgasm. The earth does not have to move, nor do orgasms have to occur at all, much less in a chain, for a person to enjoy a sexual experience. Lots of things, from individual differences to the emotional context of the sexual encounter, contribute to any one woman's response and how she feels about it.

Variations in the male orgasm have received little attention from the public or from sex researchers. But some observers think that men, too, can have multiple orgasms—that is, repeated climaxes, with or without ejaculation, during a single act of intercourse. According to Wardell Pomeroy, who worked with Kinsey:

> A man's experience of multiple orgasm is somewhat different from a woman's. In the male, each orgasm is distinct; after ejaculation the penis again grows turgid, excitement builds, and another climax is achieved. With women, however, multiple orgasm is often experienced as waves of more and more intense climaxes, each blending into the other. . . . The man's experience might be compared to the up-and-down levels of a graph, the woman's to widening concentric circles. (Pomeroy 1976, p. 204)

Pomeroy estimated that only about 20 percent of adolescent boys have this ability, which declines with age.

Researchers Mina Robbins and Gordon Jensen (personal communication) have brought the male multiple under scientific scrutiny. They found a young man who said he often had repeated orgasms without ejaculation, prior to his final, most intense orgasm with ejaculation. They brought him into their laboratory with his female companion, hooked him up to a polygraph, and found all the signs and symptoms of sequential orgasms: increased respiration and heart rate, muscular tension, urethral and anal contractions. After each climax, the man's erection lessened slightly for fifteen or twenty seconds, and then the next build up to another orgasm began. Robbins and Jensen (1977) have since interviewed thirteen men, aged twenty-two to fifty-six, who report the same capacity for multiples. By ceasing to thrust just before the moment of ejaculation, they apparently are able to control internal responses that are usually involuntary. The final orgasm, with thrusting, is the most intense, is accompanied by ejaculation, and is followed by a refractory period. So the male multiple is more common than previously assumed, though again, no one is sure just how widespread it is.

the vaginal-clitoral debate

When people aren't worrying about whether women should have orgasms at all or whether they should have one or many, they are worrying about what kinds of orgasms are normal, natural, and right. According to Freud and his followers, young girls concentrate on the clitoris for sexual satisfaction, but as they mature the vagina is supposed to become more important. Clitoral orgasms, it was thought, are active, vigorous, immature, and typical of women who deny their true femininity. For Freudian Helene Deutsch (1945) a clitoral orgasm was rather like a good sneeze: "In some cases the vigorous 'antimotherly' orgasm—as it may be termed—successfully realizes the woman's unconscious intention; by expelling the inflowing semen the woman can keep both the man and the undesired child away from her body." The mature vaginal orgasm, in contrast, was mellower, more ladylike:

> The typical function of the vagina during intercourse is passive-receptive. Its movements have the character of sucking in and relaxing, with a rhythm adjusted to that of the male partner. In the vast majority of women, if they are not disturbed, the sexual act does not culminate in a sphincterlike activity of the vagina but is brought to a happy end in a mild, slow relaxation with simultaneous lubrication and complete gratification. (Deutsch, reported in Moore 1961, p. 592)

As Masters and Johnson later showed, Deutsch's physiological description was far off the mark. But Deutsch, like Freud, had no qualms about speaking of the "vast majority" of women.

Kinsey was one of the first critics of Freud's theory that mature women get sexual satisfaction from vaginal, not clitoral, stimulation. He noted that the theory assumed the vagina is sensitive to pressure and stimulation. To test this assumption Kinsey asked five gynecologists to touch 879 women on the clitoris, vaginal wall, cervix, and other parts of the genital anatomy. Few women were even conscious of a touch on the vaginal lining or the cervix, but almost all were very sensitive to a touch on the clitoris. This is just what one would expect, said Kinsey, given that the vaginal tissues contain few nerves. In fact, the interior of the vagina is so insensitive that operations can sometimes be performed on it without anesthesia.

One problem with Kinsey's study was that the examined women were not sexually aroused; perhaps the vagina becomes more sensitive than the clitoris during intercourse. Masters and Johnson got around this problem by having volunteers use the artificial penis to simulate intercourse. This allowed them to observe the vagina and clitoris during orgasm. As we've seen, both organs are involved in sexual response, and the actual contractions of orgasm occur in the muscles encircling the lower vaginal walls. But Masters and Johnson found that no matter what the site and source of stimulation—vagina, clitoris, or breasts; penis, hand, or vibrator—the clitoris is "the primary focus for sensual response in the human female's pelvis."[3] Masters and Johnson concluded that it is useless (at best) to perpetuate the distinction between vaginal and clitoral orgasms.

But the controversy was not over. Before long some perceptive writers were pointing out that the physiological measurements that Masters and Johnson took were one thing but subjective experience was another. Women continued to report orgasms that felt different. For example, in a survey of 103 educated, articulate, and sexually active women, Barbara Seaman (1972) learned that some women always required direct clitoral stimulation to reach orgasm, while others swore that for a good orgasm they needed something—preferably a penis—in the vagina. Some women were certain that they experienced their orgasms in the clitoris, others were just as sure the site was the vagina. For a third group the site was sometimes the vagina and sometimes the clitoris. Some of these women felt that the vaginal variety was more restful or complete; others preferred the clitoral kind.

It is possible that Seaman's respondents actually shared the same experience but applied different labels to it. On the other hand, it is a bit presumptuous to decide that women don't experience what they say they do. Seaman reasonably pointed out that we ought to avoid confusing the physiologically observable aspects of an experience with the total experience:

> Today we know that all female orgasms are similar physiologically, which is an interesting medical fact but should not be a revolutionary

[3]The clitoris is the only organ in the body that has sexual pleasure as its *sole* purpose. Sex education books often neglect this fact, however. Many teach—incorrectly—that the vagina is analogous to the penis and is the main source of sexual pleasure for women.

one. Did the public go into paroxysms when some nineteenth-century doctor discovered that all dinners are digested the same way? No, because the public *knew* that all dinners do not taste the same and that a feast of Boeuf Bourguignonne or Homard en Coquille is an entirely different *experience* from a hasty meal of brown bread and water. (Seaman 1972, p. 62)

This brings up to the nub of the problem: Which sort of orgasm reaches the standards of French cuisine, and which is merely plain and ordinary fare? Seaman refused to answer that one, concluding wisely that "the liberated orgasm is any orgasm a woman likes."

You'd think the matter would stop there, but the labeling game goes on. Josephine Singer and Irving Singer (1972) took the novel position that there are not two but three varieties of female orgasm. The *vulval orgasm* is the one Masters and Johnson reported. The *uterine orgasm* occurs only during intercourse, and it does not produce the contractions of the vulval variety. Masters and Johnson missed this type of orgasm, the Singers believed, because it is emotionally very intense, and the atmosphere in the laboratory does not lend itself to such intensity of experience. Finally, the *blended orgasm*, as its name implies, combines elements of the other two types.

The most recent reincarnation of the vaginal-clitoral debate involves the Grafenberg spot, named for the physician who first reported it in the 1940s. According to John Perry and Beverly Whipple (1981), the "G-spot" is a small, sensitive area in or behind the front wall of the lower vagina, about two inches from the entrance. Perry and Whipple say the spot swells when stimulated by a penis or finger, though it is not clear why. They also claim that stimulating it triggers a nonclitoral orgasm that seems identical to the Singers' uterine orgasm. Further, some women with a Grafenberg spot expel a fluid through the urinary opening. Perry, Whipple, and their colleagues have argued that this fluid is neither urine nor vaginal secretions. A chemical analysis of the fluid from one such woman seemed to suggest that it resembled prostatic secretions in men (Addiego et al. 1981).

Articles on the G-spot, as well as a popular book on the subject, have been full of unverified assertions. But the first effort to verify Perry and Whipple's ideas scientifically (by a research team that included Whipple) has produced little supporting evidence. In a careful laboratory study of eleven women, six of whom claimed to be "ejaculators," all the women were examined by two gynecologists who did not know which women thought they ejaculated (Goldberg et al. 1983). In addition, the women masturbated to orgasm and any ejaculated fluid was collected. The physicians found an area similar to descriptions of the Grafenberg spot in only four of the eleven women—and only two of the four had said they were ejaculators. Moreover, although six women did emit a substance through the urinary opening, the researchers could detect no difference between any of the emissions and urine.

This study is important not only because it is the first rigorous attempt to substantiate the Grafenberg-spot hypothesis, but because it alerts us to the power of the media to create a phenomenon where none existed before. Goldberg and his colleagues reported that many of the women who initially volunteered for the study "seemed to be susceptible to suggestion. After hearing mass media accounts of female ejaculation, they thought they may be ejaculating. In fact they were merely lubricating" (1983). Finally, the anatomical structure of the G-spot—if it does exist—remains a mystery, and there is no evidence that all or even most women can learn to respond to its stimulation. (Some women respond sexually to massaging of the knee, but this doesn't mean that all women do—or want to.)

The vaginal-clitoral controversy and the hoopla about G-spots are not simply matters of scholarly disagreement or amusing misconceptions. People persist in arguing that one kind of orgasm is better or healthier than another, which shows that personal interests and emotions are at stake. Indeed, the very argument that orgasm is necessary to health is just as much of a value judgment as the idea that orgasm is detrimental to health; the fact that modern scientists can bring modern technology to the study of sex does not free them from their moral and intellectual predilections. Writer Robert S. Wieder (1983) has lamented "the recent decline of sexual literature into fad diets for the Id, perpetuating a kind of Orgasm-of-the-Month-Club that seemed to have run its course after Vaginal, Clitoral and Battery Powered. . . . The G spot premise merely panders to our contemporary pushbutton psychology, and would replace tenderness and affection with a kind of bloodless proficiency at sexual engineering."

sex in mind and action

Kinsey shocked the world when he discovered that in almost every area of sexual behavior women were far from being as sexless as the Victorians had hoped. But neither were they as sexy as the Victorians had feared. Men were more active than women on all measures of sexual activity—sexual fantasies, responses to erotica, masturbation, premarital and extramarital sex, and homosexuality. Do these differences survive?

sexual fantasies

In Kinsey's sample, more men than women reported fantasizing about sex, though women were as far from being asexual in mind as they were in deed. Kinsey was especially interested in fantasy during masturbation. He found that 89 percent of men who masturbated fantasized but only 64 percent of the women did, and the men did so much more regularly. The figure for women may be higher today, however, because sexual fantasy is becoming recognized as normal and appropriate for both sexes. In fact, although men may still fantasize more than women during masturbation, there is some evidence that women fantasize as much as or even more than men during intercourse (Hessellund 1976; Sue 1979). Perhaps women need fantasy more during intercourse when physical stimulation is not effective enough to bring on orgasm.

Indeed, recent books on female sexuality encourage women to use fantasy to enhance their sexual experiences. E. Barbara Hariton (1973), a psychologist, interviewed a group of upper middle class housewives and discovered that 65 percent had sexual fantasies during coitus; 28 percent reported occasional thoughts that could be considered fantasy. Many people, including some psychotherapists, have assumed that women who fantasize during sex are neurotic, bored, unhappy, or frustrated, but Hariton found no evidence of emotional instability, unhappiness, or neurosis among the women who fantasized. Instead they tended to be creative, nonconformist, and sexually active and satisfied.

In their fantasies, people of both sexes tend to imagine forbidden activities or partners, but certain themes are more characteristic of one sex than of the other (Hunt 1974; Sue 1979). Men are somewhat likelier than women to think about group sex, sex with a stranger, forcing someone to have sex, or overcoming a woman's initial resistance. Women are somewhat likelier than men to think about romantic situations or about being overpowered. Fantasies involving force, by the way, usually do not include physical violence or psychological degradation, and therefore should not be thought of as rape fantasies. For both men and women fantasies are a way of mentally playacting certain cultural erotic roles or of experiencing a side of oneself that one cannot or would not want to express in real life. Indeed, most fantasies have little to do with reality. Many women who occasionally fantasize about being dominated sexually are themselves assertive, independent, and professionally successful (Hariton 1973; Singer and Switzer 1980).

responses to erotica

Kinsey reported that men and women differed considerably in their responses to erotic stimuli. Far more men than women reported being turned on by pornography and erotic materials. For example, 54 percent of the men said they had been aroused by photographs, drawings, or paintings of nude figures, compared to only 12 percent of the women. Although almost half of the men who heard erotic stories reported being aroused by them, the same was true for only 14 percent of the women—and more women than men said they were offended. Even Kinsey, who soon stopped being startled by the sexual preferences of his interviewees, was surprised at how few females reported being turned on by erotic stories. The only kind of psychological stimulation to which women seemed more susceptible than men came from ordinary movies. Kinsey attributed this result to the romantic or emotional atmosphere that is part-and-parcel of erotic scenes in most movies.

But in a series of studies at the University of Hamburg, Gunter Schmidt and Volkmar Sigusch (1973) observed how college students reacted to sexually explicit stories, slides, and films. On the average, men reported slightly more sexual arousal to the materials than women, but in both sexes there was a lot of variation from individual to individual; 42 percent of the women who saw the films and slides were more aroused than the average man. Women were also more likely than men to describe themselves as shocked or disgusted by the erotica. In general, though, the sexual and emotional reactions of the men and women were more alike than different.

Most important, the majority of both women and men in the German studies reported physiological signs of sexual arousal to the erotica. When Schmidt and Sigusch grouped all kinds of reactions together—in men, pre-ejaculatory emissions, erections, and ejaculation; in women, vaginal lubrication, genital or breast sensations, and orgasm—they found that 80 to 91 percent of the men and 70 to 83 percent of the women had been aroused.

There are problems in generalizing from these results. College students are more permissive toward sexuality than many other groups, and those in northwestern Europe seem to be more permissive than their American counterparts. Studies such as Schmidt and

Sigusch's do show, though, that there is nothing inevitable about a sex difference in reactions to erotic materials.

It may have occurred to you that women may be more likely to lie or at least to be evasive about their responses to pornography. Or they may be less sensitive to physiological signs of arousal. Julia Heiman (1975), a psychologist, got around these problems by recording the actual physiological responses of college men and women while they listened to taped erotic stories. Males wore a flexible circlet (rather like a rubber band) around the base of the penis. The device, called a strain gauge, is filled with mercury and measures blood volume and pressure pulse, recording the slightest sign of an erection. Women got a newly designed device called a photoplethysmograph, a small acrylic cylinder containing a photocell and light source. When inserted just inside the vagina, the photoplethysmograph registers changes in blood volume and pressure pulse, early indications of sexual arousal.

The students listened to four kinds of tapes: erotic stories about explicit sex; romantic versions of the same stories; stories that were both romantic and erotic; and control stories that were neither erotic nor romantic. In general, the women were as likely as the men to be turned on physiologically while listening to the erotic stories, and for both sexes straight sex was more arousing than romance alone. Further, there was no evidence that these women preferred romantic-erotic stories to ones that were simply erotic. In fact, when the students evaluated the stories subjectively, the women rated the erotic ones as more arousing than did the men.

Although previous findings of a sex difference in response to pornography may have been due to women's difficulties in recognizing or admitting arousal, it's also possible that a real change has taken place since Kinsey's day. Women today are exposed to more erotica than they were then, and the content of the material is becoming more female-oriented. It is more permissible than it once was for a woman to enjoy magazines like *Playgirl*, to go to pornographic movies, and even to hang pictures of nude males on her bulletin board. Familarity does not always breed contempt.[4]

---

[4]And then again, sometimes it does. Many feminists, while endorsing erotic images of sensuality and freely offered sex, condemn the sexual sadism against women featured in many pornographic films, books, and magazines (see Steinem 1978). There is good reason for this concern; Evidence is accumulating that violent pornography can promote sexually aggressive behavior or foster apathy toward the sexual aggression of others (Malamuth 1981).

masturbation

In our great-grandparents' eyes, masturbation was not only evil and disgusting but downright dangerous. Victorian physicians warned that stimulating yourself sexually could lead to acne, blindness, impotence, insanity, coughing spells, muscular convulsions, fever, and warts. Some worried that masturbation would drain men of semen, which they regarded as a scarce substance to be hoarded carefully and dispensed stingily on special occasions. Like an engine without fuel, it was thought, a man low on semen would soon stop running. For this reason, many experts also condemned nocturnal emissions (wet dreams) and too frequent coitus. Special horrors were reserved for the autoerotic woman. In addition to the usual illnesses, she would suffer loss of flesh, gastric and uterine disorders, emaciation, and bad breath. She risked turning into a pale, ugly, filthy nymphomaniac who would die a lingering death.

In the post-Victorian period, masturbation, like other forms of sexual expression, became somewhat more acceptable—for males. In females stimulation of the labia and clitoris, the commonest type of masturbation, was deemed immature and masculine. Freud, whose writings greatly influenced sexual standards, considered the clitoris a stunted penis and felt that the sooner a woman accepted this fact and turned to bigger and better things, the happier she would be.

Because of the strong taboos against masturbation, most people in the pre-Kinsey era believed it to be quite rare. Kinsey set off shock waves when he announced that the practice was more popular than baseball. Virtually all of the men in his sample (92 percent) had masturbated, and quite frequently at that. But what really stunned people was Kinsey's report that 62 percent of the females he interviewed had masturbated, almost all to the point of orgasm. In Hunt's *Playboy* sample, about the same overall proportions of men and women had masturbated as in the Kinsey sample, but women were beginning to do so earlier and with greater frequency.

Thus, masturbation is widespread, but many women still never do it. Furthermore, in Kinsey's study practically all males who masturbated began during adolescence, but many females did not discover masturbation until their twenties, thirties, or even forties. These facts are important, because masturbation appears to play a crucial role in sexual development. It is the most common source of the first orgasm, and, according to Kinsey, the most important source of orgasm for young, single people.[5] And it provides a person with an opportunity to become familiar with his or her unique responses to sexual stimulation, free from social and performance pressures inherent in sex with a partner.

What are the consequences for women if they miss this opportunity? The factor that best predicts whether a women will have orgasms during marital coitus is whether she has had any orgasms, by whatever means, before marriage. Since the largest number of women achieve premarital orgasm through masturbation, masturbation is strongly related to the ability to have coital orgasms after marriage. Kinsey found that a third of all females who never masturbated to orgasm before marriage failed to reach orgasm in coitus during the first year of marriage, and in most instances during the first five years. Only 13 to 15 percent of those who did masturbate before marriage were totally unresponsive during the early years of marriage. Kinsey was aware that these statistics did not *prove* that masturbation makes coital orgasm easier, because those who masturbated before marriage might have been more erotically inclined in the first place. But he believed that there was a causal connection. In his section on female masturbation he wrote, "In many a specific history it appeared that the quality of the marital response was furthered by the female's previous knowledge of the nature of a sexual orgasm." He also observed the opposite, namely, that a girl who avoids sexual arousal throughout childhood and adolescence— "withdrawing from physical contacts and tensing her muscles in order to avoid response"—becomes conditioned, and she does not shed these inhibitions easily after marriage.

Kinsey's view is so widely accepted today by sex therapists and educators that masturbation has been transformed from a "perversion" into a treatment for sexual problems. Many maintain that it is especially useful for women who have never experienced orgasm by any means; by masturbating, the women learn what arouses them, then transfer the lesson to intercourse (Barbach 1975). Some therapists also prescribe masturbation for men who want to acquire better control over their sexual responsiveness. However, while we

[5]In Kinsey's sample, 40 percent of the females experienced their first orgasm during masturbation, 27 percent during coitus (premarital or marital), 24 percent during petting, 5 percent during an erotic dream, 3 percent during homosexual activity, and 1 percent during "psychological stimulation." Sixty-eight percent of the males ejaculated for the first time during masturbation, 13 percent during a nocturnal emission, 12.5 percent during coitus, and about 4 percent during homosexual activity.

think it is clear that masturbation does help people learn about their own responses and overcome inhibitions, it has not been convincingly demonstrated that the lessons of masturbation invariably do transfer to intercourse following therapy (see Payn 1980). The modern emphasis on the joys of self-pleasure may be the antithesis of the Victorian emphasis on the dangers of self-abuse, but in either case we must separate personal preferences from statistical generalizations.

premarital and extramarital sex

The respectable Victorian girl was expected to "save" herself until marriage, so that she could present the precious gift of virginity to her husband. If he also saved himself for her, so much the better, but it was understood that many young men would not achieve that goal. Today a majority of Americans have a more favorable view of premarital sex, especially if the partners feel strong affection for each other (Hunt 1974; Tavris and Sadd 1977). Yet approval is far from universal. Recently the Vatican reaffirmed its position that "every genital act must be within the framework of marriage." And a few years ago, when Betty Ford told an interviewer that she would not condemn her daughter for having a premarital affair, her tolerant attitude created somewhat of a furor.

The furor came years too late. Kinsey found that while most women born before 1900 (86 percent) had been virgins on their wedding nights, by the 1950s virginity was honored more in word than in deed. Nearly half of the married women in Kinsey's sample had coitus before they were married. (The figures for men were even higher: 98 percent of those with a grade-school education, 85 percent of high-school graduates, and 68 percent of those with some college had had premarital intercourse.) On the other hand, Kinsey did not find that premarital sex had become a casual matter for women. Over half of the women who had sex before marriage had only one partner, almost always the fiancé. A third had two to five partners, and only 13 percent had more than five. For most of the women Kinsey interviewed, premarital sex occurred in the context of a serious relationship.

During the 1960s discussion flourished about whether premarital sex was still on the increase. Some sociologists argued that since the 1920s behavior had not changed nearly so much as attitudes about sex; people were not acting differently, they were simply talking more openly and tolerantly (Reiss 1960, 1969; Bell 1966). This view eventually gave way before mounting evidence of real

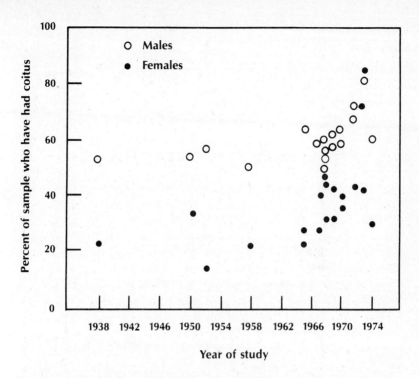

Figure 3. Each point represents the result from a study of premarital intercourse among college women or men. Although findings vary, taken as a whole they reveal a clear upward trend starting in the mid-1960s.
SOURCE: Offir 1982; originally adapted from Hopkins 1977.

behavioral change beginning in the mid-1960s (see Figure 3). Since most males had always had premarital experience, women accounted for most of the change. In Kinsey's study, less than a fifth of nineteen-year-old single women said they had had intercourse. In contrast, a national study of over 4,000 young unmarried women conducted in 1971 found that almost half the nineteen-year-olds were no longer virgins (Kantner and Zelnik 1972). And a replication only five years later found that over half were now nonvirgins, and intercourse was beginning at a slightly younger age on the average—16.2 years, versus 16.5 in 1971 (Zelnik and Kantner 1977).

The trend away from female virginity, then, has continued (see also Jessor et al. 1983). Various studies produce somewhat different tallies, depending on their methods and samples (see Table 4), but the inescapable conclusion is that the virgin bride is following the route

Table 4. Premarital Intercourse Among Women

Study and year[a]	Subjects	Percentage reporting premarital intercourse
Kinsey et al. 1953 [1938–1949]	Unmarried women age 19	18–19%
Hunt 1974 (Playboy survey) [1972]	Married women ages 18–24	81
Kantner and Zelnik 1972 [1971]	Never-married women age 19	46
	white women only	40
	black women only	80
Jessor and Jessor 1975 [1972]	Unmarried fourth-year college women	85
Tavris and Sadd 1977 [1974] (Redbook readers)	Married women ages 20–24	91
	Married women under 20	96
Zelnik and Kantner 1977 [1976]	Never-married women age 19	55
	white women only	49
	black women only	84
Jessor et al. 1983 [1979]	Unmarried and married women ages 23–25	86[b]

[a]Period of data collection is given in brackets.
[b]Frances Costa, personal communication.

The figures on premarital intercourse depend in part on the age and race of the respondents and whether they were married or still single at the time of the study. It is clear, though, that American women are becoming more like American men, who almost all have intercourse by the time they marry.
SOURCE: Adapted from Offir 1982.

of the buffalo and becoming a statistical rarity. Men are still more likely than women to have sex before marriage, but the gap is narrowing and may soon disappear altogether.

But merely counting virgins can be misleading. When we go beyond the general numbers, we find that an important difference between men and women is still alive: Though fewer women today demand to be engaged before agreeing to sex, women who have sex before marriage (and marry fairly young) are still likely to have as partners only the one, or maybe two, men they love; men are more likely to sleep with the many, or any, they like. In Hunt's survey, half the married men reported at least six premarital partners, while over half the married women with premarital experience reported only one. The average number of partners may have increased somewhat for women in the past decade: In Kantner and Zelnik's 1971 sample, 61 percent of sexually experienced teenage women had had only one partner; but by 1976 the number had shrunk to only half. (Remember, since these women were single, the numbers do not indicate total number of partners before marriage.) But at the same time, only 11.3 percent of the white teenagers reported six or more partners, and only 6 percent of the black teenagers did so.

We see similar trends in extramarital sex. In recent years Americans have become more tolerant about extramarital sex; while only a few believe it should be encouraged, an equally small number think it is always wrong under all circumstances. Studies find that the majority of people regard adultery the way they regard eating garlic: It's fine for them, but they don't want anyone near them to do it—especially their spouses.

Kinsey found that men were more likely than women to have sex not only before marriage but outside of it. Though he did not present exact statistics, he estimated that about half of the husbands he interviewed had intercourse with a woman other than their wives at some time during their married lives. In contrast, only about one-fourth of the wives had sex with someone other than their husbands. Even this percentage of women is inflated because Kinsey included a disproportionate number of divorced women in his calculations, and they were more likely than never-divorced wives to have had ex-tramarital sex. When Hunt recomputed Kinsey's statistics, taking this overrepresentation into account, he estimated that the incidence of extramarital sex in Kinsey's time was closer to one woman in five.

Since Kinsey's time, however, changes have occurred among women, most dramatically among young women. In Kinsey's sample, only some 8 percent of married women under age twenty-five had had extramarital sex, but in Hunt's study about a quarter had. A generation ago, only a third as many young wives as husbands reported an extramarital experience, but today three-fourths as many young wives as husbands do. Unfortunately, more recent studies have used only special populations, such as the readers of a particular magazine, so it is hard to say how many women overall now have extramarital affairs, but many estimates put the number as high as 40 or 50 percent (for example Rubenstein 1983).

Women, then, may soon be—if they are not now—as likely as men to have at least one extramarital experience. Again, though, differences between men and women in number of partners and in motives remain. It could be that men have more partners because they have more opportunities; a *Redbook* survey (Tavris and Sadd 1977) found that employed wives are more likely to have sexual affairs than unemployed wives (though some smaller studies have found the opposite). But it is also possible that women enter extramarital liaisons, like premarital ones, less for lust than for love. For women, having sex outside marriage is still strongly correlated with marital dissatisfaction (Tavris and Sadd 1977). Men are more likely than women to pursue novelty for its own sake and to try to distinguish emotionally the casual encounter from the serious commitment of marriage.

homosexuality

Until the Kinsey study, people assumed that homosexual behavior must be very rare and that it would attract only the "sick" or "perverted." Kinsey redefined the whole question. Homosexuality, he said, is not an either-or matter: "The world is not to be divided into sheep and goats." Sexual behavior falls along a continuum, with the exclusively homosexual and exclusively heterosexual at the two ends and all mixtures in between. Some people enjoy coitus with a partner of the opposite sex but prefer same-sex relationships; some go through a lengthy period of exclusively homosexual activity and then become exclusively heterosexual; some have homosexual fantasies but no corresponding experience; and so on. Kinsey decided to avoid the label *homosexual* and instead to describe frequencies of homosexual behavior and ratios of homosexual to heterosexual experiences.

In Kinsey's sample, only 4 percent of the males were exclusively homosexual throughout their lives. However, by age forty-five about 37 percent of all men had experienced at least one homosexual encounter leading to orgasm. When Kinsey considered all erotic response, whether or not it involved orgasm or even sexual contact, fully half of the men said they had experienced homosexual arousal. Kinsey, to say nothing of the American public, was astonished by these findings.

In this area of sexuality, too, the figures for women were lower. By age forty-five, 20 percent had had a homosexual experience, and the percentage fell to 13 percent when only encounters leading to orgasm were counted. Only 1 to 3 percent of the women said they were exclusively homosexual.

Many researchers are unhappy with Kinsey's statistics on homosexuality. A few believe his figures are too low, because some people with homosexual experience were probably unwilling to admit their behavior. But others, like Hunt, have argued that the figures are too high. Kinsey sought out homosexuals to interview, so they were overrepresented in his sample. Further, his startling 37 percent figure for men included many who had a single exploratory experience, usually during adolescence. Hunt calculated that only about one in ten males in Kinsey's sample was "more or less exclusively homosexual" for three years or more after the age of fifteen. The female percentages were also inflated, because single women, who are more likely than married women to have homosexual experiences, were overrepresented. All in all, concluded Hunt, homosexual behavior is not as common as Kinsey's data indicate, nor has it increased much during the past two decades, though it has definitely come out of the closet.

Whatever the precise figures, surveys consistently find that males are more apt to try a homosexual experience and to be exclusively homosexual than females are. In a *Psychology Today* survey, 4 percent of the males but only 1 percent of the females said they were exclusively homosexual; 66 percent of the females but only 48 percent of the males said they had never had a homosexual experience and never would (Athanasiou, Shaver, and Tavris 1970). Males also report more partners. Kinsey found that 22 percent of the male homosexuals but only 4 percent of the females had had eleven or more partners; Hunt's figures were 8 percent and 1 percent, respectively.

In a survey of homosexuals in the San Francisco Bay area, psychologist Alan Bell and sociologist Martin Weinberg (1978) discovered even more dramatic differences. Most lesbians reported having had fewer than ten sexual partners, and almost half said they had never had a one-night stand. But the *average* male in this study reported hundreds of partners, many of them in one-night stands; over a quarter reported a thousand or more partners. A few of these men may have been exaggerating; also, gay people in San Francisco, which is known for its acceptance of homosexuality and for a gay male subculture dedicated to "cruising," (searching, in public places, for a sexual partner), may not be representative of the national gay population. But gay men obviously have far more partners than do gay women.

As one might expect, given the above figures, lesbians are more likely than gay men to form long-term relationships (although a majority of both sexes have had at least one such relationship, and both sexes say they value love and companionship). In the *Psychology Today* sample, 60 percent of female homosexuals but only 33 percent of male homosexuals said they were currently living with a lover. In the Bell and Weinberg study, about half the males, as opposed to three-fourths of the females, were in a relatively stable relationship at the time they were interviewed. Some writers think this difference between gay men and women reflects traditional attitudes toward love versus lust, attachment versus novelty, and thus has less to do with whether one is straight or gay than with whether one is a man or a woman. Is there something naturally promiscuous about men and something naturally more loving about women? Or does society encourage recreational sex for men and relational sex for women?

perceptions of sex and love

We have seen that in terms of sexual physiology, males and females are not drastically different: Both undergo similar bodily changes; some percentage of both can apparently have multiple orgasms, if effectively stimulated; both use the same terms to describe the subjective experience of orgasm—tension, muscle spasms, temporary loss of awareness, warm feelings of release. Now it seems that differences in sexual behavior are fading, particularly in such areas as premarital and extramarital sex. Among many Americans, expressed sexual attitudes and actual sexual behavior have changed over the past few decades almost as rapidly as the cost of living.

But when we dig below the surface of the sexual statistics, we find some old, familiar themes.

sexual motives

When psychologist Judith Bardwick (1971) asked some college women why they made love, she got answers like the following:

> "He'd leave me if I didn't sleep with him."
> "Right now to please him."
> "Well, a great strain not to. Fairly reluctant for a while, but then I realized it had become a great big thing in the relationship and it would disintegrate the relationship. . . . I wanted to also."

"Mostly to see my boyfriend's enjoyment."
"I gave in to Sidney because I was lonely."

Few of Bardwick's interviewees said that they made love because *they* wanted to and because they physically enjoyed sex. Bardwick concluded that most of them accepted sex as the price of a romantic relationship or as a way to prove their love. Whereas previous generations of women had said no to premarital sex because they feared they would lose the man if they said yes, Bardwick's work suggested that many young women were beginning to say yes because they feared they would lose the man if they said no. Bardwick's anecdotal observations, though reported some time ago, continue to be supported by those of other psychologists and educators.

Thus, although more women are having premarital sex than ever before, their reasons often differ from men's. The differences show up in the very first experience with intercourse: Women's first experience is more likely than men's to occur in a committed relationship or with someone they love (Athanasiou, Shaver, and Tavris 1970; Christensen and Gregg 1970; Jessor et al. 1983). Women are still far less likely than men to seek sexual adventure for its own sake.

Further, when young women have sex, sexual gratification is sometimes the farthest thing from their minds. In one study, 23 percent of college women said that during their first premarital experience they yielded because of force or a sense of obligation rather than personal desire; only 2.5 percent of the men said the same (Christensen and Gregg 1970). And the old stereotype that women use sex to get love while men use love to get sex has some truth in it. In a survey on sex roles, more than half of the men but only 15 percent of the women said they had told a sex partner they cared more for her or him than they really did in order to have sex. In contrast, a fourth of the women but very few of the men admitted using sex to bind a partner into a relationship (Tavris 1973).

In an imaginative study, Terry Smith Hatkoff and Thomas E. Lasswell (1977), borrowing a typology of love first proposed by Canadian sociologist John Alan Lee (1974), had several hundred volunteers rate themselves on a paper-and-pencil "love scale." They found that men scored much higher than women on items designed to measure a "ludic" approach to love. In Latin *ludus* means "a game." The ludic approach seems to have more to do with sexual conquest than it does with romance, commitment, interdependence, or other aspects of love; in fact, most people probably would not consider it a kind of love at all. Hatkoff and Lasswell described the typical ludic lover as

> a person who "plays" love affairs as he or she plays games or works puzzles—to win, to demonstrate his/her skill or superiority. A ludic lover may keep two or three or even four lovers "on the string" at one time. Sex is self-centered and exploitative rather than symbolic of a relationship. . . . Such a person usually enjoys love affairs, and hence rarely regrets them unless the threat of commitment or dependency becomes too great. (p. 223)

This does not mean that most men are ludic types; on the contrary, most people of both sexes prefer to have sex in a loving, committed relationship (Rubenstein 1983). But it does explain why you can think of more male ludic lovers, from Casanova to Hugh Hefner, than female sexual adventurers.

The greater tendency of men to separate sex and love may result as much from social pressures as from individual desires. In Hunt's survey, 60 percent of the males and 37 percent of the females thought premarital coitus was all right for men even without strong affection, but only 44 percent of the men and 20 percent of the women gave the same privilege to women. Study after study confirms that women risk stronger disapproval if they choose to be ludic. Young men who have many sexual partners are known as rakes, playboys, studs—terms that are more positive than negative. But young women who have multiple partners are branded "easy lays," "sluts," and worse. Little wonder that young women, though sexually more active than ever before, must still worry about their reputations and try to preserve at least the appearance of chastity. Conversely, there are strong pressures on young men to "score"—to have as many sexual partners as possible. One young man we know felt he needed therapy because he liked sex only with the woman he loved.

the mixed messages of courtship

"I am twenty-one, a newly minted college graduate, and my roommate and I take a celebration trip to Mexico. She is blond, demure, very feminine. We meet two men: a CPA who believes in the emancipation of women (he chooses me), and an unemployed bullfighter who does not (he chooses my friend). The four of us have dinner, dance, tell stories, laugh; later, the bullfighter drives us on a tour around the city. Everyone is happy until the bullfighter tells my friend that he loves her and desires her desperately. She politely refuses. His demeanor changes at once: the gentle, whimsical fellow becomes a demented madman. Careening the car wildly along the road, shouting all the while at the object of his lusts, he drives us into the countryside. None of us, not even his compadre, can stop him.

"Suddenly he stops the car and drags my friend out by her arm. As she stands, shaking, he drops his pants to reveal his private accoutrements. 'Look at me!' he demands. 'Can you still refuse my manhood?' Somehow, she can. After a few more tense minutes, the bullfighter shoves her back into the car and takes us home.

"The next day the CPA calls to apologize to me. 'This is the problem with Mexican men,' he says sadly. 'We must teach our boys to be hombres, real men, not these brutal machos. Will you have dinner with me?' He is so woebegone that I agree.

"The bullfighter calls to apologize to my friend. If she spurned his sexual overtures, she must be a real virgin. He asks her to marry him, or at least to have a drink. She does not agree.

"Postscript: I have dinner with the CPA. He attacks me in the street on the way back to my hotel, and I have to claw his face to escape. I get away with one last image of his eyes, suffused with loathing and rage." (From Tavris 1982)

This particular incident, which happened to an American woman in Mexico, could have involved people of any ethnic group in the United States, where "date rape" is far from rare. How does it happen that men and women miscommunicate so badly? The answer, it seems to us, is that many men and women remain obedient actors in a dating script straight out of the 1950s—and unfortunately they often don't understand each other's lines. In spite of the sexual "liberation" of women, men are still expected to initiate the social action, whether making a date or a pass, and women are still expected to accept or refuse (McCormick 1977). The problem is that men and women often unconsciously disagree on what constitutes a sexual invitation or a sexual refusal.

A group of researchers at UCLA interviewed over four hundred Los Angeles adolescents, aged 14 through 18, about their expectations regarding dating and sexual relationships (Zellman et al. 1979; Giarrusso et al. 1979). These young people had grown up with the "sexual revolution." Almost all had at least some dating experience, and a majority (71 percent of the males, 51 percent of the females) had had sexual intercourse. Yet boys and girls were as unalike as their fathers and mothers before them in the way they viewed dating partners and dating situations. Here are some of the differences:

1. Boys are more likely to regard tight or revealing clothing as a signal that a person desires sex—especially when such clothing is worn by a girl. In other words, when Anita wears the latest tight designer jeans she may simply be trying to keep up with her fashion-conscious girlfriends, but Joe may conclude she's trying to seduce him.

2. Girls are less likely than boys to feel that a female who accepts a date with a known Don Juan is implicitly agreeing to have sex. On the other hand, girls are more likely than boys to feel that a male has a right to expect sex from a girl who has a "bad reputation."

3. Boys are consistently more likely than girls to regard particular locations or activities as signals for sex. Thus a male may assume his date wants sex just because of where he finds her, when in fact she intends nothing of the kind, and we get the classic confrontation: She says she doesn't want sex, but she goes to his apartment for a drink, because she wants him to know that she's interested in him—or maybe she's just thirsty. He, however, assumes that her acceptance of his invitation means she wants him to make a pass. He makes it, and when she turns him down, he puffs up with righteous anger. After all, didn't she lead him on, act like a tease, and then capriciously change her mind? She feels betrayed too: She *told* him she didn't want sex, and then he went and ruined the evening for both of them.

4. Girls view a variety of verbal, physical, and romantic actions in a less sexual light than boys do. Consider such activities as talking about sex, playing with a date's hair, tickling or wrestling with a date, telling a date how sexy, good looking, or understanding he or she is, and staring into a date's eyes: To a boy these are likely to be signs of sexual interest; to a girl, they are likely to be signs of affection. Girls are also more likely to distinguish between males and females who do such things. They feel that if a girl tells a partner he is good looking or that she loves him, her words are less indicative of sexual interest than the same message would be coming from a boy.

5. When the teenagers in the study were asked whether it was ever permissible to hold a girl down and force her to have sex, most agreed that it was not. But when they were confronted with nine specific situations (for example, "The girl has led the guy on," or "He's so turned on he can't stop"), only a minority rejected forced sex—otherwise known as rape—in all the situations. And once again, startling sex differences appeared. Males are much more tolerant about forced sex than females are. More girls than boys (44 percent versus 24 percent) condemned it in all nine situations, and males were more accepting than females in each specific situation. Both sexes, though, think that if a boy forces a girl with a bad reputation into having sex, then she "deserves" it.

In sum, young women see the world of male-female relationships in a less sexualized way than young men do. As the researchers noted, this difference virtually guarantees a continuing battle of the sexes: first, because males and females misread each other's sexual and emotional signals; second, because males are more likely to endorse the idea of sexual force, making the battle a literal as well as a figurative one. Obviously, though, there is more to sexual relations than sexual skirmishes, and so we turn now to the question of how men and women view the emotional connection between the sexes.

romance versus intimacy

Women are supposed to be the more romantic sex. After all, they are the ones devouring the gothic novels and swooning over the soap-opera seductions. (Men, practical lunkheads that they are, supposedly wouldn't recognize a romantic thought if it sat on their heads, whistling Dixie.) But romantic fantasy, like sexual fantasy, does not necessarily tell us what a person values or wants in real life.

Psychologist Zick Rubin was among the first to study the stereotype of male-female differences in romance. In the spring of 1972 he and his colleagues Anne Peplau and Charles Hill recruited 231 college couples who were going together. They gave the students extensive questionnaires and then followed up with further questionnaires and some interviews in late 1972, 1973, and 1974. Unexpectedly, they found that men tended to fall in love more quickly and easily than women, and that men rated the desire to fall in love as a more important reason for having entered the relationship than the women did. When Rubin looked up some earlier studies of love and attraction, he found the same pattern.

At the end of three years, 103 of the couples (45 percent) had split up. The researchers asked these students why their relationship had crumbled and who had been the one to end it. In most instances, there had been a breaker-upper and a broken-up-with, although the two ex-lovers did not always agree on who was which. Women were somewhat more likely to end the relationship; further, men reported feeling more depressed, lonely, and unhappy after the end of the affair than women did (Hill, Rubin, and Peplau 1976). In Rubin's words, "Man proposes, woman disposes."

More recent studies have continued to find that men are the more romantic sex. Hatkoff and Lasswell (1977), for instance, discovered that men are not only more ludic than women but also more romantic (the researchers used the word *erotic*)—they believe in love at first sight, hope to fall in love, and want to know everything about their beloved from the first moment (without worrying that this onslaught of information could shatter their idealized image of the loved one). Ludic and erotic styles of love and sexual attraction are not as incompatible as they may appear; actually, it's the old pedestal-gutter syndrome in new disguise. When men regard women as "sluts" or playthings, they can completely separate sex from love; when they think they've found the romantic ideal, they elevate the woman onto a pedestal, to be worshipped, protected, and pursued.

It's not, of course, that women cannot be romantic or ludic, but this polarity seems to be more characteristic of men. Nor is it the case that women have no emotional investment in romantic liaisons, or that once in a relationship they do not experience it as intensely as do men. They do, but at the same time they seem less likely than men to allow themselves to be swept away by their emotions at the start of a relationship. Often they first judge the suitability of the prospective lover, and only then (if he passes the test) do they permit themselves to feel love. Emotions may seem to have little to do with economics, but sociologist Arlie Hochschild (1975) has argued that for many women love does have an economic motive—marrying the best breadwinner—and for this reason women are more likely than men to talk themselves into or out of love, depending on the situation, and to seem obsessed with finding love and keeping it. (Women's magazines frequently offer advice to their readers on how to get their men to love them again, a topic rarely mentioned in men's magazines.)

Thus, in the Hatkoff and Lasswell study, women scored higher than men on "pragmatic" love. The pragmatist is unable or unwilling to invest love in love objects deemed unworthy. She assesses her own "market value" and tries to make the best possible "deal" for herself. She checks out future in-laws and thinks ahead about such issues as family size (Hatkoff and Lasswell 1977). The pragmatist may also walk out if her love is not returned. In the Hill, Rubin, and Peplau study (1976), men ended relationships when they had become relatively uninvolved, but women ended them both when they were uninvolved *and* when they were highly involved. Why would someone who is still in love end a relationship? One possibility is that women care more about the quality of an affair and thus are readier to say "Love me or leave me." But another is that women are more goal-oriented (that is, pragmatic) than men: They are less likely to stay in an affair for love's sake if it isn't going to meet their long-range objectives. If a woman's status and income are going to depend on her husband's, she must be careful to whom she gives her heart and not waste time on a relationship that's going nowhere. As sociologist Willard Waller said (1938), "A man, when he marries, chooses a companion and perhaps a helpmate, but a woman chooses a companion and at the same time a standard of living. It is necessary for a woman to be mercenary."[6]

But wait, you say: Women no longer have to be so mercenary; these days they can earn money in their own right. What does this portend for the future of romance? Some writers predict that as the sexes spend more time together, romantic love, which depends on a longing for the unfamiliar and on delayed sexual gratification, will fade away. Says one, "The notions of agony and ecstasy traditionally associated with this kind of love have become meaningless—in fact, quaint" (Kinget 1977).

The evidence, however, shows that if anything, women are apt to become *more* romantic, not less. Almost two decades ago, William Kephart (1967) asked college students whether they would marry a person who had all the qualities they desired but whom they did not love. Two-thirds of the men said no, but only a quarter of the women ruled out the possibility. Only a decade later, in a replication of the study, this sex difference had nearly disappeared. Everyone was more romantic, and especially women: 86 percent of the men and 80 percent of the women indicated that they would hold out for love (Campbell and Berscheid 1976; see also Berscheid, in press). This makes sense in light of economic changes since the 1960s; now that most women plan to work and earn money, they feel they are free, like men, to marry for love. Another long-standing sex difference seems to be biting the dust.[7]

Romance, however, usually flowers at the start of a relationship, and implies little or nothing about how the sexes get along once they are committed to a long-term relationship. Do men and women differ

[6]When Scottish scientist Lord DeWar described love as "an ocean of emotions, entirely surrounded by expenses," he may not have realized that he had touched on the difference between romantics and pragmatists. If more men indulge in the emotions, more women coolly consider the surrounding expenses.

[7]Although some feminist writings have been antiromantic, profeminist women are generally no less romantic than their traditional counterparts (Greenblat and Baron 1983). Americans of all philosophical persuasions accept romantic love as the proper basis of marriage, despite evidence that romantic love is always ephemeral. However, the idea that love and marriage go together like a horse and carriage is not common historically or cross-culturally.

in their willingness to nurture a relationship, worry about it, invest in it? Conventional wisdom says yes. Even the strong-willed Scarlett O'Hara, in *Gone With the Wind*, wound up begging Rhett Butler to stay. He, of course, didn't give a damn.

Once again, however, the real differences seem to lie more in the way people interpret situations than in the value they place on them. Both sexes consider love and family to be high on their list of priorities, and in the last twenty years men in particular have rated family life higher than they used to (Veroff, Douvan, and Kulka 1981). Both sexes, as Rubin and others have found, are miserable about losing love and affection. But just as boys and girls interpret sexual signals differently, so it appears that men and women interpret love and intimacy differently. What to a man may be a clear sign of love ("Well, I'm here with you, aren't I? I took you to Acapulco, didn't I? What more do you want?") will not seem so to a woman who wants verbal reassurance and heart-to-heart conversations as a sign of caring ("You never *talk* to me"). Both sexes may want intimacy, but they often seem to attach quite different meanings to the word.

For example, some men seem to equate female-style intimacy with smothering and entrapment, while some women, seeking feelings of closeness, regard the male reaction as a fear of commitment. A study in which college students wrote stories in response to a series of pictures clearly revealed this sex difference (Pollack and Gilligan 1982). Men were more likely than women to write violent scenarios when the picture depicted affiliation between people; when the pictures were about achievement, the reverse was true. In response to one picture that showed a couple sitting on a bench by a river, more than a fifth of the males produced grim stories about homicide, suicide, stabbing, kidnapping, or rape, while *none* of the females' stories for this picture contained violent imagery.

These findings don't mean that men hate women, only that they tend to see danger in relationships. "The danger men describe in their stories of intimacy is a danger of entrapment or betrayal, being caught in a smothering relationship or humiliated by rejection and deceit," says Gilligan (1982). Women, in contrast, regard intimacy as a safe harbor from isolation and loneliness (see also Rubenstein and Shaver 1982). In other research, too, men seem ambivalent about emotional attachment and expression, perhaps because these imply vulnerability (Dion and Dion 1977). But in certain other cultures, such as Japan, both sexes seek interdependency in their intimate relationships, and this is not regarded as a sign of weakness (Doi 1973; Hall 1983). The

Japanese even have a special word, *amaeru*, which has no equivalent in English, to denote both sexes' need for attachment and dependency.

For years, physicians and poets chatted knowingly about sex without benefit of the physiological facts. Since Masters and Johnson came along, people have been chatting more knowledgeably about the physiological facts, but they rarely put these facts into a psychological context. Just as a lack of physiological data once led to misguided and biased advice about sex, so physiological facts are not enough to illuminate the emotional context of sex, for sex is more than a matter of hydraulics. Masters and Johnson, so often accused of making sex mechanical, have said that when you treat sex as an exercise to be performed according to a set of directions, "you are dissecting and removing and depersonalizing the whole sexual experience." Sexual liberation requires more than dispelling physical hangups and freeing the body to respond. It also involves freeing the mind so that both sexes can enjoy—or reject—sex on the basis of choice, not coercion.

In the rest of this book, we discuss some attempts to account for the sex differences (or lack of them) described in Chapters 2 and 3. Since some supposed differences never existed, and others are changing rapidly in today's rapidly changing world, we find that the important task is really to explore each perspective's *strategy* for understanding men and women. It is easy to get bogged down in small particulars ("Which sex has more pimples?")—particulars that can change from year to year—and to lose sight of the larger issues ("Why do people keep insisting that women have more pimples, despite evidence to the contrary? Are pimples caused by pimple hormones or by a cultural preference for potato chips?"). Our understanding of the human condition depends not only on the facts we can muster but on the interpretations we bring to them.

II | *The sexes: Explaining the inequalities*

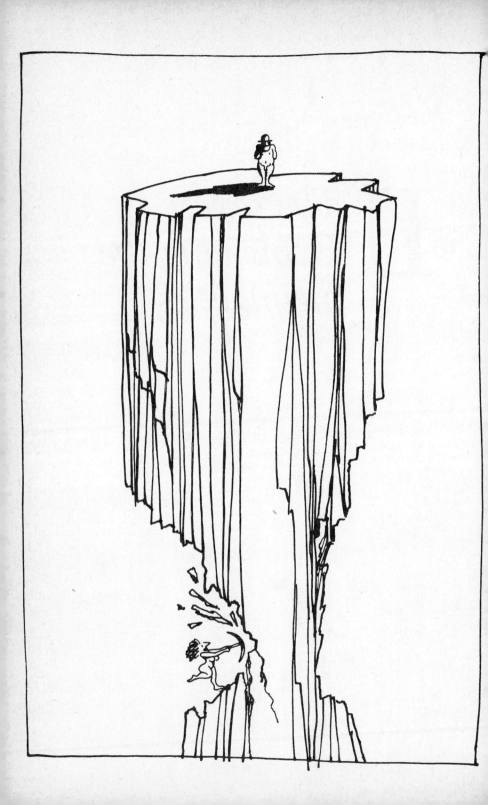

4 Genes, hormones, and instincts: The biological perspective

Of all the perspectives on sex differences and sex roles, perhaps none is as susceptible to oversimplification, distortion, and political misuse as the biological one. Consider, for example, these very recent incidents:

1. In a talk to a college audience, James Neely, a surgeon turned self-appointed authority on sex differences, reviewed some complicated research findings on male-female brain differences. Physiology, concluded the doctor, equips men and women for specific kinds of work. Men's brains give them the analytic acumen to be lawyers. Women can do well at some professions too, but their brains also happen to suit them beautifully for housework.

2. Argentina's military junta launched an invasion of the Falkland Islands in a sovereignty dispute with Great Britain. British Prime Minister Margaret Thatcher immediately dispatched troops in a successful campaign to regain control of the islands. In the United Nations, Panamanian Foreign Minister Jorge Illueca, who supported the Argentines, got up to explain that Thatcher's belligerence could be attributed to "the glandular system of women."

3. In a book called *The Compleat Chauvinist*, Edgar F. Berman maintained that women are intellectually inferior and emotionally unstable. Berman, physician to the late Hubert Humphrey, had taken the same tack during the 1968 presidential campaign, when he publically fretted about the havoc menopausal women might create were they to win political office ("If you had an investment in a bank . . . you wouldn't want the president of your bank making a loan under those raging hormonal influences"). This time he cited biological "evidence." Some sample chapter titles from his book: "The Brain That's Tame Lies Mainly in the Dame," "Testosterone, Hormone of Champions," and "Meno: The Pause That Depresses."

You can see why many people who hope for greater equality between the sexes are less than enthusiastic about the biological perspective. For centuries the sexual status quo was defended with arguments that women's inferior position was God-given or instinct-driven. Today, too, those who regard sex differences as natural and necessary are apt to feel that the basic features of femininity and masculinity are somehow wired in at birth, with experience playing only an auxiliary role. People's positions regarding biology and their political preferences are intertwined: Although some people who emphasize biology also advocate sex-role equality, a conservative position is more typical. And although some feminists emphasize and even extol the biological differences between men and women, most tend either to minimize sex differences or attribute them solely to social learning (see Tavris 1973).

Political views affect not only the kind of research that scientists choose to do but also the way people react when they hear the results. Biological determinists may greet each bit of evidence supporting the biological perspective by proclaiming, "It's the genes!" or "It's the hormones!" much as a beer maker might boast, "It's the water!" Environmentalists, on the other hand, often dismiss biological explanations as sexist without ever bothering to examine the scientific record. Although they may readily admit that external chemicals (drugs) can alter consciousness and behavior, some refuse even to entertain the notion that internal chemicals (hormones) can do the same. Ironically, both sides seem to share certain simplistic and questionable assumptions—for example, that biological factors are somehow more real than psychological or social ones, or that biologically based sex differences are inescapable.

Articles on the biological contribution to gender have cropped up of late in almost every popular magazine, from *Psychology Today* to *Playboy*. Yet ordinary folk are often confused about the issues and have only the haziest notion of what *biological* really means. If you press them, you find that they are not quite sure what a gene is, or just which hormones are supposed to influence which behaviors. An aim of this chapter is to clarify what the controversy over biology is all about. Although we cannot include all the details of biological research in a book like this one, we do have to introduce some technical terms and concepts at various points. If you are willing to read those sections carefully, you will find that you don't have to be an endocrinologist or geneticist to understand and evaluate the basic issues raised by biological research.

Biological theorists trace sex differences to the brain, that unassuming, pinkish-gray, squishy mass of tissue where every thought, emotion, and nonreflexive act originates. However, different theorists approach sex differences in the brain from different angles and at different levels of analysis. They can be divided conveniently into four subgroups:

    1. Sociobiologists, sometimes called Darwinian psychologists, are more interested in the evolutionary history of our species than they are in the firing of specific neurons or the flow of specific hormones. Although the gene is their primary unit of analysis, they leave actual genetic details to others and concentrate instead on constructing elaborate arguments for why sex differences must be genetically based. The sociobiology camp includes members of several disciplines, including anthropology, sociology, psychology, comparative biology, and physiology.

2. A second group, composed of endocrinologists, physiologists, physiological psychologists, and other researchers, focuses on how sex hormones produced before birth influence behavior and personality after birth. Their work includes laboratory experiments with animals and clinical observations of human beings who have prenatal hormone abnormalities.

3. A third group, also composed of both medical and social scientists, examines how sex hormones produced after the onset of puberty affect mood, behavior, and mental functioning.

4. Finally, a fourth group studies the brain itself. Some researchers directly examine brain tissue taken from animals; others infer human sex differences in brain organization from people's performance on various perceptual or mental tasks.

As you read, keep in mind that there is a great deal of overlap among these groups. Sociobiologists assume that hormone and brain researchers will document the genetic differences they believe evolved over millions of years. Hormone researchers assume that the chemical substances they study affect behavior by altering the way the brain works. Brain researchers, in turn, believe that many of the anatomical phenomena they observe can be traced to the action of sex hormones. The hope of many biological theorists is that the threads and strands of biological research will someday coalesce.

sociobiology: Darwin with a twist

Sociobiology is an extension of Charles Darwin's theory of evolution, which provides the organizing paradigm for all the biological sciences. In *On the Origin of Species* (1859) Darwin asked why species come to be the way they are and why species that are similar in some ways differ in others. He answered those questions in part with the law of natural selection: Within a given species (including our own), individuals who possess traits that are adaptive in the species' environment are likely to stay alive until they can reproduce and pass their genes on to the next generation. As a result, such individuals increase in number; the natural environment "selects" them, and eventually their traits spread throughout the population. Individuals who lack adaptive traits, in contrast, tend to die before reproducing, so their brand of genes—and their traits—become extinct.

Sociobiology is in large part the brainchild of Edward O. Wilson, a Harvard expert in entomology (the study of insects). With sociobiology, attention shifts from the species to the individual and from physical traits to psychological ones. Sociobiologists believe that nature has bred into each one of us a desire to pass along our genes, and that much and possibly all of our behavior is motivated by this innate impulse to see our personal genetic code survive (Wilson 1975, 1978). If we cannot actually promulgate our own genes, we try (though not necessarily consciously) to get the genes of our close relatives perpetuated. Darwin argued that evolution favors particular physical traits, like the ability to stand on two legs or grab objects with the forefinger and thumb, if they help the species survive. Wilson's view is that evolution also favors certain genetically based psychological traits and tendencies if they enhance the odds of an individual passing along his or her genes. As certain kinds of genes (and thus behaviors) spread, they eventually affect the development of whole cultures.

Sociobiological explanations have been offered for everything from altruism (concern for others) to xenophobia (fear of strangers) and have been applied both to animals and to human beings. What concerns us here, though, is the sociobiological claim that in the human species, male dominance, the sexual double standard, and maternal behavior are all rooted in biology. They evolved, say the sociobiologists, as strategies for adapting to an environment that molded human nature for millions of years, and they survived because they increased the reproductive success or "fitness" of our ancestors. True, the environment has changed, and various features of masculinity and femininity may no longer be so important. But evolution works at a snail's pace, and for a long time we will be stuck with our evolutionary legacy.

One of the most controversial sociobiological theories has to do with the double standard. Sexual infidelity has historically been viewed as a greater aberration in women than in men. Sociobiologists trace this fact to differences in the reproductive efficiency of the sexes (Symons 1979; Fisher 1982). In theory, an individual male, if he has the stamina, can father hundreds and even thousands of offspring by copulating with a number of different females. The more wild oats he sows, the more genetic success he reaps. But for a woman the reproductive facts of life are different. She produces a mature egg only once a month. Furthermore, a single act of intercourse can lead to nine months of pregnancy, the risks of childbirth, and years of bringing up baby. Since childbirth is not something she can go through thousands of times, and since she doesn't want to waste any of her precious eggs, it behooves her to be fussy about whom she chooses as a sexual partner. She can't accept just anyone's 50 percent contribution to her offspring's genes.

Once a female has a partner, it is also in her interest to do whatever she can to keep him around so that he can help her keep her offspring alive. One thing she can do is provide regular sex. Of course, in the sociobiological scheme of things, a male will only want to stay with the female if he can be reasonably sure that he is the father of the aforementioned offspring; he doesn't want to support someone else's genes. So the female also throws sexual fidelity into the bargain. He gets sex and female monogamy, she gets the bacon he brings home for their hungry brood, they both get their genes passed on, and *violà!* the nuclear family is born. The only hitch is that since the male can never be absolutely sure he is the father of his mate's offspring (she may cheat), he will still be tempted to ensure the promulgation of his genes by straying now and then—which leads us, at last, to why male adultery seems more "natural" than female.

The number of adherents to sociobiology is growing steadily, and the popular press has taken to calling it a new science. Sociobiology appeals to many people because it provides coherent explanations of disparate facts. It holds out the promise of accounting not for specific behaviors in a piecemeal fashion, but for human nature itself. But it also has some glaring deficiencies. We turn now to three of the most serious.[1]

the data gap

Although sociobiologists' theories about animal behavior draw on many empirical facts, their theories regarding human social behavior usually rest on very thin evidence—too thin, critics say, to

---

[1]For an excellent collection of essays on these and other issues in sociobiology, written by both supporters and detractors, see Barlow and Silverberg 1980.

support the heavy superstructure of inferences that sociobiologists try to erect on them. Most of humankind's time on this earth has been spent in hunting and gathering; presumably these activities have affected individual traits and social organization. However, the artifacts unearthed by archeologists reveal more about how hunting-and-gathering peoples made tools and constructed shelters than about their social and mating customs, which are the central concern of sociobiology. As for the genetic evidence, it is even more tenuous. Genetics clearly contribute to the behavior and temperamental traits of animals, as animal breeders well know. Most scientists suspect that genes also contribute in some way to temperament and ability in human beings, but they do not know how large or small that contribution is. As paleontologist Stephen Jay Gould (1980) has pointed out, direct evidence about the genetics of human behavior is hard to come by; long generations make historical studies difficult, and breeding experiments analogous to those conducted with animals are ruled out ethically. Whatever influence genes do have on human behavior is bound to be exceedingly complicated. Specific genes or gene combinations have never been linked to specific behaviors or psychological traits, much less to social customs like monogamy or the double standard—and nobody knows how to go about establishing the existence of such links.

Sociobiological speculations are always interesting, sometimes amusing, and occasionally titillating, but the paucity of evidence on which they rest has prompted Gould (1980) to dub them "Just-So-Stories" and another critic to describe them as "fairy tales" and "works of imagination" (Powledge 1982).

dispensable genes

The evolution of human societies is not precisely analogous to the evolution of species. People, unlike cabbages and dinosaurs, have minds and language, which permit learning and communication. Their social evolution means rapid change, and continuous adaptations over time, but not necessarily "progress" (Wispé and Thompson 1976). Human beings can deliberately speed change up, slow it down, or alter its direction. Cultural and technological change can influence and even overcome the impact of a group's biological heritage. Poor eyesight would affect the survival chances of a New Guinea hunter, but a nearsighted editor in the jungles of New York can survive quite nicely with glasses.

Thus many social scientists agree with sociobiologists that if a custom or behavior survives for a long period of time it must be functional for individuals or the group as a whole; but they insist that human adaptation can be explained by cultural factors rather than genetic ones (see Chapter 8). The fact that a custom or behavior is widespread or even universal does not necessarily imply that it is genetically based (Silverberg 1980). Certain environmental problems and conditions are common to all human beings, and we might expect to find some common cultural solutions and adjustments that have nothing to do with genetic tendencies.

For example, why are parents the world over willing to devote themselves to their offspring when they could be out carousing and cavorting instead? Sociobiologists say this parental altruism is wired in genetically: In a sense, it is the genes, not the kids, we're concerned about; the children just happen to be where the genes are housed. The same behavior, however, is just as plausibly explained, at least in part, by a nongenetic desire to insure that someone will support us emotionally and physically in our old age ("I made your oatmeal and drove you to soccer practice; now you can pick up my medicine and drive me to the park"). This explanation, like the sociobiological one, regards parental devotion as basically selfish, but it does not tie that behavior to a "parenting gene," the existence of which has never been established.

of biology and baboons

Sociobiology's greatest weakness is that it derives its theories about human nature almost entirely from observations of our evolutionary cousins, the monkeys and apes. Sociobiologists argue by analogy: Because these primates are so like ourselves but do not undergo the intricate and intensive learning process that we do, their behavior can tell us about our own biological inheritance. Since this argument by analogy is so essential to sociobiology, let us consider it in some detail.

Much of the behavior of nonhuman primates is *sexually dimorphic*, that is, more typical of one sex than the other, and certain primate species behave in ways that fit human stereotypes remarkably well. For instance, in some baboon species of Kenya, the males are clearly the more aggressive sex. They not only hold the top positions in the dominance hierarchy of the troop but they interfere in the fights of others, keep the peace, protect the troop, and form alliances with other males (DeVore 1965). Some writers have claimed that the adult males deserve credit for keeping the group socially stable. Male rhesus monkeys are also macho. Within a few months of birth the males are noticeably more active and aggressive than the females. They threaten each other by stiffening their bodies, staring each other down, retracting their lips, and baring their teeth ferociously—not unlike drunken cowboys in a saloon. When male rhesus monkeys play there is lots of rough-and-tumble body contact. In comparison, females are calm and passive. They play more gently and are more likely than males to retreat or go rigid when approached by another animal. These sex differences emerge at an early age, when males and females do not differ much in size.

One way to find out whether such sex differences are learned or innate is to raise some monkeys in isolation, so that they have no adults to imitate. The pioneer in this sort of research was psychologist Harry Harlow, who wanted to know what would happen to infant monkeys that grew up without their mothers' protection, comfort, and affection. He raised generations of rhesus monkeys either in complete isolation or with inanimate surrogate mothers—some made of bare wire, some covered with cuddly terrycloth.

When Harlow put the monkeys who grew up with the surrogate mothers into a specially constructed playroom, they behaved appropriately for their sex: By the second month of life the males were more aggressive and the females more passive (Harlow 1962, 1965). Harlow concluded that sexual dimorphism must be innate in the rhesus monkey:

> It is illogical to interpret these sex differences as learned, culturally ordered patterns of behavior because there is no opportunity for acquiring a cultural heritage, let alone a sexually differentiated one, from an inanimate cloth surrogate. When I first saw these data, I was very excited, and told my wife that I believed that we had demonstrated biologically determined sex differences in infants' behavior. She was not impressed and said, "Child psychologists have known that for at least thirty years, and mothers have known it for centuries." (Harlow 1965, p. 242)

Harlow believed that his results applied to human beings. "If you are not interested in human applicability," he said, "then there is no sense in studying monkeys." Harlow saw an obvious similarity between little simians and young children. He told of a school picnic for second-graders, at which the girls simply stood around or skipped about hand in hand but the boys, like little male monkeys, tackled and wrestled with each other. Although none of the girls chased the boys, some of the boys did go after some of the girls (Harlow 1962).

Even before sociobiology emerged on the scene, many anthropologists, ethologists, and psychologists freely generalized from animal studies to human beings. Lionel Tiger, in *Men in Groups* (1969), and Tiger and Robin Fox, in *The Imperial Animal* (1971), maintained that there is a fundamental difference between males and females in all primate species including *Homo sapiens*. Robert Ardrey, Konrad Lorenz, and Desmond Morris all wrote popular books that attempted to explain many human phenomena—war and territoriality as well as sex differences—by comparing us to our evolutionary neighbors. Psychologist D. O. Hebb claimed that anyone who worked with chimpanzees was bound to see how clearly their sex differences are reflected in ours. "It might do some good if all psychologists worked with chimps before they were turned loose on people," Hebb said.

> You see, the female chimpanzee is the smarter of the two. If the male gets mad at you, he blusters and openly charges. But if the female gets mad, it's all milk and honey until you get within reach. . . . If the female is caged with a larger animal she can't dominate, she manipulates the situation. . . . I think we can see the same sex difference in people. Women are better than men at manipulating social situations. They don't run away from the bigger male, but stick close and see if there is a way that they can turn the situation to their benefit. (Quoted in Hall 1969, p. 22)

Analogies between human and animal behavior are tantalizing, but they are also risky. Two species may behave in an apparently similar fashion, but that does not necessarily mean that the determinants of the behavior are the same for both (Sherif 1979). A particular behavior might be biologically determined in chimpanzees, for example, but only weakly biological or even wholly cultural in human beings, who have the ability to create social rules governing their own behavior and to communicate those rules in language. Furthermore, apparently similar behavior may not be so similar after all when you examine it closely. For example, many primates, including human beings, commit infanticide. Does that mean that the impulse to kill infants is genetic? Not really. In nonhuman primate species, infanticide usually occurs when a male who wants to mate with a female dispatches any suckling infants that were sired by his predecessor. This makes good sociobiological sense: The female who is no longer nursing comes into heat so the male can impregnate her, and the rival's genes are eliminated. But in the human species infanticide is usually carried out against one's *own* offspring rather than someone else's—a practice that seems in direct conflict with the sociobiological principle that our chief motive in life is to perpetuate our genes.[2]

Rape is another example. Biologist Randy Thornhill (1980) has proposed that rape is biologically adaptive for males who cannot attract mates—as a last-resort method for getting their genes passed on. As evidence he cites the example of the male scorpionfly, who will force a female to copulate when he lacks the proper resources—a dead insect—for courting her. (Thornhill's use of the word *rape* to describe insect behavior is an interesting bit of anthropomorphizing; the word implies something about the participants' intentions, but who knows what goes on in a scorpionfly's head?) How well does this explanation fit the facts of human rape? Not at all. Human rapists are motivated more by hostility and aggression than by the urge to copulate. In fact, most rapists have access to a consenting sexual partner; in one study of rapists, many were married and were having regular intercourse with their wives (Groth and Burgess 1977). It is true that rapists are often men who are socially subordinate or inept; but middle-class and well-off men, who can certainly afford to court a woman in the expected manner (with candy and flowers, not a dead insect, of course) also rape. Finally, the genetic theory does not explain why many rapists verbally and physically abuse their victims—and some even murder them, thus destroying their own precious genes. In light of these facts, cultural and psychological theories are far more plausible.

One of the most perplexing problems for those who wish to generalize from animal to human behavior is to decide which species to use as a standard. Sometimes a researcher's personal opinions about human sex differences influence that choice. It is interesting that sociobiologists have tended to select their examples from species where males are clearly dominant and aggressive and to ignore the many species in which females are assertive and even dominant (Weisstein 1982).

Primate behavior varies much more widely than most people realize. It is true that male rhesus monkeys in the wild are, by human standards, very poor fathers. They show no interest in newborn infants and may behave viciously if an infant gets too near. Male owl

---

[2]In our society stepfathers are often the agents of infanticide. But in many other societies biological fathers and mothers most often commit the act. Infanticide sometimes seems to be an extreme response to an inadequate supply of food or living space (Divale and Harris 1976).

monkeys and marmosets, on the other hand, often carry infants, giving them to their mothers only for nursing. It is true that in some species dominance is an issue only for males; but female dominance exists among all the social lemurs ever studied (Hrdy 1981). It is true that in some species females always bend to the will of males, but in others they do not. For example, female lemurs may grab food from a male, push him, or cuff him on the ear (Jolly 1972). Finally, it is true that male baboons outrank females in the dominance hierarchy, but gibbons do not seem to have such a sex difference. Are we more like rhesus monkeys or owl monkeys, more baboonish or more gibbonish? People who think we are biologically programed like our primate cousins must pick and choose among species, depending on what they would like to demonstrate.

Jane Beckman Lancaster, an anthropologist, has pointed out that assumptions about human beings can also influence what a researcher notices about a particular primate society. For example, most ethologists have emphasized the role and importance of male animals, which are large and conspicuous, in dominance hierarchies. But among several macaque species, mother-infant pairs determine the dominance hierarchy. Lancaster (1973) wrote: "These studies have come up with the startling conclusion that one can place almost any monkey in the group dominance hierarchy on the basis of its mother's identity and its birth order among its siblings. Among these macaques, the young monkeys take their ranks directly from their mothers." Similarly, among the Amboseli baboons, a mother's rank predicts her male offspring's diet, activities, ability to displace other animals, and so forth (Hausfater 1980).

Individual action is not the only way to express power; some female primates have discovered that in unity there is strength. Among the vervet monkeys that Lancaster studied, females band together and gang up on males who are monopolizing a food source or frightening an infant. Even the highest ranking male will turn and run during such an encounter. And Shirley Strum's research with baboons in Kenya indicates that social stability, long thought to be the males' responsibility, is actually in the fuzzy hands of the females. The female baboons form lasting bonds with other members of their sex and tend to stay with their troop for life, while males frequently shift alliances (Strum 1975). Lancaster noted that among terrestrial monkeys, which travel across large territories to find food during all seasons, "it is the old females who are likely to hold the troop's valuable knowledge about range resources—especially the sources of food and water during bad years—for they are the only group members who have spent their entire lives in that area."

Recall that sociobiologists believe that females tend to stay sexually faithful and males tend to stray because a female's reproductive efficiency is enhanced by snagging a good provider while a male's is enhanced by the opportunity to sow his wild genes. But not all primate males are playboys, and not all primate females are one-man women (so to speak). In monogamous species neither sex strays. And in nonmonogamous species where males happen to be in good supply, females tend to mate with as many males during estrus as they can fit into their social calendar (Weisstein 1982).

The female chimpanzee is a prime example of the nonmonogamous female. She may have coitus fifty times a day during the peak week of estrus. She flirts and flaunts her charms in the most provocative way to attract a male, stimulating him to perform a series of copulations. When she is done she leaves him panting on the ground and proceeds to seduce another male. A female may emerge from estrus with wounds inflicted by weary males who have had enough (Sherfey 1973). If we examine the female chimpanzee's behavior through sociobiologically colored glasses, we might be tempted to conclude that females are genetically programed to be promiscuous and that culture has imposed on them extremely unnatural restraints.

For all these reasons we think that observations of other primates, though thought-provoking, cannot provide conclusive evidence one way or the other on the question of whether human behavior is biologically based. That does not mean there is no such basis. At this point, we need to ask just how biological factors might operate in human beings to produce sex differences. One possibility is that genes and hormones program those differences even before birth. Another is that hormones make men and women different in adulthood.

prenatal factors

genes and gender

In human beings the female ovum and the male sperm each possess twenty-three chromosomes, threadlike bodies that contain genetic material. When ovum and sperm get together to form a fertilized egg cell, the result is forty-six chromosomes, aligned in twenty-three pairs. One of these pairs determines the sex of the embryo: it consists of an X chromosome from the mother and either an X or a Y chromosome from the father. The sex chromosome from the father determines the sex of the child. If he contributes an X, the child has two Xs and is a girl; if he contributes a Y, the child has an X and Y and is a boy. The X chromosome is much larger than the Y and carries more genetic material.

Some human traits and conditions, such as hemophilia and color blindness, are said to be *sex-linked*, which means that the genes for the trait are partially or totally carried on one of the sex chromosomes. Sex-linkage is almost always through the X chromosome, because the smaller Y chromosome carries less genetic material. In fact, only one trait not directly related to gender is thought to be carried on the Y chromosome: hairy ears. Because sex-linked traits are nearly always carried by the X chromosome, and because a boy always gets his lone X from his mother, sex-linked characteristics are transmitted from mother to son, not from father to son.

As we mentioned earlier, no one has yet been able to demonstrate a direct connection between specific genes and specific sex differences. For some years there did seem to be indirect evidence that one difference might be due in part to a genetic, sex-linked trait. This was the ability to identify embedded figures, to imagine objects in three dimensions, and to see faces in clouds—the spatial-visual ability discussed on pages 51–52. Several studies reported patterns of spatial-visual ability within families that were consistent with a genetic explanation (for example, Yen 1973; Bock and Kolakowski 1973). We reported these findings in the first edition of this book, and pointed out that they were not easily explained in terms of cultural factors or experience. Subsequent studies, however, have failed to replicate the original ones (for example, Loehlin, Sharan, and Jacoby 1978; DeFries et al. 1979; see also Petersen 1980). As a result, interest in a simple genetic theory of spatial-visual differences has faded.

Over the years there has also been speculation that aggression might be linked in some way to the Y chromosome. Various studies found that men with an extra Y chromosome wound up in institutions like prisons and mental hospitals more often than chance would predict (Gardner and Nieu 1972; Jarvik, Klodin, and Matsuyama 1973). But more recent evidence suggests that although XYY men are impulsive, they are not unusually aggressive toward others. Their behavior problems and their overrepresentation in institutions may be due to low intelligence rather than aggressiveness (Witkin et al. 1976; Baron 1977).

prenatal sex hormones

If genes do produce sex differences in behavior or ability, they are likely to do so indirectly rather than directly, by programing the activities of the sex hormones. Like other hormones, sex hormones are secreted by endocrine glands. Their effects are particularly noticeable during fetal development and at puberty.

the developmental relay race   Until an embryo is about six weeks old, there is no way to tell whether it will become male or female without examining the chromosomes in its cells. Every embryo contains tissue that eventually will develop into either testes (the male gonads) or ovaries (the female gonads); a genital tubercle that will become either a penis and scrotum or a clitoris and labia; and two sets of ducts, one of which will become the internal reproductive structures appropriate to the embryo's sex. In males the Wolffian ducts develop into the vas deferens, the epididymis, and the seminal vesicles. In females the Müllerian ducts develop into the Fallopian tubes, the uterus, and the inner two-thirds of the vagina. (In each sex the ducts that do not develop eventually degenerate except for vestigial traces.)

The sexual differentiation of the embryo proceeds like a relay race, to use John Money and Anke Ehrhardt's simile. The first lap, at six weeks, is run by the genes. If the embryo is genetically male (XY), the testes begin to form; if it is genetically female (XX), the ovaries will appear a few weeks later. Once the testes or ovaries have developed, they take over for the second lap: The sex hormones that the gonads manufacture determine which set of internal reproductive structures and external genitals the embryo will have. In males the dominant sex hormones are called *androgens*. The most potent androgen is *testosterone*. In females the major sex hormones are *estrogen* and *progesterone*. Researchers used to think that these hormones belonged exclusively to one sex or the other, but now they know that everyone has some of each. Males produce some estrogen in the testes and adrenal glands, and females produce androgens in the ovaries and the adrenal glands.

Nature's plan, in a nutshell, is that the embryo will become a female unless two extra factors make it male. The first is the Y chromosome, which turns the embryo's unisex gonads into testes; if the Y is lost, the fetus will become a female with Turner's syndrome. The second is the male sex hormone testosterone. If the testes cannot produce this hormone, the result is not a neuter organism but one with female genitals. As far as endocrinologists can tell, the anatomical development of the female fetus does not require the female hormone. All that is necessary is the absence of male hormones.

Animal studies suggest that there is a second critical period, after anatomical gender has been determined, when the presence of testosterone influences the development of the brain. Experiments with rats and guinea pigs show that testosterone during this period affects the hypothalamus, which is responsible, among other things, for controlling the pituitary gland. In adults the pituitary gland in turn stimulates the ovaries to release eggs and secrete estrogen and the testes to produce androgens. It turns out that no matter what the original genetic sex of a rat happens to be, if it gets a dose of testosterone at the critical period (which for rats is during the first few days after birth) its brain will always be sensitive to male hormones and insensitive to female ones. If it does not get testosterone at this period, its brain later will be sensitive to female hormones. There are striking effects on the animal's sexual behavior.[3]

In nonhuman primates, as in human beings, the critical period for sexual differentiation occurs before birth, so experiments have to be done with fetuses. In the early 1960s a group of researchers injected testosterone into pregnant rhesus monkeys and thereby produced "masculine" female offspring (Young, Goy, and Phoenix 1964; Goy 1968; Phoenix, Goy, and Resko 1968). These females, the researchers observed, threatened other monkeys more than normal females do; they initiated more rough-and-tumble play; they were less likely to withdraw when another monkey approached them; and their sexual behavior was much like that of males. Apparently rhesus monkeys are born with a hormonally determined predisposition toward certain sex-typed behaviors.

Of course, as we argued earlier, findings from animal studies

[3]For example, female rats treated with testosterone after birth will not behave like sexually normal females when they grow up, by arching the back and elevating the pelvis, even if you give them injections of female hormones. If you give them more male hormones at maturity, they will go through the whole male sexual ritual of mounting another rat and, undeterred by the fact that they don't have male genitals, they will make thrusting motions (Levine 1966). Similarly, male rats that have been castrated at birth (the testes are removed so that no testosterone is produced) later respond to injections of female hormones by trying to behave sexually like females (Young, Goy, and Phoenix 1964; Levine 1966).

may or may not hold true for people. Fortunately for science, it has been possible to make use of some of nature's errors to understand better the relative contributions of hormones and experience to human behavior.

hermaphrodites On rare occasions during fetal development, the hormone system goes wrong and produces a *hermaphrodite*, an organism that has both male and female tissue. True hermaphrodites have one ovary and one testicle, or a single organ containing both types of tissue. The external genitals are usually ambiguous in appearance—the individual has what could be a very large clitoris or a very small penis. (Remember that the genitals develop from the same original tissue in the embryo.) A *pseudohermaphrodite* has only one set of gonads—testes or ovaries—but its external genitals are either ambiguous looking or in actual conflict with its internal system. Thus it may have ovaries and a penis. True hermaphroditism is extremely rare in human beings; in this century only about sixty cases have been reported worldwide. Most of the cases in medical literature, including the ones to be described here, are pseudohermaphrodites. Following the practice of most writers on this subject, we will use the term *hermaphrodites* to refer to both kinds.

In genetically female human fetuses hermaphroditism usually occurs for one of two reasons. First, the female fetus may produce too much androgen because of a malfunction of the adrenal glands. This error occurs too late to affect the internal organs but in time to change the appearance of the genitals, and the baby is born with the *adrenogenital syndrome*. Doctors can suppress the further production of androgens after birth by administering cortisone. If this is not done, the child develops a masculine appearance and body build. Second, the fetus may be exposed to a synthetic hormone that has a masculinizing effect. A few decades ago some pregnant women took such a hormone, progestin, to avert miscarriage, and a few of their babies were born with *progestin-induced hermaphroditism*. Needless to say, the hormone is no longer prescribed for pregnant women.

Fetuses that are genetically male can also develop into hermaphrodites, having genitals that are ambiguous or that look more like a clitoris than a penis. A rare, genetically caused metabolic error may prevent the fetus from manufacturing androgen, which is crucial for male development. Or a genetic defect may cause the cells of the fetal organs to be insensitive to androgen. The testes produce testosterone normally, but the body cannot use it, so neither the internal reproductive organs nor the genitals develop normally. From the outside the baby usually appears to be female. This condition, known as the *androgen-insensitivity syndrome*, cannot be treated by administering androgen after birth, because the cells remain incapable of responding to the hormone. In still other cases, the fetus produces testosterone normally and its cells are able to respond to it, but an enzyme deficiency prevents the fetus from converting the testosterone to dihydrotestosterone, a derivative necessary for the normal development of male external sex organs.

If one could show that the hormonal imbalance that affects the physical appearance of hermaphrodites also alters their psychological makeup, that would be a feather in the cap of the biological determinists. Let's see what the scientific record shows. The strongest evidence for the biological argument to date comes from a study of genetically male hermaphrodites in two isolated villages in the Dominican Republic (Imperato-McGinley et al. 1974; Imperato-McGinley et al. 1979). These individuals had the enzyme deficiency disorder described above. They were born with internal male structures, but with a clitorislike sex organ, undescended testes, a closed vaginal cavity, and a labialike scrotum. Eighteen were raised as girls and were subsequently studied by a team of Cornell University researchers. Childhood for these hermaphrodites was apparently uneventful, but as they approached adolescence they began to realize that they were different from other girls. Not only did they fail to develop breasts, but they discovered masses of tissue in their groin or labialike scrotums—masses that turned out to be their testes, which were finally descending. At puberty their bodies began to produce a flood of testosterone, right on schedule. (Remember, these genetic males had no trouble with testosterone, but only with a prenatally produced derivative.) As a result, they suddenly started to develop male characteristics, such as muscles and deep voices. Most startling of all, in each of them what had seemed to be a clitoris turned into a penis.

An environmental determinist would say that despite the dramatic transformation of their bodies, these people should have remained psychologically female because that is how they were reared. But that is not what happened. Only one of the eighteen subjects decided to remain female; she married and expressed her hope for a sex-change operation. Another subject decided that he was male but he kept dressing as a female. All the others gradually adopted a male style and male sex role. Though the transition was sometimes rough, they grew up to become farmers, miners, and woodchoppers, and they found female sexual partners.

What conclusions can be drawn from this fascinating study? The researchers who conducted it believe it demonstrates the importance of both prenatal and pubertal sex hormones for gender identity and sex-typed behavior. They argue that prenatal testosterone created a male brain, which, because of an unusual genetic condition, stayed closeted throughout childhood in a female body. At puberty a new surge of testosterone completed the task of physical masculinization and at the same time activated inborn masculine brain patterns. The subjects' true gender identity and behavioral tendencies could then emerge.

The most serious problem with the study is that the subjects were not actually observed as children or adolescents; all the data came from interviews with the adult hermaphrodites and their relatives, and it is unclear just how many or which people were contacted. (Two subjects were already dead at the time of the report.) Because of this limitation, it is hard to be sure how consistent the rearing of the subjects actually was. Furthermore, the children's genitals were not really completely female, but ambiguous in appearance. Members of a highly traditional society probably would not respond neutrally to that kind of ambiguity (see Rubin, Reinisch, and Haskett 1981). (Indeed, some villagers now ridicule children affected with the disorder by calling them *guevote*, "penis at twelve," or *machihembra*, "first woman, then man.") And once the children sprouted penises, other people may have encouraged them to become male. If so, the psychological metamorphosis from female to male may not be quite as astounding as it seems.

To add to the confusion, findings from studies of children in the United States do not jibe with the Dominican one: American children with the same enzyme deficiency usually remain female even after their bodies become male (Rubin, Reinisch, and Haskett 1981). And in studies that do suggest a hormonal contribution to gender, the results are much weaker. In the best known of these, Money and Ehrhardt (1972) investigated a group of twenty-five hermaphrodites who were genetically female and who had undergone corrective surgery on their enlarged genitals and had been raised normally as girls. Those with the adrenogenital syndrome had received cortisone therapy as well. Money and Ehrhardt matched these androgenized girls, who ranged in age from four to sixteen at the time of the study, with a control group of normal girls who were similar in age, IQ, socioeconomic background, and race. They interviewed all the girls and their mothers and gave them many psychological tests.

Although the androgenized girls definitely considered themselves female, Money and Ehrhardt judged them more likely than the controls to regard themselves as tomboys, to play outdoor sports and games, to wear pants and shorts instead of dresses, and to prefer "boys' toys" to dolls. Most of the androgenized girls were unenthusiastic about babysitting and taking care of small children, and unlike the control girls they were more concerned about their future careers than with marriage. However, they were no more aggressive than the girls in the control group, and they showed no special pattern of cognitive skills (Ehrhardt and Meyer-Bahlburg 1981). In general their behavior was not terribly unusual for little girls.[4] Since the original report, some of the girls have grown up, married, and had children, and they have turned out to be good mothers (Money 1978).

As for the reported tomboyism, critics point out that Money and Ehrhardt relied heavily on interview data, which are notoriously susceptible to distortion and bias. True, the girls described themselves as tomboys and their mothers reported them to be very energetic and active. But we do not know whether an impartial observer would have noticed behavioral differences between the androgenized girls and the control girls. In addition, although the researchers attributed the self-reported tomboyism to a masculinizing effect of the male sex hormone on the fetal brain, upbringing could also have played a role. That is, the mothers of the androgenized girls may have reacted to their energy with the attitude, "Well, yes, she's very active, but that's probably natural, considering the extra dose of androgen she got before birth," while the mothers of the controls may have discouraged the same behavior as too masculine.[5]

Finally, in one other type of hermaphrodite study, researchers compare pairs of hermaphrodites who are born with the same physical condition but who are assigned to different genders. In one case the doctors and parents decide the child is to be reared as a boy; in the other they decide the child should become a girl. One child goes

---

[4]No one really knows how common tomboyism is (or even *what* it is). According to one study, most little girls report themselves to have been tomboys at some time, and most women, looking back on their childhoods, recall having been tomboys (Hyde, Rosenberg, and Behrman 1974). Behavioral studies are needed to find out whether these self-reports reflect reality.

[5]There is not much direct evidence on boys. Ehrhardt and Baker (1974) reported that when boys receive too much androgen before birth, they differ in only one way from their normal brothers in the family: according to their mothers, they are more energetic. Money and Ehrhardt found that when genetic males with the androgen-insensitivity syndrome are raised as girls they become stereotypically female, but in such cases it is impossible to separate the effects of learning from the possible effects of the androgen deficit.

home in a blue blanket and the other in a pink one. If prenatal hormones are the strongest influence on gender identity, one of these decisions is right and the other is tragically wrong. But if environment is more critical, the success of either decision rests on the consistency with which the parents raise the child.

Money and Ehrhardt have described several such pairs. For example, two genetically female hermaphrodites, both born with the adrenogenital syndrome, had surgery early in life to correct their enlarged clitorises. But whereas one was feminized and raised as a girl, the other underwent "penis repair" and was raised as a boy. According to Money and Ehrhardt, both children grew up secure in their respective gender roles. The girl was somewhat tomboyish, but she appeared attractively feminine to those who met her. The boy was accepted as male by other boys and expressed a romantic interest in girls.

Such studies show that fetal hormones do not determine one's gender identity in any automatic way. Money and Ehrhardt, whose other work tended to demonstrate the power of prenatal hormones over environmental influences, wrote, "Matched pairs of hermaphrodites demonstrate conclusively how heavily weighted is the contribution of the postnatal phase of gender-identity differentiation. To use the Pygmalion allegory, one may begin with the same clay and fashion a god or a goddess."

sex hormones in adults

During childhood girls and boys do not differ much in their levels of androgen and estrogen, which are fairly low in both sexes. But at puberty the testes begin to increase their production of testosterone, and the ovaries increase production of estrogen. The result is reproductive fertility and the development of secondary sex characteristics. Boys grow pubic and underarm hair; their voices deepen; their genitals get larger; their testes begin to produce mature sperm. In girls the first sign of puberty is usually breast development, followed by *menarche* (the onset of menstruation). Girls' bodies also begin to produce male sex hormone, though not nearly as much as boys'. Adrenal androgens seem to be responsible for the growth of pubic and underarm hair in girls (Money and Ehrhardt 1972).

Many endocrinologists—and nonprofessionals—believe that the sex hormones have psychological as well as physiological effects on human beings. Fluctuating hormones, they argue, are responsible for emotional ups and downs, especially in women, and may even help explain some of the status differences between the sexes. Most of the empirical research in this area has dealt with the effects of menstruation, which is a regular, visible, cyclic reminder of the role of hormones in reproduction.

menstruation and mood

As we described in Chapter 1, throughout history men have reacted to menstruation with a mixture of awe, pity, disgust, and fear. Superstitions about menstruation die hard, and even in the sophisticated United States many people of both sexes still feel uneasy about this basic biological process. As social psychologist Karen Paige has pointed out, the term *sanitary napkin* implies that menstruation is unsanitary, and menstrual blood is considered unclean and disgusting. In a recent national survey commissioned by the Tampax corporation (Tampax, Inc., 1981), 12 percent of the men and 5 percent of the women—representing fourteen million people in the general population—said that menstruating women should try to stay away from other people, and over a quarter of the respondents insisted that women look different during their periods. A student informed us that she and her female classmates at parochial school were asked to stay home at the beginning of the menstrual period. The nun who made the request was afraid that menstrual odor would distract and disturb the boys.[6] News stories about the toxic shock syndrome and a slight increase in the explicitness of ads for sanitary napkins and tampons have probably brought the subject more into the open, but *menstruation* is still not a word customarily used in polite conversation. Instead, many women resort to euphemisms: "It's that time of the month," or "Aunt Flo is here," or one is "on the rag" or "riding a white horse." Southern women speak of "falling off the roof"; French women say "the English have arrived."

Even those who do not fear menstruation may regard it as a physical or mental handicap. In the Tampax survey, one-third of the respondents said menstruation affects a woman's ability to think, and over a quarter said that women cannot function normally during their periods. Although most of the women (81 percent) claimed they

---

[6]Actually, it doesn't. In laboratory tests, men have been unable to recognize menstrual odor (Karen Paige, personal communication).

could function as well at work when menstruating, a third of the males did not believe it. The menstruating female is also said to be unusually vulnerable and fragile. It used to be conventional wisdom that one must not wash one's hair or go swimming during one's period, and a girl could feel entirely justified in asking to be excused from physical education classes (even though exercise is a good remedy for cramps). Some girls still accept these restrictions.

Even more common is the assumption that menstruating women are emotionally unstable and hard to live with. In fact, a whopping 87 percent in the Tampax survey thought that women are particularly emotional during their periods. Here is what psychologist Kenneth Moyer said, summing up the prevailing view of many husbands and social scientists:

> Although in humans violent and aggressive behavior is overwhelmingly committed by the male, any husband can testify that women are not immune to hostile feelings and aggressive tendencies. Feminine hostility has, of course, many causes, but there is now good evidence that there is a periodicity to the irascibility of women and that it is related to the hormonal changes occurring over the course of the menstrual cycle. . . . Emotional instability is characteristic of a number of women during the premenstrual period. (Moyer 1974, pp. 358–59)

Despite the negative folklore that surrounds it, the biology of menstruation is quite straightforward. Each month the pituitary gland, under the control of the hypothalamus, sends out a chemical message (a hormone) that signals a woman's ovaries to increase their production of estrogen.[7] The estrogen causes rapid growth of cells in the lining of the uterus and signals the pituitary to release a second substance, which causes one of the follicles in the ovary to rupture and release an egg (ovulation). After ovulation, which usually occurs midway between periods, the follicle that released the egg changes form and becomes a temporary gland that secretes progesterone, another female hormone. Progesterone, the "pregnancy hormone," helps prepare the lining of the uterus to receive the egg, should it be fertilized. If conception does not take place, a decrease in estrogen and progesterone occurs, along with degeneration of the now unnecessary uterine lining. The result is the menstrual flow. After menstruation the entire process begins anew.

---

[7]*Estrogen* is actually the term for a class of female hormones, analogous to male androgens. Just as testosterone is the most potent of the androgens, estradiol is the most active of the estrogens. In nontechnical discussions, however, *estrogen* is the commonly used term.

Estrogen reaches its peak at or just before midcycle, dips, rises again, and then falls off before menstruation. Progesterone remains low until midcycle and then rises after ovulation, reaching a peak a few days before menstruation; then it drops dramatically. These curves are shown in Figure 4.

The periodic fluctuation in female hormone levels has led many researchers to look for relationships between shifting hormones and shifting moods. In 1939 two psychoanalysts, Thérèse Benedek and B. B. Rubenstein, published the first study of the relation between hormone levels and emotional states. Based on reports from fifteen women in therapy, they concluded that at midcycle, when estrogen is high, the women were happiest and most self-confident; just before and during menstruation, when the hormones ebb, the women became passive, narcissistic, anxious, and tense (Benedek and Rubenstein 1939a, 1939b).

Thus was folklore enshrined as science. Psychologists hurried to document further the symptoms that collectively became known as the *premenstrual syndrome*. Unfortunately, they could not agree on how to define the syndrome. Some of them included dysmenorrhea (unusually painful menstruation, generally from physical causes) as well as other physical complaints such as headache and backache. Others restricted the definition to emotional symptoms such as irritability, depression, hostility, and anxiety. In addition, these researchers used vastly different methods to study the syndrome. Some simply asked women whether they experienced various problems at menstruation, ignoring the possibility of fallible memories and self-fulfilling prophecies. Others asked women to keep a daily diary. Still others examined what women spontaneously said about themselves or their lives at various points in the cycle. Some of the best-known studies, like Benedek and Rubenstein's, generalized from women in therapy to all women.

In one well-known study, psychologists Melville Ivey and Judith Bardwick (1968) had twenty-six college women relate memorable experiences from their lives into a tape recorder. Each woman spoke for five minutes on four separate occasions—at midcycle (ovulation) and at premenstruation, for two months. The researchers scored the stories for emotional themes related to death, mutilation, guilt, separation, shame, and diffuse anxiety—and for some positive themes, such as self-esteem and optimism. They discovered that anxiety and hostility were significantly higher at premenstruation than at ovulation, while the stories at midcycle reflected a high level of self-esteem and confidence.

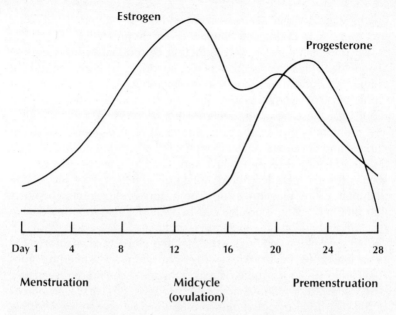

Figure 4. During the menstrual cycle, hormone levels rise and fall. Estrogen peaks at midcycle, dips, rises again, and then falls off before menstruation. Progesterone rises after midcycle, peaks a few days before menstruation, and then declines abruptly. Several studies find a relation between phases of the menstral cycle and changes in mood.
SOURCE: Adapted from William D. Odell and Dean L. Moyer. *Physiology of reproduction*. St. Louis: The C. V. Mosby Company, 1971.

The alert reader may have noticed a methodological problem. Ivey and Bardwick's women were aware that the research in which they were participating had something to do with the menstrual cycle, and this might have biased them to respond in a particular way. Bardwick countered this objection by citing the case of one woman, interviewed on the fourteenth day of her cycle, when ovulation and optimism would be expected. She told a story with dismal themes of death, mutilation, and separation. The next day she began to menstruate, two weeks early. This single example, however, does not rule out the possibility that a general bias was operating in the study.

Recently, despite the cultural discomfort with menstruation, the premenstrual syndrome, now abbreviated PMS, has been the topic of newspaper stories and television talk shows. Interest has focused on medical attempts to treat the syndrome (which is still vaguely defined). Some doctors administer progesterone or vitamin B-6. Others use drugs that counteract the effects of hormonelike substances called prostaglandins. (Overproduction of prostaglandins seems to account for at least some cases of dysmenorrhea; it brings on uterine contractions and thus cramps. But remember, PMS encompasses a whole host of symptoms, not just severe cramps.) Some patients report that these treatments relieve their depression and irritability. The problem is that most of the studies of such patients have been clinical and unscientific. The true effect of any drug remains obscure unless you administer an inactive substance, or placebo, to a control group. Ideally, people should not know whether they are in the treatment or the placebo group. The history of drug research shows that time and again the supposed benefits of some drug have been due simply to people's expectations and faith.

In sum, half a century's work on the premenstrual syndrome has been flawed by faulty methodology and unfounded interpretations (see Parlee 1973 for a more detailed critique). Even those researchers who believe that mood changes are strongly correlated with phases of the menstrual cycle are not sure how many women are affected. Estimates of the incidence of the premenstrual syndrome among women in the U.S. range all the way from 15 percent to 95 percent, depending on how the syndrome is defined and who does the defining (Paige 1973). And not every study has found anxiety and depression to be higher before menstruation. For instance, Harold Persky, using a battery of psychological tests, found little change in mood across the menstrual cycles of twenty-nine normal, healthy women (Persky 1974).

Suppose, though, that mood changes are associated with the menstrual cycle for at least some women. What might the causes be? Many researchers automatically assume that hormones must produce the emotional swings, and work is now going on to pin down the exact physiological mechanisms involved. Possibilities range from altered levels of the enzyme monoamine oxidase (MAO), which could affect the nervous system, to hypoglycemia (low blood sugar). Some scientists believe that aldosterone, an adrenocortical hormone, is involved, perhaps through its ability to cause water and salt retention. (See Ruble, Brooks-Gunn, and Clarke 1980 for a review of physiological interpretations.)

But, as statisticians like to say, correlation is not causation. When two variables, A and B, tend to occur together, it does not mean that A is causing B, or vice versa. It is also possible that another factor, C, is causing both A and B. Or that C causes A but D causes B, and both

C and D are caused by E—well, you get the point. The premenstrual syndrome (B) may be caused by physiological factors alone (A), but psychological (C) and cultural explanations (D) are also possible. When you consider the thousands of years of mystery, ritual, and taboo surrounding menstruation in all societies, it would be astounding if the negative feelings that the phenomenon evokes were purely physiological in origin.

Several studies suggest that at least some of the distress that women report premenstrually results from their own beliefs and expectations. In the first (Beumont, Richards, and Gelder 1975), one group of women reported the usual cyclic changes in pain and emotional state, but a second group of women, who had undergone hysterectomies, did not. Women in this second group still had their ovaries, so their hormones were fluctuating normally, but since they had no uterus they did not menstruate. Although the number of women studied was small, the results suggest that menstrual symptoms depend in part on women's awareness of which stage of the cycle they are in.

In a second study (Ruble 1977), young women were falsely told that the experimenter could predict the onset of menstruation by reading an electroencephalogram (EEG), which measures brain wave patterns. The women, who thought they were participating in contraception research, each gave their menstrual history. Experimental sessions were then scheduled so that all of the women would actually be about a week away from menstruation. On the day of the experiment EEGs were purportedly taken. (Actually, the machine was on but no EEG was run.) Half the women were then told that their periods were due in a day or two, while the others were told it was a week to ten days away. Finally, all the subjects were asked to report the degree to which they were experiencing forty-eight symptoms often associated with menstruation. Those who thought their periods were about to begin reported more water retention, pain, and changes in eating habits. Remember, in reality all the women were in approximately the same phase of the cycle, so hormone differences cannot account for these results.

In another study (Burke, Burnett, and Levenstein 1978), both men and women filled out a questionnaire asking which physical and emotional symptoms they were feeling that day. The men and half of the women knew that the study concerned menstruation, and their forms were even titled "Menstrual Distress Questionnaire." The remaining women were told that the study had to do with daily fluctuations in health, and they were given the same forms without the title.

Once again, the results showed how expectations can influence people's perceptions of their own physical and emotional condition. In the group of women that knew menstruation was being studied, premenstrual women had higher scores (more reported distress) than those who were between periods. But in the group that was blind to the real purpose of the study, the scores of premenstrual women and women who were between periods did not differ, and the scores of these women *also did not differ overall from those of men*!

Finally, in a recent experiment (Parlee 1982), seven women completed mood and activity questionnaires every day for ninety days, without knowing they were in a study of menstruation. The data for individual women revealed few significant mood or activity fluctuations. When the data were combined, six out of ten possible types of fluctuation did emerge, but in a direction opposite from what you might expect. Depression/dejection, fatigue, deactivation/sleep, and confusion were *lower* premenstrually than at ovulation, and confusion and anger/hostility were lower during menstruation than at ovulation. Only general activation was higher in the premenstrual phase. When questioned at the end of the study, these women *said* they were more anxious, irritable, depressed, and tense premenstrually—but their own daily reports showed otherwise. As the researcher wryly noted, the daily reports seemed to suggest what might be called a "premenstrual elation syndrome."

Outside the laboratory the anxiety that emerges with each menstrual period may be due in part to anxiety about menstruation itself. Paige (1971, 1973) explored this hypothesis in a clever series of experiments. She found that menstrual anxiety was directly related to the amount of flow a women reported during her period. Among women taking birth-control pills, those who had a reduced flow were less anxious at menstruation than women whose flow remained unchanged by the pill; but those who still had a normally heavy flow were just as anxious at menstruation as nonpill women. Paige explained her results by suggesting that women who have less of the "mess, worry, and fuss" of menstruation are less apprehensive about it and therefore feel less menstrual anxiety. (However, some people think it is also possible that the women with reduced flow had different hormone levels to begin with, which were responsible *both* for reduced flow and lower anxiety. The pill does not necessarily produce identical hormone levels in all women.)

Paige also thinks women learn to use menstruation as a way of explaining physical discomfort or psychological stress actually caused by other events. "When a woman feels irritable and has backaches during her period," she wrote, "she may attribute these feelings to the fact that she is menstruating, while if she has the same feelings after a hard day's work, she will attribute them to the tensions of the job. . . . None of the symptoms that women report during menstruation are unique to menstruation; most are common reactions that both men and women have to psychological stress" (Paige 1973). In a study of 352 unmarried college women, Paige found that women who reported having menstrual problems were more likely than others also to report psychological stress, aches and pains, and illness not associated with menstruating. Apparently women who regard menstruation as an illness are most anxious and nervous in general and are most likely to respond to any stress with physical symptoms. Some psychoanalysts have argued that menstrual distress is a sign that a woman is denying her true femininity. According to this view, the ambitious, career-minded woman (whom many analysts consider unfeminine) should report the worst symptoms. Paige's research found this assumption incorrect. "On the contrary," she said, "the traditionally feminine woman is the one who tends to get the cramps and the blues."

This line of research makes it clear that we must go beyond raging hormones to understand why some women get the menstrual blues and others don't. Paige and Paige (1981) studied a large international sample of tribal societies, and they found that while all of them have some menstrual taboos and myths, in some cultures women do not report any menstrual symptoms. They don't even know what the enthnographer is talking about when he or she inquires about such symptoms. Women in one tribe began reporting symptoms to health officials only after the arrival of Western female missionaries.

In short, all sorts of factors may account for reactions to menstruation, which differ among individuals within a society, and across societies: variations in hormone levels, diet, exercise, attitudes, and pain tolerance. The most important is probably cultural context, which determines the reactions that are socially acceptable. But not all menstrual distress is "psychological." Doctors do not yet know much about the causes of menstrual cramps, for example, or about why many women stop having such cramps after childbirth. The lack of information, unfortunately, does not stop some gynecologists from dismissing women who have pain during their periods as whining hypochondriacs. Researchers are trying to find out how the mind and body work together in producing a range of symptoms; the object is not to make women feel guilty, neurotic, or unliberated for having them.

Now the big question: So what if women get the menstrual

blues? Studies have shown that people who are highly anxious do poorly on difficult intellectual tasks, though a moderate amount of anxiety seems to energize people. Certainly, depressed people are not motivated to do their best. Therefore, we must consider the possibility that premenstrual distress, whatever its causes, leads to poor intellectual performance in women. Lots of people think it does. Lionel Tiger worried that "an American girl writing her Graduate Record Examinations over a two-day period or a week-long set of finals during the premenstruum begins with a disadvantage which almost certainly condemns her to no higher than a second-class grade. A whole career in the educational system can be unfairly jeopardized because of this phenomenon" (Tiger 1970). Mercy! Does this mean that menstruating women will have to be excused both from physical education classes *and* from final exams?

Let us relieve the female reader's anxiety at once by answering no. Study after study has failed to find a relationship between menstruation and intellectual performance. The one piece of research that seemed to support Tiger's worry was inconclusive. In 1960 physician Katherina Dalton reported that in a group of English schoolgirls, 27 percent got poorer test grades just before menstruation than at ovulation. But Dalton did not say how *much* worse they did, nor did she report any statistical tests that would have determined whether the results were reliable or due to chance. Besides, 56 percent of the girls in the study showed no change in test grades, and 17 percent did better at premenstruation—a fact that several writers have overlooked when citing this study.

But psychologist Sharon Golub did a much more extensive study in which she gave a number of psychological and mental tests to fifty women, once during the four-day period before menstruation and once two weeks later. Golub found, along with everyone from Benedek to Bardwick, that the women's anxiety and depression increased significantly at premenstruation. But she did not find any corresponding decreases in test performance. On eleven of the thirteen tests of intellectual ability there were no menstrual-cycle effects. On one of the remaining tests women who were first tested at midcycle did better at midcycle; on the other, most women did better premenstrually (Golub 1975). It seems that monthly mood changes are not great enough to affect a woman's ability to think and work. As Julia Sherman (1971) dryly put it, "Women apparently are motivated [during menstruation] to carry on as usual."

Well then, if menstruation doesn't make women dumb, perhaps it makes them dangerous. This notion is gaining acceptance in both the United States and Europe. In France severe premenstrual tension can qualify as temporary insanity in criminal cases, and in England it is deemed an extenuating circumstance. In one English case a barmaid got off with probation after threatening to kill a police officer, even though she had a long criminal record and had already been given probation once, after stabbing another barmaid. Her defense was that PMS turned her into a "raging animal" unless she underwent progesterone treatments. In another case a woman walked out of court free after her conviction for manslaughter. After an argument with her lover she had driven her car into him, but she convinced a judge that premenstrual tension resulted in diminished responsibility. Similar defenses are beginning to crop up in U.S. courts as well.

A great deal has been made of the dramatic correlations between premenstruation/menstruation and the incidence of antisocial behavior among women. Half of the women who commit suicide, half of those who commit crimes, and almost half of those admitted to hospitals for psychiatric reasons are either menstruating or about to (Dalton 1964). At first glance, these are impressive statistics. Given a random distribution, one would expect only 29 percent of all female suicides, crimes, and psychiatric admissions to occur during the eight days before and during menstruation. Some people have concluded that females go a bit berserk during menstruation.

But remember, correlations can be interpreted several ways. The crime statistic, for example, really tells us only that women who commit crimes (and get caught) are more likely than chance to be in the premenstrual/menstrual phase. It does *not* tell us that all women in this phase are more likely than usual to commit a crime. It is possible that those women who are already predisposed to commit a crime are pushed over the edge at this time; for others, premenstrual tension may set off a burst of creativity or sustained work. Another fascinating but often overlooked interpretation of the correlation is this: Being arrested, having an accident, or entering a hospital are all highly stressful events, and great stress itself can bring on an early menstrual period. Physician William Nolen (1975) noted that it is not uncommon for stress to provoke a period two weeks early. So it may well be that the popular notion that menstruation "causes" women to commit crimes, have accidents, and have psychiatric difficulties actually works the other way around: Committing a crime, having an accident, or entering a hospital may "cause" earlier menstruation.

Finally, it would be a mistake to assume that menstruating women are more anxious, tense, or antisocial than the average man. A few studies of the premenstrual syndrome have used men as comparisons. Persky (1974) reported that menstruating women score about the same on various pyschological tests as their male classmates. As we already mentioned, Burke, Burnett, and Levenstein (1978) found that men's overall "distress" scores did not differ from those of women if the women did not know menstruation was being studied. In another study, men's reported moods and difficulties with concentration varied as much as women's over a five week period. Also, men scored lower than women overall on tests designed to reflect feelings of well-being and positive emotions (Wilcoxon, Schrader, and Sherif 1976).

We are worried about the recent trend toward letting women get away with murder—literally—because it's their "time of the month." We cannot see how social justice or sexual equality are advanced by allowing women the condescending legal loophole of diminished capacity at menstruation. By the same reasoning, a person blind with rage or grief because of a spouse's betrayal ought to be excused for assault or murder. In rare cases a severe hormonal imbalance may cause emotional problems, personality changes, and even antisocial behavior, just as tumors and other physical disorders do. But in most cases our society expects people to manage their moods and assume responsibility for harming others. Furthermore, since crime, accident, and suicide rates (though not suicide attempts) are much higher for males than for females, researchers and clinicians might do better to study men at all weeks of the month than to worry so much about women during one critical week.

menopause and melancholy

Psychologists do not yet know very much about the psychological consequences of menopause; but ignorance about the topic has not prevented writers from pontificating about it. Women are in a double bind. For thirty years they are unreliable because they menstruate; then they're unreliable because they stop menstruating.

Menopause occurs most frequently when women are in the late forties, though it can begin earlier or later. The ovaries gradually atrophy and stop producing estrogen and progesterone (this is called the *climacterium*). Menstrual bleeding stops and the woman becomes infertile, although sometimes ovulation continues for a year or two after the end of menstruation. The adrenal glands continue to produce some estrogen, but the level falls to about one-sixth of what it was before menopause.

The menopausal symptom most often reported is the hot flash or flush. The woman suddenly feels warm from the waist up and perspires profusely; then, when the flash is over, she may feel chilled. Hot flashes seem to be due to a hormone imbalance. As estrogen declines, the pituitary gland releases an excessive amount of the hormones that stimulate the ovaries. This affects the vasomotor system, which regulates the diameter of the blood vessels.

Estrogen seems to be important for many functions in a woman's body, and when it falls off a number of physical effects may occur. The mucous lining of the vagina becomes thinner and less elastic, and it is more easily eroded. Sometimes there is pain during intercourse, but the probability of painful intercourse is greatly reduced if a woman has had regular sexual relations. The bones lose some calcium, and some women develop "dowager's hump" as the vertebrae compress. Some doctors believe that lowered estrogen is related to the increase in susceptibility to heart disease and cancer in postmenopausal women; before menopause women are much less vulnerable to these diseases than men. Other complaints common during menopause include headache, nausea, fatigue, heart palpitations, and backache, all of which may or may not be linked to a reduction in estrogen.[8] As if those woes were not enough, a few researchers argue that lowered estrogen levels affect the hypothalamus, and through it, the rest of the central nervous system, which causes the menopausal woman, like the premenstrual woman, to feel depressed and anxious.

The symptoms of menopause can be rather upsetting to a woman who has grown up in a society that makes a fetish of youth. But menopause is made even worse by the gloomy writings of some medical "experts." For example, David Reuben (1969), who will tell you everything you wanted to know even if he doesn't know it himself, wrote, "Without estrogen the quality of being female gradually disappears. The vagina begins to shrivel, the uterus gets smaller, the breasts atrophy, sexual desire often disappears, and the woman becomes completely desexualized." Reuben serenely announced that during menopause a woman "comes as close as she can to being a man." She grows facial hair, her voice deepens, and her features become coarse. "Not really a man, but no longer a functional woman, these individuals live in the world of intersex."

As Barbara Seaman pointed out in *Free and Female* (1972),

---

[8]Several doctors have reported dramatic success in treating certain menopausal symptoms with estrogen replacement therapy (see *Feminine Forever* by Robert Wilson). However, prolonged treatment is discouraged by the Food and Drug Administration because of an apparent link between synthetic estrogen and uterine cancer.

Reuben's description is both insulting and inaccurate. Most women continue to enjoy sex during and after menopause, sometimes more than they did when they had to worry about pregnancy. The other signs and symptoms Reuben described are considerably exaggerated. "If a woman were to believe one-quarter of the repulsive things Dr. Reuben has told her about herself," said Seaman, "she would not feel very lovable and would hesitate to expose her coarse and hairy face and hairless head in public, much less reveal her atrophied breasts and shriveled vagina to a man." Fortunately, many women haven't read Reuben and have a sexually active old age.

Though the physical symptoms associated with menopause are fairly well defined, no one is quite sure how many women suffer from them. This is because menopause is often studied (if at all) using special groups of women, such as those in therapy. So we don't know much about the majority. Recent estimates are that about three-fourths of all women experience some discomfort during menopause, but that very few are incapacitated by it. Bernice Neugarten (1967, 1975) asked 100 normal women what changes during middle age worried them the most; only four mentioned menopause. Widowhood, getting old, fear of cancer, and having children leave home caused greater concern. Neugarten thinks that "the change" has received a worse press than it deserves. Most of the women in her study rated the experience as more unpleasant for other women than for themselves. This might mean that they are denying their own distress, but it could also indicate that the real menopause is not as bad as the expected one.

It is hard to assess theories about the psychological problems that may come from the menopause because they cannot easily be separated from problems of aging in general (Perlmutter 1978). Certain symptoms have been blamed on menopause when they almost certainly should not have been. Aging can be agonizing for both sexes, not because of hormones but because of attitudes and society's limited roles for older people. Testosterone levels in most men decline gradually, not abruptly, yet men, too, often go through a turbulent emotional period during their forties and fifties—the "male menopause." They do not have a visible physical change to which to attribute their emotional state, as women do with menopause, so few researchers have looked for hormonal explanations of their mid-life crisis.

As Paige pointed out in her explanation of menstrual ailments, there are many sources of irritability and depression that have nothing to do with hormones. If a woman experiences vaginal discomfort during intercourse, and if her spouse is less than understanding, that alone could make her cross. So could reading Dr. Reuben. Pauline Bart (1971) and other sociologists have reminded us that menopause occurs at a stage in life that is difficult and depressing for women whose sole identity has come from being a wife and mother; children leave the nest when most women are in their midforties. A woman's self-esteem and the way she regards aging will certainly affect her response to pain or discomfort during the "change of life."

For some women, menopause is a difficult time, whether for physiological reasons or mental ones. But others barely notice it. Seaman tells about her mother-in-law, a busy novelist, mother, and grandmother, who at the age of fifty-two was asked by her doctor when she had had her last period. She suddenly realized that it had been months, went home and checked the medicine cabinet, and discovered that the box of Kotex she had bought the summer before was almost full. That was her menopause. Though physicians often blame menstrual distress on psychological hangups, many assume that all menopausal women suffer hormonally caused symptoms. And they don't listen. One woman's doctor asked her, "Do you find that you are nervous and depressed?" "No," she replied. "Here," he said soothingly, "have this prescription filled; it will help."

testosterone, temperament, and thought

If fluctuating estrogen levels affect the female psyche, perhaps fluctuating testosterone levels affect the male. Do men have raging hormones? This is a simple, straightforward, obvious question, but one that hardly has been studied. One reason for the lack of attention, until recently, was that methods of measuring testosterone in the blood were very unreliable. Another reason, we think, is that it rarely occurred to researchers that *male* mood swings could be hormonally caused. Without a visible sign, such as menstruation, few scientists thought to ask whether testosterone fluctuates regularly and whether it is related to changes in mood or behavior.

Male sex hormones do affect behavior in some species. If you inject testosterone into immature male mice, which normally are not very aggressive, they become as aggressive as adult male mice. In several rodent species aggressiveness drops when the male is castrated and rises agin when male hormones are injected. Biological determinists often use such animal data to argue that the male's testosterone is responsible for his dominance over weaker males and females. Not all animals are alike, though. In dogs castration does not lessen aggressiveness, nor does it affect a dog's position in a dominance hierarchy (Moyer 1974).

Robert Rose and his colleagues (1971) carefully observed the social interactions of thirty-four rhesus monkeys who were living together in a compound, and they collected blood samples from which they could analyze testosterone levels. They found that high testosterone levels were correlated with aggressiveness (which consisted mostly of threats and chasing rather than of real fighting) and with dominance rank in the group. However, monkeys that submitted to their "superiors" did not necessarily have low testosterone. This result is not as contradictory as it seems, because an animal can be both aggressive to its subordinates and submissive to higher-ups in the hierarchy. Rose and his colleagues also discovered that aggressiveness did not lead automatically to dominance; the most dominant animal, for example, ranked only twelfth in aggressiveness.

This study recalls the old refrain, correlation is not causation. Testosterone may cause aggressiveness, or being aggressive may cause testosterone to shoot up. When Rose, Gordon, and Bernstein (1972) paired two male monkeys who were low in dominance with females they could dominate and have sex with, the males' testosterone levels went up. Then the researchers put each male in with an established group of males, who lost no time in attacking the newcomer and putting him in his place. The poor monkeys' testosterone levels fell drastically and stayed low for weeks after they were taken out of that competitive cage.

The evidence on the relation between hormones and behavior in human males is no simpler than that from animal studies, and is more meager. In one study, Harold Persky and his colleagues (1971) gave eighteen healthy young men (age seventeen to twenty-eight) and fifteen healthy older men (age thirty-one to sixty-six) a battery of psychological tests and measured their testosterone levels and rate of testosterone production. For the younger men, but not for the older, both hormone measures were related significantly to hostility and aggression. Before we start worrying about letting a man with high testosterone run for public office, we must note that at least one study did not replicate Persky's (Meyer-Bahlburg et al, 1974). Another study, with prison inmates, had mixed results: The men's plasma testosterone levels were unrelated to aggressiveness as measured by psychological tests and to their history of aggressive acts in prison. But men who had high testosterone levels were more likely to have committed violent crimes as adolescents than men with low testosterone levels (Kreuz and Rose 1972).

Testosterone levels do fluctuate in human males, but over time the peaks and troughs are not as reliable or regular as the estrogen shifts in women. Charles Doering and his colleagues (1974) at Stanford University measured testosterone in a group of twenty young men, taking blood samples every other morning for two months. In addition to giving psychological tests, they had the men keep a daily diary of moods and events. They found that each man's testosterone level fluctuated considerably from day to day and week to week. Of the twenty men, twelve had regular cycles, ranging in length from eight to thirty days. It is not clear why some of the men showed these cycles and others did not. For the group as a whole, self-reported depression and testosterone were positively related, while self-reported hostility and testosterone were weakly correlated. (A later report [Doering et al. 1975] indicted that the relation between depression and testosterone was weaker than originally reported, and that the correlation with hostility was not statistically significant.) But for individual men every kind of relationship showed up. That is, for one man high testosterone might go along with increased hostility, while for another high testosterone might predictably be related to *low* hostility. Further, some men whose plasma testosterone changed a lot did not show great mood swings.

Finally, some researchers believe that testosterone accounts in some way for sex differences in mental ability. The findings here, however, are also confusing. Consider just one example: A recent study (Hier and Crowley 1982) reported that boys with a severe androgen deficiency during puberty grew up to have below-normal spatial ability—so perhaps male sex hormones are necessary for the full development of this ability. But in another study, males with a masculine body build, which is usually assumed to reflect high testosterone levels, had weaker spatial ability than males who were physically more androgynous (Petersen 1976).

It's hard to know what to say about testosterone-behavior studies beyond what Doering et al. (1975) concluded in their study of testosterone and mood: "These findings . . . provide sufficient encouragement for further work."

the maternal instinct

In most animal and human societies females do most of the child care. Some explain this fact by postulating a maternal instinct or a biologically programed "readiness" to mother. Fathers learn to love their children, to be sure, but mothers are merely doing what comes naturally.

There is some controversy about what an instinct is. According to traditional definitions, an instinct is a genetically fixed behavior pattern that is performed automatically by every member of a species, even if an individual has been raised in isolation and has never seen the behavior in question. Styles of nest building are instinctive in some birds. A young wolf instinctively howls in a certain way, whether or not it has heard the howl of another wolf. Spiders will spin an elegant web without a blueprint or demonstration. Chicks produce the usual chick sounds even if they are deafened right after hatching.

By this definition, human mothering is too complex to be considered an instinct. There are hundreds of different behaviors that go into infant and child care—feeding, supervising, cleaning, teaching, dressing, and providing piano lessons, to name a few—and none of these activities can be called instinctive in the narrow sense. Even the desire to become a mother does not appear in all human females, and not all females who want and love babies are instant experts at caring for them. One of the first American psychologists to reject the notion of a maternal instinct, John Watson, took a cold, hard look at young mothers and said this:

> We have observed the nursing, handling, bathing, etc. of the first baby of a good many mothers. Certainly there are no new ready-made activities appearing except nursing. The mother is usually as awkward about that as she can well be. The instinctive factors are practically nil. (Quoted in Shields 1975, p. 571)

Many contemporary ethologists prefer to explore biological factors that may *predispose* an animal or person to have offspring and care for them. Their idea is that although females are not born knowing how to mother, they acquire maternal behaviors more easily and rapidly than males, under natural conditions. Much of the research on this issue has been done with lower animals, and the clearest results come, as usual, from rats and mice. After female rats give birth, they immediately set about doing rat-motherly things. They nurse, build a nest for the young, retrieve pups that wander off, and so forth. Virgin rats also will react maternally, but it takes them longer to get started. If you inject them with blood plasma taken from rats that have recently given birth, however, their maternal behavior begins more readily (Rosenblatt 1967, 1969). Perhaps it is the balance between progesterone and estrogen that is crucial to a rodent's responsiveness to newborn animals. Prolactin, which causes milk production, may also be involved.

But hormones aren't the only influence. Male rats usually stay out of the baby-care business and sometimes even attack newborns, but if helpless newborn rats are inflicted on them for five or six days, they relent and begin to lick and retrieve them, though not to feed them or to build nests (Rosenblatt 1967). Strangely enough, it seems that testosterone, the male hormone, stimulates maternal behavior in male rats when it is injected directly into the preoptic area of the brain. Rats treated in this way build nests and retrieve and groom the young (Fisher 1956).

Parenthood for primates depends more on learning. The female monkey's tendency to mother an infant will not survive if she has missed out on having a good parent herself. The female monkeys that Harlow reared in isolation refused to care for their own young when they became mothers. Wild female chimps who have never assisted at a birth are sometimes frightened by the sight of their own infants. H. Hediger (1965) reported that a female chimp at the Zurich zoo took one look at her baby, uttered a piercing cry, tore up the umbilical cord, and ran away. Other zoo animals, totally inadequate at infant care, carry their babies upside down, which prevents them from finding the nipple. The infant may have to be taken away from these clumsy mothers and raised by a human being, but sometimes an observant mother watches the zookeeper or another animal and learns what to do. An animal usually improves as a mother with her second infant, and while some of this improvement may be due to physical maturation, learning may be as important. Sometimes the chimps learn the wrong lesson, though. One female, whose first baby's umbilical cord had been cut by the zookeeper, patiently waited for his assistance after delivering her second.

Because the female of the species bears the young and nurses them, research has concentrated more on mothers than on fathers. But in many species males take an active part in infant care. Male mice regularly help care for their young. Some male birds, such as penguins, take their turn sitting on the egg and feeding the young after they hatch. The male kiwi has complete charge of incubating the egg, which takes ninety days. In wolf packs, males may aid in feeding by regurgitating food, and in one zoo group, the dominant male helped carry and clean the pups, suffering no loss of wolfhood in the process (Ginsburg 1965). Young adult male hamadryas baboons often hug young infants and take them away from their mothers.

Primate males can learn to become good fathers even if they are not fatherly in the wild. Gary Mitchell and his colleagues (1974) showed that the male rhesus monkey, ferocious father though he normally is, can become intimately attached to an infant in a laboratory. Mitchell et al. paired adult males with orphan infants of both sexes and waited apprehensively to see what would happen. The males did not immediately embrace their new charges, but eventually they warmed up and became exemplary parents. They played with their adopted children, groomed them, and protected them from the incursions of meddlesome researchers.

Some ethologists today object that studies of animals in abnormal environments (such as labs and zoos) are not a fair test of the animal's readiness to mother. This readiness, they say, emerges only in the species' natural environment. They acknowledge that all primates are tremendously flexible in their ability to learn but say that this does not mean there are no biological differences between the sexes. The true measure of biological predispositions, they believe, is not what an animal *can* learn but what it most easily *does* learn in the wild. Thus while male monkeys can learn to care for infants, as Mitchell showed, they are relatively slow and reluctant learners compared to females, and they are not affectionate parents under natural conditions.

This approach has the advantage of getting us away from older, fixed notions about an automatic maternal instinct. But the argument is difficult to validate with human beings: What are the "natural conditions" for our species? Another problem is that arguing that instinct is equivalent to readiness means there is no way to demonstrate the instinct does *not* exist. If the maternal behavior occurs, then the conditions must have been right; ergo, a maternal instinct. If the behavior does not occur, then the conditions must have been wrong; ergo, there's still an instinct, but it wasn't activated. It's like saying we all have an instinct to eat lasagna, but conditions allow Italians to express that instinct more readily than Chinese.

It is interesting that so many people are so reluctant to give up the notion of instincts, especially the maternal variety. When most scientists finally agreed that human beings have no instincts in the traditional sense of the word—behaviors inevitable for all members of a species—the next step was not to drop the idea but to redefine it.

Ultimately, biological theories must deal with the many examples of unmotherly behavior that dot human history. Infanticide has been a popular method of population control, and as we've pointed out, often it is the mothers who do the killing. Lloyd DeMause, who spent five years studying the history of child care, reported that infanticide was common in ancient Greece and Rome, and that "every river, dung heap, and cesspool used to be littered with dead infants." A priest in 1527 admitted that "the latrines resound with the cries of children who have been plunged into them" (DeMause 1975). The practice of killing unwanted children continues in many tribes today, to say nothing of the current epidemic of child abuse in this country.[9]

In sum, the evidence that biological factors contribute to the readiness to mother is persuasive for many animal species, but for human beings direct evidence does not exist. Until more evidence is gathered, we think the folk notion of a maternal instinct should be abandoned. The idea that all normal women want and need to be mothers has led to much guilt and suffering among women who cannot or choose not to have children. Too many women (and men) who would have been happier without children have been pressured into having them, with sorry results. Belief in the existence of a maternal instinct surely is not crucial to the preservation of the species; many people will continue to want children and to produce them. And perhaps fewer new mothers will be shocked at how much they have to learn and more new fathers will be eager to participate in caretaking if there is less talk about woman's "natural superiority" in this field.

sex differences: a matter of gray matter?

All of the studies discussed so far have directly or indirectly sought sex differences in the brains of men and women. It is time to ask what these differences might be.

[9]See Una Stannard's article, "Adam's Rib, or The Woman Within" (1970), for a witty argument—that although women have the babies, it's the men who have the maternal instinct:

Men, not women, have historically shown the most compassion for children. It was women chiefly who killed children, and not just illegitimate children. . . . Although women had always had the opportunity to observe infants and were presumably supplied with a maternal instinct to guide them, they had not learned how to take care of them. . . . [Children] had always died in such great numbers and disease was not the chief killer; it was maternal ignorance and neglect.

When the supposed maternal instinct met the social ostracism that came with having an illegitimate child, instinct yielded. Great numbers of Victorian women, in the heyday of the female ideal, killed their own illegitimate children.

One way to approach this question is to examine the brains of male and female organisms in the laboratory. Research using human brain tissue is just now beginning. In the first study to report a structural sex difference in the human brain, physical anthropologists Christine de Lacoste-Utamsing and Ralph L. Holloway (1982) dissected fourteen autopsied brains and found that a section of the tissue connecting the two cerebral hemispheres (the splenium of the corpus collosum) was larger and more bulbous in females than in males. This finding has been replicated with brains from human fetuses that ranged from 26 to 41 weeks of development (Baack, de Lacoste-Utamsing, and Woodward 1982). In another study (de Lacoste-Utamsing and Woodward 1982) a second difference has emerged. In the human brain the ratio of parietal cortex volume to frontal cortex volume is larger in the left hemisphere than in the right—and this left-right difference seems more pronounced in females than in males (though statistical data have not been published as of this writing).

Improved techniques may make it possible to study structural brain differences in living persons in the near future. However, except for the studies just described, the bulk of the direct research on the brain to date has been done with animals. Sex differences have been found in many brain regions, but they are concentrated in areas known to be involved in reproduction. Here are some of the key findings from this highly technical area:

1. Specific receptors for sex hormones exist in the cells of various brain regions in a number of species (see Goy and McEwen 1980). When hormones pair up with receptors during a critical period in brain development, they direct nerve cell growth in ways that depend on the sex and species of the animal. The resulting nerve cell structures appear to be permanent. Curiously, in rats testosterone seems to influence brain development in a male direction after the hormone has been converted by the rat's body to estrogen, usually thought of as a female hormone (McEwen 1976, 1982). Sex hormones also influence the production of neurotransmitters, chemical messengers that allow brain cells to communicate with one another. Sex differences in amounts of neurotransmitters and neurotransmitter enzymes in rat brains have been reported by several researchers (see McEwen 1983 for a review).

2. In male rats synaptic connections (connections among neurons) in the preoptic area of the hypothalamus are denser than in females (Raisman and Field 1973).

3. When slices of brain tissue from the hypothalamus of a newborn mouse are treated with testosterone the cells produce more and faster-growing outgrowths (Toran-Allerand 1976, 1978, 1980).

4. Male rats have larger and more numerous nerve cells in the preoptic area of the hypothalamus than female rats do. But if you give females testosterone or castrate males shortly after birth they develop brain structures more characteristic of the other sex (Gorski et al. 1978; Gorski et al. 1980).

5. In male rats the right half of the cerebral cortex is significantly thicker than the left in most areas; in females the opposite tends to be true, though most of the left–right differences in thickness are not significant. But if you remove a female's ovaries at birth you can reverse the pattern, and if you castrate a male at birth reversal occurs in most of the cortical areas involved (Pappas, Diamond, and Johnson 1978; Diamond et al. 1983).

In another approach to the study of brain differences, people do various perceptual or mental tasks, and from their performance the researcher infers what parts of their brains are most active or are working most efficiently. Several researchers believe that the brains of males are more *lateralized* than those of females; that is, they believe that when males do certain tasks they are more likely than females to rely on one side of the brain more than the other. For example, when different words are presented simultaneously to the two ears, right-handed people generally discriminate words presented to the right ear a bit more accurately—indicating superior word perception in the left hemisphere of the brain. In men, this right-ear advantage is reportedly stronger than it is in women. This particular sex difference has not shown up in studies of children, but another one, involving vision and the sense of touch, has. Right-handed children, aged six to thirteen, touched pairs of objects that were hidden from view, using the right hand for one object and the left for the other. The objects had meaningless shapes and could not be easily labeled. Then the children tried to pick the shapes out of a visual display. There were no sex differences in overall accuracy, but the boys did better with objects they had touched with their left hands (and presumably processed with their right hemispheres), while girls did equally well with both hands (Witelson 1976; but for conflicting findings see Cioffi and Kandel 1979).

Such results could simply be due to differences in how hard males and females try on a particular task, or to differences in the strategies they use (Bryden 1979). But many brain researchers think the findings can be explained physiologically: Male brains are said to function more *asymmetrically* than female brains. In female brains, various perceptual processes are presumably represented more equally in the two sides of the brain (McGlone 1980; Levy 1981).[10]

Sex differences in brain organization are also suggested by what happens to people who suffer brain damage. Ordinarily the left hemisphere of the brain specializes in languge, math, logic, and other linear operations, while the right hemisphere excels in visual processing, musical perception, and other nonlinear tasks. Several studies report that when men suffer damage to the left hemisphere they tend to show a loss in verbal IQ, but when the damage is in the right hemisphere they lose nonverbal skills, including spatial-visual ones. Women also score more poorly on various tests after brain damage, but the nature of the loss is not related clearly to which side had the damage (McGlone 1978; Inglis and Lawson 1981).

The apparent male-female difference in brain lateralization may be due to different rates of neurological maturation (Petersen 1980). Many researchers believe girls mature more quickly than boys, although the evidence on this is ambiguous. Lateralization takes many years to develop. If maturation begins earlier in girls it may also end earlier, and this may cut the lateralization process off sooner in girls than in boys. (A similar argument is sometimes used to account for the fact that females are, on the average, shorter than males; puberty begins and ends earlier in girls, so they stop growing sooner.) However, the exact course of lateralization during childhood for *either* sex is a matter of scientific dispute (Maccoby 1980).

Now for not one, but two, $64,000 questions:

1. Do anatomical sex differences in animal brains (and possibly in human brains) have anything to do with lateralization differences in human beings?

2. Do reported brain differences have anything to do with sex differences in verbal ability, mathematical ability, spatial-visual ability, cognitive style, temperament, or any other human trait or ability?

---

[10]Originally some researchers thought that the two halves of the brain, like yin and yang, had complementary qualities associated with gender. The right hemisphere was associated with the "feminine" qualities of emotion, inspiration, intuition, and passion, the left with the "masculine" abilities of analytic thinking, logic, and reason. It is now clear, though, that female traits do not fall neatly into one side of the brain while male traits bunch up in the other. In the vast majority of people the left side handles speech production ("female") but is also responsible for various kinds of mathematical and analytic operations ("male"). Similarly, the right side is said to be intuitive ("female") but also handles spatial-visual relationships ("male").

The answer is the same for both questions: *No one has the foggiest idea.* The brain findings are intriguing in their own right, but at this point no one is quite sure what they mean. What is the psychological implication of larger or smaller cells in the preoptic area of the brain, either for rats or for people? What are the advantages or disadvantages of a larger splenium in the corpus callosum? If lateralization is less complete in females, what difference does it make? Is lateralization good for people, bad, or beside the point?

Like all creative scientists, researchers in this area have offered speculations that go beyond their data—some more freely than others. One hypothesis is that the two brain hemispheres communicate more rapidly and efficiently in women than in men because of lateralization differences (see Levy 1981). This could enhance a female's ability to integrate sensory information in complex situations and pick up details that men might miss or ignore. Men, in contrast, may be able to home in on just those items of information that are relevant for a particular problem, and ignore distractions. Why should these differences have developed? Possibly because they were needed for the specialized roles that males and females played in hunting-and-gathering times (Ralph L. Holloway, personal communication). Males presumably needed to focus in on spatial-visual tasks, such as computing the trajectory of a spear. Females presumably needed cognitive flexibility to respond quickly to five demanding children, a pig roasting on the fire, and sundry threats to her offspring (see also Diamond et al. 1983).

These speculations ignore the fact that general differences in cognitive style have not been strongly supported by psychological research, except in a few artificial visual tasks (see Chapter 2). However, most brain researchers emphasize that their speculations are just that. They admit that the link between physiology and psychology is still missing—that connections between brain structure and sex differences in behavior or personality are, as Levy put it, "intuitive rather than scientifically proven" (quoted in Durden-Smith 1980). Unfortunately, though, it is the speculations rather than the careful caveats that tend to make headlines. Thus an article in *Science '82* (Konner 1982) proclaimed in a subtitle that sex differences "start in the genes, trigger the hormones, shape the brain, and direct behavior"; another, in that venerable scientific journal *Cosmopolitan*, breathlessly began: "Flash: Authorities now say nature, *not* nurture, makes him thump and thunder while you rescue lost kittens and primp" (Hackler 1982). Readers can easily get the mistaken impression that links between hormones, brain differences, and psychological or behavioral differences are established fact.

evaluating the biological perspective

The evidence for some biological influence on some sex-typed behavior is substantial enough to warrant serious attention, even though the findings from animal studies are more conclusive than those from studies of people. Biological determinists make us confront the fact that biologically speaking, men and women are not exactly alike, and they probe the logically possible relations that may exist between biological and psychological differences. Their work reminds us that we are not disembodied minds.

However, although biology may influence behavior, neither genes nor hormones lead to specific actions in any simple, direct way. Cultural variability shows that our bodies are not straitjackets for personality (see Chapter 8). And research reveals that experience and learning can override biological factors to a remarkable degree: Hermaphrodites with the same physical condition can successfully be assigned to different genders. High testosterone does not make all men violent and sex-mad, nor do low estrogen and progesterone make all menstruating or menopausal women anxious and depressed. Bodily changes interact with social ones; people interpret and label—or ignore—the feelings caused by changing hormone levels according to cues provided by the social context (Mandler 1984; Averill 1982).

As a child develops, many interactions between biological potential and the environment are possible. Jacquelynne Parsons (1980) pointed out that neurological immaturity may make boy infants more irritable than girls. Adults may regard this behavior as naughtiness and even punish it; in response, boys may become aggressive. Or, because boy babies are born with stronger neck muscles than girls, adults may think they are stronger all over and handle them less gingerly; as a result, boys may become somewhat more active than girls, and eventually more aggressive. In other words, the way a particular biological attribute manifests itself in life depends on how a child is trained and treated by others. And conversely, life experiences affect the way neurons grow and connect with one another in the brain.

Looking for political and social implications in biological research is a little like reading tea leaves: You are apt to find whatever you are hoping for. Biological determinists are fond of pointing out that inborn spatial-visual differences might account for superior male performance in architecture and geometry. But then, why not leave the sewing to men, too? After all, following a dress pattern requires plenty of spatial-visual ability. Similarly, biological theorists often argue that because women have verbal skill and social sensitivity they are great at raising children and hosting cocktail parties. But might not these same skills make them top-notch politicians, journalists, ambassadors, and disarmament negotiators?

Many people believe that to say a trait is sex-linked means that *all* men and *no* women have it, or vice versa. This is obvious nonsense; baldness is sex-linked, too, but not all men go bald. Therefore, whether or not a trait or talent is distributed equally among men and women should not dictate whether an individual who has the ability may act on it. After all, we do not discourage boys from learning to read because the average boy finds reading more difficult than the average girl. Even if male-female differences in mental ability were *entirely* due to biological differences, that would be no reason to limit educational or vocational opportunities by gender (Levy 1981).

In truth, biology cannot tell us how to educate children or organize society. Even sociobiologist Donald Symons admitted, "There is nothing in the evolutionary view of life that tells us what is right or wrong, or that favors determinism over free will, or that even casts any light on the problem" (interview with Keen, 1981). Symons pointed out that although he believes hunting for game helped to mold human nature, and although he thinks human beings have an instinct to pass on their genes, he himself is a vegetarian and is childless by choice.

Because all researchers tend to become immersed in the viewpoint of their own field, some biological researchers tend to exaggerate sex differences or even assume differences that have not been documented. Unfamiliar with the psychological literature, they busy themselves constructing theoretical mountains out of empirical molehills. Or, as we have seen, they leap from findings on brain cells to complex behavioral differences, a logically invalid approach known as *reductionism*. Biologists always say they recognize the importance of learning. But a scientist whose research is designed to show that hormones can make a female rat behave like a male, or a male rat behave like a mother, is naturally going to think that a biological approach to behavior is the most interesting and useful one. Similarly, most learning theorists say that of course biological dispositions matter, but a scientist whose research is designed to show that people are amazingly malleable depending on their experience or environment naturally tends to pooh-pooh biological arguments. Like the blind men who tried to describe an elephant, each of these research traditions is capturing just one piece of the total picture.

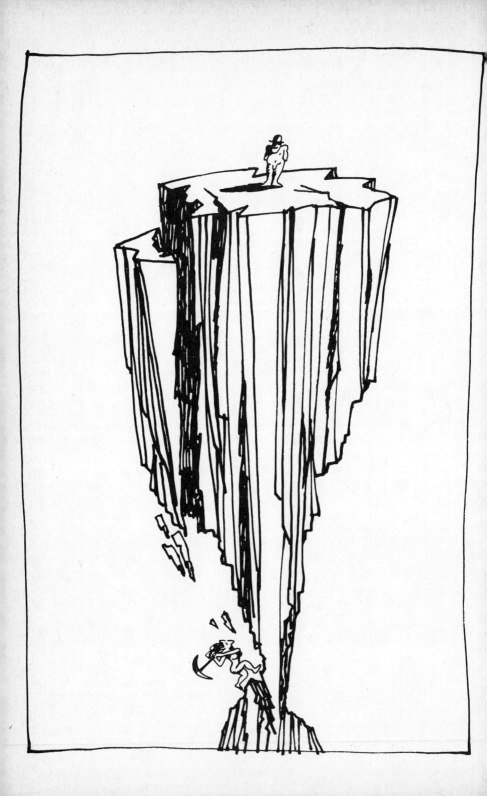

5 | Freud, fantasy, and the fear of woman: The psychoanalytic perspective

"What do you want to have a chapter on Freud for?" several friends asked us. "No one gives a hoot about him. He's just a historical footnote, a Victorian Viennese chauvinist." We do not think that Freud's legacy can be overlooked, however, because it permeates so many modern attitudes. Many therapists and social workers apply a Freudian world view to their treatments of clients and patients; Freudian language has infiltrated everyday speech. ("What a castrating woman!" "I guess I did that unconsciously." "He repressed his guilt." "Oops, a Freudian slip." "You're regressing to childhood again." "I don't need to have sex with you; I can sublimate.")

We also believe that a careful dissection of Freud's theory of psychoanalysis is important because it has profoundly affected the lives of men and women. In recent years criticism of Freud and his methods has become more vociferous, both from psychologists whose research debunks some of Freud's major premises and from feminists who challenge what they see as patriarchal notions. It *matters* whether Freud's ideas about "vaginal" versus "clitoral" orgasms are correct, because so many women and men want to have the "right" sexual experience. It *matters* whether childhood incest really occurs or is, as Freud came to believe, only a girlish fantasy—it matters to the victims of incest whose therapists tell them that "all girls, Freud teaches, dream of sex with their daddies."

The argument about Freud's theories has been lively and impassioned. Writer Eva Figes, for example, believes that Freudian ideology has been a major weapon in the enslavement of women: "Of all the factors that have served to perpetuate a male-oriented society, that have hindered the free development of women as human beings in the Western world today, the emergence of Freudian psychoanalysis has been the most serious" (Figes 1970). And the Nobel Prize–winning scientist Peter Medawar calls psychoanalytic theory "the most stupendous intellectual confidence trick of the twentieth century" (Medawar 1975).

But Juliet Mitchell, a scholar and feminist, wrote an energetic defense of Freud, arguing that his work—as opposed to popularized

Freudianism—is essential "for challenging the oppression of women. . . . However it may have been used, psychoanalysis is not a recommendation *for* a patriarchal society, but an analysis *of* one" (Mitchell 1974). Other social scientists and clinicians find no conflict between psychoanalytic thought and their own commitment to feminism and equality between the sexes (Miller 1976; Chodorow 1978).

Those who believe that Freud was arguing for patriarchy cite, among other evidence, the patronizing letter he wrote to his fiancée, Martha Bernays:

> It is really a stillborn thought to send women into the struggle for existence exactly as men. If, for instance, I imagined my sweet gentle girl as a competitor it would only end in my telling her, as I did seventeen months ago, that I am fond of her and that I implore her to withdraw from the strife into the calm uncompetitive activity of my home. It is possible that changes in upbringing may suppress all a woman's tender attributes, needful of protection and yet so victorious, and that she can then earn a livelihood like men. It is also possible that in such an event one would not be justified in mourning the passing away of the most delightful thing the world can offer us—our ideal of womanhood. I believe that all reforming action in law and education would break down in front of the fact that, long before the age at which a man can earn a position in society, Nature has determined a woman's destiny through beauty, charm and sweetness. Law and custom may have much to give women that has been withheld from them, but the position of women will surely be what it is: in youth an adored darling and in mature years a loved wife. (Freud 1961)

Echoes, indeed, of centuries of male talk about woman's tender attributes and her destiny to be sweet, charming, and sexy.

But Freud did not deny that changes in upbringing, law, and custom could change female destiny, and allow women to earn their livings too. He even suggested that might not be so bad. Moreover, he never tried to stifle the career ambitions of his daughter Anna, who became an eminent psychoanalyst in her own right. In fact, Freud warmly welcomed a significant number of women into the psychoanalytic sanctum, including Karen Horney, Clara Thompson, Ruth Brunswick, Lou Andreas-Salome, Helene Deutsch, and Jeanne Lampl-de Groot, and he often referred patients to female therapists when he felt they would be better served by a woman. Nor did Freud invariably brainwash his female patients into adopting traditional roles. One of his most famous patients, Anna O., became a social worker and active feminist after her hysterical symptoms were resolved. Her real name was Bertha Pappenheim, and she was later to write, "If there is any justice in the next life, women will make the laws and men will bear the children" (quoted in Sulloway 1979).[1]

The difficulty in finding the "real" Freud, therefore, is that we must get through a series of layers: what Freud himself said originally, what he said later, what his followers did with what he said, what his detractors thought he said, and what his defenders wish he had said. In this chapter we begin with the core of the matter, Freud's theories of the unconscious and of psychosexual development, with special attention to the controversial Freudian concept of penis envy. Next we consider some criticisms of these ideas and discuss a complementary idea, men's fear and envy of women, which has been developed by later psychoanalytic writers. Finally, we evaluate the larger framework and perspective of psychoanalysis and its approach to sex differences. (Note, though, that we are not discussing all of Freud's theories or his contributions in other areas of human behavior.)

the unconscious

To follow Freud is to journey through the mind and explore the realm beneath our daily thoughts and conscious actions. The map he used to chart his course took its signs and signals from unlikely sources—fantasies, dreams, free associations, slips of the tongue, myths, and folklore—which most of his predecessors considered trivial or irrelevant. The recurring themes in these diverse sources, which one might expect to be idiosyncratic, persuaded Freud that there are universals in human experience and that the mental transformation of those universals lives in the deep recesses of the mind. Conscious thought is merely the tip of the iceberg. To skeptical colleagues and others who were accustomed to equating *mental* and *conscious*, Freud argued that the unconscious was the wellspring of the mind, the font of human motivation and energy. Moreover, he said it was

[1]Pappenheim's attitude toward psychoanalysis remained unenthusiastic, and she would not allow the orphaned girls and unwed mothers in her care to be psychoanalyzed. "Psychoanalysis," she once remarked, "is in the hand of the physician what the confessional is in the hand of the Catholic clergyman; it depends on the person applying it and the [specific] application whether it is a good instrument or a double-edged sword" (quoted in Sulloway 1979). This observation is just as true today.

possible to identify the laws that govern this subterranean territory.

The mental apparatus, according to Freud, consists of three parts: the *id*, which serves as the reservoir of the instincts or libido (the psychic energy that fuels sexual and aggressive drives); the *ego*, which is the rational control mechanism; and the *superego*, which is the internalized voice of authority in both its rewarding (the ego ideal) and punishing (the conscience) aspects. These three structures develop sequentially and represent different desires. The id says, "I want, now"; the superego says, "You can't have it; it's bad for you"; and the ego, mediating, says, "Well, maybe you can have some of it—later." As a result, there is an inevitable war within every individual as he or she grows up. Defeat for the ego creates a disturbed person, perhaps one who is governed primarily by the impulsive, hedonistic id and seems to have no conscience; or one who is so inhibited by the authoritarian force of the superego that he or she cannot express any of the life energies.

Freud came to his conclusions about the unconscious and the origins of neurosis after years of studying patients who had bodily or mental disturbances (such as paralyzed limbs, tics, obsessive habits) but who showed no evidence of organic illness. As the patients talked, he came to believe that their fantasies and childhood memories had more power over them than their real experiences. He theorized that their symptoms represented mental conflicts, not physical ailments, and that his task as therapist was to help dredge up those conflicts from their unconscious depths.

Not that the conflicts are ever fully resolved. Tension between self-expression and self-denial always exists within a person, as it always exists between an individual and society. Every child must learn to control and redirect the libidinal impulses, to replace the *pleasure principle* that governs infancy with the *reality principle* of maturity. Analogously, societies must control and redirect the sexual drives of their members for the greater good of the group. The greatest cultural and artistic achievements of the human mind, Freud said, are expressions of sexual energy sublimated in this way:

> We believe that civilization has been built up, under the pressure of the struggle for existence, by sacrifices in gratification of the primitive impulses, and that it is to a great extent forever being recreated, as each individual, successively joining the community, repeats the sacrifice of his instinctive pleasures for the common good. The sexual are among the most important of the instinctive forces thus utilized: they are in this way sublimated, that is to say, their energy is turned aside from its

sexual goal and diverted towards other ends, no longer sexual and socially more valuable. (Freud 1960, p. 27)[2]

The sexual sublimation that civilization requires takes a heavy toll on everyone, Freud wrote, but the worst victims are women. The double standard at least allows men some sexual freedom before marriage (and after), but women are supposed to repress every sexual urge and inclination until their wedding night, at which time sexual bliss is to arrive full-blown. This impossible demand on women, said Freud, along with widespread sexual ignorance, lack of safe contraception, and unrealistic pressures for marital fidelity, were responsible for many sad cases of female frigidity and unhappiness. Unfortunately for women caught between their desires and their sense of duty, the only way out is neurosis. The civilization trap makes infidelity unthinkable, even when that would be, according to Freud, "the cure for nervous illness arising from marriage" (1908, p. 195). After all, nothing protects a woman's virtue as securely as illness. Freud's analysis of the wife's dilemma and how it becomes transformed still stands as a poignant indictment of some marriages:

> Consider the very common case of a woman who does not love her husband, because, owing to the conditions under which she entered marriage, she has no reason to love him, but who very much wants to love him, because this alone corresponds to the ideal of marriage to which she has been brought up. She will in that case suppress every impulse which would express the truth and contradict her endeavours to fulfil her ideal, and she will make special efforts to play the part of the loving, affectionate and attentive wife. The outcome of this self-suppression will be a neurotic illness; and this neurosis will in a short time have taken revenge on the unloved husband. . . . A neurotic wife who is unsatisfied by her husband is, as a mother, over-tender and over-anxious towards her child, on whom she transfers her need for love. (Freud 1908, pp. 203, 202)

For a man who basically shared the patriarchal biases of his society, Freud expressed considerable sympathy for the plight of modern

[2]Freud was trying to describe, without moralizing, what he considered to be an inevitable conflict between individual desires and social needs. "I must confess that I am unable to balance gain against loss correctly on this point," he said (1908, p. 196). When pressed, Freud generally sided with the reality principle over the potential anarchy of the pleasure principle, but he also acknowledged the need to reform sexual morality. Many people who were attracted to psychoanalysis in the 1920s and '30s, however, read Freud as saying that sexual repression and sexual sublimation were unequivocally bad and caused all manner of ailments. They set about remedying that matter at once.

woman, and he was fully aware of the ways in which culture, custom, and law shape human destinies and desires.

At the same time Freud maintained that cultures and economic systems come and go while the unconscious goes on forever. To Freud the unconscious was primary. The cultural system derives from it, not vice versa. This point is very important for understanding the psychoanalytic explanation of sex and status differences. The unconscious is the battleground for the forces of order and anarchy, and from the resolution of that war come patriarchal law and civilization. "Where id is," wrote Freud, "there must ego come to be" (1933, p. 80). To Freud the anatomical distinction between the sexes *as the unconscious interprets it, not as the rational mind regards it*, was responsible for the historical fact of male supremacy.

the psychosexual stages of development

Freud hypothesized that the sex differences he observed in personality and power were a result of an invariant sequence of stages in a child's development. While the specific form and length of each stage might vary in different societies, the psychological significance of the sequence was fixed and universal. The question he confronted was how civilization, personified by the parents, could transform the savage infant filled with surging libidinal desires into a properly socialized man or woman.

Freud maintained that sexual energy expresses itself from the moment of birth and takes different forms as a human being matures.[3] In the first three years of life, Freud said, babies discover different erotogenic zones, or areas of sexual gratification: first, the *oral*, in which pleasure is centered in the mouth and sucking; second, the *anal*, in which pleasure comes from defecation; and third, the *phallic*, in which boys get their primary erotic pleasure from the penis and girls from the clitoris. During the phallic stage (from about age three

[3]It is commonly believed today that Freud's theory of infantile sexuality was shocking and heretical to his Victorian colleagues and that Freud was shunned professionally because of it. In fact, Freud's ideas on this subject were neither original with him—he borrowed heavily from Wilhelm Fliess and Albert Moll, among others—nor especially shocking to Europeans. It was Freud himself and his devoted coterie of followers who perpetuated these two myths (see Sulloway 1979; Drucker 1979). In America, however, Freud's ideas about infantile sexuality were shocking, and newspapers and libraries often censored Freud's lectures and papers.

to age six), children develop the *Oedipus complex*, the resolution of which establishes proper sex-role identification and other personality traits. This complex gets its name from the Greek legend in which Oedipus unwittingly kills his father and marries his mother. During the Oedipal phase of development, Freud said, there is a sort of love triangle within the family. The child wishes to possess the opposite-sex parent and perceives the same-sex parent as a rival. Freud was certain about how the Oedipus complex occurred and was resolved in boys, but its female equivalent perplexed him.

the Oedipus complex

In boys, Freud argued, the Oedipus complex follows this course. The boy feels an intense attachment to his mother, who, after all, has been the more nurturant parent, and he harbors an incestuous wish to possess her sexually and to displace his father in her affections. His father becomes a competitor, a hated rival. The child's sexual gratification at this age comes from masturbation and his pride at possessing a penis, which he assumes everybody has. When he sees a naked girl or woman for the first time he is shocked. Since she does not have the precious organ that is giving him so much pleasure, she must have been castrated. If it happened to her, it could happen to him— and his father could be the one to do it. (If his parents have warned him that masturbation will make his penis drop off, this conclusion will be strengthened.) The panic of *castration anxiety* forces the boy to repress his desire for the mother. He yields to the superiority of his powerful father and transforms his feelings of rivalry into positive identification with him. In this way, the boy regains confidence that he'll keep the prized penis; giving up a few impertinent impulses is a small price to pay. He incorporates the father's authority and standards into his newly formed superego, so that conscience and the incest taboo are assured of victory over the narcissistic drives of infantile sexuality. At this point the boy enters the latency phase of late childhood, a time when sexual instincts are relatively quiescent. During the next few years he has some sexual rest and relaxation before puberty, which leads to the stage of mature genital sexuality.

Girls too go through an Oedipal stage, Freud supposed, but with far different results. Whereas the boy worries that he *might be* castrated, the girl, after seeing a penis for the first time, worries that she already *has been* castrated. As Freud described it, "When she makes a comparison with a playfellow of the other sex, she perceives that she has 'come off badly' and she feels this is a wrong done to her and a ground for inferiority" (1924a, p. 178). She is, to say the least, angry that she lacks the marvelous male organ and has an inferior clitoris. She blames her mother for this deprivation, rejects her, and seeks to displace her in her father's eyes. She becomes daddy's darling.

The problem for girls, said Freud, is that they do not have the powerful motivating fear of castration to break up their incestuous feelings and instill a strong superego. As far as girls are concerned, the worst has already happened: They have lost the penis. Thus *penis envy*, not castration anxiety, motivates the resolution of the female Oedipus complex. The girl hopes her father will give her a penis. When this wish remains unfulfilled, she finds a compensation: "Her Oedipus complex culminates in a desire, which is long retained, to receive a baby from her father as a gift—to bear him a child. . . . The two wishes—to possess a penis and a child—remain strongly cathected in the unconscious and help to prepare the female creature for her later sex role" (Freud 1924a, p. 179).

consequences of penis envy

The Oedipus complex in females doesn't die a quick and merciful death; it just fades away. Freud (1924b) speculated on the consequences for women's personalities and behavior as follows:

1. Women have weaker superegos than men because they have less motivation to incorporate the conscience of paternal authority. As Freud mused,

> I cannot evade the notion . . . that for women the level of what is ethically normal is different from what it is in men. Their super-ego is never so inexorable, so impersonal, so independent of its emotional origins as we require it to be in men. (p. 257)

2. Women feel inferior to men and contemptuous of other women:

> After a woman has become aware of the wound to her narcissism [realizing that she lacks a penis], she develops, like a scar, a sense of inferiority. When she has passed beyond her first attempt at explaining her lack of a penis as being a punishment personal to herself and has realized that that sexual character is a universal one, she begins to share the contempt felt by men for a sex which is the lesser in so important a respect. (p. 253)

The origin of male contempt for women is the same: Men disparage the sex that lacks the essential organ. As Freud put it, a boy's reaction to female anatomy is either "horror of the mutilated creature or triumphant contempt for her."

3. Women develop a personality constellation that is characterized by masochism, passivity, vanity, and jealousy. Masochism—feeling pleasure in pain—is a female trait because the girl's frustrated attachment to her father teaches her to accept the female predicament. That is, she must accept the painful realities of first intercourse, passive sexuality, and childbirth, and she must even learn to get erotic pleasure from them. (Masochistic fantasies and behavior can also occur in men, of course, but in that case they represent a desire to play a "feminine" role.) To avoid the grief of rejection by the father, the little girl must develop her threatened ego and self-esteem by making herself loved and adored—by becoming a passive love object rather than an active love seeker.[4] If she cannot have a penis, she will turn her whole body into an erotic substitute; her feminine identity comes to depend on being sexy, attractive, and adored. Female jealousy is a displaced version of penis envy.

4. Women learn to give up their infantile gratification from masturbation of the clitoris and to prepare for adult gratification through vaginal intercourse. Freud assumed that little girls are unaware of vaginal sensations. However, he theorized that in the course of the Oedipus complex they begin to get less pleasure from "masculine masturbation"—stimulation of the clitoris—probably because the girl realizes that "this is a point on which she cannot compete with boys and that it would therefore be best for her to give up the idea of doing so" (p. 256). This realization is essential for her acceptance of femininity and vaginal receptivity. As we said in Chapter 3, Masters and Johnson have discredited the vaginal-clitoral distinction on physiological grounds, but we should note that Freud was talking about a *psychological* transference from clitoris to vagina as much as a physiological one.

For Freud, the resolution of the girl's Oedipus complex answered some questions about femininity that many contemporary observers still raise: why women so readily submit themselves to male authority (father, husband, boss); why their primary source of self-esteem and identity is sexual attractiveness rather than intellectual accomplish-

[4]This was the only sense in which Freud considered women passive. He was otherwise adamant against what he considered the facile equation of masculine-active and feminine-passive. "Even in the sphere of human sexual life you soon see how inadequate it is to make masculine behaviour coincide with activity and feminine with passivity. A mother is active in every sense towards her child. . . . Women can display great activity in various directions, men are not able to live in company with their own kind unless they develop a large amount of passive adaptability. . . . We must beware in this of under-estimating the influence of social customs, which similarly force women into passive situations" (Freud 1933, p. 115).

ment; why they seem so willing to endure pain and humiliation for the sake of love and to sacrifice self-interest for the sake of lover, husband, or children. These characteristics were necessary, Freud thought, if women were to take their place in partriarchal culture and willingly accept the pains of childbirth and the self-sacrifice entailed in caring for children.

"anatomy is destiny"

At this point it is important to clarify what Freud meant by his famous cry "Anatomy is destiny." He borrowed the phrase from Napoleon, who was a consummate misogynist, but he did *not* use it to mean that biology dictates the kind of person we will become or that we are hopeless prisoners of our sex. Freud's theory of psychosexual development did not rely on biological imperatives such as the maternal instinct or female hormones to explain why women and men assume different roles. In fact, he dissociated himself from many of his woman-hating colleagues. When Paul Moebius sought physiological causes for women's intellectual inferiority, Freud argued instead that the lack of female achievement had a *social* reason: "the inhibition of thought necessitated by sexual suppression" (1908, p. 199). Also, as noted earlier, Freud was well aware that child development takes place in a societal context. He even observed that the resolution of the Oedipus complex in girls had more to do with "the result of upbringing and of intimidation from outside which threatens her with a loss of love" (1924a, p. 178) than was the case for boys.

What Freud *did* mean by "anatomy is destiny" is that sex-role development begins with the child's unconscious reactions to anatomical differences, precipitated by the shocking discovery that one sex has a penis and the other does not. Remember that Freud was not talking about a literal, rational response to sex differences. When he said that women envy men or that men fear women he did not mean they do so consciously. He was trying to describe how a real anatomical fact is dealt with by the mind in profound, unconscious ways. He continually disparaged the efforts of feminists—male and female—to persuade people that the sexes were equal, because he believed psychological effects must follow from the fact that women would never have the beloved penis.

Although men and women could never be psychologically equal, said Freud, neither were the sexes as opposite as had been assumed. One of the most important themes in Freud's work is that human traits and behaviors are not dichotomous categories—normal/abnormal, homosexual/heterosexual, masculine/feminine—but continua. We all carry both sides of each of these pairs, though in different degrees. To a world used to thinking in terms of mutually exclusive opposites this notion was (and still is) startling.

Freud maintained, for example, that no one passes clearly and cleanly through the stages of development and comes out normal at the end; we remain a mixture of influences from each stage. Rather than being determined by one event, however traumatic, a person's adult character is over-determined, the result of many experiences and innate motivations. All of us are to some extent normal and to some extent neurotic; unless our behavior reaches a self-defeating extreme, we need not be concerned about it. Freud reminded his colleagues that every lover could be said to have an idiosyncratic preference, fetish, or "perversion" of some sort—and, indeed, "the less repellent of the so-called sexual perversions are very widely diffused among the whole population, as every one knows except medical writers on the subject" (1905a, p. 51). Freud went further still. Forty years before the American Psychiatric Association decided that homosexuality was not an illness, Freud wrote to a woman who was devastated by her son's sexual preference:

> Homosexuality is assuredly no advantage, but it is nothing to be ashamed of, no vice, no degradation; it cannot be classified as an illness; we consider it to be a variation of the sexual function. . . . Many highly respectable individuals of ancient and modern times have been homosexuals, several of the greatest men among them. . . . It is a great injustice to persecute homosexuality as a crime—and a cruelty too. . . .
>
> What analysis can do for your son runs in a different line. If he is unhappy, neurotic, torn by conflicts, inhibited in his social life, analysis may bring him harmony, peace of mind, full efficiency, whether he remains homosexual or gets changed. (Freud 1961, pp. 419–20)

To a world firmly convinced that masculinity and femininity were polar opposites, Freud argued that these concepts, like homosexuality and heterosexuality, overlapped. "In human beings pure masculinity or femininity is not to be found in a psychological or a biological sense. Every individual on the contrary displays a mixture of the character traits belonging to his own and to the opposite sex" (1905b, pp. 219–20n). If you consider that researchers are only now getting around to agreeing with this statement and giving an official name (androgyny) to the psychological blend of masculine

and feminine, Freud seems remarkably prescient. To the extent that
we all begin with a bisexual potential and behave in both stereotypical "male" and "female" ways throughout life, and to the extent that
biology does not confine us to a rigid set of traits and talents, anatomy
is not destiny. To the extent that the unconscious interprets the significance of our sex organs, Freud believed it was.

attacks on penis envy

No sooner did Freud commit his provocative theory to paper than
criticism began. As you might expect, female psychoanalysts were
not too happy with Freud's emphasis on penis envy as a motivation
for women. The argument began in 1922, when Karen Horney wrote
"On the Genesis of the Castration Complex in Women," and it
continues to this day. Some critics have denied that penis envy exists
at all. Some have maintained that the concept is to be taken symbolically rather than literally, as denoting women's envy of male power
and status. What women envy, according to this line of thought, is not
the penis itself but the prerogatives that go with having one. As
psychoanalyst Clara Thompson put it, "It is the male who experiences the penis as a valuable organ and he assumes that women also
must feel that way about it. But a woman cannot really imagine the
sexual pleasure of a penis—she can only appreciate the social advantages its possessor has" (quoted in Miller 1973).

Most of today's psychoanalysts concur. Jean Baker Miller (1976),
for example, argued that women's exclusion from "the serious world
of work," their belief that men have a "special, inherent ability" and
strength, have fostered a *learned* dependence on men that for many
years was confused with penis envy. "Women have felt as if men had
something they did not," wrote Miller, "and they certainly did." But
that something is not the penis, but power, experience in the real
world, and opportunities. Finally, a few analysts have argued that
while women do envy the penis, Freud overlooked the fact that men
envy the womb; each sex, in other words, envies the unique organs
of the other.

a social metaphor?

Horney's rebuttal of Freud stressed social realities. To assert that
one half of the human race is discontented with the sex assigned to it,
she began, "is decidedly unsatisfying, not only to feminine narcissism

but also to biological science." Horney accepted Freud's notion that anatomical differences have psychological consequences, but she emphasized that the latter are strongly influenced by the real-world disadvantages that women endure, "the actual social subordination of women." It is impossible, she said, to judge the weight of unconscious motives like penis envy in the psychology of women as long as women are kept in second-class roles.

Horney also asked some tough sociological questions about the psychoanalytic assumption that femininity requires masochism. Instead of assuming that girls automatically turn masochistic at the realization that they lack a penis, she maintained, one ought to look at the *circumstances* that make women emotionally dependent on men. First, is it in fact true that women in all cultures, and only women, seek pleasure in the pain of self-sacrifice and exploitation? (No.) Second, are there social explanations of masochism to be considered? (Yes.) Women in most cultures, Horney pointed out, have few opportunities for sexual and professional expression. They are restricted to roles that emphasize or are built on emotional bonds—the family, religion, charity. Further, they are usually economically dependent on men and psychologically dependent on the family for self-esteem and fulfillment. A complete psychology of women, Horney said, must include these social facts as well as the anatomical ones. Otherwise, psychoanalysis will do no more than add another ideology to buttress the existing patriarchal establishment:

> There may appear certain fixed ideologies concerning the "nature" of woman; such as doctrines that woman is innately weak, emotional, enjoys dependence, is limited in capacities for independent work and autonomous thinking. One is tempted to include in this category the psychoanalytic belief that woman is masochistic by nature. It is fairly obvious that these ideologies function not only to reconcile women to their subordinate role by presenting it as an unalterable one, but also to plant the belief that it represents a fulfillment they crave, or an ideal for which it is commendable and desirable to strive. (Horney 1967, p. 231)

Then Horney turned the whole problem of penis envy around and argued that if we are really to understand why men have kept women under control and why the sexes distrust each other, we must look at men's envy and fear of women. Many of her male patients, she said, revealed an intense envy of pregnancy, childbirth, nursing, and motherhood, and simultaneously feared these mysterious, bloody abilities of woman. Men cope with this envy and fear with the psychological mechanisms of denial and defense. By glorifying the male genitals they compensate for their inability to give birth; by fighting to maintain superior status they control their fear of woman's sexual power; by treating women with superficial love and adoration they conquer their dread.

"Dread of what?" one may ask, and Horney's answer takes us back to anatomy:

> The clearest aspect of this dread is revealed by the Arunta tribe. They believe that the woman has the power to magically influence the male genital. This is what we mean by castration anxiety in analysis. It is an anxiety of psychogenic origin that goes back to feelings of guilt and old childhood fears. Its anatomical-psychological nucleus lies in the fact that during intercourse the male has to entrust his genitals to the female body, that he presents her with his semen and interprets this as a surrender of vital strength to the woman, similar to his experiencing the subsiding of erection after intercourse as evidence of having been weakened by the woman. (Horney 1967, p. 116)

Freud had observed, though not emphasized, the same "fear of women" in an essay on the widespread taboo of virginity:

> Wherever primitive man has set up a taboo he fears some danger and it cannot be disputed that a generalized dread of women is expressed in all these rules of avoidance [the sexual and reproductive taboos on women]. Perhaps this dread is based on the fact that woman is different from man, for ever incomprehensible and mysterious, strange and therefore apparently hostile. The man is afraid of being weakened by the woman, infected with her femininity and of then showing himself incapable. . . . In all this there is nothing obsolete, nothing which is not still alive among ourselves. (Freud 1918, pp. 198–99)

Shades of Samson and Delilah, Enkidu and the courtesan. Women sap your strength!

Both Horney and Freud are saying that during intercourse adult males may suffer a resurgence of the castration anxiety that originated during the Oedipal period. This time, however, the one who wields the guillotine is not the father but the man's sexual partner. After all, the man unconsciously believes that females have already suffered castration, no doubt for some terrible wrongdoing; they are not to be trusted. Further, the man has committed his erect penis, the symbol of his very masculinity, to the dark interior of the female body, from whence it will emerge a mere shadow of its former self. Sex may be overwhelmingly pleasurable, but it is also a risky operation.

Men may fear women, then, because of what women might do to them, but they also dread what women can do that they cannot— the mysterious processes of menstruation, conception, childbirth, nursing. In the view of many psychoanalysts the "otherness" of these female activities from the male viewpoint, combined with the obvious importance of childbirth to the perpetuation of the species, provokes large amounts of resentment, envy, and fear.

We now have two hypotheses about the reason for status differences between the sexes, which seem to be about 180 degrees apart: (1) women, lacking the prized penis, the symbol of power and pleasure, stand in awe and fear of men and therefore come to accept their inferior status; (2) men, lacking the mysterious womb, symbol of the power of procreation, and frightened by the figurative loss of the penis during intercourse, stand in awe and fear of women and must therefore force them into inferior status. Note that while the feelings of one sex toward the other are the same (awe and fear), the female's response is to knuckle under while the male's is to assert himself.

How would you evaluate the truth of these ideas? Which, if either, has more merit? We will consider two efforts on the part of contemporary psychoanalysts to investigate the effects of woman-envy and woman-fear. Each stepped outside his clinical practice to reach for rich mines of data: Bruno Bettelheim, in *Symbolic Wounds* (1962), took evidence from schizophrenic boys and primitive tribes; Wolfgang Lederer, in *The Fear of Women* (1968), went to myths, fables, art, and folklore.

men's envy of women

Bettelheim began to develop his ideas about womb envy by observing the rituals that four schizophrenic boys developed upon reaching puberty. Their monthly ceremonies had four aspects that intrigued him: secrecy from adults; the fact that the boys cut themselves in a secret part of their bodies; the loss of blood; and the boys' belief that the ritual was necessary for adult sexual satisfaction. Struck by the similarity between the boys' rites and the initiation rites of many primitive societies, which use the rituals to mark the adolescent's passage into the adult community, Bettelheim supported his theory of womb envy with examples of several kinds of male rites that mimic or compensate for menstruation and childbirth.

1. *Circumcision and subincision.* In many primitive tribes circumcision takes place at puberty, with various magical rituals welcoming the boy to manhood. Bettelheim noted that many circumcision rites involve not only painful self-mutilation but symbolic sacrifices of the foreskin, blood, or teeth to women:

> Among the Western Arunta, the foreskin is presented to a sister of the novice, who dries it, smears it with red ochre, and wears it suspended from her neck. In some tribes, after a boy has been circumcised, the blood from the wound is collected in a shield and taken to the mother, who drinks some of it, and gives food to the man who brought it to her. (p. 93)

Religious sacrifice always assumes that the donor will get something in return: a good harvest, a victorious battle, an A in algebra, a share in supernatural power. In the case of male puberty rites, the rewards include a sense of manhood and a feeling of participation in female mysteries.

Subincision is a rare and radical surgery that makes men seem anatomically more like women. During some initiation ceremonies the underside of the penis is slit, sometimes an inch and sometimes the whole length; and in many cases the healed wound, which may even be called "vulva," is reopened periodically and bleeds. This is perhaps the most extreme effort on the part of men, Bettelheim argued, to reproduce the female sex organs and symbolize the cyclic nature of menstruation:

> Statements made by the people themselves confirm such an interpretation. The Murngin say: "The blood that runs from an incision and with which the dancers paint themselves and their emblems is something more than a man's blood—it is the menses of the old Wawilak women." (p. 105)[5]

2. *Couvade.* According to Bettelheim and other psychoanalysts, men in tribal societies could cope with the ultimate miracle, childbirth, in two ways. The first was to deny the woman's contribution to conception and view her simply as a passive receptacle, a fertile field for the man's seed. The homunculus theory of sperm (that the sperm carries a complete miniature person who grows in the womb) reflects this "so much for you, ladies" opinion of women. It has appeared in countless cultures, from the Pilagá of South America to the ancient Greeks, and was not completely discredited in Europe until the mid-nineteenth century.

---

[5]In Chapter 8 we will discuss the problems of trying to explain social customs by what people say about their behavior, and we will also consider the economic—rather than symbolic—functions of such rituals.

The second strategy was for men to take on the actual or symbolic role of life giver and try to upstage the women. *Couvade* is a childbirth ritual that gives men the starring role. In a typical couvade, the woman has the baby and shortly returns to work. Meanwhile the father takes to bed with moans and groans, follows various taboos about what he may and may not eat, and receives guests. Sometimes the man appears actually to experience all the signs and symptoms of pregnancy and labor that his wife does, and he may take longer than she to recover. Among the Arapesh, a tribe studied by Margaret Mead, "the verb 'to bear a child' is used indiscriminately of either a man or a woman, and child-bearing is believed to be as heavy a drain upon the man as upon the woman" (Mead 1963). An Arapesh father grants life to his child as literally as its mother does, though with more freedom of choice. When the baby is born, he directs the women who are attending the birth either to wash it (and let it live) or not to wash it (and assure its death).[6]

Some anthropologists explain couvade rituals as a male effort to establish social paternity: "That's *my* kid; I bore him." Bettelheim concluded that couvade is the closest a man can come to the experience of childbirth, even though he can mimic only its superficial aspects. "Women, emotionally satisfied by having given birth and secure in their ability to produce life, can agree to the couvade; men need it to fill the emotional vacuum created by their inability to bear children."[7]

3. *Ritual transvestism.* When the wearing of women's clothes by men is made into a ritual, it gives boys an officially sanctioned chance to play female—in particular, the role of mother. In one New Guinea tribe the male sponsor of the boy to be initiated dresses up in widow's weeds, binds his stomach to imitate pregnant women, and wanders around the village calling for his "child" in a squeaky falsetto. According to Bettelheim, such rituals allow men to institutionalize and regulate their envy of women. Some tribes also allow girls to dress as males on symbolic occasions, but this is less

[6]Arapesh men as well as women, reported Mead, spend much time in child care and raising infants; the male role doesn't stop with couvade. If you comment about a middle-aged man that he's good looking, the Arapesh are likely to reply: "Good looking? Ye-e-s, but you should have seen him before he bore all those children."

[7]Lest you think that couvade is a quaint custom of primitive tribes, consider the popularity of natural childbirth in this country, and the renewed participation of the father in the whole process. Is Lamaze a modern couvade?

common than ritualistic male transvestism. (When transvestism is not part of a ritual, of course, it is socially disapproved for both sexes, though in men it is likely to be regarded as a sign of sexual perversion while in women it may be greeted with a relatively benign understanding that they are merely trying to acquire some of the male's superior status.)

4. *Rebirth.* According to Bettelheim, it is now widely accepted "that initiation is a symbolic rebirth, usually with the male sponsors acting the part of those who give birth to the initiates. . . . Again and again, in tribe after tribe, anthropologists report puberty rituals in which rebirth plays a prominent part. Among more sophisticated peoples, it is sometimes an abstract, symbolic drama. Among others it is a frank acting out of childbirth." Some initiation rites go to great extremes to duplicate birth: The boys must spend time in womblike huts, curl up in the fetal position, submerge themselves in water. The adult men behave like mothers, caring for the infants, and at the end of the ceremonies the boys are reborn as men. Bettelheim concluded that ritual rebirth, like the couvade, gives men a sense of full participation in the creation of new life.

5. *Separation.* Many initiation rites, in both primitive tribes and American fraternities, require absolute secrecy. Women and children must never know the dark and brooding deeds that go on in the men's world, and the boys are threatened with various tribal equivalents of hellfire and damnation if they tell. The common psychoanalytic interpretation of the severity of initiation rites in general, and of the male-bonding nature of them in particular, is that the rites serve to break Oedipal ties; the mother's power over the boy must be severed so that he can follow in his father's footsteps. Another explanation, which follows the same lines but is somewhat more sociological, is that the boy, who has typically spent his childhood being cared for by women, now must learn to be a man and to value male activities. By going through a difficult and painful initiation procedure, boys come to identify with the male role and feel closer to other men. They can finally assert themselves against those mysterious females (Burton and Whiting 1961; for a criticism of this view, see Parker, Smith, and Ginat 1975).

Secrecy is the final piece in Bettelheim's jigsaw puzzle of initiation rites. Secrecy, after all, should convince outsiders that the insiders are really onto something; it suggests that they have magical powers and are superior creatures. The male creation of secrets that are kept from women parallels the ultimate secret that women keep from men: how to have babies. The fact that male initiation rites exclude women persuaded Bettelheim that they are not simple celebrations of *rite de passage* and that their main function is symbolic rather than educational.

Bettelheim did not look for the reasons behind initiation rites in a culture's economic system, kinship structure, or sex-role patterns. Nor did he deal with the facts that not every society has all the above initiation rites for its boys and that some do not have any. His explanation for these rituals began with unconscious needs, and he shared with Freud the premise that men and women are psychologically bisexual. Therefore, he concluded, they will seek to express their sexually opposite traits in whatever ways society allows. Some cultures regulate the expression of femininity in boys with limited ceremonies like those described above. Others try to inhibit such expressions totally. Bettelheim believed that it is human nature for each sex to envy the other, and that the closer we come to allowing men and women to express both masculinity and femininity, the better off everyone will be.

men's fear of women

According to Bettelheim, envy between the sexes implies mystery and perpetual difference. According to Lederer (1968), fear is the force that keeps the sexes apart. To support his case, Lederer explored the major themes of human mythology, which reveal, he said, not what women are really like but what men have imagined women to be.

In the beginning was the earth goddess, symbol of fertility. The first deities that mankind worshipped were female, the source of life and food. Figurines and statues created in the woman-worshipping cultures have many breasts and are fat and voluptuous. There are few thin-hipped, thin-lipped fertility dolls. Mother Earth—she creates life, nurtures it, feeds her children. What's so scary about her? Well, for starters:

1. *Menstruation.* This is the greatest mystery, Lederer believed, and accounts for the widespread fears of the menstruating woman, who supposedly can blight crops, contaminate men, infect food, and cause all manner of mishaps and mayhem. Lederer thought this mystery explains why in some places women are relegated to special menstrual huts for the duration of their periods and must be ritually cleansed before they can rejoin the community.

2. *Sexual treachery and insatiability,* female characteristics we reviewed in Chapter 1.

3. *Power.* Women destroy as well as create. Earth mothers who give life can also take it away, and they can get very bloodthirsty if they do not receive the proper sacrifices:

> The fertility of the Mother demands the blood of men, the Earth needs to be fertilized with corpses if she is to revitalize the dead from her full breasts; and if she is to bring forth new life, new crops, new infants, then she demands the sacrifice of infants. Thus we universally find, *wherever on this earth the Great Mother ruled, that child sacrifice was brought in her honor.* (p. 132)

Ambivalence toward the powers of the Earth Mother is perhaps best represented by Kali, the Black One, the "Great and Terrible World-Mother" of India. "She is black with death," wrote Lederer, "and her tongue is out to lick up the world: her teeth are hideous fangs. Her body is lithe and beautiful, and her breasts are big with milk." The Snake Woman of the Aztecs, too, granted fertility only with terrible blood sacrifices "in which the victim's hearts were torn out of their living chests, and their flayed skins worn by the priesthood." Note the symbolic connection between the blood required for the sacrifice, the blood that is the symbol of life, and the mysterious menstrual blood of women. Since it is obvious that Kali, the Snake Woman, and their myriad counterparts did not actually speak to their believers, concluded Lederer, we must be dealing here with powers that men attributed to women.

Mother, good dear mom, a horrifying creature? Yes, the theme is common. There are far more female ogres and monsters than male in myth and fairy tale. Lederer did an informal survey of two hundred of Grimms' fairy tales and came up with the following tally: sixteen wicked mothers or stepmothers to three wicked fathers or stepfathers; thirteen treacherous maidens who kill or endanger their suitors to one evil suitor who harms his bride; twenty-three wicked female witches to two wicked male witches. (The three emphatically good women or mothers in the tales were slightly outnumbered by five emphatically good fathers.) Dad is a nice guy; mom, more often than not, is a witch.

In the course of time, Lederer theorized, came the Patriarchal Revolt. Men replaced their fearful worship of the all-demanding Earth Mother with allegiance to male gods. New myths of creation specified that men, not women, were responsible for the creation of the world and of life. The male gods created man first and woman as an afterthought, from man's rib, thumb, foreskin, urine, or—as recounted by a sixteenth-century German poet—from a dog's tail. Thus began the era of misogynistic religions.[8]

The idea that woman-as-mother is not only nurturant and fertile but ruthless and bloodthirsty is as common, and as paradoxical, as the idea that woman-as-lover belongs either on a pedestal or in the gutter. The ultimate fear of woman, Lederer wrote, came from her link not just with the mysteries of life but with the inevitability of death. According to Lederer, woman-worship and woman-loathing are reflections of the same fundamental male dilemma and insecurity.

We've come a long way from penis envy. If Freud thought it was an essential concept in his theory, Bettelheim balanced it with womb envy—and Lederer dismissed it altogether. There is no evidence from myth, anthropology, or clinical psychology, he argued, that women want a penis of their own; they just like to borrow one once in a while for intercourse, and *that* they have always been able to do. The desire for a penis does not appear in girls' play or women's dreams, in female fantasy or delusion, except in rare and unusual cases. The evidence indicates, Lederer concluded, that "the literal, physical possession of a penis is a matter of no consequence to women. They are, in fact, rather amazed at the fuss we men are making about the little appendage." Whatever would Freud say!

Whereas Bettelheim believed that each sex should experience and express both its masculine and its feminine aspects, Lederer concluded that opposites attract. Despite his denial of penis envy, he agreed with Freud that equality between the sexes is neither possible nor desirable, because the sexes are unique and hence eternally different. Equality would deprive us of that tingle of mystery and difference; worse, women would lose their magic appeal:

> Today our defensive strategem is the cry for equality. And in promoting loudly women's equal status, we fondly hope that she will thereby feel promoted, and not just kicked upstairs. For under the cloak of "equal rights" we attempt to deny the specifically feminine. To make women equal means: to deprive her of her magic, of her primordial position; and means further: to deprive Shiva [the masculine component of the Hindu god Shiva-Shakti] of Shakti [the feminine component], and Man of his inspiration. (p. 285)

The main business of woman is to inspire man—an odd conclusion

[8]But not everywhere. There are still tribes in the world today that worship the creative power of women and whose creation myths celebrate the mother of life (see Sanday 1981).

for someone who has written an entire book detailing the dire conse-quences of man's fear of woman. Lederer refrained from arguing that men *should* fear women, but unfortunately he failed to explain how, if men continue to view women as magic vessels, their fear and hostility can subside. Indeed his own fantasies, both wishful and hostile, appear to have remained intact:

> Woman, anyway, has no use for freedom: she seeks not freedom, but fulfillment. She does not mean to be a slave, nor unequal before the law; nor will she tolerate any limitations in her intellectual or profes-sional potential; but she does need the presence, in her life, of a man strong enough to protect her against the world and against her own destructiveness, strong enough to let her know that she is the magic vessel whence all his deepest satisfactions and most basic energies must flow. (p. 285)

Lederer has thrown out the concept of penis envy, yet still maintained that it is woman's lot to fulfill her biological destiny under the care and protection of a strong male.

evaluating psychoanalysis

How do we evaluate the relative worth of psychoanalytic theories of sex and status differences? Do the modifications of Freud's work represent advances, side steps, or irrelevant elaborations?

Some of Freud's earliest critics, who were sympathetic to some of his insights but could not accept them as literal truths, suggested gently that the best way to regard psychoanalysis was as an elegant metaphor—a set of literary perceptions rather than scientific ones. Havelock Ellis was one of these: Freud, he said, was a great artist, not a scientist. Freud, feeling insulted, replied that of course he was a scientist, committed to recording his meticulous observations and deducing general principles in a calm, unbiased way. It wasn't *his* fault if the people who disagreed with him showed neurotic defenses and resistance to the unpleasant truths he revealed. However, he did admit, sometimes with coy humility, that he was dealing in theory, not in the empirical evidence that people today require of science. "If you reject this idea as fantastic and regard my belief in the influence of lack of a penis on the configuration of femininity as an *idée fixe*, I am of course defenceless" (Freud 1933, p. 132).

The common objections that have been raised against psycho-analysis include these (adapted from Sulloway 1979):

1. Psychoanalysts support their arguments by saying "We know from psychoanalytic experience that . . ." and then leave the burden of proof to others.

2. Freud, his disciples, and many modern psychoanalysts have ignored evidence and opinions that disagreed with their views.

3. Freud and his followers never published statistics supporting the efficacy of their methods.

4. Freud and his group ignored all the work done before them, notably on the unconscious and infantile sexuality, and then they made unwarranted claims about their own originality.

5. Freud and his followers spoke and wrote as if their theories were proven, making their critics seem intolerant and foolish.

6. Psychoanalysis quickly became not a scientific approach but a religious sect, with all the characteristics of one: a charismatic leader, "a fanatical degree of faith, a special jargon, a sense of moral superiority, and a predilection for marked intolerance of opponents."

Such criticisms began to flourish as psychoanalysis grew, and they have returned with renewed force recently because of new discoveries, experiments, and statistics. Let's consider a few of these.

reality or fantasy? the "seduction theory"

Imagine that you are Freud, treating a young woman for her hysterical symptoms. She tells you that as a very young child she was molested sexually by her father. What would you conclude about the effect of this experience on her later psychological health?

In his early work Freud concluded that early sexual traumas would have a devastating effect: A child would unconsciously repress the horror of the incestuous act, and this repression would emerge eventually in neurotic symptoms. But *so many* of his women patients incriminated their fathers and other male relatives that Freud began to feel uneasy about this "seduction theory" and quickly abandoned it. Actually, he didn't abandon it so much as turn it inside out. He decided that his patients were not telling him about *real* seductions and sexual traumas, but were merely *fantasizing* about them:

> Almost all my women patients told me that they had been seduced by their fathers. I was driven to recognize in the end that these reports were untrue and so came to understand that the hysterical symptoms are derived from phantasies and not from real occurrences. (Quoted in Rush 1980, p. 83)

The entire edifice of Freud's female Oedipus complex came to rest on this shift of belief: "I was able to recognize in this phantasy of being seduced by the father," said Freud, "the expression of the typical Oedipus complex in women." Because men did not complain of having been seduced by their mothers, Freud had to conclude that the female fantasy was peculiar to their sex.

Freud was faced with the questions of whom and what to believe: the woman patient or her male relative, the recollection of a childhood event or an adult denial (and many of the men who were denying what Freud's clients said about them were Freud's friends). Notice what the consequencs were of Freud's choice: Women who were telling the truth about their incestuous experiences were told that it was all in their minds, while the adult molester was ignored entirely. Yet the evidence was there in Freud's day that most of these women were indeed telling the truth, unpalatable as that truth was to Freud. "Freud's seduction theory of neurosis was based upon many *true* instances of traumatic seduction," reported historian Frank J. Sulloway (1979), "instances confirmed by independent testimony of the seducer or by some other reliable witness."

Modern survey research, free to ask about once-taboo subjects, has found a startlingly high incidence of incestuous experiences among women and men in all socioeconomic groups and geographic regions. In a Midwestern university, for example, 21.4 percent of the students in one study (Story and Story 1982) reported having had sexual relations with a member of their families; of the female victims, 41 percent had had sex with their fathers, grandfathers, or stepfathers. (Most of the male experiences were with a brother or sister.) Similarly, in a study of 796 New England college students (Finkelhor 1979), 19 percent of the females and 9 percent of the males had been sexually molested as children; 96 percent of the offenders were male.

College students are not the only samples to report such sexual abuse. In another study of 521 Boston families, sociologist David Finkelhor reported that nearly one parent in ten (9 percent) said that their own children had been victims of attempted or actual sexual abuse; nearly half of the parents knew a child who had been a victim of sexual abuse; 15 percent of the mothers and 6 percent of the fathers had been sexually abused as children themselves; and 94 percent of the abusers were male (*The New York Times*, February 2, 1983; see also Finkelhor 1982a, 1982b). Finkelhor thinks that the total number of victimized children is at least double the number reported, because most abused children do not tell their parents or anyone else about it. And if the amount of incest and sexual abuse of children seems high nowadays, says social worker Florence Rush (1980), imagine what it must have been in Freud's day, when Victorian erotica celebrated the "sensuous little girl" as a desirable sex object.

The terrible repercussions of Freud's decision to discount the testimony of his female patients have lasted to this day. As Rush observed, people who haven't a clue about Freud's theory of infantile sexuality or penis envy readily subscribe to the idea that "children are sexy; that they participate in, and even instigate, their own molestation; and that, in the famous words of every child molester, 'the kid really asked for it'" (Rush 1980). When Rush was studying social work, she was taught never to deal with the *real* fact of a girl's sexual abuse by her father. Nor was she to help such girls see that their fathers were the ones who should feel ashamed and guilty of their actions. No, said the supervising psychiatrist, the girls would actually have *wanted* their incestuous affairs. Their feelings of shame would not come from being victims of their fathers, but from their own "deep, unconscious, incestuous" wishes to possess their fathers (or, it seems, any older man). Rush described the experience of one fifteen-year-old girl who had been "felt up" by her dentist at every visit over a period of five years. Finally she told her mother, who sent her to a therapist (a common parental reaction, unfortunately). "I told my therapist, but he hardly talked about it," said the girl, "and finally [he] said I was disturbed because deep down I really enjoyed it. I didn't talk about it anymore" (from Rush 1980).

The fate of the seduction theory illustrates an important problem in psychoanalytic theory: the tendency to reduce individual problems to mental perceptions and fantasies and to disregard a person's actual experiences and the influences of the person's real environment. Further, an individual has little recourse against the analyst's interpretation of what he or she "really" feels. If you agree with the analyst, your case supports the theory. If you disagree, you're just being neurotically defensive. This is hardly a scientific method of proof.

science or art?

Many contemporary psychologists have little patience for the fanciful word castles of Freudian theory and for the intramural bickering and debates among his followers. Quite apart from the matter of testing specific ideas within psychoanalytic theory, there are other problems with the approach as a whole:

1. *Drawing universal principles from the experiences of patients living in a specific class and culture.* Many critics of Freud have commented on this point. How, they asked, could he possibly conclude that the Oedipus complex was universal when he knew little about family structure in other societies? Some post-Freudian psychoanalysts have tried to strengthen their interpretations by seeking data from anthropology. But most simply assume, as Freud did, that the stuff they find in their own patients' dreams and free associations is the stuff of human nature.

2. *Using the retrospective memories of patients to construct developmental sequences.* Freud and his followers did not observe random samples of children at different ages in order to postulate a theory of development. Instead they worked backward, recreating the significant childhood stages and themes from the patients' adult recollections. The room for distortion is vast. No one's memory is infallible, and the memories of adult patients, who by definition have psychological problems, are particularly suspect. To the argument that memory is a poor guide to reality, Freud replied that memory was the very reality he sought. This approach might be fine for treating the patient, but it is dubious as a basis for theoretical principles that supposedly apply to everyone's unconscious reality.

3. *Generalizing from neurotic patients to all human beings.* Freud formed his theory about human development from reconstructions of his patients' early lives and fantasies. He assumed that normal people go through the same stages and crises that neurotics do, and that neurotics just get bogged down along the way. Thus, if a woman patient adored her father and was jealous of the male role, she simply had an especially bad case of the penis envy that all women feel. Freud based much of his speculation about castration anxiety and the Oedipus complex on the case of Little Hans, a five-year-old boy whose father had been a patient of Freud's. Hans was understandably confused about sexual anatomy because his mother had told him that women have penises too. Yet Freud thought nothing of concluding that all children expect both sexes to have the male organ.

Such reasoning is characteristic of many clinicians, who assume that their patients represent the larger population. For example, despite Freud's generous remarks, clinicians and psychiatrists defined homosexuality as an illness for many years, because the homosexual patients they saw tended to be unhappy and to experience conflicts and guilt in connection with their homosexuality. Not until psychologists studied homosexuals who were not in therapy did the homosexuals-are-sick idea begin to fall apart.

Another problem with generalizing from one's experiences with patients is that the nature of the relationships between particular therapists and particular patients helps determine how problems are defined and what patients reveal. Karen Horney's male patients showed signs of womb envy; Sigmund Freud's male patients did not. Lederer's patients never indicated penis envy; Freud's patients did.

4. *Evaluating subjective, personal interpretations.* Freud recognized that this criticism would be made immediately—that people would feel that dreams, fantasies, and myths are open to many readings. He tried to argue that the symbols expressed in these unconscious forms were, like hieroglyphics, a language that followed clear rules. While some translators would obviously be more skilled than others, their interpretations ultimately would have to agree, as long as they followed the grammar of the unconscious.

Since Freud was the one laying down the rules, he tended to stamp "correct" mainly on interpretations that matched his own. If some analyst found no evidence of castration anxiety in his patients, Freud blamed the analyst's faulty powers of observation, not the theory. He remarked:

> One hears of analysts who boast that, though they have worked for dozens of years, they have never found a sign of the existence of a castration complex. We must bow our heads in recognition of the greatness of this achievement, even though it is only a negative one, a piece of virtuosity in the art of overlooking and mistaking. (Freud 1924b, p. 254n)

There is nothing wrong with trying to distinguish the merits of one interpretation over another on the basis of intellectual zip, theoretical neatness, or personal preference, which is the way one might decide, say, whether Laurence Olivier's rendition of Hamlet or Richard Burton's is better. But those are not *scientific* ways to judge conflicting ideas, much less to select the one that is nearest the truth.[9]

For example, consider Karen Horney's theory of the origins of the castration complex in women. She agreed with Freud that girls do have castration fantasies, but she disagreed that they are the result of penis envy. She said that penis envy, while unconscious, is not that

[9]All scientific interpretations involve a degree of subjective judgment and face problems with bias and generalizability. But psychoanalysis has tended to make a virtue of its methodological deficiencies, instead of trying to correct them.

deeply hidden in the mind. The motivating fantasy that really gets the guilts churning is the girl's desire to have intercourse with her father. Horney has now posed a cause-and-effect question that speculation alone cannot settle. Does envy of the penis cause the little girl to desire her father and identify with him, as Freud thought, or does the fantasy of sleeping with him lead to penis envy, as Horney thought?

experimental evidence

Psychoanalysts argue that verification and modifications of their theories can come only from clinical settings and from the raw materials of the unconscious: dreams, play, folklore. They maintain that attempts to subject their concepts to the cold methods of experimental psychology are doomed to fail, because experiments can measure only conscious, overt behaviors and attitudes. The truth that psychoanalysis reveals, they say, is deeper than anything you'll find in a lab. Like the existence of God, the validity of psychoanalysis can't be proved. It is a matter of faith.

Still, efforts have been made to translate some central psychoanalytic concepts into terms that can be studied experimentally. Psychologists have devised projective tests that try to measure unconscious processes, such as the Thematic Apperception Test (TAT) and the Rorschach Ink Blot Test; they have developed various projective tests for children too. Others have made behavioral predictions based on psychoanalytic theory and have tested them, despite the possibility of error in moving from an abstract and complicated theory to specific behavior and back again. Neither line of research has had clear-cut results. One reason is that the researchers often have as much difficulty agreeing on the interpretation of the tests as analysts do agreeing on the meaning of their patients' dreams.

For example, although studies that have tried to find support for the *literal* interpretation of penis envy have produced equivocal and ambiguous findings, considerable data suggest that both women and men value the male role more highly than the female role. In survey after survey, more women than men report having wanted to trade places with the opposite sex, and both sexes tend to agree that men have an easier time of it in society and have more advantages.

As for the *symbolic* interpretation of penis envy, believers and nonbelievers alike resort to children's spontaneous expressions to bolster their opinion. The classic demonstration of castration anxiety, for example, is the little boy's shocked reaction to seeing a naked girl for the first time: "Mommy, she doesn't have a penis!" We are pleased to report two modern examples that counter Freud's theory. One writer reported that her young daughter, on seeing a naked boy for the first time, rushed to tell her, "Mommy, John Frederick doesn't have a vagina!" But the most damning blow to the penis-envy theory comes from the little girl who took a bath with her young male cousin, observed the differences in silence, and said nothing until her mother tucked her in bed that night. "Mommy," she said softly, "isn't it a blessing he doesn't have it on his face?"

Researchers have also tried to demonstrate the universality of the Oedipus complex. Again, when the concept is interpreted literally rather than as a metaphor for the struggle between infantile pleasures and societal demands, the evidence falters. Between the ages of three and six, supposedly the years of marked conflict, both sexes prefer the mother. Some little girls go on to identify with (that is, to take on the traits and goals of) their fathers rather than their mothers, but no data show that these girls are the neurotic victims of unresolved Oedipus complexes (Mahl 1971). As Freud himself admitted, "In general our insight into these developmental processes in girls is unsatisfactory, incomplete and vague" (1924a).

Sociologist Nancy Chodorow's approach (1978) used psychoanalytic concepts in a new way, arguing that neither biology nor role training can explain why women become the mothering, nurturant sex or why the sexes are not symmetrical in status and personality qualities. Unlike traditional psychoanalysts, Chodorow does not think anatomy is destiny or that sexual inequality is inevitable. But she does believe that "feminine and masculine psyches" develop differently as a result of unconscious processes, particularly those of the early mother-infant relationship. Because mothers are the first and primary love objects for their sons *and* daughters, because "mother and father are not the same *kind* of parent," the quality and intensity of a child's relationship to them differs. The early and asymmetrical triangle of child and parents forms the basis, said Chodorow, of female "connectedness" and comfort with intimacy and of male independence and reluctance to become close to others.

It seems clear that some parents do treat their opposite-sex children seductively; that sexual tensions do thrive in many families; and that young children do have sexual impulses. But social scientists have not demonstrated that family love triangles and their effects are inevitable, that families deal with them in the same ways, or that children's motivations are exclusively or even primarily sexual. Some contemporary psychoanalysts are trying to modify Freudian theory in light of these and other new findings (for example, many have aban-

doned the notion of a latency period in a child's sexual development), while maintaining the basic language and assumptions of
psychoanalysis (see Blum 1977). Still, the Oedipus complex remains
an illuminating metaphor or an unfounded hypothesis, depending on
your point of view.

existential identity and vulnerability

Even though few mainstays of Freud's theory have been verified
empirically, the theory has the virtue of raising some difficult questions about the relationship between men and women. For example,
few other branches of social science even acknowledge the important themes of existential identity and vulnerability.

Many writers, from Margaret Mead and Sigmund Freud to
Simone de Beauvoir and Norman Mailer, have said that one *is* a
woman; one *learns to be* a man. Femininity is a function of the
female body. Women are secure in their roles by virtue of their
reproductive function and the monthly reminder that they are female.
But masculinity must be learned, earned, and constantly rewon. It is
thus much more fragile than femininity. Further, if women are born
female but men must define themselves as male, then femininity is
the given and masculinity is deduced from it. That is, in order to have
a secure sexual identity, men must define themselves and their proper
spheres of behavior as the opposite of what women do (see Chapter
6). As Mead put it:

> A girl *is* a virgin [or] a mother. . . . Stage after stage in women's life
> histories thus stand, irrevocable, indisputable, accomplished. This
> gives a natural basis for the little girl's emphasis on *being* rather than
> *doing*. The little boy learns that he must act like a boy, do things, *prove*
> *that he is a boy, and prove it over and over again*, while the little girl
> learns that she *is* a girl, and all she has to do is refrain from acting like a
> boy. (Mead 1968, pp. 182–83)

This line of reasoning, tenuous though it may seem, does suggest
why equality—a world in which men and women do the same things
and share the same desirable traits—would be deeply threatening to
men. If they must base their sexuality and selfhood on being different
from women, their historically consistent and virulent reaction to
feminism and movements for women's rights is somewhat under-
standable. Conversely, it may be that men feel insecure *because* their
identity rests on vague standards of masculinity defined in terms of
what they can't do (womanly things) rather than what they should do.

If men make civilizations because they can't make babies, then naturally they will resent female efforts to usurp their role. Since they can't take over the female role, sharing can only mean that they get less. But if the premise itself is faulty (as it would seem to be, since conception requires sperm), then both sexes could define their roles and choose their activities on some basis other than sex. Logically, there is no reason to assume that reproductive and nonreproductive activities are analogous just because both are "creative."

Many psychoanalysts believe that the anatomical difference between the sexes will always entail mystery, no matter how much physiology we study or how many naked bodies we observe. Further, mystery invariably evokes interest and attraction, as well as fear and hostility. If you could wipe out the mystery, they imply, you might get rid of all that is fearful in sexual attraction but lose all that is fun, too.

The psychoanalytic perspective also holds that men and women have different kinds of sexual vulnerabilities that are anatomically determined (though the sexes are equally susceptible to emotional hurt). For women, sexual anxieties are bound up with fears of being overwhelmed, violated, impregnated, raped. For men, sexual anxieties are linked to performance and fear of impotence. Each sex's fears have objective bases—rape and impotence do occur—but psychoanalysts argue that these fears also act on an unconscious level, influencing in subtle ways the quality of male-female relationships.[10]

The twin themes of identity and vulnerability contribute in some measure to the tension and outright hostility that is often evident between the sexes. Freud and the other early psychoanalysts deserve much credit for deromanticizing the Victorian vision of men and women dallying in idyllic and nonsexual love relationships, and for probing the earthy origins of the sexes' animosity, passion, and lust. The psychoanalytic perspective puts more emphasis than any other approach on the emotional qualities of male-female relationships.

In the opinion of many critics, however, psychoanalysis overemphasizes the dark side of life. No matter where Freud looked he saw conflict between love and hate, creativity and destructiveness,

---

[10]It is interesting that there are more jokes reflecting the male's fear than the female's. "All the woman has to do is lie there and fake it," men grumble. "There's no way to fake an erection." They tell many impotence and "castrating women" jokes:

A man, frustrated at his girlfriend's reluctance to sleep with him, finally in exasperation unzips his pants, takes out his organ, and shouts at her. "Look at me! Do you know what this is?" "It looks like a penis," she replies coolly, "only smaller."

sex and death. After a lifetime of thought he concluded that such conflicts are inevitable, both within and between individuals, and that the chances for permanent peace were virtually nil. His emphasis on subterranean, unconscious processes accounts for the mood of sexual envy, fear, and distrust that immersion in psychoanalytic theory tends to generate. Not all psychoanalysts have been as pessimistic as Freud. Karen Horney (1967) offered one reason that the sexes might ultimately get it together after all: "Love succeeds in building bridges from the loneliness of this shore to the loneliness on the other one. . . . Here is the answer to the question posed initially of why we see love between the sexes more distinctly than we see hate—because the union of the sexes offers us the greatest possibilities for happiness."

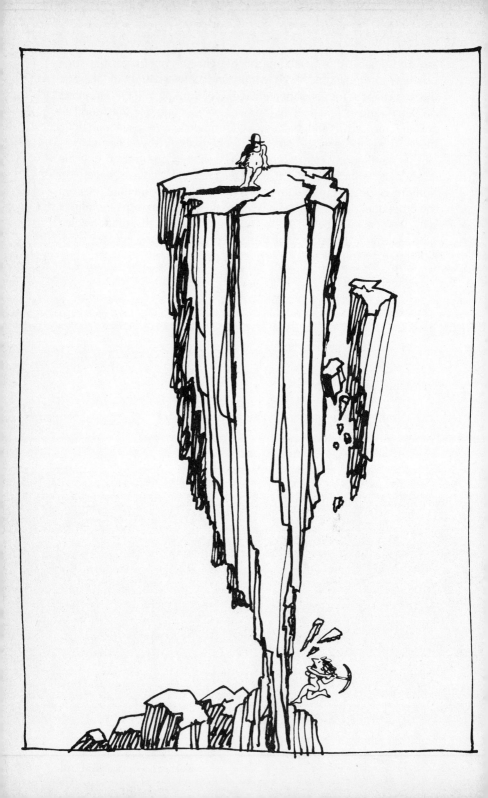

6 | Getting the message: The learning perspective

If you were to wake up tomorrow and discover that you were a member of the other sex, how would your life be different?

Researchers at the Institute for Equality in Education recently posed this question to some 2,000 students in grades three through twelve (Baumgartner 1983). Despite all the efforts of reformers to reduce the impact of sex roles during the past decade, most of these students were sure that a change in gender would alter their lives immediately and dramatically. A twelfth-grade boy said, "I would drop my math class and take more classes like cooking, English, and ones that would make me look good as a girl." An eleventh-grade girl said, "I would take classes like drafting and woodshop, and I wouldn't take Home Economics." Girls said that if they were boys they would go out for football. Boys said that if they were girls they would try to become cheerleaders. (As one fourth-grader put it, "When you're a girl, you cheer sports instead of joining them.")

Although 90 percent of girls in high school today can expect to work outside the home for twenty-five years if they marry and forty-five years if they don't, the students in this study didn't seem to know it; many thought a boy's main task in life was to pursue a career, a girl's to pursue a husband. When they mentioned specific jobs, the jobs were usually stereotyped ones. Girls said that if they were males they could be professional athletes, mechanics, construction workers, pilots, engineers, race car drivers, forest rangers, dentists, steelworkers, architects, stunt men, coal miners, geologists, farmers, sports commentators, draftsmen, and bankers. Boys said that if they were females they could be secretaries, housewives, nurses, cocktail waitresses, social workers, teachers, stewardesses, interior decorators, child care workers, receptionists, models, beauty queens—and prostitutes. Boys said their career options would narrow; girls said theirs would expand.

The students also thought a change of sex would alter their own personality traits and the way other people treated them (see Table 5 for a summary). A few boys saw certain advantages to these changes ("No one would make fun of me because I'm afraid of frogs"). And some of the girls were less than eager to become boys. In general, though, girls thought they'd be better off as males, while boys wanted no part of being female. Grammar-school boys, especially, tended to view girlhood as a fate worse than death. Some gave their essays titles like "The Disaster," "The Fatal Dream," or "Doomsday." And they often made remarks like the following:

"If I were a girl, everybody would be better than me, because boys are better than girls." (Third-grader)
"Girls can't do anything fun. They don't know how to do anything except play with dolls." (Fourth-grader)
"If I woke up and I was a girl, I would go back to sleep and hope it was a bad dream." (Sixth-grader)
"If I were a girl, I'd kill myself." (Grade unspecified)

Clearly, sex-role stereotypes are alive and well and living in the hearts and minds of American schoolchildren. How did they get there? The learning perspective says that thousands of childhood experiences eventually fit us for a social system in which males go one way, females another.[1] It also says that the basic ingredients of personality are set in childhood (some proponents even say within the first few years of life) and that virtually from the moment of birth boys and girls take different roads to different personalities. This view implicitly accepts the idea that stereotypes about the sexes have a strong basis in reality: that men are more independent and aggressive, for example, and women are more nurturant and emotional. But it also says that there is nothing biologically inevitable about these differences; they are learned from books, films, parents, and other people. As a result, no sooner have children learned to speak than they can tell you who wears dresses and who does not, who plays with baby dolls and who wouldn't touch them with a ten-foot pole, who will grow up to become a nurse and who a doctor. Children also learn many subtleties of personality and behavior, even how to sit, stand, and talk, that mark them as feminine or masculine as surely as do bows and britches.

The learning perspective has intuitive appeal because it fits personal experience better than other approaches. People can't recognize the effect of a prenatal hormone on their behavior. Few can remember having an Oedipal conflict when they were four. But almost all of us can recall events from childhood that seem to

---

[1]We are using the word *learning* in a broad sense to refer to the process of socialization, in which a child acquires through experience the traits and behaviors a culture or subculture deems appropriate.

Table 5. Schoolchildren's Perceptions of Life as the Opposite Sex

	Representative responses (grade levels in parentheses)
As boys, girls would expect to	
Be more assertive and self-reliant	"I think I would be more outspoken and confident." (tenth)
Show less emotion	"I would have to stay calm and cool whenever something happened." (tenth)
Become more aggressive	"I could beat up people." (sixth)
	"I'd probably need to start cussing . . ." (eleventh)
	"I'd have to be more (rowdy, macho, smart-alecky, noisy, etc.)" (various)
	"I'd kill my art teacher, instead of arguing with him as I do now." (eighth)
Have more freedom	"I could stay out later." (unspecified)
	"There would be fewer rules." (unspecified)
	"I'd be trusted more when driving." (unspecified)
Think less about appearance	"I wouldn't have to be neat." (fourth)
	"I wouldn't have to worry how I look." (sixth)
	"If I woke up tomorrow and I was a boy . . . I would go back to bed since it would not take one very long to get ready for school." (tenth)
Be freed from treatment as a sex object	"[I'd no longer have to experience] leers while walking down the street." (eleventh)
	(Many girls noted that they would not have to worry about rape.)
Perform different duties at home	"I would take out the garbage instead of doing the ironing." (twelfth)
	"I wouldn't have to babysit." (sixth)
Spend more time with and be closer to their fathers	"I could go hunting and fishing with my dad." (sixth)
	"My dad would . . . teach me how to work with wood." (sixth)
	"My father would be closer because I'd be the son he always wanted." (sixth)
	"If I were a boy, my Daddy might have loved me." (third)

As girls, boys would expect to

Be quieter and more reserved	"[I'd have to] . . . wait for others to talk to me first." (tenth)
	"I'd have to be (nicer, more polite, goodie-goodie, like a lady, etc.)." (various)
Be less active	"Instead of wrestling with my friends, I'd be sitting around discussing the daily gossip." (unspecified)
	"I would play girl games and not have many things to do during the day." (unspecified)
	"I would have to hate snakes. Everything would be miserable." (unspecified)
	"I couldn't climb trees or jump the creek." (unspecified)
Be more restricted	"I'd have to come in earlier." (unspecified)
	"I couldn't have a pocket knife." (unspecified)
	"I couldn't throw spit wads." (unspecified)
Worry more about appearance	"I couldn't be a slob any more. I'd have to smell pretty." (eighth)
	"I'd have to shave my whole body!" (sixth)
	"I would use a lot of makeup and look good and beautiful, knowing that few people would care for my personality . . ." (twelfth)
Be treated as sex objects	"If I were gorgeous, I would be jeered at and hear plenty of comments." (twelfth)
	"I'd have to watch out for boys making passes at me." (third)
Worry about violence against females	"I'd have to know how to handle drunk guys and rapists." (eighth)
	"I would have to be around other girls for safety." (eleventh)
Perform different duties at home	"I would dust the house instead of vacuuming." (fourth)
	"I would be the one who has the kid." (eighth)
Do fewer things with their fathers	"I would not help my dad wash the car or gas up the car." (fourth)
	"I would not be able to help my dad fix the car and truck and his two motor-cycles." (sixth)

SOURCE: Baumgartner 1983.

explain, post hoc, why we are what we are, or why we never became what we wanted to. For example:

1. Did your parents encourage you to have a paper route when you were younger, or to babysit?

2. Could boys take cooking in your school and girls take shop? Which did you take?

3. Did you go out for Little League? Other sports? What did your parents think about your athletic abilities? Did you ever try out for football? Cheerleader?

4. Did anyone ever give you a toy nurse's kit? Doctor's kit? Chemistry set? Tea set?

5. Did anyone ever tell you that if you worked hard you could be an astronaut? Policeman? President of the United States? What was your earliest ambition?

6. Did your mother often talk to you about how wonderful it would be to marry and have children when you grew up?

In its broadest outlines, the learning perspective has to be right. As we noted in Chapter 1, activities and occupations labeled feminine in one society are labeled masculine in another. A Chinese woman can operate a crane or fly a plane without defending herself by insisting, "I'm not one of those weird women's libbers." A Danish man who happened to be a dentist would be a minority in a "woman's" occupation. Since cultural norms for men and women vary so drastically, the process of socialization, which transforms infant savage into civilized adult, must explain a lot about sex differences. No gene determines that boys shall play football and girls shall wave pompoms.

But this common-sense perspective also has some uncommon problems. It is one thing to say that sex differences are learned, and something else again to say precisely how this learning takes place. "I treat all my children alike!" parents like to claim (though they will probably think that *their* parents played favorites), and finding out whether people do what they say can be as hard as catching fish bare-handed. Also, the learning perspective makes some debatable assumptions about masculinity, femininity, and the stability of attitudes, behaviors, and personality traits across time and place.

In the first part of this chapter we consider three major theories of socialization, efforts to explain the process by which girls supposedly become girlish and boys boyish. In the second part we look at the content of that process—at the messages, both explicit and subtle, that surround children in the home, in the classroom, and on the playground. Finally, we examine some recent criticisms of the learning perspective and some new trends. The research, it turns out, confirms some parts of the perspective, but not others.

socialization theories: two sexes and how they grow

social-learning theory

The basis of much contemporary research on sex typing is social-learning theory, a product of the behaviorist school of psychology. Behaviorists emphasize observable events and their consequences rather than internal feelings or drives. Years ago they formulated a set of principles to describe simple learning in animals; later they applied these principles to the complex learning skills and social behavior of people (thus the term *social*-learning theory). Behaviorists believe that all learning, including how we learn to be masculine or feminine, can be explained with the same basic rules.

The most important learning principle is that *behavior is controlled by its consequences*. An act that is regularly followed by a reward, or reinforcer, tends to occur again; an act that produces punishment—or is ignored—drops off in frequency. In the animal lab, for example, a hungry rat that gets a tasty morsel when it presses a bar will probably press the bar again. A rat that gets an electric shock when it presses the bar will soon stop pressing. The same principle works with people. If parents reward little girls for playing with dolls ("What a sweet little Mommy you are!"), girls will tend to play with dolls. If adults punish them for playing with baseball bats ("You don't want *that* for Christmas, silly"), girls will not develop much interest in Little League. Whether the rewards and punishments are handed out deliberately or not, the effect is the same.

With human beings direct on-the-spot reinforcement is often unnecessary because language offers some convenient shortcuts. For instance, parents can tell their daughter that they disapprove of her hitting other children and that they like it when she helps in the kitchen. Anticipated rewards and punishments affect behavior just as real ones do. As psychologist Walter Mischel (1966) wrote, "A man does not have to be arrested for wearing dresses in public to learn about the consequences of such behavior." In addition, children can learn about the consequences of what they do by observing what happens to other people. Being the intelligent little persons that they are, they participate vicariously in the experiences of others and draw their own conclusions.

Most learning theorists feel that reinforcement alone cannot explain how children learn everything that their sex is expected to do and not to do. Parents would be kept busy twenty-four hours a day rewarding and punishing, rewarding and punishing, for each detail of behavior. Besides, most adults are not aware of the many mannerisms, gestures, and speech habits that are part of their sex roles. Such nuances, say the theorists, must be learned through imitation. Children do a lot of apparently spontaneous imitating; possibly they copy other people because adults have rewarded them for copying in the past, or perhaps they are simply natural mimics.

Most studies of imitation (or *modeling*) have been done in the laboratory rather than in real-life settings, and in the laboratory psychologists can often predict what sorts of models children will choose to imitate. For example, they tend to imitate adults who are friendly, warm, and attentive (Bandura and Huston 1961). They also imitate powerful people, that is, adults who control resources that are important to the child, whether intangibles like the privilege of playing outside or tangibles like cookies and toys (Bandura, Ross, and Ross 1963; Mischel and Grusec 1966). Because parents are the most nurturant and powerful people in a child's world, they are assumed to be very effective models.

In order to explain how girls become feminine and boys masculine, social-learning theory assumes that children copy people similar to themselves—in particular, the same-sex parent and friends. As Mischel (1970) observed, "Boys do not learn baseball by watching girls and girls do not learn about fashions from observing boys." But research has not confirmed this key assumption. When children in an experiment have a chance to copy adults, they show no consistent tendency to mimic one sex more than the other. Researchers who have tried to correlate more global personality traits of parent and child (rather than concentrating on a particular action) do not find that children resemble the same-sex parent more than the opposite-sex parent or other adults (Maccoby and Jacklin 1974; Smith and Daglish 1977).

One plausible explanation for the discrepancy between theory and data is that children observe both sexes, but as they grow older they are most likely to do what they have learned by imitating same-sex models, because that path leads to reward and the other to punishment (Bandura and Walters 1963; Mischel 1970). "Both men and women know how to curse or to fight or use cosmetics or primp in front of mirrors," Mischel commented, but they don't do these things equally often. A three-year-old boy may innocently dress up in his mother's clothes and makeup, but if he does so at age fifteen he'll be in trouble.

Also, parents may be potent models, but children grow up with many influential people, not all of whom agree on what behavior is appropriate. (One of us recalls a favorite uncle who could be counted on to give her a really good "boy's toy" amidst all the dolls and clothes on her birthday.) For that matter, parents often do not agree on how to treat their children. Children have an entire smorgasbord of models to copy—parents, teachers, friends, siblings—with the result that each of us is a unique composite of many influences. Children must sift through conflicting demands and expectations, often finding, for example, that they cannot please their parents and friends at the same time. They have to figure out why something they did pleased their mother but angered their father, and why they were punished for fighting at one time but not another. And they have to deal with the fact that the behavior a parent displays may not be the one the parent rewards.

cognitive-developmental theory

Social-learning theory views the child from the outside. It describes how the child is shaped by external events but has much less to say about what goes on in the child's head. Lawrence Kohlberg (1966, 1969) proposed another approach, which emphasizes how children think. As learning theorists see it, children (and adults) of all ages learn things in the same ways—through reinforcement and modeling. But cognitive theory, like psychoanalytic theory, says that all children pass through certain *stages of development*, and that the way they learn depends on the stage they have reached. The Swiss psychologist Jean Piaget showed that children's ability to reason and their understanding of the physical and social world change in predictable ways as they mature. Kohlberg argued that these changes affect the way they assimilate information about the sexes.

Thus, although two-year-olds can apply the labels "boy" and "girl" correctly to themselves and others, their concept of gender is very concrete. Preschool children rely on physical features such as dress and hairstyle to decide who falls in which category. Girls are people with long hair; boys are people who never wear dresses. Many children at this stage believe they can change their own gender at will simply by getting a haircut or a new outfit. They do not yet have the mental machinery to think of gender as adults do. All the reinforcement in the world, Kohlberg argued, won't alter that fact.

By the age of six or seven, children understand that gender is permanent. This is a consequence not of rewards and punishments, in Kohlberg's view, but of a growing ability to grasp that certain basic characteristics of people and objects do not change even though less basic ones may. Just as the amount of water remains the same when it is poured from a short fat glass into a tall thin one, a woman remains a woman when she wears pants. Children at this age know that they are and always will be female or male. Now their task is to find out what to do to bring their actions into line with the label.

A child's desire for consistency can lead to rigid insistence that the rules seen as appropriate for males and females be obeyed. Children seek a tangible sign to distinguish girls from boys, women from men, and themselves from the opposite sex. A girl may reason, for instance, that since boys wear pants but girls often wear skirts, she'd better stick to skirts. One colleague recalls that as a small child she was the despair of her liberated relatives when she insisted on wearing dresses instead of practical jeans.

Research finds that children between about five and seven are especially uncompromising about the shoulds and should nots of sex roles. In one study of four- to nine-year-olds, psychologist William Damon (1977) asked children questions about a boy named George, who liked to play with dolls even though his parents opposed it. The youngest children thought George should go ahead and do whatever he wished. But by the age of five or six, children viewed George's behavior as beyond the pale, primarily because others would disapprove and might punish or ridicule him. (One little boy thought it would be all right for George to play with dolls if no one could see him.) Then, at six or seven, another shift occurred, as children began to distinguish between arbitrary social rules and fundamental issues of right and wrong. These children thought George would be unwise to play with dolls because it would cause him embarrassment, but they did not think he should be punished for it.

Consider, too, this exchange that one of us (C.W.) had with her son Jason and his friend Nick when both boys were six. They had been saying that it was better to be a boy than a girl because boys could do more things.

C.W.: What could you do if you were girls that you can't because you're boys?

JASON: Have a vagina.

C.W.: What else?

JASON: Be a mother.

C.W. What do you think boys can do that girls can't?

JASON: Be a father.

NICK: Be a doctor.

C.W. But women can be doctors, too.

NICK: [*patiently, as if to a slow child*]: No, those are called nurses.

Eleanor Maccoby (1980) has suggested that children at this age may exaggerate sex roles "in order to get them cognitively clear." The same sort of exaggeration and overgeneralization has been noted in other areas of cognitive development as well.

Social-learning theory says that girls learn feminine behavior and boys learn masculine behavior because they are rewarded for doing so. Cognitive-developmental theory takes a different position: It assumes that children and adults try to maintain a coherent and balanced picture of themselves and the world, in which beliefs, actions, and values are congruent. The knowledge that gender is permanent motivates the child to discover how to be a competent or "proper" girl or boy. As a consequence, she or he finds female or male activities rewarding. Reinforcements and models help show children how well they are doing, but essentially children socialize themselves.

Despite the differences between social-learning and cognitive-developmental theory, it is often hard to choose between them when explaining an observation. For example, one study found that bright children preferred dolls of the same sex as themselves—regarded as a sign of sex typing—at younger ages than children of average intelligence (Kohlberg and Zigler 1967). Another (Connor and Serbin 1977) found that preschoolers with high verbal IQ scores were more likely than others to prefer sex-typed classroom activities. The cognitive interpretation is that the bright child matures earlier in mental capacity and therefore understands and assimilates sex-role demands faster than the average child. That is, the bright child goes through the same developmental stages in the same order as other children, but more quickly. The social-learning interpretation is that intelligent children need fewer lessons (fewer reinforcements) before they know what is expected of them (Mischel 1970).

identification

Many psychologists believe that a third process accounts for sex-role learning: the tendency of children to identify with the same-sex parent. The child wants to be like the parent and copies his or her values, mannerisms, personality, and ambitions, not just specific acts. Because of identification, children develop a stronger emotional commitment to their sex role than to behavior that is not tied to their masculinity or femininity. Freud's theory of psychosexual development (Chapter 5) is an identification theory *par excellence*, and it was Freud who first introduced the term. Freud believed that children incorporate ("introject") large chunks of the same-sex parent's personality into their own, mainly as a way of reducing the anxiety and conflict caused by Oedipal desires. Today most theories of identification do not give such a central place to sexual motivation. Instead they emphasize the child's desire to be similar to someone of the same sex; to be like someone who is powerful; to enjoy vicariously the position of someone who has status; or to reproduce the feelings experienced when the model gave the child love and attention. In some theories, attachment and dependency cause identification; in others identification leads to attachment and dependency. This approach encompasses more than the behaviorists' emphasis on specific acts. Instead of counting reinforcements and situational forces that cause a boy to strike back at the neighborhood bully, identification theories leapfrog over particular events and concentrate on a global personality trait, the boy's aggressiveness.

Most identification theorists have had much more to say about boys than about girls. An assumption underlying much of their work is that a nonmasculine boy is doomed to be a social and psychological misfit. (As psychologist Joseph Pleck [1981] pointed out, even some "male liberation" books have warned about the dire consequences of "an insecure sense of masculinity." We will have more to say about this assumption later on.) These theorists believe that identification is a riskier, more failure-prone business for boys than for girls. Infants of both sexes, they note, start out with a stronger attachment to the mother than to the father, since she does most of the child care and provides most of the nurturance. For girls, identification is relatively simple; they just continue the attachment to the mother.[2] But in order for boys to become masculine and enter the world of men, they must break away from their mothers and identify

[2]Freud would disagree; see Chapter 5.

with their fathers. This is difficult; girls have many examples around them of what women do, but boys have a much vaguer idea of what men do; they are surrounded by female relatives and teachers in their early years. Psychologist David Lynn (1966) wrote that "the father as a model for the boy is analogous to a map showing the major outline but lacking most details." A boy knows he should *not* be a sissy but has a harder time figuring out what he *should* be. He may turn to fiction and symbolic models, following a fantasized stereotyped image of the male role instead of identifying with a real person, as girls do.

Several writers have suggested that the salience of the mother and the relative invisibility of the father in the family produce problems for both sexes (Dinnerstein 1977; Chodorow 1978; Baumrind 1980). Girls, they say, establish a strong, symbiotic relationship with their mothers that prevents them from being autonomous and self-confident and establishing a perspective of their own; it's hard to explore the world if you're tangled up in apron strings. Psychologist Lois Hoffman (1972) even suggested that perhaps "girls need a little maternal rejection if they are to become independently competent and self-confident." Boys, on the other hand, hoping to become independent "little men," struggle against the temptation to merge with their mothers. In the process they not only stifle their own "feminine" qualities, but also come to denigrate those who actually are feminine: women. Their hostility toward women causes them personal problems later on, in their intimate relationships with the other sex, and it also leads to continued social subordination of females.

Pleck (1981), who reviewed the meager research bearing on these points, concluded that there is little evidence to support them. He also observed that although such ideas seem consistent with feminist politics—in that they imply we'd all be better off if fathers were more involved in child rearing—they also hold the victims of male hostility responsible for it. Father reaps the credit when a boy becomes masculine (he provided a good model for identification), but poor old mom gets the blame for the boy's psychological problems and her own inferior social position. As Pleck noted, there is a much simpler explanation for negative attitudes toward women: They justify male privilege.

The general concept of identification is plausible, but in practice it is hard to say when identification has occurred. Often people use the term loosely, as in, "I respected my father, but I identified with my mother." Psychologists define the term differently, depending on who is theorizing. For one it means that a child wants to be like a parent; for another, that a child actually behaves like the parent; for a third, that a child feels closest to the parent. You can see how hard it is to interpret this concept. If you walk, talk, and bake like your mother, if you have her endearing mannerisms and infuriating habits, but you have the literary tastes of your father and want to be an accountant like him, with which parent have you identified? In addition, in some studies people say they are most like one parent but feel closest to the other. Clearly, the idea that girls learn to be feminine by identifying with their mothers and boys learn to be masculine by identifying with their fathers is too simple.

Even when a child does turn out like a parent, identification is not necessarily the process responsible. Indeed, the child's behavior may not be based on the parent's at all. Psychologist Albert Bandura (1969) illustrated this point with a parable about a big-game hunter who came face to face with a hungry lion. "As he prepared to shoot the onrushing beast, the gun jammed. Helpless and terrified, the hunter promptly closed his eyes and began to pray rapidly. Moments passed and, much to his surprise, nothing happened. Puzzled by this unexpected turn of events, the hunter cocked his head and slowly opened his eyes to find the lion also bowed in prayer. The jubilant hunter loudly exclaimed, 'Thank God, you are responding to my prayers!' The lion promptly replied, 'Not at all. I'm saying grace.'"

All three socialization theories give us some good ideas of how sex typing occurs in general, but it is hard to predict how any given child will turn out. A child does not copy the parents in a mechanical way. The child may follow in the parent's footsteps only if the parent is wearing comfortable shoes—and is satisfied with his or her life path. If a mother chronically complains about her fate, her daughter may vow, "I'll never be like her!" Or the mother may seem happy enough, but her daughter may imitate the father for reasons that have nothing to do with gender. Perhaps she just likes him more. Maccoby and Jacklin tell of a little girl who held tenaciously to the belief that only boys could become doctors, even though her own mother was a physician. Apparently she was influenced more by the attitudes and behavior of people outside her family than by the real-life model who was closest to her.

It is easiest to play quarterback on Monday morning, and all these theories can trace an individual's adult behavior to childhood antecedents after the fact. A social-learning theorist would look at the person's history of rewards and punishments—all that family attention for good grades and apathy for making the team (or vice versa). An identification theorist would try to see which parent the person resembles most, especially in values and ambitions. A cognitive theorist would point to the child's mental processes and ways of assimilating information. Although learning, cognitive, and identification theories emphasize different aspects of sex-role learning, many psychologists help themselves to a little of each.

We turn now from sex-role theories to sex-role messages. What do children learn about the content of male and female roles in this society, and how are the messages transmitted?

sources of socialization

parents: perceptions and lessons

Many parents feel that they know their babies quite well when the infants are only a day or two old. "She's such a contented little dumpling," they say, or "He's quite an assertive little man." With such remarks sex typing begins. Psychologists Jeffrey Rubin, Frank Provenzano, and Zella Luria (1974) interviewed thirty first-time parents, fifteen of girls and fifteen of boys, within twenty-four hours of the baby's birth. Each baby had been routinely examined after birth by hospital personnel for physical and neurological characteristics such as color, muscle tone, and reflex irritability, and there were no objective differences between males and females, even in size. Yet the parents of girls rated their babies as softer, more finely featured, smaller, and more inattentive than did the parents of boys. Fathers especially were influenced by the gender of the child. They described their sons as firmer, larger-featured, better-coordinated, more alert, stronger, and hardier than the mothers of sons did; men thought their daughters were more inattentive, weak, and delicate than the women did. There was only one exception. Mothers rated sons cuddlier than daughters, and fathers rated daughters cuddlier than sons—a finding that Rubin et al. called the Oedipal Effect.

Of course, it is always possible that the infants really did differ in ways that the hospital personnel had missed. But consider another study, by John and Sandra Condry (1976). They showed men and women a videotape of a nine-month-old infant reacting to a teddy bear, a jack-in-the-box, a doll, and a buzzer, and had them rate the infant's pleasure, anger, and fear in each situation. Half the adults thought they were watching a male and half thought they were watching a female. The supposed sex of the child made little difference in the case of the teddy bear (the infant was obviously pleased with it) or the buzzer (the infant cried intensely the whole time). But when the infant was shown the jack-in-the-box and responded with agitation and eventually tears, it was another story: The "girl" was seen as more fearful than the "boy," while the "boy" was seen as angrier than the "girl." "If you think a child is *angry*," wondered Condry and Condry, "do you treat 'him' differently than if you think 'she' is *afraid*?"

That is the important question: whether parents' differing perceptions of boys and girls affect how they treat them. The answer is, it depends. The pressures on boys and girls to act in certain ways are uneven and unequal—with more flexibility generally granted to girls. Until adolescence it is more permissible for girls to behave like tomboys than for boys to behave like sissies, an observation that draws many explanations. One is that parents fear that boys who prefer traditionally feminine activities may become homosexual; another is that masculinity is a more precarious identity than femininity, so boys must stick carefully to the rules. Some sociologists explain the matter in terms of status and power: Lower-status groups, whether women or minorities, are understood to aspire to the status above them and forgiven when they try to move up. When a higher-status person takes a step down, however, society's pressures are brought to bear on him.

Almost all parents encourage some sex-typed behavior in their children, for example by buying more trucks than dolls for boys and more dolls than trucks for girls. Jerrie Will, Patricia Self, and Nancy Datan (1974) observed eleven mothers as they played, one at a time, with a six-month-old child. Taking advantage of the fact that male and female infants look much alike, the researchers told six of the women that the child was a boy named Adam, and the other five that it was a girl named Beth. Then they looked to see which of three toys—a doll, a train, or a fish—the women would offer the child. Those who thought they were playing with Beth handed her the doll more often than those who thought they were playing with Adam, and "Adam" got the train more often than "Beth" did. Afterward, two mothers commented that Beth was a real girl, because she was sweeter and cried more softly than a boy would. In fact, Beth was a boy. The notable thing was that all of the women claimed to believe that males and females are alike at this tender age, and none said she would treat her own son and daughter differently. On the contrary, nine insisted that they encouraged rough play with their daughters, and ten said that they encouraged their sons to play with dolls.[3]

Many people believe that adults punish boys who behave like girls more than they do girls who behave like boys, and there is at least some evidence that this is so (Pleck 1981). Another common assumption, that fathers are more insistent on sex typing than mothers are, also seems to be true—especially if the child in question is a son (Langlois and Downs 1979, cited in Maccoby 1980). But when we turn to tests of the assumption that parents grant more autonomy or freedom to young boys than to young girls, we find a surprise. Most studies, Maccoby and Jacklin reported, do not support the assumption. In fact, some research shows that parents claim to restrict preschool boys *more* than girls. They set firmer rules for boys; they are more apt to lay down the law with boys and to make sure it is obeyed. Possibly parents think that boys are more rambunctious and therefore keep closer tabs on them.

Research on the origins of aggressiveness is also somewhat surprising. Although boys tend to be more aggressive than girls, some studies find that parents actually punish boys who fight more often than girls, or at least they say they do.[4] Perhaps girls fight less than boys because they are punished more consistently for doing so. Or perhaps boys fight more than girls because parental attention can be reinforcing even when it takes the form of spankings and scolding. Further, when parents spank boys for being aggressive, they are modeling the very behavior they presumably would like to get rid of:

---

[3]The overall package of research on parent-infant exchanges is contradictory. Some studies find that mothers touch boy babies more often than girls; some find that they touch girls more; some find no difference. The same is true for studies of how much the mother talks to the child and of how quickly she responds to the baby's cries and coos. The kind of attention a parent gives to a child varies with social class and the age of the child. Highly educated mothers respond more quickly to the sounds and cries of female infants, but the reverse is true for less well educated mothers. Parents may hold or touch a child of either sex more at one age than another, although in general parents tend to regard daughters as more fragile than sons and treat them more gingerly (Maccoby and Jacklin 1974). The data don't give any strong indication of how, or even whether, such parental behavior is related to the child's behavior later in life.

[4]Most research on aggression is based on interviews with parents. Sometimes parents and children are observed at home or in a laboratory, but Maccoby and Jacklin found no studies in which researchers watched how parents actually react when their child brawls with other children outside the home.

"Hitting is bad" (whack!). Keep in mind, too, that Americans are ambivalent about aggressiveness and violence, especially in males. Parents may convey to their sons, but not to their daughters, a covert admiration for feistiness.

teachers: the hidden curriculum

Fortunately, some good observational studies are being done in schools. One study of teachers and children in fifteen nursery-school classrooms supports the position that adults do treat boys and girls differently, but in subtle ways. Even people who talk equality sometimes remain unconsciously traditional. Psychologists Lisa Serbin and K. Daniel O'Leary (1975) trained observers to record exactly how and when preschool teachers spoke to the children. They were especially curious to find out how the teachers responded to boys and girls who were aggressive or dependent. Here are three of their main findings.

1. Teachers did reward the boys for being aggressive, but not by saying, "Terrific, Tommy, clobber him again." They responded over three times as often to boys who misbehaved as to girls who misbehaved. When they rebuked the girls, it was briefly, softly, out of other children's hearing. When they scolded the boys, they called public attention to their naughtiness—which only inspired the boys to continue in their ways. Serbin and O'Leary described a typical encounter:

> John was a five-year-old bully. When someone didn't follow his directions or give him the toy he wanted, John lost his temper. He pushed, shoved, shouted, and threw things. When we first watched John in his classroom, he was playing peacefully with another boy at building a Tinker-Toy tower.
>
> Then John asked the other child for a piece of material the boy was using. When he was refused, John began to tear the tower apart. The other boy protested, and John raised his hand threateningly. The other children across the room instantly sang out in chorus: "Teacher, John's hitting!" Mrs. Jones looked over and ordered John to stop. She strode across the room, pulled John away, and spent the next two minutes telling him why he shouldn't hit people. Five minutes later, John was hitting another classmate. (p. 57)

One can easily conjure up an image of John, thumbs in lapels, basking in the limelight. Serbin and O'Leary explained that the example shows how teachers can reinforce exactly the behavior that's causing a problem: "For John, as for many children, being disruptive is an effective means of getting a far larger dose of attention than good behavior can bring." The solution, incidentally, was to ignore the bullying. When the teacher learned to overlook John's aggressiveness, it stopped.

2. Teachers did reward the girls for being dependent, but not by saying, "How nice, Sally, that you're tugging on my skirt." They responded more often to girls when they were nearby than when they were out of arm's reach, and rarely sent the girls off to work on their own. In contrast, the teachers paid the same amount of attention to boys whether they were close to them or not, and encouraged the boys to do independent work.

3. All fifteen of the teachers paid more attention to boys. Boys were twice as likely as girls to get individual instruction on a task: They got more tangible and verbal rewards for academic work, and they got more help than girls did when they asked for it. The sort of help the boys got was the kind that creates independence and capability. A child's ability to solve problems is related to the amount of detailed instruction an adult gives. The best instruction teaches how to solve the problem without actually providing the answer. Now consider what happened in one classroom that Serbin and O'Leary observed, when the children were busy making party baskets. When it was time to attach the paper handles, the teacher showed the class how to use the stapler. Then she held the handle in place so each boy could staple it himself. But if a girl failed to staple the handle on her own initiative, the teacher simply took the basket and attached the handle for her.

Serbin and O'Leary believe that the teachers' unwitting encouragement of the boys' aggressiveness explains why more boys than girls have reading problems and learning disabilities: Their rowdiness prevents them from paying attention when they should. On the other hand, the extra instruction they get helps their problem-solving skills. Girls, praised for staying close to their mothers and teachers, learn more easily to talk and read, but not to solve problems on their own. Other researchers find that parents, too, pay more attention to boys, both punishing and praising them more. Why this is so is not known. Maccoby and Jacklin (1974) wrote, "In some situations boys appear to be more attention-getting, either because they do more things calling for adult response [such as breaking lamps and catching frogs] or because parents and teachers see them as having more interesting qualities or potential."

Maccoby and Jacklin's comment points to the chicken-or-the-egg problem common to all scientific endeavors. Some teachers and parents react more harshly to boys' aggressiveness than to girls'. Does that explain why more boys than girls fight, or do adults react to boys more harshly because boys are more aggressive to begin with? Parents usually say the latter; most will tell you that it's easier to raise a daughter than a son. "She'll sit and play quietly for an hour while he tears the house apart, plank by plank," they complain, shaking their heads in amused resignation (or dismay). One teacher in Serbin and O'Leary's study said that it was harder for her to ignore boys because "boys hit harder." We can't know for sure whether she was influencing the child's act or whether he was influencing hers—or both.

As children get older, teachers and other school personnel can directly influence their academic attitudes and ambitions. For example, a recent review of the literature on math achievement (Eccles 1982) found that teachers, counselors, and parents all reward boys more than girls for learning math, and encourage boys more to enter math-related careers. (In one study, counselors unapologetically admitted *discouraging* girls from taking math courses! And in Baumgartner's study, one teacher *insisted* there were more boys than girls in his math class—until he checked his roll book and found there were more girls.) In math and science courses, teachers tend to interact with and praise boys more, especially when teaching students who are mathematically talented. Advanced math courses in high school are more likely to be taught by men (Fox 1977), which means that students see few female role models in this field. It is hardly surprising that by high school girls have more negative attitudes toward math and are less likely than boys to appreciate its usefulness.

Of course, if children can learn sex roles in school, they should be able to unlearn them there, too. Even one math teacher can inspire a girl to be interested in math if the teacher gives sincere praise for good work and explicit advice about the usefulness of math in high-paying, high-status jobs (Casserly 1979). And nothing about children's classroom behavior is impervious to change. Using praise and attention as rewards, preschool teachers can get girls to be more independent and both sexes to play more with each other and select both boys' and girls' toys (Serbin and Connor 1979a). The effects are surprisingly rapid; simply by moving into a particular area and giving attention to a particular type of play, a teacher, within minutes, can eliminate sex differences in play patterns that were "obvious" all semester. When the teacher withdraws attention or praise, children tend to revert rapidly to their previous sex-typed behavior. Still, the fact that such behavior can be eliminated quickly shows the enormous impact of the environment—including the teacher—on children's day-to-day conformity to sex roles.

Teachers who want to reduce sex typing cannot do so with intentions alone, for belief does not automatically translate into behavior. The fifteen teachers in Serbin and O'Leary's study were not aware that they were treating boys and girls differently. Neither was the staff of a nursery school that Carole Joffe (1971) observed, in which there was a deliberate attempt to avoid sex typing. Despite the egalitarian philosophy, the teachers and the mothers who worked with them perpetuated the stereotypes. They complimented girls on their dresses but said nothing when the girls wore pants, and they seldom commented on the way boys were dressed. They praised the boys for defending themselves well in a fight, for being "brave little men," though the school had a rule against fighting.

In some homes and classrooms, the overt sex-role philosophy of the past has gone underground, and the message parents and teachers communicate to children are as complicated as they are subtle. A parent, teacher, or a casual observer may miss them, but children do not.

sex typing as child's play

Unlike long division or geography, the lessons of socialization do not have to be formally taught. Children may pick them up from their daily experiences as naturally as a plant takes in carbon dioxide from the air. For example, several writers believe that the toys children play with can affect their later cognitive ability. When they play house, children rehearse verbal skills; when they build things with Legos and Lincoln Logs, they practice spatial-visual skills.

Although there have been few studies on this issue, a preference for "masculine" classroom activities and toys does seem to be correlated with spatial-visual ability among preschoolers (Connor and Serbin 1977; Serbin and Connor 1979b). As usual, it is hard to prove the direction of cause and effect. It does seem reasonable, though, to assume that at the very least, when children in a toy store notice chemistry sets, doctor's kits, and race cars under the sign "Boys' Toys," and tea sets, nurse's kits, and dolls under the sign "Girls' Toys," they pick up some sort of message about what's expected of them.

Children learn how to behave not only from parents but from peers. Janet Lever (1976, 1978) watched fifth-graders playing during recess, in physical education classes, and after school. She noticed that boys played outdoors more than girls did; it's easier to run around and be independent outdoors. Also their games were more competitive and demanded a higher level of skill. When disputes arose, boys typically settled them by quarreling or repeating the play. They seemed to relish their debates, and everyone, from the star player to those on the sidelines, took part. Girls played in smaller groups, often with just a best friend, and their disputes tended to end the game. Again, cause and effect are hard to untangle; boys may learn to be competitive by playing certain games, or they may choose certain games because they are competitive, or both. It's quite possible, though, that boys' play teaches them about organizing groups and resolving conflicts by applying abstract "rules of the game," while girls' play teaches them more about cooperation and sensitivity toward specific individuals (Gilligan 1982).

media messages

Anyone who reads, watches television, or goes to the movies can verify that media stereotypes are far from subtle. Everywhere one goes, one runs smack into the same images of women and men; yet they are so ubiquitous, so "natural," that people don't always realize they are there. There is no mystery to the media's message about what each sex should do and be; like the purloined letter, it is right there in front of us all the time. This section discusses the images of males and females in books and television, but much of what the research shows also applies to magazines, songs, movies, newspapers, and professional journals.

children's books: fairy tales about the sexes Preschool picture books, grammar-school readers, textbooks in science and social studies—all are populated primarily by males. When Women on Words and Images (1975a), a New Jersey group that studies sexual stereotypes, surveyed 134 children's readers published up to 1972—a total of 2,750 stories—it discovered these ratios:

Boy-centered to girl-centered stories	5:2
Adult male to adult female main characters	3:1
Male biographies to female biographies	6:1
Male animal stories to female animal stories	2:1
Male folk or fantasy stories to female folk or fantasy stories	4:1

The same group also looked at 83 books published after 1972 (Women on Words and Images 1975a). The ratio for biographies had improved markedly, to 2:1, but the ratio of boy-centered to girl-centered stories had worsened, to 7:2 (for similar findings, see St. Peter 1979).

The WWI study, like others, found that boys and men in children's readers monopolize the traits that Americans regard highly: ingenuity, bravery, perseverance, achievement, sportsmanship. Boys make things. They rely on their wits to solve problems. They are curious, clever, and adventurous. They achieve; they make money. Girls and women are incompetent and fearful. They ask other people to solve their problems for them. They typically react to a crisis by dissolving in a puddle of tears. They spend most of their time baking cookies and sewing, and they are constantly concerned about how they look, which boys never are. In story after story, girls are the onlookers, the cheerleaders, speaking such lines as "Oh, Raymond, boys are much braver than girls," and even accepting humiliation and ridicule. In sixty-seven stories one sex demeans the other—and sixty-five of these involve hostility of males against females. Boys exclude girls from groups, show them up as scaredy-cats, and make fun of their domesticity. The girls often join in the derision of their sex: "I'm just a girl, but I know enough not to do that"; "Even I can do it and you know how stupid I am."

Grammar-school readers offer many models for boys to emulate, but few for girls—a difference reflected in the responses of Baumgartner's schoolchildren when they were asked what it would be like if they were the other sex. WWI tallied 147 occupations for boys (including astronaut and cowboy), but only 26 for girls (including circus fat lady and witch). In the 134 books examined, only three working mothers appeared—and in one, a young bully's bad behavior is chalked up to the fact that his mother wasn't home during the day to take care of him. For that matter, mothers, whether working or not, usually come out as mindless, dull, and punitive. Lenore Weitzman et al. (1972) explored the roles of women in prize-winning preschool picture books and found that women are the wives of the kings, judges, adventurers, and explorers, but they themselves are not the rulers, judges, adventurers, and explorers. Even eminent women have a way of fading into the background. One study of grammar-school textbooks in California recorded an illustration of Marie Curie, the Nobel Prize–winning chemist, peering from behind her husband's shoulder as he and a male colleague conferred (U'Ren 1971).

To be sure, some changes are taking place. In the post-1972 books examined by WWI, for example, there were some competent girl characters and some boy characters who expressed emotions.

Most major textbook publishers now have guidelines for depicting girls and women. Firemen are becoming firefighters, policemen are becoming police officers, and women are gradually shedding their aprons (*New York Times*, April 30, 1978). Since 1972 California textbook regulations have banned "descriptions, depictions, labels, or retorts which tend to demean, stereotype, or be patronizing toward females." But millions of unrevised books are still in use because school systems often order new texts only when the old ones wear out. And even recently produced materials may be biased. When a presidential advisory council examined materials used by the pre-school program Headstart, it discovered that girls were shown playing with dolls, talking on the telephone, doing domestic chores, or looking out the window, while boys were shown hammering, sawing, and otherwise being active and curious (*Los Angeles Times*, January 24, 1978).

Portrayals of males and females in children's books have little link with reality. Nearly two-thirds of all women with school-age children work outside the home, but they are rarely found in these books; further, even the most dedicated housewife does more than wash dishes and bake brownies. Nor are the boy characters' adventures remotely related to what adult men (or real boys) do; they rescue people, protect their mothers from grizzly bears, leave home to pan for gold. They don't prepare to become what most real boys will become—insurance salesmen, factory workers, plumbers, office workers, teachers, and the like. The exaggerated male figures in children's fiction are not meant to be realistic, of course; they are supposed to teach values, such as persistence and courage. The important point is that female characters portray these positive qualities less often.

television: truth down the tube   Almost everyone in America watches television, children more than anyone else. In a national sample of viewers, George Gerbner and Larry Gross (1976) found that half of the twelve-year-olds in this country watch an average of six or more hours per day. The typical teenager today has spent more time in front of the tube than in school. Television programing has truly become a "universal curriculum."

Television programs are children's textbooks in motion; the same stereotypes and sex ratios prevail. Three-fourths of all leading characters on prime-time network TV are male (Women on Words and Images 1975b). On weekend dramatic shows, the ratio of men to women reaches five to one (Gerbner and Signorielli 1979). Children's programing is a chauvinist's dream come true. Not only do male central characters outnumber females, but they get to have most of the fun (Sternglanz and Serbin 1974; McArthur 1982). Males solve problems, exercise creativity and imagination, give orders, and help or save others, and they are likely to be rewarded for their actions. Females are more deferential, passive, and compliant; instead of issuing orders, they obey them. They are far less likely than males to express an intention to do something and to then follow through. Not all images of males are positive; most villains are male. And not all images of females are negative; female characters often hug and kiss, cooperate with others, and share. But both as heroes and villains, it is the males who have an impact on the course of events.

On adventure shows aimed at children and adults, men portray freewheeling cops, private eyes, and secret agents; women in these shows tend to be interested mainly in romance, their families, or the boss's welfare. Women are also victims—but they are less likely to risk victimization if they are married, which may imply that if women want to be safe and secure, there's no place like home (Gerbner et al. 1980). To land the job of TV heroine, a woman must still be slender, attractive, and young. Male adventurers during the past decade, while often attractive (Magnum), have also been fat (Cannon), bald (Kojak), old (Barnaby Jones), or plain (Quincy).

Until a few years ago most TV women didn't have jobs outside the home. Then, during the early 1970s, Mary Tyler Moore broke new ground with her portrayal of a competent woman holding a responsible job among men. Soon there was Wonder Woman, Police Woman, and the Bionic Woman (though we might note that Wonder Woman, when she wasn't saving the world, worked as a secretary, and the Bionic Woman, when she wasn't lifting boulders with her little finger, taught elementary school). Today most women on TV work; there have been lawyers *(Hill Street Blues)*, police officers *(Cagney and Lacey)*, waitresses *(Alice)*. But many TV heroines unmask the villain by accident or luck, or because a male partner bails them out of a jam. When women succeed, many of these programs seem to say, it is not by virtue of their own talents. (As we saw in Chapter 2, many women attribute their success to luck instead of to skill; these TV programs encourage the tendency.) And, although there are now programs about single parents, there are hardly any showing people successfully combining marriage, parenthood, and a career.

It would be a mistake, however, to assume that *only* women come across badly on TV. In comedy series, in contrast to adventure shows, men and women appear in nearly equal numbers, and men are as likely as women to be dingbats. In fact, often it is the wives who are wise, witty, and patient, and who end up deflating their husbands' puffed-up egos. Possibly men get their comeuppance in situation comedies because sitcoms ridicule everybody, or because the family is the female's domain and the male role at home is ambiguous and changing, an easy target. The point is that, overall, there are many more competent and admirable men on TV than there are women.[5]

The big question, of course, is whether sex stereotypes in the media contribute to sex differences in real life. If children are exposed to endless images of dependent females and assertive males, can we assume that they will ape what they see? The connection is not quite as simple as that. After all, people who saw Bonnie and Clyde rob banks and kill people on film did not dash out to do the same. But evidence is mounting that television images can affect attitudes and behavior. In the past, it was hard to show that laboratory findings extended to the real world. And while surveys often found that heavy TV viewers held a more stereotyped view of men and women than other people, no one knew whether television created those attitudes or whether people with such attitudes were simply attracted to television. (The same problems cropped up in studies of television violence and antisocial behavior.) Recent experiments, though, are beginning to tease out the relationship between cause and effect and extend laboratory findings to the real world.

For example, Michael Morgan (1982) had teenagers fill out a short sexism questionnaire, first in 1975 and then again in 1977. By giving the questionnaire twice to the same subjects, Morgan was able to find out if heavy TV viewing was associated with an *increase* in sexism over time. In general, boys were more sexist than girls— especially boys with low IQ scores. But the effect of television was most apparent among the subjects who were least sexist to begin

---

[5]Commercials are another breeding ground for stereotypes. We are all familiar with the harried housewife who agonizes over waxy yellow buildup and ring-around-the-collar. In ads about cleaning products, women speak more, but 96 percent of the authoritative voice-overs are male (Women on Words and Images 1975b). Men tell women how to care for sick children, bake a cake, wash dishes, and read dog-food labels. True, more recent commercials have begun to break away from the old stereotypes, showing wives who work, husbands who cook, and daughters who play football and provide their mothers with dirty clothes to wash. And overall, neither sex is especially intelligent or likeable in commercials. Yet in general, men are still given more status. When males endorse products, it's because of their authority or expertise; when women do so, it's because they are product users (McArthur 1982).

with—girls with high IQs! That is, boys were sexist with or without television, but TV tended to bring intelligent, nonsexist girls into the sexist mainstream. After two years, girls who were heavy TV watchers became more like boys in their attitudes toward women.

Most adults probably regard TV portrayals as cartoons, exaggerations, flights of fancy. Somehow many of us have been able to withstand the onslaught of dumb blondes and fearless hunks. But children and adolescents may be less skilled at distinguishing reality from fantasy; therefore they may be more susceptible to images of violence and sex-role stereotypes. Television alone cannot account for sexist attitudes; it must interact with other factors, such as family background, parents, intelligence, books, and personal heroes. But each program a child sees may be like a drop of water falling on a rock: A single drop has little effect, but given the right conditions, if enough drops fall, the rock's shape will change.

subliminal communication

Children can pick up sex stereotypes and norms not only from books and film but by observing how people around them behave in social situations. At dinner time, which parent sits down at the head of the table? In restaurants, who goes through the ritual of approving the wine? On family outings, who drives the car?

Sex differences in status are apparent even in the way we talk and write (Lakoff 1975; Thorne and Henley 1975; Parlee 1979; Mayo and Henley 1981). Most laymen, though, are not aware of this. And there you see the problem. Can women be laymen? Feminists believe that the use of *men* or *mankind* to refer to humanity, and the use of *he* to refer to any person, sex unspecified, communicates the notion that *male* and *human* are synonymous while females are outsiders. It is no accident, they say, that feminine forms can never be used in the general way that masculine forms are, that we never say "All women are created equal," "No woman is an island," or "These are the times that try women's souls." As Simone de Beauvoir wrote some thirty years ago:

> A man never begins by presenting himself as an individual of a certain sex; it goes without saying that he is a man. The terms *masculine* and *feminine* are used symmetrically only as a matter of form, as on legal papers. In actuality the relation of the two sexes is not quite like that of two electrical poles, for man represents both the positive and the neutral, as is indicated by the common use of *man* to designate human

beings in general; whereas woman represents only the negative, defined by limiting criteria, without reciprocity. . . . Thus humanity is male and man defines woman not in herself but as relative to him; she is not regarded as an autonomous being. (1953, pp. xv–xvi)

Some linguists think that feminists simply have a case of pronoun envy; but in practice, masculine forms are not nearly as neutral in the generic sense as these linguists claim. Wendy Martyna (1977) has shown that even when people seem to be using *he* to include both sexes, they often are really thinking about men only, which may become apparent from context. Thus two psycholinguists, discussing, of all topics, how pronouns are used to indicate status and power, wrote, "The progressive young Indian exchanges the mutual T [a kind of pronoun] with his wife" (Brown and Gilman 1960). As if all progressive young Indians were male! School texts are notorious for this sort of thing, as when they talk about "that language spoken by the educated professional and his wife" (Burr et al. 1972). Janet Hyde (1984) has shown that "gender neutral" *he* is understood by children as masculine and affects their sex stereotyping of jobs.

The sexes learn early about styles of speaking, too. Girls aren't supposed to curse or speak too assertively, and some words are off limits for one sex or the other. Women may use certain adjectives *(adorable, lovely, divine)*, adverbial phrases *(awfully nice)*, and euphemisms *(powder room)* that men must avoid. Men give orders more directly, using true imperative forms *(Open the window; Shut the door)*, whereas women soften their commands by disguising them as questions *(Would you mind opening the window? Could you please shut the door?)*.

The way we address other people depends both on how intimate we are with them and on how powerful we are in comparison with them (Brown and Ford 1961). Because gender is related to intimacy and power, we should expect forms of address to be different for men and women. In keeping with the pedestal-gutter syndrome, men are at once respectful toward women (they are not supposed to offend the ladies by swearing) and overly familiar. One of us recalls a telephone conversation during which a man, an attorney whom she had never met, kept calling her "doctor." "Please, let's be more informal," she suggested. "OK, dear, now where were we?" he shot back. It's a rare woman who would address a male colleague with a cavalier "honey" or "doll." Coming from a woman, such terms are likely to be construed as a bid for sexual intimacy, not power.

Communication does not need to be verbal to be effective. Nancy Henley and Jo Freeman (1976) argued that a clear message of which sex has more power is transmitted in touches: Females, they maintained, are touched more than males are, and this marks them as subordinate. Of course, people touch each other for many reasons—to be friendly, to show affection, to initiate sex—but touch also functions to show who outranks whom. In our society, touch implies privileged access to another person. For example, who would be more likely to touch the other by throwing an arm around the shoulder or putting a hand on the back: teacher or student, master or servant, policeman or accused, doctor or patient, minister or parishioner, executive or secretary? "As with first-naming," noted Henley and Freeman, "it is considered presumptuous for a person of low status to initiate touch with a person of higher status." Thus, they continued, when male diners pat waitresses, or a male professor touches a female student, the intent is not necessarily sexual. But if a woman touches a man, her gesture, like the familiar "honey" or "dear," usually will be interpreted as a sexual overture even when it is not, "since it would be inconceivable for [her] to be exercising power."

Henley (1970) supported this thesis with personal accounts of what happened to her when she broke the usual pattern of who initiates touching. (Readers may try a small experiment for themselves by deliberately touching a person of higher status.) She also asked a male student, unaware of her theory, to observe and record touches in an outdoor setting. Apart from lovers, he noted, men were more likely to touch women than women were to touch men. Perhaps children use such nonverbal signals along with more obvious ones, like who makes decisions, to figure out which sex is more powerful.

Other sex differences in both verbal and nonverbal communication also seem to be related to status. Here are some findings:

1. In conversations between two women or two men, both speakers tend to interrupt each other equally often. But in male-female conversations, men do almost all of the interrupting (Zimmerman and West 1975).

2. Women seem to work harder than men to keep a male-female conversation going; for example, by asking questions. Men often squelch a topic raised by a woman by giving a minimal response, such as "yeah" or "umm" (Fishman 1978).

3. In male-female discussions, women tend to gaze more at men than the reverse. Although a fixed stare can sometimes signal dominance, gazing while listening usually indicates either attentiveness to what is being said or an attempt to please (Francis 1979).

4. In male-female conversations, men tend to speak for longer periods, while women tend to laugh and smile more. Men who laugh and smile a lot are more likely than other men to describe themselves as sociable, friendly, and affiliative. But women who laugh and smile the most are more likely than other women to describe themselves as uncomfortable in the particular situation, and retiring and deferential in general (Francis 1979).

Besides learning about power and status from people's words and deeds, children may draw inferences about sex differences in personality. They may decide that females are more nurturant and empathic because their mothers usually comfort them when they're hurt, encourage lap-sitting, and rock them to sleep when they're sick. They may conclude that males are the more aggressive sex, because their fathers most often roughhouse with them, toss them into the air, and accept their invitations to play touch football. Children probably generalize from personal experience to reach conclusions about the "natural" traits and duties of men and women.

learning about sex

Although volumes have been written on the development of sex differences in personality and mental abilities, few learning theorists have paid much attention to the development of differences in sexuality. As psychologist Robert Sears (1979) has noted, as far as sexual behavior is concerned, "the period from six to sixteen is virtually a terra incognita." The precise ways in which society conveys expectations regarding sexual behavior remain to be pinned down by empirical research.

It is easy to imagine, though, how the general lessons of sex-role socialization might help account for the sex differences we described in Chapter 3—differences in how males and females interpret intimacy, attribute meaning to sex, select partners, and conduct themselves during courtship. No one needs to sit down with a boy or girl and explain the double standard in so many words. If children learn from parents, teachers, and the media that males are expected to initiate activities, that lesson may later transfer to dating and marriage, where males tend to be both the initiators and the choreographers of sexual activity. If children learn that dominance and submission are normal in male–female relationships, whether on the playground or in the office, then images of dominance and submission may later invade their erotic fantasies and affect their actual behavior. And the media, of course, provide plenty of models for how lovers are supposed to act.

Sociologists John Gagnon and William Simon (1969, 1973) have proposed a general explanation of how experience shapes male and female sexual behavior. Their theory acknowledges an indirect biological contribution to sexual differences but emphasizes the impact of culture. Like many other researchers, Gagnon and Simon believe that adult sexuality is conditioned in part by adolescent experiences with masturbation and that sex differences in sexuality are linked to the fact that boys masturbate more than girls. The increase of male hormones at puberty may cause a boy to have frequent erections even when he is not preoccupied with erotic activities or thoughts, so his attention is directed to his genitals. At the same time, the social demands of the American masculine role, which emphasize aggressiveness, achievement, and conquest, encourage the boy to experiment. For most boys, experimentation begins with masturbation, a purely physical experience detached from images or feelings of romantic love. Boys commonly masturbate in front of other boys—the one who ejaculates first or farthest may even be hailed as a winner—and many learn about masturbation from friends before they try it. The encouragement of his peers motivates a boy to experiment some more. Sex becomes a way to confirm one's status among other males, especially, according to Gagnon and Simon, for working-class boys.

For girls, anatomy and cultural rules produce another pattern entirely. It is much easier for a girl to ignore her genitals and to remain ignorant about them. The sign of male arousal, an erect penis, is easy to interpret, but women often need experience to learn to recognize and understand their own arousal. Girls are less likely than boys to discover and practice masturbation; if they do, they usually make the discovery on their own and talk about it to no one. Many women refer to the vagina and clitoris as a vague area "down there"; men have many words to call their genitals, and none of them are vague.

For both anatomical and social reasons, then, Simon and Gagnon think that girls are less likely to learn about physical sexuality and orgasm. What they do learn about is romance, attractiveness, and the importance of catching a mate: "While boys are learning physical sex, girls are being trained in the language of love and the cosmetic values of sexual presentation through training in dress, dancing and other display behavior. . . . At no point is sexual expression valued in itself, independent of the formation of families" (Simon and Gagnon 1969). Boys, we might add, are more likely than girls to take communal showers and nude swimming lessons as well as to have conversations about sex, experiences that give them different associations with sex from the ones girls learn. In short, many boys learn to think of sex as an achievement while many girls learn to think of it as a service to the male.

Note that Gagnon and Simon's argument is not that males have a sexual advantage over females. Each sex emerges from adolescence with its own area of expertise. Males, on the whole, are more familiar and comfortable with the physical aspects of sexuality, but females, on the whole, are more familiar and comfortable with intimate relationships and the language of romantic love. The challenge for both sexes, in late adolescence and adulthood, is to bridge the gulf in sexual perceptions and purposes.

some consequences of socialization

The messages of socialization, overt and subtle, teach children what toys are okay to play with and which jobs are all right to aim for. The lessons hit home within the first few years of a child's life. But that's the way it has been in virtually every society in history. Why now are so many people arguing that separate-but-equal treatment of boys and girls is discriminatory and unfair?

It wasn't always so. In the 1950s and 1960s, when the socialization perspective first gained popularity, scores of psychologists spent thousands of person-years trying to discover how parents turn out "properly" sex-typed children. Most implicitly assumed that good parents communicate the rules effectively and that sex-typed children are well adjusted and happy; woe to the girl who wanted to play baseball or to the boy who wanted to be a nurse. Joseph Pleck (1981) has suggested that such views grew out of the trauma of the Great Depression of the 1930s. Millions of men were unable to play their designated role of family provider. "If holding a job to support a family could no longer be counted on to define manhood," said Pleck, "a masculinity-femininity test could." Never mind that the psychological tests designed to gauge mental health were developed using small or oddly selected samples (such as imprisoned rapists), or that scores from one test often failed to correlate with those of another.

Gradually, though, psychologists (and others) began to suspect that sex typing had its darker side. A negative consequence for females was that they grew up thinking they were not quite as good as males, or maybe that they were not worth very much at all. As we saw in Chapter 2, girls and women often are less confident than boys and men in specific situations, especially those involving competition and comparison with others.

There is also some evidence that women hold their whole sex in less regard than they do men: In survey after survey, women say that if they could choose the sex of a firstborn or only child, it would be a boy. (Men are even more likely to prefer a male.) Also, more females than males suspect that the grass is greener on the other side of the gender fence, and say they have fantasized about being a member of the other sex. Females may not think males are superior; they may simply perceive that it's a man's world. It's possible, though, that envy leads to a belief that males really are more valuable human beings, that a man's destiny matters more than a woman's. In any case, as Baumgartner's study showed, it's an envy that starts at an early age.

Many psychologists believe that when people disparage the group they belong to they reveal a hatred of themselves. Self-disparagement is not uncommon among minorities, who are exposed to the same cultural images of their groups as the majority is; there are anti-Semitic Jews and white-supremacist blacks.[6] Helen Mayer Hacker (1951), in a classic essay on women as a minority group, observed, "Like those minority groups whose self-castigation outdoes dominant group derision of them, women frequently exceed men in the violence of their vituperations of their sex."

Sex-role socialization is not such a blessing for boys, either. Pleck (1981) reexamined some older studies of masculinity and discovered that although researchers assumed "masculine" boys were psychologically healthy, their findings sometimes said just the opposite. For example, one study found that boys who were judged highly masculine were often absent from school. Instead of seeing this truancy as a cause for concern, the researcher decided that absenteeism must be a healthy attempt to establish independence! In another study the researchers offered a case history to illustrate the superior sexual adjustment of masculine males. The young man in this case had dated often in high school and college, which at first

[6]The pioneering social psychologist Kurt Lewin described minority group self-hatred some fifty years ago, long before the subject came to national attention.

glance might seem healthy. But he also admitted dating only so he could "get laid," and not because he actually liked the girls he took out. He may have been popular, but he was also predatory.

Pleck noted that "adjustment" depends on a society's values, especially those of the middle class, and at least some aspects of the traditional masculine role are not useful in middle-class life. An organization man, for example, cannot go around flexing his muscles (at least, not too obviously). He needs to cooperate, to be sensitive to others, and to influence others instead of bullying them. Pleck also argued that the rigidity of the male role has been a burden to many men, causing grief to those who fail to fulfill its vague standards.

Thus, both sexes, if they try to live up to sex roles, are put in the same position: They're damned if they do, and damned if they don't. Are there any other choices?

the androgynous alternative

Until a decade ago virtually all socialization studies assumed that masculinity and femininity are mutually exclusive features of personality, that the higher you are on one trait the lower you must be on the other. Then, in the early 1970s, psychologists began to reconsider; perhaps masculinity and femininity were not opposite poles of a single continuum after all, but rather two separate dimensions (Constantinople 1973). If so, people should be able to possess both kinds of traits.

To explore this possibility, psychologist Sandra Bem (1974) had Stanford University students rate themselves on a checklist of terms that described socially desirable but stereotypically masculine or feminine qualities. Half came out traditional, but 15 percent were cross sex-typed; that is, they scored higher on traits associated with the other sex than on those associated with their own. More important, 35 percent were *androgynous*: They scored about the same on masculine and feminine qualities. Other researchers soon refined and redefined the concept of androgyny. Janet Spence and her colleagues (who formulated their ideas at about the same time as Bem) added an especially important modification: In their work (and since 1977 in Bem's as well), *androgynous* refers to people who score high on both masculine and feminine traits, while those who score *low* on both are called *undifferentiated* (Spence, Helmreich, and Stapp 1975; Spence and Helmreich 1978).

One of Bem's goals (though not Spence's) was to show that

androgynous people are psychologically healthier than others because they can be masculine or feminine as the situation requires. They might be nurturant and sympathetic on one occasion, assertive and independent on another. In contrast, Bem argued, sex-typed individuals are restricted to a narrow range of behavior. A "real woman" won't try to change a fuse; a "real man" doesn't diaper babies or (they say) eat quiche.

Androgyny was an idea whose time had come. It quickly spawned scores of research reports, books, magazine articles, symposia, and workshops. Some therapists started to talk about encouraging their clients to be more androgynous. The concept was appealing not only because it supports an egalitarian philosophy but because it recognizes that people do not divide up neatly into either-or categories. Indeed, androgyny started what scientists call a *paradigm shift*—a complete change in the way researchers view a problem and conduct studies. But androgyny also has its problems. Psychologists Faye Crosby and Linda Nyquist (1978) have summarized some of the most serious ones, including the following:

1. It's as hard to pin androgyny down with a simple questionnaire as it was in the past to measure masculinity and femininity. (For details, see Kelly and Worell 1977; Walkup and Abbott 1978.) Which items do you put on a scale when any given item may be important to one person's self-concept and irrelevant to another's? How can you be sure your particular item will measure the critical features of such all-encompassing dimensions as masculinity and femininity? (One group of critics recently suggested that on androgyny tests "masculinity" is really just dominance/poise, and "femininity" is really just nurturance/warmth [Lubinski, Tellegen, and Butcher 1983].)

2. Because of methodological problems, the four tests now in general use may not measure exactly the same thing. Some researchers find that people are often classified differently by different tests. Thus Judy may score as masculine on one test and androgynous on another.

3. In their enthusiasm for the concept of androgyny, researchers have sometimes made exaggerated claims for it. As Crosby and Nyquist noted, in a rapidly growing research area "one researcher's fancy becomes another's fact." Thus, it is widely assumed now that "androgyny is better," but not all studies show this. In fact, the evidence seems to say that people with masculine traits—those who score as *either* androgynous *or* masculine—have the highest self-esteem; they also have higher subjective well-being, lower stress, and greater social effectiveness (Lubinski, Tellegen, and Butcher

1983).[7] Spence (1983) feels that no firm conclusions are possible yet about whether androgynous and/or masculine people have better psychological health overall; the data show only that sex-typed feminine women are not better off than androgynous ones, as a previous generation believed.

4. Androgyny researchers, like their predecessors, assume they know what psychological health is. They differ only in what sorts of behavior they identify as appropriate. But how do you decide when assertiveness, for example, is adaptive and when it is self-serving or socially insensitive? Bem (1975) found that androgynous men were likelier to play with a fluffy little kitten than sex-typed men were; she considered the androgynous men's kitten preference to be adaptive. But, as Crosby and Nyquist pointed out, there is no logical reason to judge it so, especially when the room was filled with many other interesting things to do. There is also no way to prove that "flexibility" makes a person healthier or happier than "consistency"; indeed, if flexibility is taken to an extreme, the opposite may be true—the person may have no moral spine or guiding principles.

5. Most androgyny researchers assume that people are fairly stable over time—androgynous today, androgynous tomorrow. But people can change, and so can stereotypes about masculinity and femininity. Oddly enough, most androgyny researchers hope that the stereotypes *will* change. But their tests and scales are based on the opposite assumption.

beyond androgyny

Most critics of androgyny research do not want to abandon the concept; they merely urge more caution in drawing conclusions. Some psychologists, though, wonder whether androgyny is really the solution to sex-role rigidity, after all. Sandra Bem, the first to popularize androgyny, was also one of the first to notice that it has a built-in flaw: Like past personality theories, it assumes that masculinity and femininity are necessary dimensions of personality. When John is active, he is said to be expressing his masculine side; when he is sensitive, he is being feminine. Yet the androgynous person is supposed to be unfettered by sex roles—which, if true, renders masculinity and femininity meaningless. Thus the concept of an-

---

[7]If masculinity scores predict behavior as well as androgyny scores, or if some additive combination of masculinity and femininity scores does so, then androgyny as a separate category becomes conceptually superfluous and empirically useless (Motowidlo 1982; Lubinski, Tellegen, and Butcher 1983).

drogyny, Bem has pointed out, "contains an inner contradiction and hence the seeds of its own destruction" (Bem 1978). Further, androgyny theory replaces "a prescription to be masculine or feminine with the doubly incarcerating perscription to be masculine and feminine. The individual now has not one but two potential sources of inadequacy to contend with" (Bem 1983).

If androgyny is not the solution, what is? In the late 1970s a few writers began to envision the possibility of transcending rather than merely combining sex roles (Rebecca, Hefner, and Oleshansky 1976; Garnets and Pleck 1978). A "transcendent" person who happened to be both active and gentle would be viewed (and would view her- or himself) not as androgynous but simply as an individual who was sometimes active and sometimes gentle. Gender would be beside the point.

In her recent writings, Bem (1981, 1983) has also been advocating a gender-free world instead of an androgynous one. Bem observes that socialization teaches us more than the content of sex roles in our culture, that is, the particular traits and activities associated with men and women. It also teaches us to perceive much of the world in terms of a male-female dichotomy. In doing this we use not just specific bits of information about sex roles but a vast, sprawling network of associations that directs and organizes our perceptions. Bem calls this cognitive structure a *gender schema*.

As Bem points out, gender distinctions touch almost every aspect of our lives. We categorize jobs, toys, sports, hobbies, household tasks, articles of clothing, and speech patterns as male or female. Other writers have noted that we even extend gender categories to inanimate objects. Angular things are male, round ones are female. Ships, countries, cars, nature, and the moon are female (and are referred to as "she"), while death, time, and the sun are male (and are referred to as "he"). Donald G. MacKay and Toshi Konishi (1982) conclude that these conventions are not arbitrary: Female entities are those regarded as fickle or requiring control; male entities are those regarded as stable or predictable. The tendency to divide the world by gender is so pervasive, MacKay and Konishi observed, that it even extends to animal species. People think of dogs and lions as male (they're strong, brave, clever) and cats as female (they're coy and domesticated). Children are often surprised to learn that in fact not all dogs are male and not all cats are female. Thus does metaphor become more real than reality.

When people organize information on the basis of gender, their observations are influenced accordingly. A newspaper reporter describes a female astronaut's hairstyle and cooking skills, although they are irrelevant to the story. A schoolteacher divides a class into a boys' team and a girls' team for a game of dodgeball. (What would people think if the teacher divided the children by hair color or race instead of sex?) Parents comment on a son's physical strength—or weakness—but don't notice either in a daughter.

Bem believes that there is nothing inevitable about the acquisition of a gender schema, noting that there are cultures in which gender is not as salient a category as in our own and the notion of what is male and female is more fluid (see Chapter 8). Bem (1983) has even proposed some strategies for preventing the development of a gender schema in children. Can you imagine a society in which gender distinctions were confined solely to anatomical and reproductive differences? Is such a society realistic or desirable? What do you think?

evaluating the learning perspective

Hardly anyone denies that children are raised differently depending on their sex. As we have seen, children are immersed in sex-role messages conveyed by language, the media, adult examples, and the inadvertent as well as the deliberate use of reward and punishment. In studying how socialization creates sex differences, however, many researchers have tried to stuff real people into pigeon holes that don't fit flesh-and-blood human beings very well. They lose sight of the fact, as Mischel (1970) observed, that "there are many different acceptable ways of being a boy or girl, and even more diverse ways of being a man or woman." The learning perspective itself allows for this range of behavior, but the demands of the laboratory often force researchers to narrow their horizons. Like trying to photograph bacteria with a Polaroid, the methods have often been too clumsy for their object.

An excellent example of the inherent dilemmas of the socialization perspective—in concept and method—comes from the fascinating research on achievement motivation.

a case in point: the achievement motive

Because of socialization, some researchers believe, boys and girls reach adulthood with different desires to achieve—and different spheres in which they wish to achieve, to meet a personal standard of excellence. These sex differences, they argue, help account for the greater prevalence of men in politics, business, science, and art. As a girl grows up, her ambitions are systematically squelched. And by adulthood, achievement motivation, or its absence, is a stable disposition of the personality.

The theory of achievement motivation, as originally formulated, was highly successful in its description of and predictions for men. But women didn't behave like men on achievement-motivation tests. Did the psychologists say, "Hmm, wonder why?" No, they assumed that women had *no* achievement motivation and dropped them from their studies. In 1958 an 873-page compilation of the research was published; the information on females was confined to a single footnote (Atkinson 1958).

In the 1960s psychologist Matina Horner came up with a novel explanation for the finding that women did not respond like men on achievement-motivation tests. She argued that women, unlike men, have a motive to *avoid* success, a fear that achievement will have disastrous consequences. Because women learn that achievement (especially intellectual achievement) is aggressive, and therefore masculine, they worry that they will be less feminine if they compete. Anxiety about this conflict makes women feel defensive if they do achieve and may prevent them from achieving in the first place. Able men do not have this problem because achievement and the masculine role go hand in hand.

To test her theory, Horner (1969) asked ninety female undergraduates to tell a story based on the following sentence: "After first-term finals, Anne finds herself at the top of her medical school class." Eighty-eight men responded to the same sentence, but about John. When Horner scored the stories, she found that most of the men (90 percent) were comfortable about John's success and saw a rosy future for him. "John is a conscientious young man who worked hard," wrote one male. "John continues working hard and eventually graduates at the top of his class."

But a majority of the stories written by women (65 percent) contained images that reflected what Horner called a fear of success. The most common theme was that Anne's academic success would bring her social rejection. She would be unpopular, unmarried, and lonely. Another was that Anne would feel unfeminine. One young woman saw particularly dire consequences for Anne: "Anne starts proclaiming her surprise and joy. Her fellow classmates are so disgusted with her behavior that they jump on her in a body and beat her. She is maimed for life." Some stories solved Anne's "problem" by having her drop out of medical school to marry a successful doctor or to enter a more "feminine" field, such as social work.

When Horner published her work, a chorus of "Aha!" went up throughout the land. Researchers thought they now understood why women had been ruining their studies. College women had a reason for their uncertain career plans. Journalists announced that an explanation had been found for women's low status in the world of work: The fault lay not in the stars but in women themselves. They might want to achieve, but they also wanted to be feminine, and the two motives were as incompatible as oil and water.

In the years that followed, dozens of follow-up studies were done all over the country and the world—Yugoslavia, Italy, Norway, the West Indies. The more data that came in, the more it appeared that the matter of women's lack of achievement was not quite solved. Criticisms of Horner's work began to appear (Tresemer 1974; Condry and Dyer 1976; Shaver 1976).

One problem was that men often showed as much "fear of success" as women, and sometimes more; so the "motive to avoid success" is not limited to women. But the sexes do seem to regard the perils of achievement differently. Women associate success with social rejection; men question the value of success in the first place. They wonder whether hard work really pays off. In their stories, John may drop out of medical school to write a novel or take a 9-to-5, blue-collar job. Or John may find that his victory is a Pyrrhic one: "He graduates with honors and hates being a doctor. He wonders what it was all for." "It's great for his parents, but he doesn't give a shit" (Hoffman 1974). Anne suffers by becoming unpopular and dateless, but John suffers by dropping dead prematurely (Robbins and Robbins 1973).

Worry about being different may cause women to feel ambivalent and guilty about their accomplishments, especially when they compete in male-dominated professions or if they have been punished for competing in the past. But men, too, sometimes feel conflict about competition and striving for success, and no one ever uses that fact to argue that they, as a sex, are unfit for jobs and careers.

More important, the stories about Anne and John could reflect not deep-seated motives but realistic assessments of the consequences of conforming or not conforming to social custom. In this view, it is not success that women fear but punishment for deviation from traditional roles. Studies that ask both sexes to write stories about John and Anne find that men and women recognize that female achievement is unusual, and that it frequently brings down punishment on the head of the achiever. In fact, men are sometimes more disturbed by Anne's number-one status than women are—they write more negative themes about her than women write about either Anne or John. So perhaps women are right to worry about the consequences of doing better than men; if they step too far toward the front of the line, they may arouse the worst in some males.

John Condry and Sharon Dyer (1976) offered an apt analogy to show that fear-of-success themes may reflect an understanding of social realities rather than fear of achievement. Suppose you gave people a description of an interracial couple who had just gotten married and were about to set up housekeeping in rural Georgia. You ask them to write a story about what will happen to this couple. If you took each story that mentioned negative consequences and labeled it "fear of interracial marriage," you would be making a serious mistake. The people who predicted bad things for the couple would not necessarily be afraid or bigoted; they might just know which way the racist wind blows.

Finally, no one has shown that fear of success actually keeps anyone from succeeding! When Lois Hoffman followed up on the young women in Horner's study nine years later, she found that their fear of success had greatly decreased. Further, women who were high or low in fear of success in the original study did not differ overall in either educational or occupational achievements. High percentages of both groups went on to get master's and doctoral degrees (Hoffman 1977).[8] Consider, too, the fact that women highest in fear of success in Horner's study were honor students. As David Tresemer (1974) observed, if the people who show fear-of-success imagery are the ones who are doing best, how deeply debilitating is it?

We have little doubt that some bright women, as the socialization perspective would predict, grow up with conflicts about what it means to be feminine and worry about whether career ambitiousness is appropriate. Undoubtedly, some who could be mathematicians solve the conflict by becoming bookkeepers. Similarly, some bright men, realistically appraising the personal costs of becoming workaholics, may decide that traditional success is less fun than finding a steady 9-to-5 job. Both, as adults, may feel unhappy or guilty about

---

[8]Women who had been high in fear of success as undergraduates were also more likely to marry, to have children, and to become pregnant for the first time when they were on the verge of success relative to a husband or boyfriend. Marriage and pregnancy may have been a way to reduce anxiety about pursuing nontraditional goals; in essence, these women decided to do it all.

their decisions (or not). However, achievement motivation and fear of success do not necessarily become ingrained personality traits, uninfluenced by the experiences of adult life.

personality and power

Most learning theorists have assumed that basic attitudes, abilities, and traits are set firmly in childhood. The learning approach does not rule out the possibility of adult changes; social-learning theory, in particular, stresses that as rewards change, so will a person's behavior. But in practice, researchers and nonprofessionals alike often think that adults are not really able to choose freely what path they will follow—they assume that the adult course was determined in the "formative years." Their conclusion, therefore, is that if you want to teach children to conform, or *not* to conform, you'd better get them young. Thus Sandra and Daryl Bem wrote:

> The free will argument [of role choice] proposes that a 21-year-old woman is perfectly free to choose some other role if she cares to do so, no one is standing in her way. But this argument conveniently overlooks the fact that the society which has spent twenty years carefully marking the woman's ballot for her has nothing to lose in that twenty-first year by pretending to let her cast it for the alternative of her choice. Society has controlled not her alternatives, but her motivation to choose any but one of those alternatives. (1976, p. 184)

Today, however, many social psychologists are reconsidering the belief that a child's personality ballot is marked in indelible ink during those formative years. The formative years, it turns out, stretch from cradle to grave. In fact, as we will show in the next chapter, achievement motivation and other feelings about work can change profoundly depending on adult experiences. There may be no point at which we can say of a person, "She (or he) lived happily (or miserably) ever after."

For example, take the matter of self-esteem. Overall, women probably have lower self-esteem than men. But self-esteem, like any other personality trait, can change with time and place. Paul Mussen (1962) found this shift in a study of adolescent boys. Those who had highly masculine job interests liked themselves better, had more self-confidence, and were better adjusted according to psychological tests than boys who had less traditional, more feminine interests. Observers rated the masculine teenagers as more carefree, contented, and relaxed. This makes sense; boys who buck their peers in adolescence risk some bad times and heavy social pressure. But because Mussen's data came from a longitudinal study, he was able to take the rare step of seeing what happened to the boys when they reached their late thirties. He found that the boys who had been very masculine as teenagers now were *less* self-confident and self-accepting than the "feminine" boys.

To the question, "Why do most women hold low-ranking jobs?" this perspective answers, "Because women have acquired certain traits—fear of success, dependence, sociability, noncompetitiveness—that limit their aspirations and their abilities." Yet personality differences do not wholly explain status differences. Whatever their childhood experiences, people grow up to face a world that assigns different tasks to women and men; one must understand the roles that adults are expected to play and the value society places on those roles. Parents and the media do not get their ideas about how boys and girls should behave from thin air. Where do these ideas come from?

Ironically, the socialization perspective, which has raised people's awareness about the ways that boys and girls can have their potentials blocked and goals narrowed as they grow up, can also be used to justify keeping the doors of opportunity shut. Sociologist Jessie Bernard (1975) wrote that defenders of the status quo can say, "Sorry, girls, too bad you haven't got what it takes; you're afraid of success and all that. I know it isn't your fault; I know it's the way you were raised; you'd be just as superior as I am if you had played with trucks instead of dolls. But what can I do about it, after all?"

In the view of Bernard and other sociologists, a thousand more studies on the development of personality differences will not give us the whole answer to the lesser status of women. As Bernard put it, we need rather to expose "the institutional structure which embalms those differences in the form of discrimination against women. The name of the game is power."

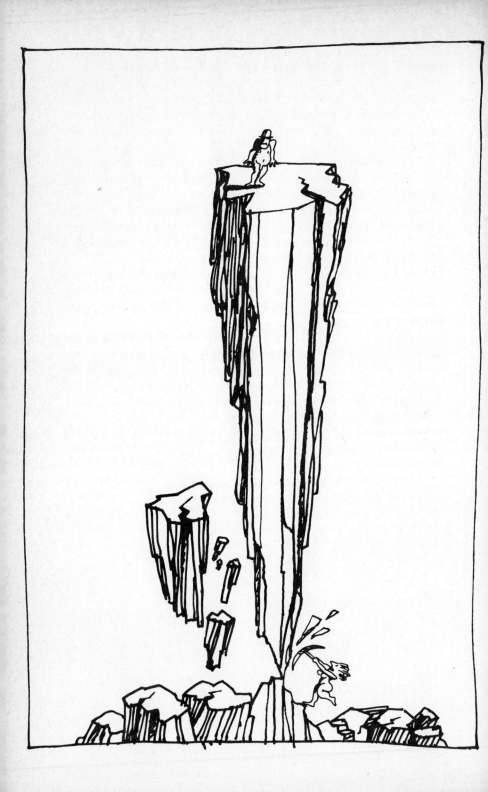

7 | Earning the bread versus baking it: The sociological perspective

Michael and Marian have been going together for two years, and both of them agree that he is the dominant one. He generally decides where they will go and what they will do, and when they disagree on something Mike usually persuades Marian that he is right with an onslaught of reason and rhetoric. But Marian is not a doormat, she'll tell you. "If there's something I really want," she confides privately, "I can get it by pouting and sulking for a few days. And I can get the world from him if I cry. He can't stand it when I cry."

John and Martha are both department managers in a large corporation, but they are as different in style as Laurel and Hardy. The people who work for John say he is fair-minded and friendly, helps his subordinates, and sees to it that work gets done. The people who work for Martha can't say the same, though. They complain that she is petty, picky about trivial rules, and petulant if things aren't done just her way. "Bitchy—a typical woman boss," one of her employees remarks. "I'll never work for one again."

Most people would explain Marian and Martha's actions by saying that women learn to get their way through indirect manipulation, so if they have to take a leadership role they don't know how to exercise power effectively. It is easiest to explain sex differences in the use of power and influence in personality terms: A person behaves in a particular way because of some internal, stable set of traits that he or she possesses. This chapter, however, shows how external forces—the people around us, the roles we play, the work we do, the situations we are in, the rules we unconsciously follow—shape and direct behavior. The most extreme form of this view, held by some social scientists, says there is no such thing as personality, that we are all malleable in the face of social pressure and the organizations we belong to.

Behavioral psychologists, such as learning theorists, also study how the rewards and punishments a situation provides can create behavior, but their focus is still on the individual. Sociologists focus on the circumstances that surround the individual. In this psychological age people are used to thinking in terms of intrapsychic drives and motives, and psychological explanations are more popular than social ones. But now we'll ask you to suspend the familiar ways of explaining sex differences and to regard their origin from an entirely different perspective.

Social pressure is like a cobweb—strong but hard to see. Some time ago, psychologist Stanley Milgram asked the city-wise New York students in his graduate seminar to do a simple little experiment. "Pick out someone on a crowded subway," he said, "and ask him to give you his seat." "Are you crazy?" replied the students. "A person could get killed doing that." One brave volunteer finally agreed to approach twenty people at random and see what happened. Rumors soon began circulating through the psychology department: "They're getting up! They're getting up!" The student reported back to the class that half of the people he asked for a seat automatically got up and gave it to him, with no excuses offered or demanded. But most surprising to the student, the simple little request had proved extraordinarily difficult, and he couldn't finish the assignment of twenty people. So Milgram decided to try it himself. He barely succeeded. "The words seemed lodged in my trachea and would simply not emerge," he reported. "I stood there frozen." When he finally got up the nerve to ask a man for his seat—and got it—he collapsed in a fit of nervous tension.

Milgram's experiment, though it may seem trivial, points out a powerful fact about human behavior. Our actions are governed by a network of rules that operate whether we are aware of them or not. Often the rules become apparent only when we try to break them. "We are all fragile creatures entwined in a cobweb of social constraints," explained Milgram. "If you think it is easy to violate [them], get onto a bus and sing out loud. Full-throated song, now, no humming. Many people will say it is easy to carry out this act, but not one in a hundred will be able to do it" (Milgram 1974).

The sociological view relies less on how people explain their own attitudes and behavior than on outside influences on their attitudes and behavior. For example, suppose you think of yourself as an assertive person who stands up for your beliefs. Now suppose you are called upon to defend a conviction of yours in the following groups: six women who agree with you; six women who disagree with you; six men who agree with you but don't like you very much; three women and three men with mixed opinions; and six men who oppose you. Would you feel as comfortable in all situations? Would you argue the same way? Change your convictions to go along with the majority? Chances are that your opinion of yourself might not change as you performed this exercise, but your behavior would (Ruble and Higgins 1976; Kimble, Yoshikawa, and Zehr 1981).

In this chapter we look at some ways that two major institutions, work and marriage, affect and create differences between women and men: differences in attitudes, goals, values, and even apparent abilities. The sociological perspective argues that the roles people play in this society as spouse and worker perpetuate sexual inequality. Since inequality is built into the system, it says, equality can come only when institutions, organizations, and roles change, not just personal attitudes.

work: grand or grind?

To understand the difference between psychological explanations and sociological ones, imagine a person who is applying for a job. Many companies have personnel psychologists who have to figure out who, supposedly, is the best person for that job; to do so, they commonly give a battery of personality tests. Their assumptions, based on psychological principles, are that people acquire their personality traits in childhood and that these traits make them either seek or avoid particular jobs. An aggressive boy who loves taking risks would, presumably, do well as a salesman for a new company, whereas a timid girl who "fears success" is best off in the unrisky job of bookkeeper.

But sociologists look at this question differently. What are the conditions of the job itself, they ask, that affect personality? In their research, they find that a timid girl who takes the sales job generally rises to the challenge—and becomes more aggressive and willing to take risks. Give that salesman the bookkeeper's job, and watch his spirits sag and his cautiousness rise.

Sociologists Melvin Kohn and Carmi Schooler (1973, 1978) have been doing long-term studies to find out how jobs affect personality. First they studied a random sample of 3,101 American men to see how certain structural aspects of their jobs (complexity, pace, pressures, fringe benefits, routinization) affect such individual characteristics as job commitment and satisfaction, anxiety, self-esteem, intellectual flexibility, and moral standards. Using complex statistics to tease out cause from effect, they found in all cases that "job affects man more than man affects job." The complexity of the job was especially important: It affected all facets of the men's psychological functioning and was directly related to their self-esteem. The reason high job complexity makes for high self-esteem, the researchers said, is that a man's job "confronts him with demands he must try to meet." The average woman, they noted, has less chance to rise to the occasion than the average man, since her work is less complex than his.

In the next phase of their research, the researchers applied the same methods to 555 married women. Again they found that women are as affected as men are by occupational conditions. For women as for men, jobs that encourage self-direction (Can you work at your own pace? Make your own decisions?) make people more intellectually active, flexible, and open, and less authoritarian. Constricted, boring, routine jobs that give employees no room to spread their wings, in contrast, dampen people's self-esteem and make them more rigid and intolerant of others. *Occupational conditions affected all women similarly*, the researchers found, regardless of the women's reasons for working, their education, their training, the number of children they had, and even whether they wanted to be working or not (Miller et al. 1979).

Other sociologists have also found that roles change attitudes more often than attitudes create roles. In 1956 Seymour Lieberman did a field study in a factory, assessing changes in workers' attitudes when some of them became foremen and others became union leaders. The workers filled out a questionnaire about their views on labor and management; fifteen months later they took the questionnaire again. The workers who had become foremen were now much more favorably inclined toward management and more critical of the union than they had been, while the new union leaders were more critical of management. Still later, some of the foremen became workers again—and their attitudes changed back to pro-union (Lieberman 1965). Most people who become managers start to think and behave like managers, not like workers in managerial disguise, even if they try hard to remember their humble origins. When a wolf wears sheep's clothing, in other words, it becomes a sheep; and vice versa.

With this way of looking at things, then, consider now three aspects of organizational structure that account for some apparent differences between men and women at work: opportunity, power, and tokenism.

opportunity

In one large corporation that sociologist Rosabeth Kanter studied, she asked 111 employees how they felt about promotion. The men were more eager to move up in the hierarchy than the women and much more certain of their ability to succeed. The women didn't want promotions, they said, if their new responsibilities might interfere with family matters.

If Kanter had stopped there, she would have come away with the excuse that many employers use to explain why they don't promote women: Women are happy where they are. But Kanter didn't stop there. She observed that men and women have dramatically different *opportunities* for promotion. In the company Kanter studied, men made up only a small proportion of the white-collar workers. Most men were trained professionals in positions that led up the steps to management. Most women, in contrast, held dead-end jobs as secretaries or clerks; the best job they could aspire to was executive secretary. When Kanter looked to see what the few women in high-ranking jobs (such as sales) thought about promotion, their achievement ambitions were no different from the men's. "Ambition, self-esteem, and career commitment were all flourishing among women in sales jobs, which are well paid and on the way to top management," Kanter (1976a) reported. Similarly, Crowley, Levitin, and Quinn (1973) found that the *desire* for promotion among American workers is largely a matter of their *expectation* of promotion. Women want promotions as much as men do, when they think they have a realistic chance of advancing.

Achievement ambitions, it seems, are directly related to one's chances of achieving; for women, the chances are low. Crowley and her colleagues found that two-thirds of all American working women never expected to be promoted. "We would guess that to avoid frustration," the researchers noted mildly, "women, like men in the same situation, scale down their ambitions." Kanter reviewed some early research on work motivation in men. She found that when men's opportunities for advancement are blocked they behave like the stereotypical female. They play down the importance of their jobs, fantasize about leaving, emphasize family life over careers, and claim little interest in higher-status work. Male auto workers, meat packers, and factory workers have the same attitudes toward achievement and work as female secretaries and typists do. Conversely, when real opportunities for advancement are offered, more people respond. Cynthia Fuchs Epstein, for example, found that as opportunities were created for women in law, their ambitions and goals changed accordingly (Epstein 1981).

Kanter also observed that the kind of job a person has determines what he or she enjoys about working. People whose work is exciting, challenging, and flexible will concentrate on it, putting in as many hours as they need to with a minimum of grumbling. If they are in an advancement hierarchy—with goals of becoming head of the department, dean of the college, manager of the business—they will do what it takes to get there. On the other hand, people whose work is repetitive and boring will be less involved with the work itself. They get more pleasure from other aspects of the job, such as working conditions, companions, opportunities for socializing. When work is dull, friends can liven it up. The result, said Kanter, is that women seem more "talk-oriented" than "task-oriented" on the job and seem to care more about external conditions than about the intrinsic demands of the assignment. People sometimes use the stereotype of the gossipy female coffee klatsch to "prove" that women are more interested in people than in work and to explain why they don't achieve what men do. But talk or task orientations probably reflect the characteristics of the job more clearly than the personality of the woman or man who holds it. For instance, in some blue-collar occupations that by and large do not extend to their employees much opportunity for creativity and flexibility, friendships take precedence over tasks (Walshok 1981). But highly mobile jobs require that a person subordinate friendships with coworkers to work demands. "The competitive corporate world requires its participants to be willing to relocate, to surpass rivals without hesitation, to use other people to advance in status," Kanter wrote. "The aggressive, striving junior executive is as much a creation of his place in the organization hierarchy as is the talkative, unambitious secretary."

A laboratory study reported by Kanter showed directly how the opportunity for advancement affects people's behavior in a group. Arthur Cohen set up some work groups of young men: The participants in half of the groups had good chances for promotion, while those in the other half had no such chances. Although members of each group had the same job to do and the same supervisors, their reactions and attitudes differed. The high-opportunity groups became much more involved with their task. "They dropped irrelevant chatter, and reported later that they cared more about the high-power people who were supervising them than about each other," Kanter reported. "The nonmobile group members, by contrast, concentrated on each other. They virtually ignored the powerful supervisors, because they had nothing to gain from them anyway. They were more openly critical and resentful of people with power."

People do not make conscious decisions to emphasize or de-emphasize their work or coworkers. They don't say, "Gee, I guess this job is a dead end, so I might as well chum up with Diane," or "No sense bothering to make friends with these branch-office hicks, since I won't need them when I'm moved to New York." People tend to feel that the decision to make friends with Diane or to avoid people in the office is a matter of personal choice that has nothing to do with the job. But such "personal choices" are part of a vicious circle. People in dead-end jobs, whether male or female, lower their aspirations to accord with reality. Employers note that the workers don't have the attitudes or the ambition to warrant promotion and dismiss them from consideration, thus confirming the employees' impression that their jobs lead nowhere. Likewise, when people are hindered by the conditions of their work from being highly productive and creative, both employers and employees tend to blame the employees—"See? They (we) are just lazy and dumb." They fail to see that productivity on the job is not just a matter of how good you are, but also of whether your job lets you be good or not (Reskin 1978).

power

Power is a hard thing to define to everyone's satisfaction. Sometimes it is used to mean influence, or the ability to get people to do what you want. Sometimes it means authority, or the legitimate right to issue orders and see that they are obeyed. The two meanings are not the same, because one person might hold a high office but lack the ability to influence others, while another might have considerable influence without being in an official position of power.

Many commentators on the sexual scene observe, with varying degrees of seriousness, that women have plenty of influence but not much authority. Women, they say, are the power behind the throne, the stage managers who make it all happen and then retreat to the wings, leaving the men to take the curtain calls. According to this line of reasoning, female power is based on womanly wiles and seductive persuasion. Tears are as effective as threats, and sexuality as powerful as strength. Since the ladies get exactly what they want, why make things even more unfair by giving them legitimate authority too? Didn't Helen of Troy have power? Carmen? Lady Macbeth?

This argument is also used, of course, to explain why women don't really "need" to have leadership positions; they have as much power as they want already, and, besides, they wouldn't be good leaders anyway. Prejudice against women bosses has been around a long time, going underground when the mood of the country is egalitarian and surfacing during times of economic competition between the sexes. In 1976 a Gallup poll found that most Americans held negative views of women bosses,[1] and a 1979 study found a continuing "preference for men as bosses and professionals" (Ferber, Huber, and Spitze 1979).

But there are negative stereotypes about male leaders, too (see Table 6), although they aren't used to keep men from being promoted. Employees can be critical of both sexes. A female leader may be "emotionally demonstrative" (a bad thing, apparently), but a male leader may be "remote, inaccessible" (Heller 1982). So there are two questions to be asked here: *Do* men and women differ in their leadership styles, and, if so, *why* do they differ?

The answer to the first question is: *Given the same job conditions*, no, men and women don't differ much as leaders. Kanter

---

[1]Oddly enough, people find it easier to accept the idea of a woman president, perhaps because that possibility is so remote. The proportion of people who say they could vote for a female president has steadily risen, from 31 percent in 1937 to 80 percent in 1983.

Table 6. Contemporary Stereotypes of Men and Women as Leaders

NEGATIVE IMAGES	
Men	**Women**
Too focused on procedures	Too focused on people
Remote, inaccessible	Emotionally demonstrative
Authoritarian, aggressive	Not assertive
Sexist	
POSITIVE IMAGES	
More humane	Relaxed, humorous
Open, friendly	Separate work and social roles
Egalitarian	Think categorically
Efficient and organized	Work independently

SOURCE: Heller 1982.

reviewed the research on sex differences in leadership and found little consistent evidence. Another sociologist, Barbara Bunker (1976), also reviewed numerous studies comparing male and female leaders and reported that the myth of the mean female boss doesn't hold up. Field studies of leaders in real-world organizations show few sex differences. For example, a study of 950 female managers and 966 male managers found that *"women, in general, do not differ from men, in general, in the ways in which they administer the management process"* (Donnell and Hall 1980; emphasis in original). They do not differ significantly in management philosophy, motivation, participative processes, competence with others, or managerial style. There are a few points of departure between male and female managers: "Under stress," the researchers noted, "males are more likely to become dictatorial and females are more likely to become conciliatory."

Moreover, the subordinates and peers of managers evaluate leaders of both sexes equally. In experimental situations, too, people are equally satisfied with male and female leaders. Workers of both sexes want a boss who is competent, dominant, and directive. If he or she is also a "nice guy," so much the better.

If men and women don't differ as much as people assume, why the assumption? One reason may be that female bosses are still rare enough to stand out. When people have a female employer they don't like, it is easiest to explain the feeling by reference to sex. But no one can dismiss a bad male boss with "he's only a man—what d'you expect?"

Kanter added another explanation. She concluded that a manager's style of leadership depends more on whether he or she has real power than on whether he or she has a specific personality trait. "Real power" means that the organization has given the person the authority to make decisions, institute them, and hand out important rewards and punishments (promotions, raises, transfers, dismissals). Power comes not just from job title or a fancy office but from membership in the informal inner circles of the company and from recognition by coworkers. Kanter concluded that a boss's style reflects his or her power. "Powerless leaders, men and women alike," she wrote, "often become punitive, petty tyrants. . . . Blocked from exercising power in the wider hierarchy, they substitute the satisfaction of lording it over subordinates. Unable to move ahead, they hold everyone back." Bosses who have real authority tend to be more flexible about rules, to share information with employees, and to try to help able ones move on to better jobs.

In one study, young men and women were put in a supervisory position, with instructions to get good work from their employees (Instone, Major, and Bunker 1983). They could use any form of influence they wished: promise pay increases; give pay increases; threaten to decrease pay; actually decrease pay; threaten to transfer or fire them; actually transfer or fire them; offer special instructions, encouragement, or help. They could apply liberal doses of praise and support, or they could bawl them out, or they could express concern and interest. Instone and her colleagues found that *men and women supervise others relatively similarly when they have equal access to power resources*, that is, when they have authority to promote or fire, praise or criticize. Men and women did not differ in their use of one strategy over another. Men were not more likely to use threat and coercion on their employees, nor were women more likely to be sweet and encouraging—or vice versa.

But the researchers did find that a supervisor's *self-confidence* was an important element in the kind of leader he or she was. Males and females with low self-confidence were most likely to use coercive tactics: to threaten and bully, to use the stick instead of the carrot on their subordinates. The stereotype of the harsh female boss, Instone and her colleagues observed, parallels the behavior of people—men, too—who have little self-assurance. And self-confidence itself depends on aspects of the job, not just the personality: It depends on whether a worker gets feedback on his or her performance, on whether the job emphasizes constant evaluation and comparison with others, and on those aspects of the job identified by Kohn and Schooler—flexibility, freedom from constraints and total routine, the chance for self-direction.

Because women are so rarely in visible positions of power, many people assume that women behave as they do because of their sex rather than because of their status. In truth, women who truly have authority behave as well or as badly as men, and men whose authority is uncertain or absent behave as well or as badly as women in similar spots. Kanter cited a study of Air Force officers which showed that men who had low status and little chance for promotion were more inflexible and authoritarian than officers of the same formal rank who had more power.

Sociologists believe that women use indirect methods of influence because they are barred from using direct ones, not because they are "naturally" manipulative and seductive. Any social group that does not have access to legitimized power develops indirect ways to influence the dominant group. Many writers have compared blacks and women in this regard; historically, both have had to rely on wiles and guile to get around the whims of the master, the white man (Hacker 1951; Myrdal 1944).

Further, the fact is that most women and minorities *are* excluded from access to legitimate power. Not just from the power of position ("I'm the boss here"), but from the informal power networks, the "old boys" circle by which company leaders bring their protégés into positions of power. The protégé system has made it difficult for women to succeed in business without really trying—unless they have a sponsor or a father in the ruling family. In a report on the ten highest-ranking women in big business in 1973, *Fortune* magazine observed that eight of the ten made it to the top because of family connections, marriage, or the fact that they helped create the organizations they now preside over (Robertson 1973). They did not start out in jobs with limited futures, nor did they have to work their way through a corporate hierarchy that discriminated against them. Cynthia Fuchs Epstein (1970, 1981) has written about the difficulties women have in getting a high-ranking sponsor to help them succeed in the academic and legal worlds. Judith Lorber (1975) has documented the reasons that women doctors earn so much less than their male colleagues and are less successful:

> The fault may not lie in their psyches or female roles, but in the system of professional patronage and sponsorship which tracked them out of the prestigious specialties [such as neurosurgery] and "inner fraternities" of American medical institutions by not recommending them for the better internships, residencies, and hospital staff positions, and by not referring patients to them. (p. 82)

Such "inner fraternities" are not relics of the past. Many men's organizations still exclude women, providing the men with a private place to do business. (The Friars Club, the Bohemian Club, and the Century Club—which number as members the cream of the political, business, and journalistic establishment—do not, as of 1983, admit women.) This is still one of the major barriers to female opportunity at work.

the trouble with tokens

What situations tend to foster stereotypic feminine strategies? Kanter (1975) would answer that the single organizational factor surest to provoke stereotyped behavior is tokenism. Women in management are often isolated from each other, working as the sole female in groups of men. All individuals who have token status, Kanter noted—whether a female scientist or a male nurse or a black executive—share certain experiences. A token is always in the limelight: Everyone notices her or him, and everything the token does is scrutinized. Coworkers tend to concentrate on qualities that make the token unique rather than on those the token shares with the rest of the group.

In his essay on being a token man enrolled as a visiting student at Wellesley College (where the sex ratio was 400 females to every male), David Kent (1980) recalled how it felt to be a stranger in a woman's world. "I didn't fit into the Wellesley system," he wrote, "so I was categorized and abused and discriminated against. . . . I could not miss a class without the professor's noticing that I was absent. In class, I was called on to present the male point of view, which always seemed to get me into deep trouble." Kent even heard the word *co-ed* applied to *himself*, and was irked by a word "we men had always despised." Naturally—it refers to the minority sex that is being allowed to be co-educated with the majority sex. It marks the sex that is different. Kent added: "I became self-conscious and insecure. I developed a deep fear of not measuring up to whatever I was supposed to measure up to; I felt the women were judging me by a set of invisible standards." All of these feelings, of course, are what token women describe when they first join an all-male organization.

Similarly, a single black person in a group of whites will have heightened visibility. Kanter (1976a) reported a study by Shelley Taylor and Susan Fiske on just this situation. Their students listened to a tape of a group discussion and saw pictures that presumably were of the participants; then they described their impressions of each member. The photos showed either one black man in an all-white group or a group that was evenly mixed, black and white. The observers' opinions of the black man changed, even though the taped discussion (hence the man's objective participation) did not. Basically, the students paid too much attention to the black man in the white group. They thought his contribution was disproportionately large, and they stereotyped his personality traits. When they evaluated the mixed groups, they were as likely to recall information about whites as about blacks, and they rated their personalities equally.

A group not only *sees* a token in a stereotyped way; it also pressures the token to *behave* in a stereotyped way. Kanter (1976b) identified a few traditional roles that a token woman can adopt if she wants to win acceptance by the group. She can play the *mother*, who is sympathetic and comforts the men, who bakes cookies for the department or office, who sews on buttons; or the *sex object*, the seductress, who provokes men to compete for her and woo her; or the *pet* or kid sister, who plays cheerleader to male ideas and adds humor without threat. If a woman does not take on one of these three roles (all of which deflect issues of professional ability and competition), she will be regarded with suspicion, even hostility. She may be viewed as an *iron maiden* who insists on her rights and her competence. The iron maiden may be asked, "You're not one of those women's libbers, are you?" Regardless of her answer, men are inclined to regard her as a hard-hearted militant.

Carol Wolman, M.D., and psychologist Hal Frank (1975) examined the token's predicament in more detail. They observed and recorded the behavior of six working groups, ranging in size from nine to thirteen members, each of which had only one female participant. Three of the groups consisted of graduate students taking a course in T-groups (group processes and dynamics) and met for thirty hours each; three groups consisted of first-year students in psychiatry and met for six months. All these people were psychologically oriented and might have been expected to be perceptive about behavior. But in four of the six groups the woman was treated as an outcast, a deviant, no matter how hard she tried to win acceptance from the group. One woman isolated herself by choice. One was eventually accepted, but with low status and only after she had presented herself to the men as naive, less competent than they, and frightened. (In time she proved to be extremely competent and her status rose.) Some of the strategies the women tried reflect Kanter's four types:

> [Betty] fought for regular membership by rationally pointing out that she didn't fit the "little sister" stereotype the group had imposed on her. This earned her a "women's lib" label. . . . She was treated as a deviant for the duration of the group, and felt frustrated and unhappy. (pp. 166–67)

> [Cora] presented herself as assertive, rational, and self-assured. The men provoked her into becoming emotional, and then defined her as deviant for being naive, bitchy, and overemotional. She felt that at times they ignored her, and at times they competed to control her as a way of establishing and maintaining their "pecking order." (p. 167)

Wolman and Frank observed that whatever the woman did to gain acceptance, the men countered by reinterpreting her efforts:

> If she acted friendly she was thought to be flirting. If she acted weak, the men tried to infantilize her, treating her as a "little sister" rather

than a peer. If she apologized for alienating the group, she was seen as a submissive woman knowing her place. If she asked for help, she earned a "needy female" label. If she became angry, or tried to point out rationally what the group process was doing to her, she was seen as competitive, in a bitchy unfeminine way. "Feminine" coping mechanisms increased her perceived differences; "masculine" ones threatened the men so that they isolated her more. (p. 168)

In short, the token woman faces a damned-if-you're-feminine, damned-if-you're-masculine dilemma.[2] Tokens thus react, understandably, with depression, frustration, or anger; they feel there is something wrong with them that has brought on the group's wrath or disdain. The male majority see things the same way; they generally feel something is wrong with the token woman to warrant their wrath or disdain.

All tokens face the same predicament: how to lose their exaggerated visibility and win the group's acceptance. Some play the stereotype expected of them; Everett Hughes (1958) found that a token black among white workers often becomes the group comedian. Others try to hide themselves and their accomplishments: Many female executives describe efforts to minimize their female attributes and fade unobtrusively into the background (Hennig and Jardim 1977). One way to reduce conflict with male peers is to let a man take credit for one's accomplishments. Kanter (1976b) reported interviews in which some women "even expressed pride that they could influence a group of men without the men recognizing the origin of the idea, or they rejoiced in the secret knowledge that they were responsible for their boss's success."

Another kind of accommodation a lone woman sometimes makes to win acceptance is available to the rare woman who makes it to the top of a male-dominated profession. Such a woman can become a Queen Bee who has no use for other women. "If I made it, why can't they?" is her attitude. Queen Bees thrive on their "unusual pet" status for three reasons (Staines, Tavris, and Jayaratne 1974):

   1. *Cooptation.* The token woman, like any other token, faces considerable pressure from the majority group to take sides, to show loyalty to the majority, and to oppose other minorities. If the token

---

[2]The experiences of the solo women in Wolman and Frank's study lend some credence to the idea that the women studied by Matina Horner and others (see Chapter 6) don't so much fear success as fear social rejection. If Anne is the only woman in her medical school class *and* gets the highest grades, she may have all the problems these female students had, times ten.

keeps arguing, for example, that more blacks or women or Jews should be admitted, members of the dominant group may find their tolerance stretched. They can admit a token or two without shaking the system, but that's all they aim to do.

2. *Rewards for being special.* The token gets ample praise and attention for not rocking the boat. Queen Bees feel special: They are highly praised for "being so feminine" yet "thinking like a man." Wolman and Frank's study illustrates the tremendously frustrating double-bind the token is in. If the men decide that she is a remarkable exception to her sex, worthy of their friendship and acceptance, what relief and pleasure she must feel! How can she risk all her gains by reminding them, "Er, fellas, a lot of other women would like to work here . . ."

3. *Excluding the competition.* The Queen Bee doesn't want competition any more than the men do. Most tokens have worked very hard to be admitted to their groups, and they don't see why it should be easier for others. It can be fun to be the one-in-a-million woman at the top. Why let in everyone else and become just one of the crowd?

With the rise of the women's movement, though, and the increasing visibility of successful women, "Queen Bee-ness" seems to be on the wane; it may have been more characteristic of earlier generations (Kulka and Colten 1982).

What happens when men become the tokens? Again, it is the structure of the group itself that creates the supposed failure of the token's personality. In one study (reported by Kanter 1976a), male nurses were the tokens in a female working world. The men were treated much like Wolman and Frank's lone females and like David Kent at Wellesley: They felt isolated and not quite accepted, and they often sensed disguised hostility and distrust from the group.

If this analysis is correct, it follows that when women and men share the same job status in greater numbers, the visibility of the token will diminish and male and female performance will be evaluated more equitably. This is exactly what happens. Two researchers (Tsui and Gutek 1982) compared managerial performance, attitudes toward women managers, and career success of 217 male and 78 female middle-level managers in a large corporation in the Midwest. Tsui and Gutek had the managers' supervisors, peers, and subordinates evaluate the managers' effectiveness and competence, and how liked and respected they were. They found that male managers were *not* rated more favorably than female managers were, either by others or by themselves. Nor were male managers liked and respected more, or considered more credible. If anything, the female managers were being promoted more quickly, catching up with male managers in income and position. Women were a bit more likely to rate themselves lower in effectiveness than their own superiors, employees, and peers rated them—which shows a lingering trace of self-doubt. But once these women had demonstrated their managerial effectiveness, they were rated by others just as the men were.[3]

Similarly, if this approach is correct, we should expect that once the structural forces that dampen job interest and ambition are removed, employees' interest and ambition will soar. This is the assumption behind many affirmative-action programs—that once organizational conditions are changed (to eliminate blocked opportunities, powerlessness, and tokenism for either sex), attitudes and motivations will change accordingly. For example, Kanter interviewed a woman who had been a secretary in a large corporation for twenty-five years:

> Five years ago, she would have said that she never wanted to be anything but a secretary. She also would have told you that . . . she was thinking of quitting. She said secretarial work was not a good enough reason to leave the children.
>
> Then came an affirmative action program, and Linda was offered a promotion. She wavered. It would mean leaving her good female friends for a lonely life among male managers. Her friends thought she was abandoning them. She worried whether she could handle the job. But her boss talked her into it and promised to help, reassuring her that he would be her sponsor.
>
> So Linda was promoted, and now she handles a challenging management job most successfully. Seeing friends is the least of her many reasons to come to work every day, and her ambitions have soared. She wants to go right to the top.
>
> "I have fifteen years left to work," she says. "And I want to move up six grades—to corporate vice president, at least!" (1976a, p. 91)

the work force and the forces on work

You rarely hear anyone say any more that "a woman's place is in the home." This is because most women aren't there. In 1953 only 26 percent of all married women held jobs, and the percentage was even

---

[3]Even this dip in self-confidence may have a job-structure cause, not a personality cause. In a study of fifty male and fifty female insurance company employees, women tended to denigrate their own abilities when they were paired on a task with a male coworker, yet to accept more responsibility for success and report greater confidence about their future ability when paired on the same task with another woman (Heilman and Kram 1978).

lower for women with children. Two decades later, in 1973, 42 percent of all wives were working, and a third of all mothers with preschool children. In 1982, 51 percent of all wives were employed, and nearly half of all mothers of preschool children (Table 7).

The old stereotype held that women work for pin money—extra frills and luxuries, rather than the family's meat-and-potatoes needs—or to mark time until they marry (white women, anyway; black women have long been accustomed to working for necessity). This stereotype had a purpose: It justified paying women less than men for the same work. "Husbands, the breadwinners, need the money more," employers could say; or "Why should I promote her? She'll just get married and quit." (Employers, it may be noted, were not paying *men* according to need—that is, giving a man with three children more money than a man with only one; nor were they promoting bachelors in preference to married men.) In fact, most women work for the same reasons that men do: They need the money and they enjoy the satisfaction (see, for example, Crosby 1982).

With all these women working, it might seem that soon women will not have to worry about tokenism and powerlessness, that both sexes are on the way to equal opportunities at work. But seeming isn't so. As we noted in Chapter 1, job segregation, in which the large majority of each sex clusters into "women's work" and "men's work," continues, with women's work bringing significantly lower pay (Treiman and Hartmann 1981). The fact that more and more women work has not yet appreciably affected another fact, which is that women earn only 60 percent of what men earn.[4] Male and female occupations in this society are, by and large, "separate and unequal" (Epstein 1976), with male-dominated occupations offering far more chances for status and promotion than female-dominated jobs. Unfortunately, the combination of lower pay for women and the tracking of women into sex-segregated jobs is creating a new class of poor families (see Chapter 1). One in three families headed by women is poor, compared with only one in ten families headed by men (there aren't very many of those, however) and only *one in nineteen* headed by two parents.

[4]As we show in the next chapter, women's work is usually valued less than men's work (in economic and prestige terms) across cultures as well as in our own. And there is a biblical precedent, suggesting that women's lower economic value has a long history. The Lord instructs Moses (Leviticus 27:1–4) to appraise individuals thus: For a male between twenty and sixty years of age, "thy estimation shall be fifty shekels of silver"; and for a woman the same age, "then thy estimation shall be thirty shekels." A 40 percent value gap even then!

Table 7. Percentages of Married Women Holding Jobs, 1960–1982

Year	All wives	Wives without children	Wives with children under 6	Wives with children 6–17
1960	30.5%	34.7%	18.6%	39.0%
1963	33.7	37.4	22.5	41.5
1968	38.3	40.1	27.6	46.9
1973	42.2	42.8	32.7	50.1
1980	50.1	46.0	45.1	61.7
1982	51.2	46.2	48.7	63.2

SOURCE: U.S. Department of Labor 1974, and personal communication 1983.

Valerie Oppenheimer (1970, 1975) argued that the labor market in the United States is actually two markets, male and female, so that the sexes rarely compete for the same jobs. Sex segregation of jobs is not just a matter of women "wanting" poorly paid service jobs (such as waitress or nurse's aide). They are the only jobs women can get. The job market opened to women in the midfifties because the country needed not just more workers but specifically *female* workers. Women, observed Oppenheimer, rarely *displaced* men, for example as teachers and typists; they merely *replaced* men when men got opportunities to move ahead. Women offered special qualities: They were cheap to hire, they were available, they were educated. Industrial society needs a pool of cheap but educated labor, and this need has kept women in low-paying, well-schooled jobs such as elementary-school teaching and clerical work. "To substitute men," noted Oppenheimer, "would require either a rise in the price for labor or a decline in the quality of labor."

What accounts for sex segregation in the labor force? It can't be enough to say that men and women are socialized differently and have different backgrounds. Women overcame their socialization sufficiently to go to work in the 1960s and 1970s; why not overcome the kind of work they had in mind, as well? Sociologists answer with reference to what they call "market forces": the trends in the economy, job characteristics, and job opportunities that direct men one way and women another. Women (correctly) perceive that they will have difficulty being employed in math and science fields, which are male-dominated, so they don't take math and science courses. High-school girls think they'll have a better chance of getting work if they learn clerical skills, so they don't learn technical skills—even though carpenters are better paid than secretaries.

Market factors exert a large influence on both sexes' choice of what skills to acquire, but in different ways. The primary influence on women's choice is *the sex composition of occupations*, an indicator of their likelihood of getting hired. The primary influence on men's choice is *the potential income of occupations*, regardless of the sex composition (Paige 1976). To determine whether the number of women in typically male occupations would affect young women's career aspirations, psychologist Madeline Heilman (1978) informed three groups of high-school students that the proportion of women in law and architecture would, in fifteen years, be either 10 percent (token), 30 percent (minority), or 50 percent (equal). The more balanced the predicted sex ratio, the *greater* the occupational interest the young women showed. And the more balanced the sex ratio, the *less* occupational interest the men showed.

At every level of educational achievement, women tend to prepare for the jobs they can expect to get, even when it means less income. Men don't enter "women's" jobs because they won't earn much money, and women don't try for "men's" jobs because they doubt they will be hired. Women aren't interested in "men's" jobs, you say? As some fields have opened up to women—such as medicine and law—women are going into them in droves. And when "women's work" goes professional and practitioners get higher salaries, as is happening in health technology, men suddenly find such jobs appropriate for them (Van Dusen and Sheldon 1976).[5]

But perhaps you believe, as some employers do, that the sex-based wage difference is deserved. After all, if women have less education, work experience, and work continuity (interrupting their careers to have children), as well as higher absenteeism, than men, they ought not to have the same income. But all of these skill factors account for only one-third of the wage gap between white men and white women, and only one-fourth of the wage gap between white men and black women. In a nationally representative sample of

---

[5]The same is true of minorities. Although white women still avoid skilled trades, the most striking change among black women in the last decade has been the virtual disappearance of household service as an anticipated occupation; black women are moving into jobs newly available to them, sales and clerical (Crowley 1982). Incidentally, one field that has opened up for both sexes, computer programing, still has few women in it, perhaps because of the "math filter" that screens women out of scientific occupations.

American families who were interviewed every year for fifteen years, researchers found that the income discrepancy between the sexes is *not* because women have fewer work skills than men do (Corcoran, Duncan, and Hill 1982). Men continue to enjoy a large financial advantage over women, even when both sexes have identical talents and training.

Another challenge to the "you earn what you deserve" idea comes from research generated by "human capital theory." This theory, first proposed by sociologist Gary Becker (1964), considers major lifetime choices—to go to college or not, what kind of schooling to choose, when to marry, whether to have children, which occupations to go into—as decisions we make about the use of our time. This time is as valuable to us as money—we allocate our time as we allocate income (hence the term *human* capital). Becker argued that some labor is more productive than others simply because more resources have been invested into training. What you earn, therefore, should be a function of the amount of time you spend on your education, your professional training, your work experience.

Becker's theory turned out to be true . . . but only for white males (Mueller 1982). For women, years of schooling and work experience are very poor measures of their human capital, that is, their marketable skills. Earnings for women do not show the typically steep rise that they do for men who accumulate experience. Indeed, the more educated a woman, the higher the rate of depreciation of her market value when she drops out of the labor force (even for a few years to have children). By the time such women have returned to work, their wages have declined significantly, regardless of previous experience.[6]

Working women lose even more in wages once they marry. Two sociologists, Donald Treiman and Kermit Terrell (1975), analyzed representative samples of American women, aged thirty to forty-four, their husbands, and other men the same age. They found that women who had never married earned far more than women who had (or did have) husbands. To be sure, single women were also better educated, had higher-status jobs, and worked longer hours than their

---

[6]Human capital theory does seem to account for career achievement, if not income, among an elite group of women professionals. The three factors now related to career success among such women are (1) earning an advanced degree, (2) accumulating years of work experience, and (3) not having child care responsibilities (Lykes and Stewart 1982). The *timing* of these three factors is relatively unimportant. Finishing one's degree and staying in the labor force are more important for eventual success than *when* a woman gets her degree or begins her career.

married counterparts, but these factors accounted for only part of their greater income. The single women got a higher return for their education, for example. Given the same number of years of schooling, single women can expect to earn three times as much per year as married women. Similarly, wives get paid less than husbands, on the average, even when their work experience and number of hours on the job are the same. Black wives, who are significantly better educated than their husbands, are paid much less than black men, again for equivalent work. As psychologist Joan Crowley (1982) summarized, "All available analyses do indicate that women pay for their time at home in the form of lower lifetime earnings and wage rates."[7]

A sex-segregated marketplace supports these salary differences by making use of the fact that most women's primary allegiance is to their families. "Women's" jobs do not require long-term commitment or extensive sacrifice of time, so a woman can take a job, quit, and return as family responsibilities change. Because service and clerical jobs exist all over the country, women whose husbands are transferred can travel with them and pick up work in the new city. Employers, for their part, do not have to provide much training for female employees or invest time and resources in them. Geographically, married women are a captive labor force. Where they work is determined by where they live, which in turn is determined by where their husbands work. Further, most wives have to consider other attributes of a job than income and interest: They want their hours to correspond to the children's school hours, for example, or they decide to work nights while their husbands are home with the kids.

In times of crisis, such as the Civil War and World Wars I and II, women have gone to work when they were needed; when particular kinds of work required the services of women (such as the white-collar jobs that became available after World War II), women have gone to work. In times of recession they are, however, the last hired

---

[7]Efforts to achieve equal pay for equal work do not touch the market forces that keep most women's incomes low—because most women do not work in sex-integrated jobs. This is why you may be hearing arguments for equal pay for *comparable* work in the next few years; an effort could be made to balance incomes across occupations, according to training, education, and skill. In 1983, Pismo Beach, California, population 5,700, became the first city to pass a comparable worth law, upgrading the job worth of its eleven female city employees. A female account clerk, for example, now earns what a male maintenance man does.

and first fired (and black women are in the most precarious economic situation). The sociological perspective predicts not that women enter the labor force in general or any given occupation in particular because their attitudes change, but rather that once women go to work, their attitudes about working follow suit.

The needs and demands of the economic marketplace, then, set limits on the work that women and men do. But as Treiman and Terrell's work suggests, there is another major barrier to equality between the sexes, a barrier that permits men's work and women's work to stay segregated. That barrier is the family.

marriage: cage or castle?

Suppose that 90 percent of the young men in this country were required to work for an influential company with branches in every state. They love the company and go to the job with high hopes and cheerful enthusiasm. After a few years managers notice that the workers are wilting. Most of them have hypertension, peptic ulcers, headaches, and insomnia. Many are lonely, anxious, and depressed. Production slows down. Some employees stop working altogether.

What's wrong? Most observers would say that something is amiss with a company that can so transform its bright young workers. If you reread the above paragraph, substituting "women" for "men," "wives" for "workers and employees," and "marriage" for "the company," you'll have the same situation in different dress. Yet while social scientists and unions have paid in blood, time, and effort to document and change the effects of bad working conditions on employees, less attention has gone to the effects of marital conditions on families.

When Betty Friedan wrote about "the problem that has no name" in *The Feminine Mystique* (1963), she hit a responsive nerve in women who were unhappy with the role of happy housewife. Since then research on women and marriage has shown a subtle change: Instead of asking, "What's wrong with women who can't adjust to marriage?" researchers have begun to ask, "What's wrong with marriage that so many women can't adjust to it?" In this section we look at the effects of marriage to see why they are so different for women and men. Because virtually all Americans marry, an understanding of sex differences in achievement, status, and power must include an analysis of the ways marriage enhances or inhibits achievement in men and women. The picture is not black and white; contemporary marriage is a complex, changing institution, and its effects come in all shades of gray.

his and hers marriages

"Every woman should marry," wrote Benjamin Disraeli, "and no man." Take any book of famous quotations, look up marriage, and you will find such a wailing from men, such a catalogue of complaints, that you will wonder why any of them went through with the awful deed. ("Bigamy is having one wife too many," the men joke. "So is monogamy.") The irony is that marriage, which many men consider a trap, does them a world of good, while the relentless pressure on them to be breadwinners causes undue strain and conflict. Exactly the reverse is true for women. Marriage, which they yearn for from childhood, may prove hazardous to their health, while the opportunities of work help keep them sane and satisfied. Let's look at this paradox more closely.

Sociologist Jessie Bernard, in *The Future of Marriage* (1972), wrote that the sexes get into marriage as they get into bed: with different desires, rhythms, and expectations. And they have entirely different experiences. Critics of traditional marriage are often asked, "What's *wrong* with raising boys to be workers and girls to be wives?" One answer rests on accumulating data showing that marriage is neither as healthy nor as satisfying for wives as it is for husbands.

Bernard gathered considerable evidence on the mental and physical health of married and single Americans. Overall, she found, married men are healthier in all ways than single men. They are even likely to get better jobs and higher pay. Single men get into more trouble than husbands: They commit more crimes, murder more often, have more traffic accidents, and kill themselves at a higher rate. Bernard recognized that perhaps marriage should not get all the credit for civilizing young men: Perhaps unhealthy, neurotic, criminally inclined men are simply not selected as mates. She tried to get around this problem by comparing married men with widowers, to see what happens when men are thrown back into the single state. "They are miserable," she reported. "They show more than expected frequencies of psychological distress, and their death rate is high." Studies that compared married clergy with celibate priests—all men

of similar background and health—found that the husbands i.
longer than the celibates.

Among women, the situation reverses: Married women show
more mental and physical problems than single women. In 1973
Walter Gove and Jeannette Tudor reviewed dozens of studies that
compared the mental health of married men and women. No matter
how they defined mental illness—as including neurotic disorders
such as chronic anxiety or only true psychoses in which a person
cannot function, such as schizophrenia, manic-depressive reaction,
and paranoia—women are less healthy than men. Further, no matter
who defines the mental illness, women are less healthy than men.
More women are admitted to mental hospitals on an involuntary
basis. And more women show up ill on community surveys, when
selection bias is largely eliminated (Russo and Olmedo 1983; Russo
and Sobel 1981).

There's a long list of symptoms that psychologists use to tell
whether people are suffering from stress and distress, including nervousness, inertia, insomnia, nightmares, fainting, headaches, dizzi-
ness, heart palpitations, and feelings of impending nervous breakdown. In the many studies that have now been done, of selected
groups as well as national samples, more women than men, and
specifically more wives than husbands, report these problems (U.S.
Department of Health, Education, and Welfare 1970; Campbell
1975; Rubenstein 1982). In particular, women are more likely than
men to suffer from depression, by a factor of two or three to one
(Weissman and Klerman 1981; Howell and Bayes 1981). Gove and
Tudor believe, as Bernard does, that women do not show these higher
rates of illness because they are women—and therefore weak, or
permitted to complain—but because of strains in the roles they are
called upon to play.[8] When Gove (1972) reviewed studies of marital
status and mental illness that were done after World War II, he found
without exception that wives were more likely to have a mental
disorder than husbands. But when he compared never-married men

[8]Some people think that the sexes don't really differ in mental illness, it's just that
women admit problems and pains more. Gove and Kevin Clancy addressed this
problem by studying the effect of response bias—for example, the tendency to give
answers that will win social approval, to agree to most questions asked, and to claim
symptoms that are considered desirable—on reports of psychosomatic illnesses. They
found that when they controlled for response bias, the sex differences in mental illness
increased. So women don't have more symptoms because they think they should have
them or are simply more willing to talk about them (Clancy and Gove 1975).

ed women, divorced men with divorced women,
n with widowed women, the men usually had the
ntal illness. It would seem that something about
n and hurts women. What is it?

why wives wilt and husbands thrive:
the housewife syndrome

The sociological view seeks to understand what it is about the structure of marriage that causes the sexes to react so differently. Not unreasonably, people tend to think there is something the matter with them if they cannot adjust to a new role, whether as spouse, parent, recruit, employee, or manager. But sociologists have managed to pinpoint some forces in the roles called for by marriage, not in the personalities of individuals, that produce sex differences in achievement, nurturance, self-esteem, and mental health.

Bernard and others believe that marriage exerts its most negative effects on women whose sole identity is as wife and mother. These women are subject to the "housewife syndrome." In a *Psychology Today* survey on happiness (Shaver and Freedman 1976), housewives reported feeling more anxious and worried than employed wives (46 percent to 28 percent); more lonely (44 percent to 26 percent); and more worthless (41 percent to 24 percent). This response from women who read *Psychology Today* is interesting precisely because these women are more affluent, educated, and aware, on the average, than most Americans. If housewives who have these benefits still show the psychosomatic syndrome, then the stress of marriage is not only a result of being poor and having to manage a household on a shoestring.

The housewife syndrome, once identified, became the subject of considerable study—and some derision. Some physicians have written disparagingly about the bored, neurotic wives who clutter their offices hoping to find a medical reason for their malaise. Housewives do consult doctors more often than men and single women do, and they are more likely to use and misuse such drugs as tranquilizers, barbiturates, and amphetamines (Fidell and Prather 1976; Bart 1971). Some writers have criticized American housewives as demanding, lazy, and domineering (see Philip Wylie's portrait of "mom" in *Generation of Vipers*). Some have argued that there is nothing wrong with marriage that a fascinating woman, a total woman, a *real* woman can't fix.

It is important to remember than there *are* many happy house-wives in this country. As the glorification of family togetherness in the fifties gave way to feminism, the political pundits swung from trying to prove that all wives are contented to trying to prove that all of them are miserable (or ought to be). The real question is, who is which and why? A study by Myra Marx Ferree (1976) narrowed down the conditions that cause a housewife to blossom or wither.

Ferree's sample consisted of 135 working-class women from the Boston area. About half of them worked outside the home, but not in glamorous professions: They were supermarket and department-store clerks, waitresses, typists, beauticians, and so on. Yet the wives who held jobs were happier and more satisfied with their lives than the full-time housewives. Ferree speculated that housewives lack the social contact with customers and coworkers, and the regular paycheck, that bolster self-esteem and create a sense of accomplishment. Housewives typically lack recognition for the work they do; for that matter, there are no clear criteria for a job well done. Among Ferree's housewives, only one in fourteen said she was extremely good at taking care of a home, while three out of four felt incompetent. Most of the working wives (67 percent) also claimed to be poor homemakers. But *not one* of the employed wives said she felt incompetent at her job, and over half said they were extremely good.

Ferree went on to see what allowed some of her housewives to feel happy with their lives and competent in their roles. The answer was that the happy housewives see family and friends regularly, and that their husbands and relatives value their work and give them moral support. They feel neither loneliness nor boredom, moods that are highly correlated with watching television and doing house-work—the primary activities of alienated housewives (Shaver and Freedman 1976; Rubenstein and Shaver 1982).

Not so long ago, housewives lived near their mothers, sisters, and other family members for most of their lives, and they formed close-knit groups that exchanged support and help as well as news and advice. In recent decades, however, high job mobility and the exodus to the suburbs have broken up the extended family and stable neighborhood patterns. When housework and child care became a solo pastime, it became a lonely one. Ferree's working wives said they had felt they were "going crazy staying home, not seeing anyone but four walls all day." Full-time housewifery, said one woman, "is like being in jail."

It was not always thus. In her comprehensive history of house-work Susan Strasser (1982) described the massive amount of productive and maintenance work that nineteenth-century housewives did: doing laundry with tubs, washboards, and flatirons; growing and preserving food; sewing and mending; cleaning filthy kerosene lamps; refilling mattresses with new straw; endlessly hauling water and tending fires; making soap and candles; and of course cooking—which, before the household use of gas and electricity, was "hard, hot, heavy, and even hazardous." Without romanticizing this hard and painful work, Strasser argued that earlier generations of housewives *did* have the satisfaction of doing work that needed doing. Modern women have less of the hard work, but also fewer satisfactions from it.

There are working conditions to a housewife's job, in other words, as there are to any other job, and these conditions can produce satisfied "employees" or unhappy ones. Ann Oakley (1974) observed that housewives who seem to have an obsessive determination to keep their homes orderly and immaculate are in fact behaving rationally:

> Faced with housework as their job, they devise rules which give the work the kind of structure most employed workers automatically find in their job situation. Having defined the rules they then attempt to adhere to them, and to derive reward from carrying them out. Since housework is not paid and husbands are by and large uncritical appraisers of their wives' work in the home, self-reward for housework activity is virtually the only kind housewives can hope to experience. (p. 95)

Sadly, self-reward is difficult, and for many wives it is not enough. Research has overwhelmingly confirmed the health benefits (to both sexes) of having two roles instead of one: work and family life. Just as unmarried men have a higher illness risk, so do unemployed women:

1. Using a national sample of 389 women aged forty to fifty-nine (206 of whom were employed full or part time, 183 of whom were full-time homemakers), researchers Lerita Coleman and Toni Antonucci analyzed dozens of factors they thought might affect a woman's well-being—that is, her self-acceptance and self-esteem, her lack of depression and anxiety. Of all those factors, including income, education, marital status, and presence or absence of children in the home, *only one* was related to self-esteem: employment. "Moreover," they added, "employment is also one of the most important predictors of physical health and lack of psychological anxiety."[9]

[9]This study was reported in the Newsletter (Winter 1982) of the Institute for Social Research, University of Michigan.

2. Using a large, representative sample of 5,000 women, white and black, interviewed in 1967 and again in 1977, researchers explored the effects of employment on health (Waldron 1982). Working women were less likely than unemployed women to report psychophysiological symptoms (a measure of lack of well-being and poor physical health), especially among women who had positive attitudes about working outside the home. Most of the unemployed women (white or black, with high or low levels of education) reported more psychophysiological symptoms than their counterparts in the labor force, and those who were worst off were those who were unemployed but wanted to work.

3. Using a random sample of 1,111 men and women in Boston, researchers wondered whether the higher rates of depression among women are a result of social roles or something specific to women (Gore and Mangione 1984). They found that *all of the differences between men and women in reported levels of depression could be accounted for by their different states of marriage and work*. That is, men were nearly twice as likely as women to be married and working full time (62 percent to 33 percent), the two-role combination that is advantageous to health (see also Baucom 1983).

4. Using a random sample of 458 English working-class women, sociologists George Brown and Tirril Harris (1978) identified several factors that predicted which of the women would succumb to clinical depression: lacking an intimate relationship with her husband, losing her mother before age eleven, having three or more children under the age of fourteen living at home, and lacking outside employment.

What happens when bright, college-educated women avoid careers and choose a traditional family path? Judith Birnbaum (1975) studied women who had graduated with honors from the University of Michigan fifteen to twenty-five years earlier, selecting twenty-nine who had married, borne children, and sought no further education or employment. For comparison, she also interviewed twenty-five married women with children and twenty-seven single women, all of whom were Ph.D.'s on the Michigan faculty or M.D.'s. Birnbaum found that of the three groups, as shown in Table 8, the homemakers had the lowest self-esteem and felt the worst about their competence—even at child care and getting along with people. They felt the least attractive, worried most about personal identity, and most often felt lonely. The only thing the professional women said they missed was enough time to do all the things they wanted, but the homemakers said they missed challenge and creative involvement.

Most poignant of all, the married professionals were happier with their marriages than the housewives who were devoting all their time to their families. In answer to the question, "How does marriage change a woman's life?" the housewives were far more likely than the married professionals to respond negatively. More than half of them (52 percent) said that marriage is restricting, burdensome, and demanding, compared to 19 percent in the professional group.

For many housewives, it seems, the absence of rewards for a job well done, social isolation, and financial dependence on their husbands create feelings of helplessness and hopelessness, which in turn lead to depression and loss of self-esteem. Work apparently gives people a sense of mastery—control over life events—that marriage and children do not provide. A housewife has relatively little control over decisions that affect her (she may have to move because of her husband's career advancement, for example), and feeling helpless is a step toward depression (Stewart and Salt 1981; Crosby 1981).

Further, many studies have shown that the more income the wife brings in, the more power she has in the family and the more she participates in decisions. This is true for wives of all races and classes. And the higher the husband's status, occupational prestige, and income, the greater his power in family decisions. So full-time housewives lack power as well as autonomy. Because the husband's income-producing job has higher status than the wife's job as homemaker, his needs and wants come first. Dair Gillespie (1976) argued that despite the egalitarian philosophy of most American marriages, husbands and wives have vastly unequal legal rights and obligations, financial resources, and power. "Women are *structurally* deprived of equal opportunities to develop their capacities, resources, and competence in competition with males," she observed.

the working-wife syndrome

Many wives today are caught in a double bind. If they do not work outside the home, they have a high chance of coming down with housewife syndrome—feelings of depression and incompetence, and psychosomatic ailments such as insomnia and stomach aches. If they do work, they have an advantage over housewives in having higher self-esteem, greater power and participation in family decision-making, and fewer psychological and physical symptoms. The catch-22 is that marriage and work are in greater conflict for women than for men: The accommodation of the job's demands to family needs rests on women. A married mother who works has two

Table 8. Some Findings on the Health and Happiness of Married Professionals, and Single Professionals

	House-wives N = 29	Mar... fess... N =	
Self-esteem score (competence in five areas: domestic, social, child care, cultural, intellectual)			
Poor to average	31%	4%	15%
Average to good	55	42	31
Good to very good	14	54	54
Mental-emotional health			
Poor to average	39	12	12
Good to very good	61	88	88
Feelings of uncertainty about who you are and what you want			
Hardly ever	34	64	58
Fairly often	66	36	42
Feeling lonely			
Hardly ever	28	72	27
Sometimes too often	72	28	73
Would like to have more friends	40	12	11
Misses challenge and creativity	42	4	0
Feels "not very" attractive to men	61	12	58
Very happily married	52	68	—

SOURCE: Birnbaum 1975.

jobs; a married father who works has one. Some women, such as the housewives in Ferree's study, take jobs that pay less or are less challenging in order to reduce pressure. They get the benefits of combining work and family with less strain—but less income, too. Other women opt for the whole show—a more-than-full-time career and a family.

How stressful and difficult is it to combine work and family? For most employed wives the psychological protection of having two roles compensates for the extra obligations, and contentment at work is positively associated with contentment at home (Crosby 1982). *Role strain*, a concept dear to the hearts of sociologists, seems to be

haracteristic of a specific group of employed wives than of all
em: namely, women who are trying to combine high-prestige
reers with having families (most female sociologists themselves, of
course, fall into this category). If we want to answer that old question—Why have so few women become famous inventors, politicians, scientists, and artists?—we need to understand the obstacles in
their way.

Traditional wives, a category that includes the vast majority of
women whether they work or not, take care of cleaning, shopping,
meals, laundry, sewing, child care and babysitters, and what Bernard
calls "stroking." Part of a wife's role is to listen to her husband's
troubles and bolster his ego. These support functions of a wife free
her husband for other concerns. Ernest Hemingway wrote novels,
and Mary Hemingway ran his estate. Einstein could pursue a problem
long into the night because Mrs. Einstein saw to dinner. Presidents
have time for politicking because their wives raised the babies.

Sociologists Rose Coser and Gerald Rokoff (1971) observed that
our primary role allegiances are strongly sex typed: "A man owes to
his profession what a woman owes to her family." The prestige
professions of men, Coser and Rokoff believe, require "selflessness
and a devotion to a calling." Think of the scientist who sacrifices
fame for the love of his work. But in another sense real professional
achievement requires great selfishness. If you are hot on the trail of a
breakthrough in biochemistry, if you have a brilliant idea for the third
chapter of your novel, if you have a legal brief that must be ready by
9:00 A.M. tomorrow, you must selfishly seize the time. If you are
worried about feeding the family, dusting the bookshelves, or cheer-
ing up your spouse who had a lousy day, you may not finish the task.

Note that we are talking about selfishness not as a personality
trait but as a *role requirement*. Most jobs require a fixed amount of
participation, and people know they can be fired if they fool around
with the rules. A male bus driver or a businessman may not want to
leave a sick wife or child in order to work, but he may feel he must.
Other careers simply are so demanding that they cannot accommodate people who would prefer to be flexible about hours and time
with family. Some men and women today are deciding that professional achievement is not worth the pressure to behave egocentri-
cally, but at the moment we are not talking about what should be or
could be, but about what is. Currently, the "is" means that fewer
women than men have been structurally able to meet the demands of
full-time careers, because women don't have wives to take care
of them.

Thus many women face a dilemma at the heart of their lives: how to strike a balance between the "selfless" pleasures of giving and loving and the "selfish" pleasures of finding their own way in the working world. Those women who do try for careers that demand more time and attention than a 9-to-5 job may receive more financial and psychological rewards than the average female worker, but they also face special dilemmas. Margaret Poloma (1972) studied fifty-three couples in which the wife was actively working in law, medicine, or college teaching, professions that are predominantly male and require extended training and personal investment. Poloma wanted to know how these women managed their roles as wives and professionals. Most of her interviewees juggled their jobs and families with four kinds of "tension-management techniques":

1. They looked at the benefits, rather than the costs, of combining career and family. As one woman explained, "I am a better mother *because* I work and can expend my energies on something other than the overmothering of my children."

2. They decided in advance which role to emphasize, in case of conflicting demands, and in virtually every case family crises took precedence over career crises. When the babysitter didn't show up or a child got sick, the wife, not the husband, missed work that day.

3. They compartmentalized the two roles as much as possible, keeping work and family distinct. Few of the women brought work home with them, for example, though their husbands did often. One lawyer wouldn't talk about her practice at home, said Poloma, so that "the children would not think that her work was more important than their father's."

4. They compromised. The wives controlled the extent of their career commitment to fit the circumstances of their family lives—how the husband's work was going, his income, the ages and number of children, the husband's support (or lack of it), and so on. "When one or more of these factors is out of kilter, the wife makes the necessary adjustment to manage role strain," Poloma found. "She generally expects little and asks nothing of the family to better enable her to adjust to family and career demands."

A decade later it is still up to the wives to resolve role conflicts, the way Poloma's interviewees did. Professional women studied by Colleen and Frank Johnson (1981) reported feelings of "being drained," "emotionally leeched," "overwhelmed," "guilty." One woman physician said: "I come home and I just don't have anything to give to Paul—that is a terrible feeling. I feel it's not worth it—I resent my job. Then I resent myself for being so damned conscientious—to give so much at work and have to be reserved at home." Men too can feel role strain between balancing home and work, of course; in a national survey of workers, about 35 percent of the men and women said that family life and job interfere with each other somewhat or a lot (Crosby 1982). But the *nature* of that interference is different for women and men. Men complain of overwork; women, of scheduling problems and exhaustion. In the Johnsons' study, when the husbands reported feeling role strain, their remarks were vague and unemotional: A man might say, "Well, occasionally it gets a bit busy, but we manage to work it out." It was the wives, though, who did most of the working it out.

Coser and Rokoff note that every time a professional woman compromises in favor of her family, or stays home to wait for the babysitter, she confirms the prejudice that women don't really want to achieve and are not really serious about their work. Thus is another self-fulfilling prophesy created: Because women do the compromising when family and career demands conflict, fewer job opportunities are open to them, and career commitments become, for some, too heavy a burden.

The good news, though, is that the unquestionable benefits of having at least two roles are outweighing the possible strains of combining them. "Role strain" is even fading from the sociological lexicon (Epstein 1983), as sociologists are beginning to study the ways that role combinations protect psychological and physical health. As Epstein concluded from her research on women lawyers:

> The essence of successful role management is that it is done in conjunction with others. Friends and relatives have to be amenable to the new rules. The successful women I have studied had in common one crucial element—the goodwill and supportiveness of others in their lives on their way to "having it all." (p. 103).

of housework and husbands

You may have wondered, in the discussion of the conflicts of working women, why husbands don't take some of the pressure off their wives. A good question—but most of them don't. In spite of the increasing number of married women who work, there seems to be no corresponding, significant increase in the number of married men who are doing more at home. The result, that many women have two jobs instead of one, is true all over the world. Yugoslavian husbands don't like household chores any more than Peruvian husbands do.

An international team of social scientists, under the direction of Alexander Szalai, a Hungarian sociologist, did an enormous study on how people spend their time. Two thousand citizens in each of twelve countries[10] filled out minute-by-minute diaries covering a twenty-four hour period in their lives. This extraordinary survey showed, first of all, that housewives have not been liberated by technology or by jobs. In countries that have a rich supply of washers, dryers, and other modern conveniences, women spend as much time on home and family chores as do women in countries where housewives still chop their own wood. The average women in Osnabruck, West Germany, has all the appliances she wants, yet she spends as much time doing housework—within a minute—as a wife in Kragujevac, Yugoslavia, who still draws water from a well (Szalai 1972).

Another sociologist, Joann Vanek (1974), found that the hours devoted to housework are remarkably constant not only across technological and national boundaries but across time as well. Today's average American housewife puts in as many hours as her grandmother did forty years ago: about fifty-three hours a week. True, noted Vanek, some jobs have become less time consuming, such as sewing, cooking, and meal cleanup. But women still spend exactly as much time—in some studies, even more time—transporting children and husbands from place to place. "Contemporary women spend about one full working day per week on the road and in stores compared with less than two hours per week for women in the 1920s," Vanek said. Parkinson's Law, which states that activities swell to fill the available time, must be operating. Vanek added that because the value of housework and the criteria for a completed job are unclear, women apparently feel pressure to spend long hours at it (see also Oakley 1974).

Working wives spend less time than housewives on daily chores, averaging twenty-six hours a week. They aren't spending less time because they're getting more help, though. Vanek found that working wives are no more likely than housewives to have paid help—and no more likely to be helped by their husbands. "Contrary to popular belief," she said, "American husbands do not share the responsibilities of household work. They spend only a few hours a week at it, and most of what they do is shopping." As a result, working wives have about ten fewer hours of free time each week than either

[10]Belgium, Bulgaria, Czechoslovakia, East Germany, France, Hungary, Peru, Poland, the Soviet Union, the United States, West Germany, and Yugoslavia.

housewives or employed men. Working wives use weekends to catch up on the cleaning and shopping. Working husbands use weekends to do odd chores, and then catch up on their rest, watch TV, or play sports. As the family grows larger, the husband's participation *decreases*. He does less child care, housework, and cooking. The wife's housework time, however, increases between 5 and 10 percent with each child, whether she works or not. These time statistics were still true as of 1983 (NOW Legal Defense Fund, personal communication): On the average, employed wives spend twenty-six hours a week on housework—their husbands, thirty-six minutes.

Why don't husbands do more? Possibly for the same reasons that little boys won't play with "girls' toys"—women's work is less valued and threatens masculinity. Possibly because housework isn't much fun. Or possibly because the wives don't want them to. Nancy and John Robinson (1975), using a national sample of American households, found that only 19 percent of the women they interviewed said they wanted more help from their husbands. The majority of American men and women are more willing to accept equality for women in the marketplace than in the home; housework, they say, is the woman's responsibility (Osmond and Martin 1975). Perhaps this is because women learn early that housework is a central part of their feminine role; indeed, single women spend one to two hours more per day on housework than single men do, and only twenty minutes less per day than do young wives without children. Single (and divorced) men, it seems, still prefer to pay a woman to do housework or to leave it undone rather than to do it themselves. In one city a man can call "Rent-a-Wife" and, for $25 an hour or $600 a week, a woman will do his shopping, chores, redecorating, and other household tasks (Strasser 1982).[11]

The roles of husband and wife currently assign the bulk of the housework and child care to women. This frees men to pursue

[11]Most married housewives don't earn anywhere near this sum from their husbands. In recent years social scientists have begun to appreciate the importance of the housewife's work and to try to assign it some monetary value. The calculations can get complicated. One way to come up with an estimate is to apply the going wage to all the jobs the housewife does, such as babysitter, cook, decorator, housekeeper, dishwasher, and chauffeur. Insurance companies, which estimate a wife's value to her family in the event of her death, put the cost of her yearly services at $25,000 (Steinem 1983). But no social scientist has figured the value of housework the way a New York jury did in 1974. A man whose wife had been injured in a car crash had to do all the housework by himself for two whole months. The jury, sympathetic to his plight, awarded him $56,000. *Newsweek*, which reported the story, could not resist remarking that not even the woman's movement had suggested that a housewife's job is worth $336,000 a year. If it were, you can bet more men would be doing it.

professional or leisure activities, but it also deprives them of something they might enjoy: time with the children. Sociologist Philip Stone (1972) used Szalai's international time data to study the amount of time spent on child care in the twelve countries. He found that women—working or not—spent far more time with children than their husbands did. In only one nation, the Soviet Union, did husbands and working wives spend the same amount of workday time with their children, and even there, on weekends the mothers tried more than the fathers did to catch up. Overall, fathers from Eastern European countries spent more time with their children than fathers from Western countries did. Can you guess how much time per day the average American father spent with his children? A half hour? An hour? Two hours? The correct answer is twelve minutes.

That startling "twelve minutes" statistic continues to show up (see Pleck and Lang 1978), although there is some debate about whether men are doing more housework and child care than they used to—and, if they are, whether they are happy about it or not. In national-sample surveys, men *are* reporting more involvement with their families and greater psychological well-being and happiness from their families than from work (Veroff, Douvan, and Kulka 1981). But one in-depth study of 160 middle-class Boston families suggests that men are happiest when they have the least to do at home.

The researchers, Grace Baruch and Rosalind Barnett, reported good news and bad news about men's domestic involvement. The greater a man's participation in his family life (from doing chores to taking care of the children), the more competent and involved he feels as a father, and the less sex-stereotyped his children are (especially his sons). But it did not seem that such fathers were motivated by love for their wives or a desire to share family responsibilities equally: The more housework and child care a man did, the less satisfied he was with his marriage, and the more he grumbled about loss of leisure and career time.[12] A massive survey of 6,000 U.S. couples found exactly the same thing (Blumstein and Schwartz 1983).

the family battleground

The sociological perspective says that to understand the reasons for the war between the sexes, we must look not to their different personalities but to their different roles, power, and statuses. When

[12]The preliminary report on this study was described in the April 1983 edition of *Second Century Radcliffe News*.

husbands and wives are hostile and abusive to each other, it's easy to look for psychological explanations ("His mother treated him badly"; "She's insecure") or to resort to name-calling ("He's a bastard"; "She's a bitch"). But psychological and physical abuse can be better explained by sociological factors than individual ones (Straus, Gelles, and Steinmetz 1980): factors such as occupation, income, unemployment, the distribution of power in the household, the concentration of decision making in the hands of one spouse.

Thus, for example, in families in which one spouse feels "underpowered"—that is, lacking in deserved power or influence—arguments and abuse are more prevalent than in families in which both spouses feel appropriately powerful (McElfresh 1982). Note that we did not mention sex of spouse in that sentence, because it doesn't matter. Whether the wife feels she has less power than she should, or whether the husband does, it is the imbalance that leads to family conflict.

Similarly, we discussed earlier that housewives who do not bring income into the family tend to have lower self-esteem than employed wives and to feel that they love their husbands more than their husbands love them (Shaver and Freedman 1976; Birnbaum 1975; Hochschild 1975). But in the 10 percent of working couples where the wife earns more than the husband, the husbands behave and feel like stereotyped housewives—their self-esteem drops, and they complain that they love their wives more than their wives love them (Rubenstein 1982).

Finally, just as Birnbaum described the psychological consequences for women who are underachievers (that is, who do not work at jobs commensurate with their education and training, or who do not work at all), so there are negative consequences for men under such conditions. Rubenstein (1982), reviewing several studies, reported that men who are working at jobs beneath their educational attainments (for example, husbands with law degrees who are driving taxis) and who, in addition, are married to women who are working above their educational level (for example, wives with two years of college who have become company managers) have a much higher than normal risk of heart disease. In such families both spouses are unhappy; their sex life tends to suffer, they often psychologically and physically abuse each other, their divorce rate is high.

It would seem to follow that equality between the sexes would be an important step toward marital harmony. On this point, two theories conflict. One says that violence against women is the ultimate weapon men use to maintain patriarchal authority; as women struggle for equality, therefore, violence against them should increase. The second theory argues that violence is a *result* of inequality, and therefore the struggle for equality will bring a decrease in violence.

Two sociologists have found that both theories are right, up to a point. Kersti Yllo (1983) and Yllo and Murray Straus (1981), reanalyzing a national random sample of 2,143 husbands and wives, found a curvilinear relationship between equality and violence. In states where women have the lowest economic, educational, political, and legal status, the rate of wife abuse is the highest. As women's status increases, violence against them decreases. But in the states in which women have relatively high status (in no state are they truly equal), the violence rate rises again, suggesting a male effort to maintain power or control (see Figure 5).

When the researchers next looked at violence by wives against husbands, the picture got clearer. As women's status increases, so does their violence against husbands. In the states in which women have very low status, the rate of violence against them is *double* the rate of their violence against husbands. In contrast, in higher-status states, the amount of violence committed by husbands and wives against each other is about the same (5.1 percent versus 5.9 percent). In the lower status states, Yllo and Straus suggested, wives are more or less forced to accept beatings from their husbands because they are economically dependent on the marriage. When wives begin to earn their own way . . . they fight back.

This interpretation suggests that income might have something to do with marital violence, and it does. As Rubenstein's overview also found, as the status of women rises and so does a wife's income, men become threatened by the breakdown of traditional roles and the rapid social change—and women do, too—which in turn produces domestic conflict and unhappiness. But, as Yllo observed, we really can't say yet whether true equality will reduce this conflict, because we haven't got there yet.

The American family is clearly in a time of transition. The traditional family, with the husband as provider and the wife as housekeeper, began in the early nineteenth century and lasted, according to Jessie Bernard (1981), until 1980, when the U.S. Census Bureau stopped specifying the man as "head of household." As the male role of the good provider became synonymous with affluence and commercial success, Bernard observed, the husband's powers grew and those of the housewife, who lacked cash income, waned.

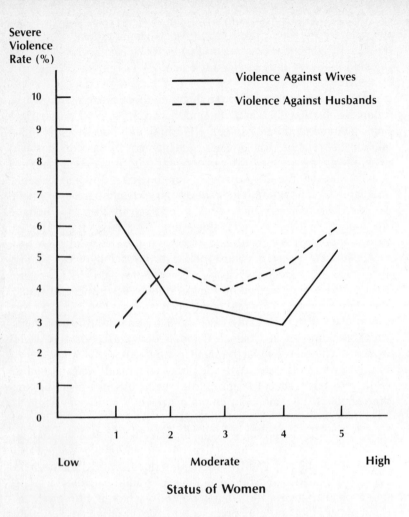

Figure 5. Violence against wives and against husbands, in relation to the status of women. The rankings of women's status are based on cumulative ratings in four spheres: *economic* (such as percentage of women in labor force and in specific occupations, income discrepancy between sexes); *educational* (such as percentage of female high-school and college graduates, of female interscholastic athletes, and of high-school administrators); *political* (such as percentage of women in state senate); and *legal* (such as no occupations barred to women, equal pay laws, unrestricted property rights for wives, state equal rights amendment). No state was truly egalitarian on all, or even most, of these measures.

SOURCE: From Yllo 1983.

Yet just as the solo role of housewife became psychologically detrimental to many women, so the single role of breadwinner or good provider had psychological hazards for many men. "As the pampered wife in an affluent household came often to be an economic parasite," wrote Bernard, "so also the good provider was often, in a way, a kind of emotional parasite."

In the past two decades, as women entered the labor force, the power and prerogatives of the good provider have been diluted—and men have become disenchanted with the constraints and disadvantages of the good-provider role (Veroff, Douvan, and Kulka 1981; Ehrenreich 1983; Pleck 1981). But this does not mean that sex-role equality is on the way. Bernard believes that the increasing numbers of employed women have put the family through a "subtle revolution": They have weakened male financial authority in the home and increased demands on men to be emotionally invested in the family, to spend more time with the children. These efforts for change have not pleased most men, says Bernard; instead they have increased the sense of the burdensomeness of marriage.

In short, Bernard concluded, "the good-provider role may be on its way out, but its legitimate successor has not yet appeared on the scene."[13]

evaluating the sociological perspective

The sociological perspective explores the ways in which all of us are products of the roles we play and the situations we are in. Our motivations and preferences may lead us to choose one job over another, or one kind of marriage over another, but it is also true that jobs and social relations will affect our feelings, attitudes, and self-esteem. In this view, men are not achievement oriented or aggressive or dominant primarily because they were raised that way or have masculine genes, but because the structure and requirements of their careers and marriages encourage and foster these qualities, withholding from them the opportunities to be more nurturant and family oriented. And women haven't the time to make it to the top of a profession unless they forego children, get outside help, or postpone career decisions until the children are grown. It was easier for Golda Meir to manage Israel as a grandmother than it would have been for her as a young mother.

[13]For a discussion of one such contender, the dual-career couple, see Chapter 9.

This perspective can give people cause for optimism, because it argues that we are not prisoners of childhood. We are not programed for life by age five (as many Freudians would say) or by age fifteen (as many developmental psychologists would say). As adult roles change, as the economy creates opportunities or restricts them, as market forces shift, then adults change too. Theories that propose a consistency between childhood experiences and adult personality were all formulated when people's lives were consistent from childhood to adulthood, when rowdy little boys grew into aggressive company managers, when passive little girls grew into dependent housewives. In recent generations many people have faced tremendous social and economic changes, and this consistency has been broken: Plenty of rowdy little boys now become laid-back lute players, and the passive little girls have learned to manage jobs, bankbooks, and families after all (see Brim and Kagan 1980). As Lykes and Stewart (1982) found, career achievement for women is no longer related to childhood factors, such as whether or not their mothers worked, their childhood ambitions, their socioeconomic backgrounds; it is related to adult experience and training.

Conversely, with the decline of the good-provider role, the criteria upon which men have based their sense of masculinity have changed. Not so long ago, no self-respecting, successful white man would tolerate having a wife who worked outside the home; such a thing was an insult to his manhood. Quite soon, it was all right for the wife to work, as long as she didn't make more money than he did. Now it is even all right for her to make more money—if she's not working in his field or in a "masculine" career. These rapidly evolving changes in masculine norms suggest that equality would not be a biological impossibility for either sex, and that people adjust their ideas of what a "real" man or a "real" woman is to accord with the needs and demands of their lives.

Thus the sociological view forces us to think about causes and effects in a different way. For example, consider attitudes about having children. In this century norms about the right number of children to have—and even about whether to have children at all— have swung wildly. Sometimes the norms have been pro-birth: It is every woman's duty to have as many children as possible. Sometimes the norms have been anti-birth: It is a woman's duty not to bring children into this troubled and overpopulated world. Sometimes the norms have emphasized the woman's duty to herself instead of her duty to her children: A talented woman should pursue her own career unencumbered by children. Sometimes the norms conflict: A woman should have children, but also liberate herself. In some generations women who wanted no children were considered sick, selfish, or neurotic; they were "childless" women. Today such women are admired, tolerated, or at worst pitied; they are "childfree" women.

Why the changes? First notice the shifts in birthrates that have corresponded to these changing norms. The most "childfree" cohort of American women was the cohort born between 1906 and 1910 (Davis 1982). Among these women, who came of childbearing age just before and during the Great Depression, fully 30 percent of the black women and 21 percent of the white women had no children at all, and 32 percent and 25 percent, respectively, had only one child. After World War II the birth rate climbed; women left the factories and went home to have babies—lots of them. The average wife in the 1950s had four children; after 1960, however, the birth rate went into a sharp and steady decline, to an eventual average of 1.8 children per family.

It has often been argued that the birth control pill and worries about world overpopulation caused the latest decline in the birth rate, which in turn caused women to enter the labor force (since they had more free time on their hands). But it is just as plausible to argue that the troubled economy (inflation) and new service jobs (which needed women) brought women into the labor force, which in turn caused the decline in the birth rate, which in turn justified having fewer children. Davis (1982), tracing the rise and fall of the birth rate among women born between 1895 and 1920, found that when women needed to limit their childbearing—specifically in the hard economic times of the Depression—they did. They didn't have the pill, perhaps, but they used every other sort of family-planning method they could. (Davis's analysis rules out other explanations for the changing birth rate, such as different ages at marriage, mothers' education, maternal and fetal health rates.)

Cause-and-effect is not a one-way street, of course, but we are arguing simply for looking in both directions. If the economy improves and "women's work" becomes superfluous, we could still see a return of 1950s' family size and a pro-birth ideology. But if women have become committed to working and to having smaller families, sex roles may continue to evolve in unforeseen directions.

One strength of the sociological perspective is also its weakness. Understanding how the system works can save people from blaming themselves when such blame is inappropriate, and it can energize people to change institutions. But is can also provide an excuse for resignation and inactivity ("Don't blame me—it's the system that makes me this way"). Which of these occurs may depend on how deeply powerless people feel—or, to put it more sociologically, on how powerless they in fact are.

Sometimes one hears that if women ran the world we would greet a humane new era. In this view, because women are more nurturant, empathic, and sensitive than men, because they are closer to birth and the mysteries of life, they wouldn't get this planet into wars and tyrannies; if mothers ruled the world, no son of theirs would ever see battle. This idea is based on the same assumption as the one that claims women are emotionally unfit for political office—namely, that the sexes are fundamentally different. But the sociological view predicts that women who are cast into positions of authority will behave just as men do, neither better nor worse. Certainly Indira Gandhi has been just as authoritarian, and Margaret Thatcher just as ready for war, as any male leader. To be sure, these women were sole females in otherwise male-dominated systems. Nowhere on earth is there a system in which men and women truly share political power or in which women dominate. If we ever get a chance to observe one, we can see whether women bring "feminine" traits to office or whether office drums "masculine" traits into them.

This chapter has argued that the way a society sets up its work and family organizations determines how men and women will behave, what their ambitions will be, what opportunities they can reach for. The next question to ask is: How did the system get to be the way it is? No one sat at a pinnacle of power and decided what work would be open to women and what to men. So now we will move to the next perspective and explore some theories about the origin and function of sex differences across societies and throughout history.

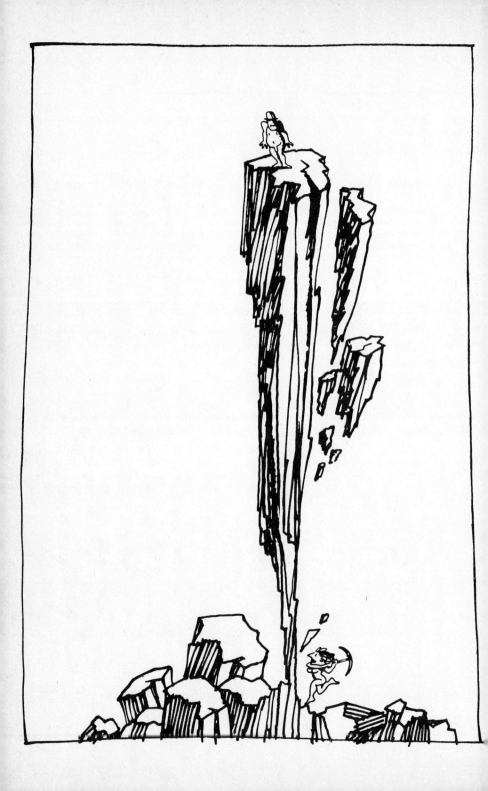

8 | The origins of roles and rituals: The anthropological perspective

In 1973 a Lebanese man choked his fifteen-year-old daughter to death because she "flirted with boys." He was given a presidential pardon. In 1977 one of the brothers of King Khalid of Saudi Arabia drowned his unmarried daughter in a swimming pool because she had been to bed with a man. He was exonerated; in fact, he was congratulated. When the Ayatollah Khomeini took power in Iran, one of his first acts, symbolizing the new regime's return to religious fundamentalism, was to restore a dress code for women. Khomeini's original decree specified the observance of *purdah*—the veiling and seclusion of wives—but the protest of thousands of women succeeded in modifying that decree somewhat. Women who work are not required to wear the veil, but to "dress modestly" with no part of the body or hair exposed.

Throughout many Islamic cultures of the Middle East and India, various versions of purdah are practiced. Purdah is the extreme form of segregation of the sexes; the word itself is Persian, meaning curtain or barrier (Fernea and Fernea 1979). Indeed, purdah is the barrier between the "women's sphere" of the private home and the "men's sphere" of public life, although sometimes purdah has been honored more as an idea than in practice: Poor village men, for example, have not usually veiled or secluded their wives because women have been needed to work in the fields or in cottage industries. But in the cities and among the wealthy classes, women have had to veil their faces before virtually any man—even men in their own households.

Thousands of miles and a century removed from the Middle East, on this continent, Iroquois women lived a very different life. They had high status and wielded significant political and economic influence. Although women could not join the highest ruling body, the Council of Elders, some of the older wives (matrons) had power to influence decisions of the Council, including those on war and peace treaties (Brown 1975; Sanday 1981). Iroquois matrons helped select, and could become, the tribe's religious leaders, and they reigned supreme in their households. The matrons guarded the tribe's treasury of stored food and valuables, and they had the right to dispense these goods, even those that had been acquired by men. An Iroquois male offended a matron at his peril.

How shall we account for the different status of women among these societies? The perspective described in this chapter represents the broadest level of explanation. It takes as its unit of analysis not the individual, not the family, not even social roles, but entire societies. Each perspective in this book raises questions for its successor: There may be biological and anatomical differences between males and females, but how do those affect personality differences? Personality differences may be learned, but why are boys and girls socialized differently? Boys and girls may learn different lessons as they grow up because their society profits from a division of labor, but why does one society divide the sexes rigidly and brutally and another not?

In trying to understand human behavior, most people cannot see the forest for the trees. The trees are the fascinating rituals (circumcision, couvade), the inconsistent attitudes (woman on a pedestal, woman in the gutter), and the apparently arbitrary sex-role assignments (women tend the chickens, men tend the cows). The anthropological perspective makes us look at the forest—the whole package of economic and environmental factors that produced a given culture and its customs. Anthropologists use tribes the way psychologists use individuals: to isolate a unit for study. By collecting and describing thousands of these social units, anthropologists have demonstrated the remarkable plasticity of human nature.

This very plasticity—the variety of male–female relations and family arrangements and sexual customs—has been and still is a source of energetic debate among anthropologists, who of course cannot help but bring their own cultural biases to the societies they observe. For many years that bias was male: Male anthropologists understandably emphasized the roles and power of men, and they often were oblivious of and insensitive to the women they studied. As women entered the field in greater numbers, they helped correct this distortion. The image of "man the hunter" was balanced by that of "woman the gatherer" (Dahlberg 1981). The idea that our species is "naturally" warlike and competitive was countered by the evidence that we are just as naturally peaceful and cooperative (Tanner and Zihlman 1976). Female anthropologists reanalyzed old studies with new results: Whereas Bronislaw Malinowski, in his famous work on the Trobriand Islanders, had emphasized male economic and political control, Annette Weiner (1976), interpreting the Trobrianders from a woman's perspective, was able to demonstrate the power that female Trobrianders had in their own right.

But even as they have shattered old myths, modern anthropologists have modern biases to contend with. One battle currently raging in the field, for example, pits those who argue that male supremacy is universal against those who believe it is not. Feminists and anti-feminists alike are to be found in both camps. Some men, such as George Gilder, use the notion of universal male dominance to argue that that's the way we are built, it's inevitable, we might as well accept it. But some feminists use the same notion to argue that although change is feasible, equality will require a long struggle. Anthropologist Michelle Rosaldo (1980) put it this way:

> My reading of the anthropological record leads me to conclude that human cultural and social forms have always been male dominated. By this, I mean not that men rule by right or even that men rule at all and certainly not that women everywhere are passive victims of a world that men define. Rather, I would . . . argue that in all known human groups—and no matter the prerogatives that women may in fact enjoy—the vast majority of opportunities for public influence and prestige, the ability to forge relationships, determine enmities, speak up in public, use or forswear the use of force are all recognized as men's privilege and right. (pp. 393–94)

As anthropologist Bonnie A. Nardi (1982) summarized the research, "There is no evidence of truly egalitarian societies. In no societies do women participate on an equal footing with men in activities accorded the highest prestige." In particular, she noted four reasons that no society so far can be considered egalitarian:

1. Childbearing is not a role that accords women prestige.

2. Men control women in marriage exchanges.

3. Male activities are universally more highly valued than female activities are.

4. Men control the political sphere and dominate politically.

Although Nardi agrees with other anthropologists that women do have key economic roles in many cultures and that they often play key roles in group rituals, she maintains that women are always dominated by men in "the decision-making sphere."

In contrast, anthropologist Karla Poewe (1980) has called the belief in universal male dominance "an ethnological delusion": "Our obsession with dichotomies and our need to ground explanations in biology have channeled studies about male–female relations into a male dominated cul-de-sac." That is, our Western tendency to see the world in either-or terms, in simple categories (male/female, nature/nurture, dominant/submissive), has blinded us to the subtleties and complexities of human life—often making us *impose* categories where none exist. Poewe argued that there is a range of possible and actual relations between men and women, ranging from male dominance and sexual antagonism to a balance of power and sexual affinity. Similarly, Karen Sacks (1976, 1979) asserted that anthropologists have been reluctant to recognize sexual equality when they see it—if a tribe's kind of sexual equality doesn't meet Western notions. Because in our society separate never has been equal, we assume that when men and women have different roles, the women must be inferior or powerless (Schlegel 1977; see also Rogers 1975).

Politics, in short, can influence the observations of contemporary feminist anthropologists even as it influenced the observations of traditionally male-biased anthropologists. We agree with Poewe's criticism of Western bias, for example, but she has a bias of her own: Marxism (which we discuss on pages 319–20, 339–42). Because many Marxists believe that the oppression of women is a relatively recent invention—a result of capitalism and colonization (Etienne and Leacock 1980)—they must find evidence showing that primitive, precapitalist tribes were egalitarian, more humane for both sexes. As Jane Atkinson (1982) noted, "A sexually egalitarian past is central in Marxist feminists' vision of a sexually egalitarian future." But this romantic view of the past is not supported by evidence.

Well then, is there no way out of the dilemma of biased observation? Yes and no. Science and understanding proceed in increments, and although we can never entirely shed the limitations of our culture in general, and our values and politics in particular, we *can* learn to be more tolerant and appreciative of how other cultures work. We can try not to impose our cultural categories on other societies, but to assemble evidence first; then we can let ourselves be surprised, for human beings are continually surprising.

For example, a fascinating new idea in anthropological research is that even as apparently basic a category as male/female may simply be a human invention rather than a universal, biological distinction (Kessler and McKenna 1978). Atkinson, who studied the Wana of Sulawesi, Indonesia, reported that "gender is not a central organizing principle of that culture" (Atkinson 1982). Societies vary enormously, it turns out, in how literally they interpret the labels "male" and "female":

1. In some cultures, such as that of Morocco, gender is absolute and rigid. A man does male things, a woman does female things, and you cross that line at your peril.

2. In some cultures, such as the Wana, the Balinese, or the Semang, gender categories are flexible and unimportant. There is a minimal differentiation of sex roles, and if a woman wants to do "man's work," or vice versa, it's no big deal to anyone (Atkinson 1982; Sanday 1981).

3. In some cultures, such as the Hua of New Guinea, gender can flow and change between male and females, old and young. The Hua believe that after women have had sufficient sexual intercourse and childbearing, they can become, in social terms, men; and older men, after ritual imitation of menstruation and childbirth, can become, in social terms, women. In their rituals, each sex becomes more like the other (Meigs 1976).

4. And in some cultures, there were and are institutionalized ways for people to change gender. Perhaps the best-known example is the custom of *berdache* among North American Indians (Whitehead 1981), where a man could become, in all major social respects, a woman. He dressed like one, behaved like one, worked like one, lived like one. There was no formal female equivalent of the male berdache, but the historical record contains frequent accounts of women who hunted and even took to the warpath when they wanted to or needed to. Some Indian fathers taught their wives and daughters traditionally male skills; one Crow girl, having practiced masculine arts as a child, rose to the position of chief of her tribe. In at least thirty African societies, such as the southern Bantu, the Ibos of Nigeria, and the Simbiti of Tanzania, a woman can literally buy herself the status of male if she has accumulated enough cows or other wealth. She may even buy herself a wife and become a legal husband: She does not have sex with her bride but arranges partners for her; the female husband is the accepted father of any children that result (O'Brien 1977).

"Biology itself is mute," wrote anthropologist Rayna Rapp (1979); "it speaks only through cultural constructions that people make of their experiences."

We could go on describing different tribal customs and cultural constructions in all their dazzling variety, and what we would gain by doing so is data on human and cultural variability. This is the dominant tradition in anthropology. As an anthropologist, you sit down with a wise village elder, for example, and ask him (or her) who marries whom, how women are treated, why men fight, and who does what work. Margaret Mead's famous books on sex and temperament are an excellent illustration of this approach. Mead wanted to know *what* the Arapesh and Mundugumor were like, and she was less interested in *why* the Arapesh were gentle and cooperative while the Mundugumor were suspicious and nasty.

But other, more recent schools in anthropology are trying to explain the whys. They are not content merely to know that the Machiguenga behave this way and the Mundurucú another way.

They want to know what forces *cause* different groups to evolve in different directions and whether there are any general principles that can explain the path taken by each. Using the descriptive data provided by field workers, these researchers seek patterns across cultures. They regard the rules, rituals, and customs of a given tribe as parts of an interlocking system; to understand why a tribe practices a particular custom, therefore, we have to understand how the whole system works and the role (or *function*) that custom plays.

This is the approach we take in the rest of this chapter. Instead of asking, Is male dominance universal? we ask, instead: What are the social and economic and political forces that make men and women in tribe A hostile toward each other, while members of tribe B get along so much better? What are the conditions that cause women's status to rise or fall? The answers go beyond informants' descriptions and explanations of their actions, because people are often unaware of the most basic rules they follow (see the Milgram subway experiment described in Chapter 7). Further, this approach requires us to regard each culture as a product of its own unique history and environment. Customs that work in a particular social and economic system cannot be exported from one society to another like cheese. You may like the way Mbuti men treat women more than the practice of purdah, but even customs you don't like have a purpose. This is why people engage in rituals that seem, to outsiders, to be irrational or painful, such as superincision (making a slit in the penis) for males and infibulation (cutting and sewing up the vagina) for females (Hayes 1975). It doesn't advance our understanding to moan, ''But why do women (or men) put up with that awful practice?'' They put up with it because it is one element in an interconnected system of kinship, population pressures, and economic dependency.

This chapter illustrates a *strategy* that can be used to think about sex differences; it does not explain every riddle and ritual mentioned earlier. Some of the studies we have chosen offer new and controversial answers to old questions. They cover a lot of territory and may seem unrelated, but they share a framework, a way of approaching the relations between men and women, that we find creative and exciting. The first section describes researchers' efforts to explain particular phenomena: the rituals of circumcision and couvade; sexual customs that range from repressive to open; female veiling and seclusion. The second reviews some theories that try to account for male dominance and variations in female status across cultures and throughout history. The third discusses the strengths and weaknesses of the perspective as a whole.

some customs in social context

social dilemmas and sexual rituals

circumcision When psychoanalysts try to explain the origin of sexual taboos and rituals, they look for answers in unconscious motives (see Chapter 5). For example, they usually account for circumcision practices in terms of castration anxiety and father-son rivalry. Some focus on the boy's motives. Circumcision, they say, represents the boy's willingness to sacrifice a part of his penis as a symbolic gesture of deference to his father's power: "If I give you this much, may I please keep the rest?" The trouble is that in no society do boys circumcise themselves, certainly not Oedipal-aged little ones. Another explanation is that circumcision represents the father's effort to head off the threat from his son, that it is a symbolic gesture meaning, "Buzz off, kid, your mother is mine." The trouble is that fathers rarely circumcise their own sons. The operation is usually done by a third party: the chief of the tribe, a doctor, the boy's uncle, and so on.

Karen Paige and Jeffery Paige (1981) have developed a theory of reproductive rituals and taboos that does not rely on unconscious mechanisms. They regard these rituals as a form of psychological warfare that people use to influence and assess the opinions and intentions of other individuals when more direct means of influence are unavailable (Paige 1977). *Rituals are used to persuade and convince other group members of one's intentions.*

If you live in a hunting-and-gathering society, your fortunes rise and fall with the prevalence of food in the forests, which may or may not be plentiful. The deer or the fish may not be abundant in a given year. People who depend on unpredictable runs of game or fish for their protein live under uncertain circumstances, and their resources are temporary, perishable, and of little value as objects to be inherited. Most hunters and gatherers do not acquire property that can be handed down from generation to generation. You can't bequeath twenty berries to your children or stash twenty fish under your bed for very long. Nor can you put a fence around forty acres of tropical jungle and try to live on the occasional wild pig or tapir that bounds through.

Now consider the advantages, and disadvantages, of settling down. Once you have some land to be plowed and animals to domesticate, you start worrying about how to protect them. One cost of wealth is the fear of losing it. If you are desert nomads, like the Bedouin, you had better keep a careful eye on your camels; in that blistering climate, they may mean the difference between life and death. If you cultivate land as your only source of food and income, you had better keep marauders and hungry neighbors away. Cows and camels can wander off; farms and fields can be raided. So property requires protectors.

Tribes that control stable economic resources face a critical social problem, the Paiges argued. Their need is for large numbers of sons to defend the group's property and boundaries against outside enemies. The danger is that some young men may break away and grab some property and camels for themselves. According to the Paiges, circumcision is a symbolic demonstration by fathers of their loyalty to the existing tribe.

The Paiges began their analysis by noting where circumcision occurs: most commonly in advanced horticultural or pastoral societies such as the Tiv of Nigeria and the Kazak of Russia.[1] Most of these societies share a common social organization, namely strong fraternal interest groups. That is, they consist of bands of related males united under common military or political leadership. These males have the power to defend property, control resources, and negotiate binding agreements over women and wealth. Since their power comes from their unity, male solidarity is essential. A son who moves away represents not just the loss of one man, but the loss of the son's sons and all their wealth and military strength. "In such societies, fission is not simply a cause for grumbling but a major political crisis," wrote the Paiges.

In hunting and gathering tribes that lack fraternal interest groups, fission is quite common. The son of a Mbuti hunter takes with him only what he can carry, and his departure means no loss of power or prestige for his father. It is only when military and political power depend on the continual expansion of males in the father's line that a son who leaves the tribe is a great threat.

The Paiges' next question was, For whom is the circumcision

[1]Some critics of studies based on samples of tribal societies point out that apparent correlations between their customs and rituals may be spurious. They argue that the process of cultural diffusion—when a society breaks up and spawns several off-shoots—accounts for such correlations. That is, if several (or many) tribes in a sample once made up a single tribe, then of course a pork taboo in one will have many of the same economic correlates as a pork taboo in another. The Paiges, however, drew their tribes from the Standard Cross-Cultural Sample, which is a stratified sample of tribes taken from 186 distinct groups around the world. Each group consists of a cluster of societies that share similar culture, language, and location. Selecting one tribe from each group minimizes the effects of diffusion.

ritual performed? They believe it is done not to solve the psycho-dynamic conflicts of the individual father or his son, but to solve the political conflicts of the tribe. By allowing his son to be circumcised, the father demonstrates publicly to his brothers, chief, and other close kinsmen that he is loyal and will not leave. When a father hands over his son to the tribal establishment he is yielding to the group's authority and power. But there are some hazards: Circumcision occasionally goes wrong even in a modern hospital; among primitive tribes, accidents are common and the child may even die. (Participants often make nervous jokes that illustrate their awareness of risk. Tiv fathers tell the circumciser: "Easy, easy, or many women will weep.") But that is the point. The ritual *must* involve risk, and risk of the man's reproductive ability at that, for it to counter the risk of fission. Circumcision is never done on the ear, or elbow, or ankle, but on the penis, organ of procreation and power.

Some anthropological explanations of circumcision regard the ritual as a rite of passage, a ceremony that initiates boys into manhood. John Whiting, Richard Kluckhohn, and Albert Anthony (1958) asserted that it serves to break a boy's emotional bond to his mother and assure proper masculine identity. One trouble with such interpretations, the Paiges said, is that the timing of circumcision rituals varies widely. Of the twenty-one tribes in their sample that practice the custom, boys are circumcised in infancy in four, in early or late childhood in ten, at puberty in six, and in late adolescence in one. This age distribution, and the fact that even members of the same culture may disagree over whether and when to circumcise their sons, persuaded the Paiges that the purpose of the operation is not to impress masculine standards on the child. The child is a passive central character; the ceremony is not for him but for the adults. Among the Thonga the clan chief orders the ceremony for all boys between ten and sixteen, and if necessary he will use force to compel them to have the operation. This is the most common pattern—a villager elder commands a reluctant father to have his sons circumcised.

The force of the ritual is made especially clear when a father disobeys. A man who does not allow the circumcision of his son is telling everyone that he can't be trusted, that he is an individualist who might leave the tribe at any time and had better be watched carefully. If he can't be counted on to sacrifice his son, at least symbolically, he certainly can't be counted on in the next war. (This is a function of many group rituals. A Mormon who drinks coffee and an Indian who eats the sacred cow are both announcing the limits of their loyalty to the group.) The Paiges described in colorful detail the politics of circumcision in many tribes. Kinsmen are constantly fighting over who should do the operation and how old the child should be. Sometimes the timing of a circumcision settles a brewing feud, or escalates one. Victor Turner (1962), who studied the Ndembu tribe of western Zambia, observed one wily old chief who revived his flagging power over squabbling factions by deciding that a circumcision ritual must be done—and he presided.

Genesis 17 describes circumcision as a social bargain between God and Abraham: "This is my covenant, which ye shall keep, between me and you and thy seed after thee: Every man-child among you shall be circumcised. . . . And the uncircumcised man-child whose flesh of his foreskin is not circumcised, that soul shall be cut off from his people; he hath broken my covenant." The God of the Hebrews was explicit about the loyalty function of circumcision. When Moses broke the covenant by failing to circumcise his son, God threatened to slay the boy. Moses' wife Zipporah cut off her son's foreskin herself to save him (Exodus 4). The ancient Hebrews, as the Paiges pointed out, were advanced horticulturalists with precisely the kind of economic and political organization to which fission is the greatest threat. Indeed, the story of Genesis is a story of fissions and feuds, of a growing tribe that needed unity and struggled with dissensions. Circumcision, like any test of loyalty, reduces the threat only temporarily. "Ritual provides a means of gaining temporary political advantage, not final political victory," wrote the Paiges.[2]

couvade   "It's a wise child who knows his own father," the saying goes, and from the biological fact that paternity is rarely 100 percent certain comes a wide range of social customs attending childbirth. In some societies women are confined in special huts or

---

[2]Perhaps you are wondering what ritual function male circumcision has in the United States. For the Jews, of course, circumcision still plays its original role. For non-Jews, circumcision apparently began as a way to prevent "masturbatory insanity" among boys—doctors believed that a circumcised penis was less sexually sensitive than an uncircumcised one (which isn't true), and that therefore a boy who was circumcised would be less likely to masturbate and thus go crazy. When that belief died, however, the ritual found a new justification: hygiene. (As Karen Paige [1978] and others have observed, the ear gets dirty too, but no one recommends ritual surgery to remove the earlobe.) Today the practice of circumcision has outlived its original rationales. There is no longer any medical, hygienic, cancer-preventing, or sexual purpose to the tradition, and even the American Pediatric Society no longer recommends circumcision as routine procedure: The risks are greater than the supposed benefits (see Paige 1978; Paige and Paige 1981).

moved to another community during childbirth; or their social contacts—especially with men—are severely curtailed; or they are regarded as unclean and dangerous, to be avoided at all costs. In other societies *men* follow the taboos and restrictions. In the most extreme form of husband involvement, *couvade*, fathers, not mothers, are expected to have labor pains and a long recovery period (see Chapter 5).

Many anthropologists have observed that the birth of a child is occasion for relatives to lay claim to the newborn's allegiance, inheritance, and eventual productive and reproductive capacity. Almost everywhere the rights of such control over the child belong to the father, but the biological father and the legal (sociological) father are not always the same person. The legal father may be the wife's brother, a clan head, a state agency, an ancestral ghost, or even a woman.

Paige and Paige (1981) regard couvade and other birth rituals as symbolic efforts to assert claims to the offspring, made necessary by the absence of more potent means of assertion, such as binding contracts and legal machinery. "Ritual is a poor substitute for legal or political action," they wrote. "A potential claimant would be ill advised to spend two weeks in a hammock or avoid turtle meat if he could claim his child by hiring a lawyer or organizing a war party." Preindustrial tribes do not have these alternatives, and for them paternity rights depend on a complex set of bargains and rituals. The Paiges hypothesized that restrictions on the pregnant woman and participation of the husband in rituals like couvade would occur in different kinds of societies. (Table 9 summarizes the birth practices found in their sample of 114 tribal societies.) They found that, like circumcision, restrictions on women are most likely to occur in societies in which men are strongly organized and can enforce the restrictions and in which wealth is exchanged at the marriage. A groom who pays a bride price expects a fertile wife. If she is barren or produces a defective child, the husband and his kinsmen may demand a refund from her father, in the form of an additional wife, some cows, even someone else's child. When males are not effectively organized, they cannot restrict women and control the birth process by careful monitoring of the female's activities and whereabouts. Without legal or military recourse, they must assert their claims another way: through ritual involvement. As they had predicted, couvade *is* more likely to occur in tribes that do not have strongly organized male groups, do not practice exchanges of wealth at marriage, and do not offer compensation to a husband for his wife's

Table 9. Birth Practices in Tribal Societies

MATERNAL RESTRICTIONS

Social (high):

Structural seclusion	Confined to dwelling during pregnancy at least two weeks prior to delivery; secluded in special hut; moved to other community during birth process.
Social avoidance	Contact with people, especially men, restricted during pregnancy. Pregnant women avoided and believed to be unclean and dangerous, evil.

Personal (low):

Sex taboo	Sexual relations with husband restricted for at least two months before delivery.
Food taboo	Eating certain foods during either pregnancy or postpartum is restricted.
Minor	Restrictions on looking at ugly objects, wearing certain clothing, working too hard, etc.

HUSBAND INVOLVEMENT

Couvade (high):

Seclusion	Secluded in dwelling during pregnancy or postpartum with or without mother and child. May also be considered unclean. Avoids others.
Postpartum work taboo	Refrains from performing normal tasks during postpartum period. Must remain close to home; contact with others minimized.
Food taboo	Refrains from eating certain foods during pregnancy or postpartum.

Minor (low):

Minor observances	Minor ritual observances, such as seeking a vision; performs birth-related sacrifices. May help wife with daily chores.
Informal	Residual category: no changes in normal behavior. No ritual observances.

SOURCE: Paige and Paige 1981.

fertility problems. Restrictions on women and the involvement of husbands are both alternative male methods of asserting paternity and protecting their rights to the child, but which method is used depends on the economic and social structure of the community.

When the Paiges argue that rituals are a form of psychological warfare designed to persuade some individuals of other individuals' intentions, they are using psychological notions to link economic condition A with ritual behavior B. Many anthropologists would be content to find simply that A and B coexist. The Paiges want to show how the bargains that live in the heads of a tribe's members solve social problems: If I go through labor with my wife you will believe I am the child's real father; if I let my son be circumcised, you will believe I am loyal; if you share your meat from a successful hunt with me, I will share mine with you when I am lucky and you are not. The idea to think about is that these psychological bargains are effects, not causes. They result from conflicts that originate in a group's economic system, not from conflicts in people's minds.

sexuality versus the system

To explain the sexual suppression of women, biological theories are frequently posed. Men have a stronger sex drive, which is why they have all those wives and mistresses and lovers. Polygyny (one man with several wives) is more popular than polyandry (one woman with several husbands)[3] because men want to have sex more often than women do; a man can satisfy many women but a woman can't quench the fires of many men. Social customs and marriage practices, this theory runs, result from this basic difference between the sexes.

For a while there was an effort to replace theories that emphasized the male sex drive with theories that emphasized the female sex drive. Psychiatrist Mary Jane Sherfey (1973), for example, basing her argument on Masters and Johnson's early reports on multiple female orgasm, decided that female hypersexuality and insatiability were at one time normal and adaptive. Observing that a female chimpanzee may have coitus twenty to fifty times a day during the peak week of estrus (her fertile period), Sherfey concluded that "something akin to this behavior could be paralleled by the human female if her civilization allowed it." Naturally, civilization couldn't allow it, not if men were going to get any work done or if women were going to tend their families, so, Sherfey reasoned, female sexuality was suppressed.

[3]Polygyny occurs 141 times more often than polyandry. In a random sample of 1,179 world societies, it was found that almost 15 percent practice monogamy; 85 percent practice limited or general polygyny; and only .6 percent—seven societies— practice limited polyandry (Divale and Harris 1976).

The major problem with Sherfey's theory, as with other biological explanations, is that it cannot account for societal differences. Women are not sexually suppressed in all cultures. Further, in societies that give women (and men) considerable sexual freedom, people still manage to get jobs, get married, and have children. And even in societies where people have large amounts of leisure time, they do not just stay home, making love day in and day out. They also enjoy a sport or two, read books, go to the movies, and plant gardens.

For these reasons, we think it is necessary to look elsewhere to explain sexual customs. A good way to begin is by asking, What is the net effect of beliefs that couples can have sex only at certain times, or that women are dirty and to be avoided, or that women are inherently lustful (or lustless)? One answer from converging lines of research is that many of these attitudes and their corresponding rituals serve to increase the chances for conception when population is low and to decrease them when population is putting pressure on resources.

sexual customs and population control   Ernestine Friedl (1975), an anthropologist, cited a study of the remarkable differences between two tribes that live in New Guinea. The highland people believe that intercourse weakens men, that women are dangerously threatening and unclean, and that menstrual blood can do all sorts of terrifying things. Sex is considered powerful and mysterious: It must not be performed in a garden or the act will blight the crops. Antagonism between the sexes runs high. Men often delay marriage because bride prices are very high, and many remain bachelors. Not so far away, another tribe has an opposite view of women and sex. They think sexual intercourse is fun and even has a revitalizing effect on men. They think sex *should* take place in gardens, as it will foster the growth of plants. The only worry men have about sex is whether they can perform as well as custom decrees and as females like. The living quarters of men and women are not segregated, the way they are in the highlands. The sexes get along relatively well.

Why the two sets of attitudes? One explanation is that the highland people have been settled a long time and have little new land or resources; a population increase would seriously strain the food supply. Sexual antagonism, fear of coitus, and an acceptance of bachelorhood are all good ways to lower the birth rate, just as prosex attitudes are an excellent way to increase it. The sexy tribe lives in uncultivated areas, and it needs more group members to cultivate the land and help the group defend itself against hostile neighbors.

Many societies have sexual rules whose effect is to lower or raise the birth rate. In some tribes heterosexual intercourse is taboo for 205 to 260 days a year, and on New Britain Island (a territory of New Guinea) men are so afraid of sex that *they* are the ones who worry about being raped (Rubin 1975). In many societies sex is taboo after a woman has a baby, sometimes for several years. Conversely, the orthodox Jewish belief that a woman is unclean during her period and for seven days thereafter assures that intercourse will occur near ovulation. Certainly the Catholic taboo on birth control contributes to a higher Catholic birthrate.

Sexual freedom or repressiveness, in other words, has its origin in nonsexual events. In many Polynesian societies boys and girls are sexually free before marriage. In societies at the other end of the sexual continuum, neither sex may have intercourse before marriage. In the middle are all sorts of variations: Girls may have sex but woe if they get pregnant, or girls may have sex only with their fiancés, to whom they are betrothed as children. In reviewing the research on premarital sex rules, Friedl found that permissiveness occurs in tribes that do not require large-scale property exchanges at marriage. This makes good economic sense. In many tribes elders control the economic resources of the group, and they determine which woman shall be exchanged for how much property. When marriages entail high bride prices that one kin group pays to another, you can bet that the buyer wants unused merchandise. Families limit the sexual activity of the young so as to increase the girl's value at marriage. With this interpretation, one could have predicted that in the United States, as marriage evolved away from being a means of property exchange with women as the pawns, and as dowries vanished and the strength of kin groups diminished, the premium on female virginity would fade. As it has.

polygyny and polyandry   Ester Boserup (1970), writing on the economics of polygyny, explained the usefulness of a man's having many wives in African tribal economies. In regions where land is widely available for cultivation, polygyny advances its development. A man with several wives gains workers for his fields and producers of his children, wealth on two counts. For their part, the wives are not unhappy with the system, or at least no more unhappy than monogamous wives are in the West. A Tiv woman expressed dismay when a visiting anthropologist, Laura Bohannan, told her that English men have only one wife at a time. "Only one? The poor wife! Who helps her hoe the fields, deliver her children, prepare the food, mend the clothes, and tend the infants?'' (Who, indeed.) In most polygynous households, conflict among the wives is minimized by a set of rules that specifies how often the husband sleeps with each wife and how often each wife must cook for the husband (Bohannan and Bohannan 1953; Lamphere 1974; Leis 1974).

Polygyny, in other words, has survival benefits in certain kinds of societies. Horticultural tribes are much more likely than hunters and foragers to allow men to have several wives, and the reason seems to be, again, the greater accumulation of property and all forms of wealth among farming societies (Friedl 1975). Women become valuable possessions, not only for the sons they can bear for defense but for the land they bring with them at marriage, which unifies kin groups. The more wives a man has, then, the more wealth he has, and the more bodies are available to tend his property. It's a matter of economics, not sex drive.

There are, however, examples of polygynous marriages in which the women are secluded and do not add to the husband's economic resources (such as in the Hausa region of northern Nigeria and some Middle Eastern groups). Still, these arrangements are not simply for the sexual pleasure of husbands. As anthropologists Lourdes Benería and Gita Sen (1981) suggested, ''Seclusion [of wives] may be an effort to control female sexuality for the purpose of identifying paternity and transmitting resources from one generation to the next.'' Indeed, a factor that undoubtedly has militated against polyandry is just this little matter of paternity and lineage. Identifying a child's mother is both easy and, in a patrilineal system, rather unimportant. When identifying a child's father is crucial for clan and inheritance purposes, a woman had better not have multiple relationships.

the puzzle of purdah

Perhaps no custom more fascinates or horrifies Westerners than the wearing of the veil, with its implication of mystery, and the general practice of purdah, the seclusion of women from the public world. Anthropologists themselves are greatly divided on the meanings of purdah, the reasons for it, and the moral evaluation of it: Is it a sign of the ultimate oppression of women or a means of women's emancipation and independence? Is it a form of female solidarity or of female enslavement? Is it profoundly different from other forms of sexual segregation or basically the same thing in (literal) disguise?

Keep in mind a few general points:

1. *Purdah* does not refer to a single practice throughout the Middle East and India. In some cultures female seclusion begins at puberty; elsewhere, seclusion begins at marriage. In some places the upper class is most likely to observe purdah; in other places it is a lower-middle-class custom (Papanek 1973). Some veiled women work in the fields or may otherwise leave the home; others must remain inside the family compound (Sharma 1978). The two elements of purdah—restricted living space and bodily covering—may be combined in a variety of ways.

2. In spite of these variations, purdah always has a common *expressed* purpose: to protect women's chastity and men's honor. Women are so sexy, so tempting, so incapable of controlling their emotions and sexuality, the men say, that they are a danger to the social order (Mernissi 1975). Purdah is the way to restrain and control them.

3. The concepts of honor and shame, which regulate the practice of purdah, do not refer so much to individuals as to the entire extended family. "It is the group, not the individual, that is socially shamed or socially honored," noted Elizabeth and Robert Fernea (1979); acts of honor or shame "affect the entire existing social equilibrium." But the sources of honor are different for males and females. Male honor rests on bravery, piety, and responsibility; if lost, it can be regained. Female honor rests on chastity and sexual purity; once lost, it can never be regained. If a woman's loss of honor is only privately known, she may get away with merely a rebuke; but once her lapse becomes public knowledge, drastic, violent action against her may be taken to "cleanse" the family name.

4. As Hanna Papanek (1973) observed, there are two principles of purdah, which she calls "separate worlds" and "symbolic shelter." The first refers to the sexually segregated division of work in societies that practice purdah: Women's work and men's work never overlap. But this segregation is not symmetrical, she added. Purdah also represents women's shelter from the outside, hostile world; it distinguishes those who are protecting from those who are protected, and sheltered women demonstrate the status of their protectors.

But what do the sheltering and seclusion of women accomplish? Ursula Sharma (1978) observed the practice of *ghungat nikalna* (veiling the face completely in front of all men senior to one's husband in age and status) in a northern Indian village called Ghanyari. Sharma equated *ghungat* with foot-binding in China, seclusion among Muslims, and the myth of the perfect housewife in the United States: All three customs, she argued, are ways of limiting women's public effectiveness (outside the home). "If males are dominant everywhere, male dominance is not everywhere the same, and *ghungat* in Ghanyari supports particular types of political and economic community among males."

But it does not much advance our understanding to say that purdah is simply another form of male dominance. What are those "particular types" of political and economic community? Anthropologist Jane Schneider (1971) argued that concerns about female chastity and family honor function to sustain the cohesion of families under particularly vulnerable economic conditions—when women are "contested resources much like pastures and water," for example, among pastoralist peasant societies, and when inheritance rules link marriage with property passed down to sons. Anthropologist Sherry Ortner (1978) suggested that concern about the purity of women and female virginity was tied to the historical emergence of stratified states. With the rise of the state and its hierarchies of class (in contrast to hunting and gathering bands), Ortner proposed, came the rise of the patriarchal extended family—and women became part of the patriarch's property.

In her large sample of world societies, Paige (1983) tested these and other theories of female chastity, finding that some elements of the theories were supported and others not. For instance, Ortner was right in one respect: Once a society becomes class-structured, control over a daughter's mate selection increases; only one-third of the classless societies exert high control over their daughters' social lives, compared to 60 percent of the societies that are stratified by social class. Second, Schneider was on the right track in suggesting that when families pass down valuable property to their sons they also resort to strong methods of chastity control and worry more about the premarital behavior of their daughters.

Paige (1983) concluded that "virginity rituals are surveillance tactics used by the powerful to protect their daughter's social reputation throughout the period of nubility." Societies based on advanced agriculture or pastoralism have economies that promote the emergence of large and powerful male interest groups—groups powerful enough to enter into high-stakes marriage bargains with each other and to enforce the terms of those bargains. What women in purdah are being "sheltered" from is not their own sexuality per se; *they are being sheltered from personal marriage choices against kin wishes,* from developing personal attachments that might interfere with a successful arranged marriage. And arranged marriages are important because they perpetuate the system of the ownership of land and other property (Papanek 1973).

In sum, said Paige, purdah is one form of chastity control; the strict seclusion of marriageable daughters is an alternative to killing or mutilating those who have premarital sex (unless, of course, the girl violates purdah), and minimizes the public need to control the daughter's virtue. Married women continue to be subject to purdah and chastity rules because, as we noted earlier, of concerns over paternity and lineage and over "correct" identification of offspring for inheritance.

Thus some anthropologists maintain that purdah is not much different from other methods of controlling female sexuality; the veil, they say, is only a tangible symbol of the barrier that exists between men and women in many cultures. Indeed, in recent years some women's voices have been raised to *defend* the veil and purdah:

1. While admitting that purdah curtails female autonomy, making women dependent socially and economically on men, Lila Abu-Lughod (1983) argued that "sexual segregation is not inherently bad for women." Abu-Lughod lived with a group of Bedouins, collectively known as Awlad Ali, who inhabit the coastal region of the Egyptian Western Desert. Instead of taking the male perspective and regarding women as the excluded sex, she adopted the women's perspective. These Bedouin women, she concluded, take responsibility for their own conformity to the rules of the tribe, so they do not feel they are ruled by men; they have full autonomy in their own realm, which is relatively unsupervised and egalitarian (among women). Bedouin women are self-assertive; they are rewarded for their independence, pride, and boldness; and because of the culture's denial of sexuality, women do not orient themselves toward men but toward other women. Abu-Lughod described a female world full of shared experience, humor, affection, and warmth. When a man enters the woman's sphere, women react the way women do in an American sorority or other women's gathering: They stop chatting, they become more formal with each other, they giggle and flirt with the men.

2. Numerous observers of Arab life think that it is a Western fallacy to impose "inferior/superior" evaluations on the Arab categories of female/male and private/public. Sherri Deaver (1980) argued that male and female, in Arab thinking, are not a continuum in which one is higher than another. Is an apple better than a pear? A tiger better than a bear? Deaver believes that Saudi men do not regard women as inferior because they view women as the "repository of family honor," nor do Saudi women regard themselves as inferior. Louise Sweet (1974), who lived in a Syrian village and other Middle Eastern communities, believes that separate can indeed be equal. Westerners persist in regarding the veil, seclusion, and the kin group's control of property as signs of male advantage, she wrote, and in misinterpreting the protection of women as "oppression." In fact, the whole system is adaptive and advantageous to women, considering the harsh living conditions (such as barely habitable deserts, flooding, droughts, male violence and feuding).

3. To Egyptian social scientist Fadwa El Guindi (1981), the return of the veil among modern Egyptian women is an important symbolic act of liberation and emancipation. "A new Egyptian woman is emerging—educated, professional, nonelitist, and veiled," she wrote. The veil allows women to be progressive *and* traditional: to become educated and to work, but also to retain the cultural standards of modesty and morality. With this one symbolic act, Egyptian women can go to college and mingle with men, yet also keep apart from men sexually and thereby "protect their virginity and honor." To El Guindi and others who disdain what they regard as the corruption, materialism, and sexual decadence of the West, the veil is a link to their own culture, allowing them to progress at the pace they want.

It seems to us that two issues are being confused here: One is the origin and function of a custom; another is whether that custom, once established, may have unanticipated benefits or symbolism for those who practice it. Without question, purdah reinforces and perpetuates male dominance in the economic and political life of these cultures. This does not mean that women can't have a great time together in their own sphere, or that they don't accept the system as it is; male Untouchables in India accept their lowest-of-the-low caste too, as God's will. Women in purdah may in fact be separate but equal in religious and cultural terms, but this form of equality does not obliterate what Papanek calls the "deepest inequality"—between those who provide shelter and those who receive it, between the protectors and the protected. (Mae West observed this point years ago, when she noted: "Every man I meet wants to protect me . . . I can't imagine what from.") The justifications for purdah sound to us like the justifications for paying American women less than men for the same job, or for arguing that women should be protected from arduous tasks such as running a country or having a good job, or for maintaining that because slavery produced warm emotional bonds among slaves it was worth perpetuating. At the same time, it is not up to Westerners to impose their philosophy on any other culture, whose policies and beliefs are integrally related to its history, economics, and extended social system. Removing the veil will not make women in purdah equal; evolution toward equality may mitigate the need for the veil.

The conflicts of values, customs, and beliefs between U.S. and Arab cultures show clearly in the following account, by an American woman living in Saudi Arabia:

> I have learned to endure some hardships and some indignities. I've learned to wear long dresses with long sleeves in public despite temperatures hitting close to 120 degrees. I've given up my right to drive. I've even learned to take my allocated seat in the back of the public bus. That is, I've learned to adapt to local custom if I wish to live there as the wife of an American businessman.
>
> Women are not employable in Saudi Arabia unless they are nurses or teachers or can be kept totally segregated from men. So when I started working, illegally, I learned that I must enter and exit the building through the back door. . . . I felt safe. Until the morning last month when someone cried out: "Hide! They're searching the building for women!"
>
> Two members of the Matawa, the quasi-official religious police, had entered our corporate headquarters building and were making a floor-by-floor sweep for "illegal" women. We were not supposed to be working, and we certainly were not supposed to be working in the presence of men. . . .
>
> We women were at the mercy of another culture's understanding of our place. To be fair, the Saudis believe that such restrictions are protective, not restrictive. They can't imagine why decent women *want* to step outside their homes, any more than I, an American woman who chafed at the defeat of something so basic as the equal rights amendment, can understand why any women want to live in segregation. . . .
>
> So I and the other women waited while men decided what was to be done about our future. . . . All 80 women employees, except for a few nurses, were laid off. If exceptions had been made, a corporate lawyer later told me with no apparent sense of irony, suits might be filed against the company for discrimination.
>
> Although our situation is ludicrous, although it is absurd, it certainly is not funny. While the men go about their important business of running this part of the world, their wives can go back to playing bridge or attending lunches (if they are properly attired)—or step into the back of the bus and go downtown to spend their husbands' paychecks. (*Los Angeles Times*, January 12, 1983)

subsistence and status: why men matter more

the Marxist model

Karl Marx was one of the first philosophers to argue that to understand behavior one had to start with the basic economic conditions of people's lives, not with the ideas in their heads. Economics, Marx thought, was the groundwork for the ideological superstructure of law, politics, custom, art, ideas. In preindustrial societies, as among hunters and gatherers, people produced or killed just what they needed. In capitalist societies, the aim is to create surplus goods that can be exchanged for labor. Preindustrial societies, Marx thought, were egalitarian; no group exploited another. But capitalism brought class structure, the emergence of an exploiting group that grew rich on the labor of workers. Marx believed that the inherent conflict between owners and workers would inevitably lead to revolution by the workers, and that a classless socialist system would be born from the ashes of the old (see Marx 1964). Although Marx was not overly concerned with sex and status differences, many writers have used his theory to account for the subjection of women around the world. As Gayle Rubin (1975) noted, "It has been argued that women are a reserve labor force for capitalism, that women's generally lower wages provide extra surplus to a capitalist employer, that women serve the ends of capitalist consumerism in their roles as administrators of family consumption, and so forth."

Marx's collaborator, Friedrich Engels (1973), took the next step. In *The Origin of the Family, Private Property and the State*, first published in 1884, Engels added sex to Marxist economics, noting that work is not the whole of human experience and that people do need to reproduce themselves. Although Engels's book shared some nineteenth-century misconceptions about the existence of matriarchies and the egalitarianism of primitive tribes, his work contributed a provocative idea: The monogamous family as an economic unit is what constrains women and assures their subjugation. Engels believed that "as wealth increased it made the man's position in the family more important than the woman's, and . . . created an impulse to exploit this strengthened position in order to overthrow, in favor of his children, the traditional [matriarchal] order of inheritance." The overthrow of "mother right," he went on, meant *"the world historical defeat of the female sex.* The man took command in the home also; the woman was degraded and reduced to servitude; she became the slave of his lust and a mere instrument for the production of children" (Engels didn't mince words). You may recall that Wolfgang Lederer, the psychoanalyst, also theorized about a patriarchal revolt against matriarchal religions, but his explanation concerned the minds of men, not the economic conditions of their households.

Just as Marx and Engels assumed a basic camaraderie between the sexes in classless societies, so they assumed that the sexes would reunite harmoniously once classless societies returned in the form of communism. Their view that ideas and relationships are shaped by the *tangible* conditions of people's lives—their property, their jobs, their involvement with work—had dramatic impact, in both politics and science. But the theory is too narrow to explain such phenomena as Yanomamo hostility to women, sexual segregation among the Kwakiutl, and the practice of genital mutilation among the Sudanese. Nor can it explain why women's work was less valued than men's work long before capitalism dawned.

We turn now to some other efforts to account for male dominance and for variations in women's status from culture to culture.

man the hunter, woman the life-giver?

Anthropologists who believe that some kind of male dominance is universal also believe that explanations for this sexual imbalance must likewise apply universally. It seems logical, they say, to start with the fact that women give birth to children and men don't. Thus, in a controversial essay Sherry Ortner (1974) theorized that societies put a higher value on all things, events, and activities that are under human control (culture) than on events they cannot control (nature). Women stand closer to nature than to culture because of their reproductive functions, which is why women and women's work are devalued, even despised.

But this neat theory was soon encumbered with exceptions. It turns out that many societies worship the life-giving functions of women; great importance is attached to the creation of life among the Iroquois, Hopi, Dahomeans, Ashanti, and others (Sanday 1981). Further, men are as likely as women to be associated with nature and natural functions in societies that celebrate men as hunters and farmers, or that worry about men's "bestial sexual passions" (remember the Victorians). Moreover, in some kinds of societies, the glorification of man the hunter is not balanced by a notion of woman the mother—the two roles are not regarded as logical opposites or even complements (Collier and Rosaldo 1981). Mothering itself is not universally admired, universally devalued, or even universally done only by women—Himalayan Lepcha men "mother" their children

(Sanday 1981). "Mothering is a social relation, much like fathering, judging, or ruling," wrote Jane Collier and Michelle Rosaldo (1981), and a culture's attitudes about it cannot be understood without looking at the "complex social whole" (see also MacCormack 1977; MacCormack and Strathern 1980).

Another explanation distinguishes domestic (female) work from public (male) work (Rosaldo 1974). Women are oppressed and lack social worth, this argument runs, to the extent that they are confined to the home, cut off from other women and the outside world. Men, by controlling the distribution of wealth in the public community, not just at home, accordingly have more prestige, status, and power. This public/private dichotomy too was quickly laden with exceptions. What, for instance, should we make of a tribe in which sexual antagonism runs high and everyone tells you that men have all the power—but in which, on closer inspection, women have influence and power too? Among the Enga, a tribe known for its hostility toward women, women play an influential backstage role in the community's economic exchange system. And among the Warlpiri, a supposedly male-dominated Australian aboriginal society, women play key roles in the politics of male initiation and marriage arrangements (reported in Atkinson 1982). Among pastoral nomads in Iran, women, who are not recognized as power holders, in fact control herds, brideprice, and goods for market (Fazel 1977). Tinker women are the political power brokers within Irish society, but they do not have power in relation to Tinker men (Gmelch 1977). These examples, observed Rayna Rapp (1979), warp the tight fit between "women = domestic powerlessness" and "men = public powerfulness."

Some anthropologists use the preceding illustrations to argue that in many cultures women *do* have equality with men, or at least that they have power in their own spheres. But we think that this view obscures an important distinction: not between domestic and public, but between *power* and *influence*. The king has power, but the queen may influence him; he has the right and position to make decisions, she may have the charm and skill to affect those decisions. The fact is that women have had varying degrees of influence, but they have rarely shared the structural bases of power along with men. Why not?

digression: a fable

Suppose you landed on an unexplored continent and discovered a species of animal called the uhurdu. They all look alike to you, but eventually you observe that some of them have a freckle behind their ears and others have a stripe on their bellies. Uhurdu live on fuzzy yellow plants that grow plentifully in their habitat, and all uhurdus gather them easily. After a few months, however, you learn that while the fuzzy yellow plants are necessary for the health of the uhurdu, they are not sufficient. Twice a year the species must eat a rare red berry that grows high above them on a steep cliff: If they don't get their dose of the berry, they will weaken and die. Now the freckled uhurdu leave for several weeks, maybe a month or even two, however long it takes to get enough berries for every uhurdu. The striped uhurdu stay behind, feeding fuzzy yellow plants to the newborn. When the freckles come back, they are greeted with celebration and carousing, and a big feast is held for all. The freckle who got the most berries is immediately surrounded by a bevy of flirting stripes.

Being a good anthropologist, you learn to speak hurdish and ask some of the creatures about their social organization. They all tell you that the freckled uhurdu are braver and more intelligent than the stripes, and more important, too. "But the stripes do important work," you object. "They produce small uhurdu, and feed them. They gather fuzzy yellow plants every day and carry loads of them to the nesting site. They make redberry pie and redberry beer and weave redberry skins for winter warmth." "True," the uhurdu tell you, "but any of us could do that. Only the freckles can reap the berries. Without the freckles' work, we would die."

It seems easy to understand why freckled uhurdu would be regarded as more valuable than striped. Their work, though less frequent than plant gathering, is unpredictable, difficult, and essential. We would not expect the uhurdu to understand nutrition any more than we would expect squirrels to know why they hoard nuts for the winter. In the process of evolution, we would say, the species learned what it took to keep themselves alive.

Some anthropologists try to apply the same kind of analysis to human societies. They explain status differences between the sexes in terms of which sex produces the most food and which sex produces the essential food (protein); as in the case of the uhurdu, these are not always the same sex. Current theories suggest that status differences develop out of the division of labor and the way that food and wealth are distributed among a tribe's members. Such explanations begin with the survival needs a tribe faced. All groups had to reproduce themselves, feed themselves, and defend themselves; if they did not, they died out. For obvious reasons, the job of reproduction went to women. For convenience, their secondary job was gathering food near home base—plant foods, usually. Men, rather by default, devoted their primary energies to hunting animal food and, when necessary, to defense. This early and inevitable division of sexual labor, such theories argue, put men in a better position to acquire and control the valuable resources.

hunters and gatherers versus horticulturalists

There are about 300,000 people on the earth today who still get food in the original way, through hunting and gathering. These tribes live on wild plants, animals, and fish, in whatever proportion and combination their environments permit. In such societies men are always responsible for hunting large game and deep-sea fishing, and these occupations always carry prestige. Women's work is gathering the staple foods and has less prestige. Sometimes women help with the hunting and fishing, but they are never in charge of these activities.

Although all hunting-and-gathering societies rely mainly on men to be the hunters, regional environments have created different patterns in the division of labor. Friedl (1975) cited four:

1. Both sexes spend most of their time gathering, usually on an individual basis; men forage for themselves, women forage for themselves and their children. Men spend only a little time hunting, and meat is rarely distributed. (Examples: the Hadza of Tanzania in Africa; the Paliyans of Southwest India.)

2. Both sexes work together to hunt, gather, and fish, though men actually kill the game. Usually, the participating households share in the proceeds; sometimes husbands and wives work as a team and keep their own food. In these societies women can join men on the hunt because game is plentiful or close; for instance, the sexes may join forces to net a large catch during heavy fish runs. (Examples: the Washo of the Great Basin of North America; the Mbuti pygmies of the African Congo.)

3. The sexes are highly segregated, with men hunting alone or in small groups and women gathering vegetables and plants near the campsite. Women contribute more than half of the food supply, but men add 30 or 40 percent, which must be distributed to the whole group. This is the most common pattern, and it points to the importance of "women's work"—gathering—as the primary means of getting food, which we tend to forget in thinking of the glamour and status of hunting. (Examples: the Tiwi of North Australia; the !Kung-san of Africa [the exclamation point represents a clicking sound].)

4. Men provide virtually all the food. This pattern, of which the Eskimos are a familiar example, is the most rare; like the other patterns, it is determined by environmental conditions. Eskimo women have no vegetable gardens to give them a source of food or income; you can't grow corn in ice. Eskimo women have no rights, political or sexual. Men frequently take the women they desire by force, whether or not the women are married; men also share the women they "own" with other men, as a form of hospitality. Because women are totally dependent on men for protection and for every subsistence need—for their food and raw materials—their self-esteem comes from their role in the family and from their husbands' social status.[4]

As you might expect, relations between men and women in these four different subsistence patterns range from quite egalitarian to supremely male-dominated. It is no coincidence that where women contribute to the economic needs of the society and work alongside men, sexual relationships are less hostile. Notice that social customs and the degree of sexual segregation of tasks reflect the kind of food the environment offers and the ease or difficulty of getting it.

why brawn gets the bacon   The usual explanations of why men became the hunters and women the gatherers rest on physical sex differences. Men were better suited to fight and hunt because they were bigger, stronger, more muscular, could run faster, had greater lung capacity, and were more motivated by hormonally based aggressive drives. Anthropologist Marvin Harris (1974) thinks that physical strength was virtually the only reason that men became the warriors and hence the dominant sex, but others take issue with the physical-strength explanation. "The labor record of primitive women does not warrant the assertion that [women] were physically weak or helpless," wrote Evelyn Reed (1975). On the contrary, the heavy burdens that women carried, the hard work they did in the fields, the labor involved in everything from construction to domestic chores, all meant that women had to be extremely strong. Reed went so far as

---

[4]In one sample of ninety hunting-and-gathering societies, the *primary* source of food was as follows (Martin and Voorhies 1975):

Gathering	52 societies
Hunting	22 societies
Fishing	7 societies
Gathering and hunting equally	3 societies
Gathering and fishing equally	3 societies
Hunting and fishing equally	3 societies

to suggest that the many burdens of women's work "gave them a high degree of endurance and the strength to lift *heavier* loads than men."

Arguments about physical strength seem pointless because they cannot be resolved, but the issue itself is important. Newer approaches suggest that those who believe the egg came first should think about the chicken. For example, perhaps it was not that men became hunters because they were stronger than women; perhaps men became stronger than women once they had to be hunters. Analogously, Friedl (1975) observed that many people assume that the number of children a woman has determines how fully she participates in the work force: Pregnancy and childbirth clearly limit her ability to work. But perhaps, Friedl said, a society's subsistence needs and its ecology set limits on how many children a woman can be "permitted" to have. In societies that require considerable female labor, an adaptive solution would be to generate taboos and sexual customs that would insure a greater spacing of children. (This has been true in 20th century America; see Chapter 7, pp. 292–93.) Indeed, in hunting-and-gathering societies such as the !Kung-san of Africa, where women contribute up to two-thirds of the tribe's food, women nurse each child for four years. Women do not regularly ovulate while they are breast feeding a child; thus female !Kung-san can travel long distances to collect food without carrying more than one child at a time. Friedl proposed that the spacing of children and styles of child rearing are everywhere adjusted to the work that women have to do. Work is not adjusted to the frequency of childbirth. There is one exception: Childbearing meant that women couldn't hunt.

Why didn't the sexes take turns searching for deer and tapirs and caring for the toddlers? In our modern, relatively flexible society, changing roles and alternating jobs seems a reasonable solution. One friend of ours thought it would be quite acceptable for tribal women to hunt now and then while the men cared for the young and very old. The only problems she foresaw were family squabbles: "You took *three weeks* and only brought back *one* deer, and now I'm supposed to catch twenty rabbits in three days?"

Friedl suggested that structural factors caused the assignment of men to hunting and women to gathering. First, women could not be hunters on a regular basis because they are the childbearers, in two senses: They bear them during pregnancy and they often carry them around (for nursing and feeding) when they are small. A society in which females were raised, along with males, to be hunters would be wasting its efforts. Girls marry at just the time they could become skilled hunters, and they spend most of their childbearing years pregnant or nursing.

When we say women couldn't hunt, though, remember that we are talking about a certain kind of subsistence hunting—the kind that requires roaming far from home for an unpredictable length of time. Childbearing is perfectly compatible with hunting small game and fishing near home. It is not compatible, Friedl pointed out, with long-distance hunting. A hunter who hopes to bag a deer cannot also plan to carry home a sack of roots and berries, much less a tearful child. Because hunting is such an uncertain activity—meat may be found quickly or only after many days and miles of travel—a tribe that let "anyone" hunt would have found a maladaptive solution. Someone reliably has to feed the tribe each day while someone else chases the game. The most important consequence of the resulting male monopoly on hunting, however, was that men controlled the valuable meat. All foraging cultures, Friedl observed, have rules to assure the distribution of meat throughout the tribe, while the plant food that women collect tended to be for their immediate households only. This distribution system meant that men acquired a society-wide network of mutual exchanges and obligations, while women's influence was limited to the family. And thus was born a sex difference in power.

When human groups began to domesticate animals and cultivate crops, events that occurred only about 10,000 years ago, the fundamental nature of subsistence changed, and so did social customs and relationships. As we said earlier, settling down meant the need for a warrior class to defend property. Friedl explained the emergence of men as fighters in the same terms that account for their role as hunters: Fighting, like hunting, occurs at irregular intervals and is incompatible with gathering and child care.

Tribal societies based on horticulture[5] permit a much wider range of sex-role variations, because both sexes can work in the fields with children beside them (see Draper 1975; Lancaster 1976). The only monopoly men seem to have in horticultural systems is that they clear the land, chopping down trees and cutting away the underbrush. After that, either sex or both may be responsible for cultivating and harvesting the crops. Friedl noted that clearing the land, unlike

[5]The difference between horticulture and agriculture is that horticulturalists prepare the soil and plant crops with a hoe and digging stick, whereas agriculturalists use plows or machines.

hunting, does not automatically give men the right to distribute food. Distribution rights vary across cultures, and women's fortunes vary accordingly.

protein and power   The idea that women get higher status when they control a tribe's economic resources is supported by the case of the Iroquois (Brown 1975; Whitehead 1981). The Iroquois depended on cultivated foods for their subsistence: Men prepared the fields and women planted and harvested the crops. The tribe's basically vegetable diet was supplemented by fish, which both sexes caught, and game, which men hunted, occasionaly joined by women. In many ways the sexes lived separate lives, even eating the daily meal apart from each other. The men were often away on war parties and hunting expeditions for years at a time. Iroquois women worked together in cohesive groups, and the distribution of food was left to the matrons, a select group of older wives. Their control over the political decisions of the Council of Elders, Brown argued, was related to their control of the provisions for the hunting and war parties. She quoted an observer who wrote, "The women could hinder or actually prevent a war party which lacked their approval by not giving the supplies of dried corn and the moccasins which the warriors required."

Some writers have attributed the power of Iroquois women to the matrilineal social structure of the tribe. But in other matrilineal societies, such as the Bemba, women did not have the status of the Iroquois women (Brown 1970). One major difference between the two tribes is that the Iroquois enjoyed rich plentiful harvests, while the Bemba endured recurrent scarcity of food. The abundant crops and stored wealth of the Iroquois women gave them a stable, predictable right to distribute resources. Among the Bemba the shortage of food led to a centralized political system in which food was distributed by the chief. In adaptive terms, both tribes made good decisions. The object of food distribution, after all, is not to give all tribe members equal status but to see that all get fed.

Peggy Sanday (1974) studied twelve societies, including the Iroquois, in which female status ranged from very high to nonexistent. She defined status as the degree to which women had the power to make decisions that affected the tribe as a whole, not just a woman's own family. She used four indicators of female status, as shown in Table 10: (1) material control—do women distribute food and wealth outside the family? (2) demand for female produce—is the work that women do valued outside the family, in the mar-

Table 10. Female Status in Twelve Societies

Society	INDICATORS				
	Female material control	Demand for female produce	Female political partici- pation	Female solidarity groups	Status scale score
Yoruba	P	P	P	P	5
Iroquois	P	P	P	P	5
Samoans	?	P	P	P	5
Crow	P	P	P	A	4
Aymara	P	P	A	A	3
Tapirape	?	P	A	A	3
Rwala	P	?	A	A	3
Andamans	P	A	A	A	2
Tikopia	A	A	A	A	1
Azande	A	?	A	A	1
Somali	A	A	A	A	1
Toda	A	A	A	A	1

A = absent   P = present   ? = information unclear or unavailable
SOURCE: Sanday 1974

ketplace? (3) political participation—do women express opinions and influence policy in official ways? (4) group strength—do women belong to solidarity groups devoted to women's political and economic interests? In some of the societies that Sanday looked at, such as the Yoruba and the Iroquois, the answer to all four questions was yes. In others, such as the Toda and the Somali, the answer to all four was no.

When Sanday compared the status of women in each society with the percentage of food they contributed, she got the surprising results shown in Figure 6. When women's contribution was very low, their status was very low; Toda women contribute 10 percent of the food, for example, and their status was lowest. So far, not startling. But Sanday found that when women's contribution was very *high*, their status was still very low. Tikopia women contribute 75 percent of the food, and they are no better off than the Toda. Female status was highest in tribes in which women contributed just about as much as men. Despite such exceptions as the Rwala and the Somali, a balanced division of labor apparently does the most to balance sexual status—perhaps because neither sex feels it is doing all or

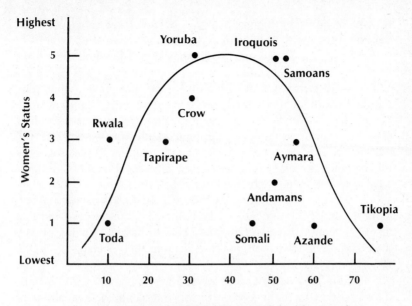

Figure 6. The relationship between female status in twelve cultures and women's contribution to group subsistence. Women have the highest status when they contribute about half of the food, not when they provide the least (10 percent)—or even the most (75 percent).

SOURCE: Adapted from Sanday 1974.

most of the work while the other is shirking or having an easier time of it.

But even that is not enough to assure sexual harmony. Orna and Allen Johnson (1975), as well as many sociologists, have found another factor that affects how the sexes think of each other: how work is organized. When the sexes are mutually dependent and work cooperatively, as in husband-wife teams, sexual antagonism is much lower than when work is organized along sex-segregated lines. Among the Machiguenga Indians of Peru, where the sexes cooperate in growing manioc, in fishing, and in recreation, husbands and wives feel solidarity with each other, not with their same-sex friends. Among the Mundurucú, women and men work in same-sex groups, and friendships rarely cross sexual lines; women feel a sense of solidarity with other women, men with men. Among the Yanomamo the women are alienated from men and isolated from each other.

Sexual antagonism is highest in this case. Such research suggests that the question of which sex is more "affiliative"—whether in terms of male bonding or female sociability—has less to do with inborn traits than with social organization.

It is still puzzling that women have low status even when they control the production of most foods. Why don't the Tikopia women behave like the male Yanomamos or Eskimos? One answer comes from our uhurdu fable: The nutritional staples of a society do not necessarily provide its protein. Women may supply 75 percent of the tribe's total calories, but the remaining 25 percent may be nutritionally more valuable. High status requires the control not just of resources but of rare resources, the most valued ones. Imagine that you control "only" 10 percent of a Bedouin tribe's resources—but that the 10 percent is their water—and you will have an inkling of why male control of protein originally gave them such power.

In sum, the connection between a tribe's economy and its customs is not a straight line. Many factors intervene: the availability or scarcity of food, population pressures, the need for warfare, the structure of work and family roles, technological inventions, and so on. Although researchers disagree about the definition (and prevalence) of male dominance, we think some conclusions can be drawn about the conditions that widen the chasm between the sexes or narrow it:

1. Male dominance is minimized when women and men share status and power; when the work of a society is interchangeably male or female; when gender is irrelevant to what the sexes do; when men and women work together (Poewe 1980; Schlegel 1977). Such integration is rare, however. In her analysis of work activities in 156 tribal societies, Sanday (1981) found that the percentage of tasks done only by women ranged from a low of 9 percent of all activities to a high of 73 percent; but the percentage of sexually integrated tasks ranged from 0 percent to only 35 percent. The sexual segregation of work is most pronounced in tribes that depend on hunting or animal husbandry; in such economies, women do more work alone—and, ironically, they do more work than men.

2. Male dominance prevails when men control the resources needed to achieve their tribe's goals, when men produce and control the critical products that women need for exchange and validation. Males and females may have (arguably) separate but equal spheres of power—e.g., in Zambia—when each sex independently owns and manages the resources necessary to achieve its goals (Poewe 1980).

3. Male dominance is exacerbated under colonization, when a foreign nation invades and controls an indigenous population, breaking up its traditional patterns and economy; capitalism, when a large class of people—children, women, minorities—can be exploited for the profits of their employers; and industrialization, which sharpens the sexual division of labor and makes status even more dependent on economic productivity (Etienne and Leacock 1980; Tilly 1981).

4. Male dominance prevails when there is a scarcity of marriageable women for marriageable men, when women are a rare resource (Guttentag and Secord 1983; Stewart and Winter 1977). A "surplus" or "scarcity" of one sex may occur for any number of reasons: war; practices such as infanticide; or migration patterns, as when men travel to work in remote areas, leaving women behind. (See Chapter 9, pp. 359–62, for the consequences of an unbalanced sex ratio in the United States.)

5. Male dominance is associated with environmental stresses, such as an unpredictable food supply, endemic warfare, chronic hunger and famine, and recent migration (Sanday 1981; Harris 1974; Friedl 1975).

How do you think the United States fits these criteria?

evaluating the anthropological perspective

Perhaps you have begun to appreciate the complexities of this perspective, in which no single custom or attitude is studied in isolation from the society as a whole. Obviously, it is easier to study a tribe of one hundred members than a nation of one hundred million. The larger and more complex a social system becomes, the harder it is to relate one part of the system to the others.

In general, any theory that says a custom exists because it has a survival function for the group has several problems. Consider the argument that male supremacy has lasted for the same reason that there are two sexes instead of one or three: If alternatives were ever tried, they didn't work.[6] This does seem to be true in the case of

---

[6]Actually, there are two sexes because two is the most efficient minimum number for the exchange of genetic information. An organism that reproduces itself gains no new material. Two sexes are sufficient for assuring the genetic recombinations necessary for variation and adaptation. A third sex would add no new genes but lots of social aggravation and sexual inefficiency.

matriarchy—no tribe has ever been dominated by male-abusing women who keep men secluded, and no tribe has ever been completely ruled by women—but it permits a "we're here because we're here" conclusion and allows for the fallacious inference that any system or social practice that survives must be good.

This inference is fallacious because social evolution is a constant process. At any one time it is hard to tell which systems and customs exist because they work and which are evolution's errors and will die. A critical issue for functionalists is to predict which is which; they cannot have it both ways. They cannot assume today that all existing customs are adaptive and tomorrow that any custom that changed was maladaptive.

Further, a custom that serves one function in society Q may have an entirely different function in society R, and a ritual that is adaptive in one culture may be irrelevant or maladaptive in another. Sexual celibacy may be a helpful custom when a society faces overpopulation but not when it brings a group's extinction (as in the case of the Shakers). A food taboo may have an ecological purpose in one tribe (the taboo on eating the sacred cow in India assures that the animals will survive to help farmers through times of drought and famine, and the products of the *live* animals are more important than the short-term benefit of eating them), but a social purpose in another (not eating meat gives some religious groups a sense of unified community) (Harris 1974).

Sociologist Alvin Gouldner (1970) once wrote that a functionalist approach is basically conservative because it nods benignly at stability (and thus at the status quo) and views change with alarm, as a sign that something has "malfunctioned." People in positions of power can use functionalist theories to justify many of the questionable practices that have had long and healthy lives: not only male supremacy but war, slavery, infanticide, and wholesale imprisonment, oppression, and slaughter of outgroups of every description. For whom are these practices functional? Theories that concentrate on the consequences of a custom for the society as a whole may miss its consequences for particular groups within that society. American slavery, for example, was certainly dysfunctional for blacks, but it benefited plantation owners and it "worked" as a basis for the southern economic system. Similarly, it is not always obvious what the costs and benefits of women's lesser status are—for a society, for its women, or for its men.

Certainly the system perspective can be used for conservative purposes, but it can also be used to illuminate the process of change.

It's a matter of disentangling *what is* from what one *would like*. Marvin Harris believes that if we can identify the rational reasons for our apparently irrational practices, and understand that these customs are born from environmental pressures, not genetic ones, we can change the conditions that create dissatisfaction, exploitation, and war. Moreover, by understanding how systems work, we will realize that we can't just blunder into another culture's way of doing things, or make changes in our own ways of doing things, without causing repercussions elsewhere. Social customs and beliefs are intricately connected, like the hundreds of bones that make up a skeleton. This fact can be used to impede change or to accelerate it.

For example, most Westerners are shocked and horrified by the practices of genital mutilation that occur in other countries. So are the women who tolerate these practices, even as they argue that they need to perpetuate them. (In her field work in Egypt, Karen Paige [in press] collected sorrowful stories from women describing their pain, tears, and protest when, as young children, they endured clitoral excision.) But as Paige observed, it is not enough to try to reason women out of this ancient tradition: "But you hate it; why inflict it on your daughters?" There are always answers: "Because she won't marry otherwise; because it's good for her; because it makes her genitals look better; because the clitoris will keep growing unless it is cut off." If the Paiges' theory of the ritual of female circumcision is correct—that the ritual has a fundamental economic and social purpose, namely surveillance over the sexuality of young women and a *public* demonstration for the kin group—then this custom will not cease simply because of argument and discussion. Indeed, it doesn't stop even when women become better educated. If kin negotiations are the reason for the ritual, then it follows that if the kinship system changes, the prevalence of the ritual will decline. And this is precisely what Paige (in press) found. Among the second generation of Egyptians she studied, more are moving to large cities and leaving the peasant countryside. With that move, there is a weakening of male kin control over daughters. (Paige measured that weakened control in two ways: first, the city families no longer go back to the villages, and the girl's immediate nuclear family, not the extended kin group, arranges her marriage; and second, city families no longer pool their economic resources with the village relatives; instead they sell off their farm property or rent it, reinvesting in urban properties and business.) With this weakening of extended kin control has come a decline in the practice of female circumcision.

Because societies, like building blocks, are assembled in different ways, a change that works to improve women's status in one culture may have an unexpectedly detrimental effect in another. In the United States birth control has had a liberating effect on women: With smaller families, women have gone to work, and their paychecks have raised their status. But Boserup (1970) observed some unexpected side effects of birth control in the rural African communities she studied. When women worked long and hard in the fields, they were valued both as workers and wives. In tribes in which hired laborers do the field work (a sign of modern "progress"), women are valued only as mothers, a lesser status, and especially as mothers of sons who will work the fields and earn money. Barren women are therefore considered useless. Effective birth control in such societies, Boserup warned, could lower the status of women even further.

The anthropological perspective, at its best, gets us away from the limitations of our own culture. It shows us that our way of life is no more natural or instinctive than any other; that what people do and believe is profoundly connected to the practical realities of their lives; that change is as much a part of the human condition as is continuity. It raises, ultimately, one of the most fascinating and important issues of our time: the control of our destiny. Do human societies evolve mindlessly, like anemones and aardvarks, or is there a place for human purpose?

9 | Conclusion: The age of alliance?

There never was a good war or a bad peace.

—*Benjamin Franklin*

Only a peace between equals can last.

—*Woodrow Wilson*

"Male supremacy is on the way out in all industrialized nations," believes Marvin Harris (1975). "Male supremacy was just a phase in the evolution of culture." Harris, an anthropologist, made his matter-of-fact assertion by taking the long view with a cultural evolutionist's eye. In the twentieth century, for the *first time* in human history, conditions have permitted societies to experiment with equality. Birth control means that women can decide when and even whether to have babies. Overpopulation means that families must get smaller. Industrialization has brought affluence to millions and provided them with the leisure time to consider less traditional roles and relationships. Warfare is largely mechanized, and males have no particular edge over females at pushing buttons to launch a deadly battle. The radically and rapidly altered conditions of life in this century suggest, said Harris, that male supremacy is just a long first act in a show that is not yet over.

Certainly it is true that many countries are addressing themselves to the "woman problem": appointing ministers to deal with the vexing question, passing laws to end the legal superiority of males, permitting women to enter occupations that were once for men only. Even Switzerland, which did not grant women the right to vote until 1971, passed an equal rights act ten years later—guaranteeing equality between men and women in the family, education, and pay. By 1980 most nations of the world had declared their formal support for the legal, economic, and social equality of women. Indeed, on December 11, 1980, the United Nations General Assembly endorsed a Program for Action for the U.N.'s "decade for women." It was interesting, though, that of the 149 representatives who spoke during the opening debate of the General Assembly, only one actually *was* a woman; and only eighteen even referred to the particular needs of women in their respective nations. In fact, reported anthropologist

Eleanor Leacock (1981), in spite of the U.N.'s brave words, the situation of women worldwide has actually worsened in recent years: Illiteracy has risen, technological development in Third World countries has had adverse effects on women's status and health, and the educational gains made by middle- and upper-income women in such nations have not been matched by employment gains.

Some attempts at egalitarianism in this century have crossed national and ideological boundaries. The Soviet Union and the People's Republic of China went through complete revolutionary overhauls that brought millions of feudal peasants into the twentieth century in remarkably few years; in Sweden and other Scandinavian countries a more equal division of labor between the sexes evolved over time; the Israeli kibbutz started from scratch as an effort to put theory and dreams of equality into practice. In the United States, movements for women's rights have come and gone and come again, bringing change and controversy in their wake. In all of these cases, the course of liberation, like that of love, has not run smooth.

The perspectives we have described in this book offer different ways of explaining both the changes in women's status and the resistance to them. We will consider first some of the national efforts at equality (in communist nations, socialist nations, and Israel and the United States), and then we will look at how the perspectives explain their successes, failures, and future prospects.

experiments in equality

the Soviet Union

In every society, wrote Marx and Engels, "the degree of emancipation of women is a natural standard of the general emancipation." The Soviet Union was the first country to try to put this belief into practice; one of the first orders of business after the 1917 revolution was to change the laws affecting women. Women quickly got the right to work alongside men, to have abortions on demand for unwanted pregnancies, and to end unhappy, arranged marriages with easy divorces. During the first heady years after the revolution, reformers were optimistic that socialism, having destroyed the economic basis of inequality, would automatically bring the demise of the patriarchal bourgeois family and liberate women. Women would take their rightful place as "productive" members of society, doing work that benefited the nation as a whole and not just the individual or the family. The state would take over the service work, child care, and household chores. As Engels wrote, "The modern individual family is based on the open or disguised domestic enslavement of the woman; private housekeeping should become a social industry." Communal dining rooms, government-run nursery schools, and professional laundries would solve the age-old problem of who does the dirty work.

In terms of the "productive work" part of this blueprint, the country's economic needs coincided with ideology. For most of this century the Soviet Union has suffered an acute shortage of men, because so many died during the revolution, a civil war, two world wars, periods of famine, and political upheavals. Before the revolution the ratio of women to men was about equal, but by 1938 it was 108.7 women for every 100 men. And the situation got worse. According to one estimate, nearly half of all the Russian men alive in 1939 died during World War II (Dodge 1966). That may be an exaggeration, but it is no exaggeration to say the country's losses were staggering. Moreover, they occurred during the decades when the Soviet Union was struggling to become a major industrial power. The government needed all the female workers it could get; its survival depended on them. And female workers it got. Today 51 percent of the work force is made up of women, and they work in virtually every sort of job. It is not unusual in the Soviet Union to see women as doctors, engineers, judges, professors, janitors, lawyers, sea captains, pilots, industrial laborers, bus drivers, and builders.

And yet Soviet working women are overrepresented in the lowest-paid, most menial jobs, such as janitors and garment workers. On the average, women still earn less than men do. The high-status jobs are all but monopolized by men, whether in science, industry, or government (Scott 1974; Lapidus 1978). And as women have entered formerly male-dominated professions, the fields have been redefined as feminine—notably pharmacy, dentistry, chemistry, and medicine (Safilios-Rothschild 1975). In politics women constitute about one-fourth of the members of the Communist Party (up from 8 percent in 1922), but on the higher rungs of the political ladder there are few women. Of the 319 full members of the Central Committee (the lawmaking body) in 1981, only eight (2.5 percent) were women, a decrease from the previous high of fourteen female members. And only one woman, Yekaterina A. Furtseva, has ever served in the Central Committee's Politburo, the ultimate seat of power, and that was only between 1957 and 1961 (*New York Times*, March 6, 1981).

Many social scientists are skeptical of Soviet claims about female equality because they observe how often ideology has succumbed to circumstance. For example, abortion was readily available after the revolution because, it was said, women should be able to control their own bodies, avoid loveless marriages, and not be slaves to unwanted pregnancies. But none of the planners realized how popular abortion would become. By the 1930s the government faced a declining birthrate, and in 1936 it did an about-face, outlawing abortion except for certain medical reasons and making divorce more difficult and expensive. Then it took positive measures to increase the birthrate: It offered premiums to women who had more than two children, payments that continued for the first four years of a child's life. Women who produced a number of children earned honors as well. A mother of five children won a Maternity Medal; seven or more children brought the Order of Maternal Glory; and ten or more won mom the title of Mother Heroine (Martin and Voorhies 1975; Field and Flynn 1970). Although the Soviet Union eventually liberalized its abortion and divorce laws again in 1966, both are, in practice, discouraged. The scarcity of contraceptives (there are no IUDs or birth-control pills, and diaphragms can seldom be found) means that many Russian women must rely on abortion to limit births, and some have as many as eight to ten abortions in their lifetimes (Knaus 1981; Morgan 1980).[1]

Perhaps the clearest rumple in the socialist blueprint concerns ideology about the family. Somehow, no one in the Soviet Union ever got around to solving the logistical problems of providing millions of families with professional laundry service, food delivery, and child care; doing so would have required shifting funds and energies away from more pressing problems. As a result, guess who does the housework and child care?

The domestic side of life is still regarded by both sexes as the woman's responsibility. Although many children go to state-run nursery schools, the nurseries are not free and not yet available to every child. So most mothers rely on friends or relatives to help them with child care, and in a crisis it is usually the mother, not the father, who compromises the job for the family (Morgan 1980; Lapidus 1978). It is

[1]To those who are concerned with the long-term consequences of overpopulation it seems surprising that a government would want to *increase* its population. But a sudden drop in births can have serious short-term results—shortages of workers in critical occupations, reduced demand for consumer goods, a relative increase in the proportion of old people. Is the drop in the U.S. birthrate associated with efforts to strike down liberal abortion laws?

usually the mother, not the father, who interrupts a career for a few years in an effort to juggle the needs of children, household, and job. And it is usually the mother, not the father, who stands in long lines at the market, prepares meals without benefit of fancy appliances, and cleans the house. The men "help out"—evoking a few sarcastic reactions from women:

> There's a bachelor I knew in three periods of his life. First when he was married and, by his own words, didn't know how to put a teapot on to boil, never mind eggs. . . . Then he got divorced. A miracle followed. He could have been a professor of homemaking. His room wasn't simply clean, it was downright sterile, and the dinners he made for friends were beyond praise. . . . Then he remarried. And immediately stopped cooking dinners, making pickles, and it took an argument for his wife to get him to go down for bread. (Russian woman quoted in Mandel 1975, p. 211)

Lenin had berated men for shirking their domestic duties. "Very few husbands, not even the proletarians, think of how much they could lighten the burdens and worries of their wives, or relieve them entirely, if they lent a hand in this 'woman's work.' But no, that would go against the 'privilege and dignity of the husband.' He demands that he have his rest and comfort." That he does. Soviet writers have considered many ways to lighten woman's burden: giving women less strenuous jobs, arranging part-time work for women or shorter working days, distributing better household appliances, building more child care facilities, and so on (Field and Flynn 1970). But they seem to be overlooking Lenin's observation that the handiest labor-saving device is a husband.

the People's Republic of China

Before the revolution of 1949, the Chinese say, all people carried three mountains on their backs—feudalism, capitalism, and imperialism—but women had a fourth burden, male supremacy. A proverb sums up the treatment of women in prerevolutionary China: "A woman married is like a pony bought—to be ridden or whipped at the master's pleasure." Women had no rights—not over their property, their bodies, or their marriages. Fathers sometimes drowned their infant daughters and sold their surviving daughters as concubines and prostitutes. Husbands could beat or even kill their wives with impunity, and landlords could rape them. When a woman married she became subject to the wishes of her husband's family forever; divorce was almost impossible, and widows were forbidden to remarry.

With the Communist victory in 1949, the new People's Republic of China produced a series of sweeping reforms. The government gave women property rights, a free choice in marriage, the right to vote, the right to divorce. It abolished polygamy, prostitution, wife buying, and female infanticide. It declared that women were economically equal to men and would get the same pay for the same work. China today has had even less time than the Soviet Union to overturn centuries of feudalism and female subordination; yet in only a few decades extraordinary changes have taken place in the status of women. Ninety percent of them work outside the home. As in the Soviet Union, women have entered jobs formerly reserved for men: They drive trucks, fly planes, and wield picks. (In 1957 China had a squadron of jet fighters run entirely by women.) They are doctors, teachers, and engineers (Curtin 1975; Tavris 1974).

Of course, the entrance of women into the work force has not been steady and uncomplicated. Work for women has depended on the country's economic growth and on its shifting economic policies, as in the U.S.S.R. Katie Curtin (1975) believes that an industrial slump in the mid-1950s was behind propaganda praising home life and the contributions of the housewife. (A postwar slump in the United States evoked the same ideology.) But when China developed an acute need for labor in 1958, and subsequently launched the "Great Leap Forward," the government proclaimed the liberating, patriotic effects of being a working woman. It set up day-care centers to make it possible for women to enter the work force in large numbers. The program was so successful that today a Chinese "housewife" is virtually an anachronism. In many places wives have gotten together to organize what they call "housewife factories," local enterprises that produce everything from embroidered pillows to insulation materials (Tavris 1974).

Yet some economic inequities are built into the system. On communes, which are huge agricultural collectives of up to 50,000 people, a system of work points determines a person's share of the collective income. The more physically strenuous the job, the more points one gets. Women earn fewer work points than men because they don't do the hardest work, because they tend to work shorter days in order to do housework (which is not regarded as productive labor), and because they don't get points for maternity leave or for days off during the menstrual period if they take them (Diamond 1975). In the cities, men still seem to wind up doing different work from women, even in the same factory, and getting more money.

Despite its reforms, the Chinese Revolution did not aim to overturn the basic structure of patriarchy (Stacey 1983). For one thing, the Chinese Communists never were as concerned as the Soviets about changing the basic nature of the family and sexual relations. The Chinese see no incompatibility between the family and female liberation; indeed, they believe the family is bedrock. Although a wave of divorces followed the revolution, ending thousands of brutal marriages, today divorce is more difficult to get, and a Chinese couple goes through considerable discussion and persuasion from colleagues and family before they make it to the divorce court. Further, the Chinese see no link between female liberation and sexual liberation. On the contrary. The Chinese are quite Victorian in their views: Before marriage, the sexual rule is "all for none and none for all"; sex, the adolescents learn, saps your strength. Abortion and birth control are available to all women. The purpose, though, is not to make them sexually free but to keep the population down and the females working.[2]

the Scandinavian countries

A policy which attempts to give women an equal place with men in economic life while at the same time confirming woman's traditional responsibility for care of the home and children has no prospect of fulfilling these aims. The division of functions between the sexes must be changed in such a way that both the man and the woman in a family are afforded the same practical opportunities of participating in both active parenthood and gainful employment.

—The Status of Women in Sweden:
Official Report to the United Nations

[2]The traditional hostility toward female infants continues, in modern guise. A new Chinese method of identifying the sex of a fetus produced an unintended consequence: Of thirty fetuses that had been intentionally aborted after the mothers knew the sex, twenty-nine were female (Campbell 1976). In addition, the Chinese policy of one-child families, designed to control the exploding population, is often defeated by parents whose first child is a girl. Many of them keep trying until they have a son. On March 3, 1983, the [Chinese] People's Daily reported: "At present, the phenomena of butchering, drowning and leaving to die female infants and maltreating women who have given birth to female infants have been very serious. It has become a grave social problem" (Li Jiangui and Zhang Xiaoying, pseudonymous Chinese students, The New York Times, March 11, 1983).

Sweden and the other Scandinavian countries have striven for sex-role equality through evolution rather than revolution, and they have instituted imaginative programs toward that goal. In the mid-1950s Sweden grappled with the issues of social and economic equality that came to America's attention years later. While many American men were struggling to be "good providers" and while their wives were trying to live up to the "feminine mystique" (Ehrenreich 1983; Friedan 1963), two Swedish sociologists, Alva Myrdal and Viola Klein, wrote *Women's Two Roles: Home and Work* (1956), a book that explored the difficulties of combining those roles and that suggested some solutions.

The role of Swedish women in the work force, like that of women elsewhere, has fluctuated with economic conditions. Between 1930 and 1946 droves of women left the labor force in what has been called a "mass flight" into marriage. "Aha," observers said. "See? Women are happier as housewives." However, their flight coincided with what a Swedish sociologist called an "enormously woman-hostile labor market during the Depression." After the Depression the economic standard was high enough for many women to afford to stay home, which has not been the case in the Soviet Union and Finland, for example (Haavio-Mannila 1975). In the 1960s a shortage of labor meant that Sweden needed its women in the work force. Accordingly, official policy shifted, child care facilities were improved, and a national educational campaign for sex-role equality began. Scandinavian women are less likely to enter "masculine" professions than women in Eastern European nations, although they make up one-fifth to one-third of the physicians and lawyers and have taken over the fields of pharmacy and, especially in Denmark, dentistry. There are numerous government-sponsored nursery schools, though not enough for the children of all working women.

Because taxes and some legislation favor the two-income family, husbands and wives are redefining the division of labor in the household. Both partners are encouraged to share housework and child care when both work, and—most radical innovation of all— husbands as well as wives have the option to stay home or work part time. But perhaps most unusual, Sweden has a paid paternity-leave program. The Swedish system offers benefits to either mothers *or* *fathers* who choose to stay home with their new infants. Parents may take up to nine months of paid work leave, and divide up that time any way they like: Either parent may stay home the whole nine months; one may take three months and the other six; both may work half time for the full nine months (Lamb 1982). And yet the proportion of fathers taking at least one month of leave (since the program was introduced in 1974) has only been about 5 percent.

Elina Haavio-Mannila (1975) compared the efforts of three neighboring nations—Sweden, Finland, and the Soviet Union—to liberate women from housework. The three countries have different ideologies about sex roles and different industrial histories, to say nothing of political philosophies. Haavio-Mannila's study was based on interviews with 430 Soviet families in three cities (Leningrad, Moscow, and Pensa); 271 families in Helsinki, Finland; and 442 families in Uppsala, Sweden. She found *no differences* among these countries in the families' division of labor. It didn't matter whether the women had outside jobs or not, or how actively the government encouraged them to join the labor force or stay at home. In 70 percent of the households, only the wife bought food, made breakfast, fed the children, and washed the dishes; in 80 percent she cooked dinner. The men were more likely to fix things around the house—and that's all. Househusbandry may be an approved way of life in Sweden, but it is far from a popular practice.

the Israeli kibbutz

Perhaps no experiment in equality has been scrutinized as minutely as the kibbutz (plural *kibbutzim*). Scarcely had the idea been planted before researchers began pulling it out by the roots to see how it was doing. The story of the kibbutz is particularly interesting because some people argue that it shows that equality is doomed, that men and women, left to their preferences, lapse into their "natural" roles.

Kibbutzim are rural communities in which members collectively own all property. The first kibbutzim were founded early in this century by young socialist emigrants from Russia and Europe, who wanted to escape what they considered the stifling atmosphere of traditional urban Jewish life. They had read Marx and Freud and were determined to set up an alternative community that would represent the best of both. The founders therefore rejected the nuclear family, which they regarded as patriarchal and antifemale, a breeding ground for the Oedipus complex and sexual hostilities. They rejected the values associated with capitalism, especially competitiveness and financial ambition, and sought instead a community based on physical labor, austerity, equality, and group loyalty. There would be no salaries and no status distinctions based on wealth. Each member of the group would get the goods and services she or he needed, regardless of the work assigned.

The decision to break up the nuclear family came about for several reasons. The founders feared that family loyalties would compete with allegiance to the larger community, and in the face of harsh external conditions for survival the kibbutz could not afford much internal dissension, family squabbling, or personal ambition. Ideologically, the founders also believed that if parents dealt with their children as friendly comrades instead of as stern disciplinarians, a more democratic bond between adults and children would result. The children would be more secure as well, because they would be children of the kibbutz, nourished and loved by everyone. Finally, the founders believed that when women were free for "productive" work like plowing fields and building roads, when they didn't have to worry about cooking meals and ironing shirts, they would become equal partners with men once and for all—politically, economically, and sexually.

The kibbutz made almost all housekeeping a collective enterprise. Kibbutz members eat together in a communal dining room; they get their clothes, toothbrushes, and soap at a communal commissary; and they send their dirty linen to a communal laundry. Though they live in private apartments, the rooms are small and do not require much care. Child rearing too is a collective procedure. Within a few days or weeks after birth, babies are brought to a special children's house, where they are cared for by a specially trained professional called a *metapelet* (nurse). Children visit with their parents in the late afternoons and on weekends, but they eat and sleep in their own quarters. A child's friends, not parents, are the primary contacts, and as a result the kibbutz child develops a strong allegiance to the peer group. All of this, however, is rapidly changing, with a significant number of kibbutzniks returning to the nuclear family arrangement (Palgi et al. 1983).

Today there are about 280 kibbutzim, representing 3 percent of the total Israeli population—a small but influential proportion. They range in size from several dozen members to over 2,000; but most have a few hundred. The kibbutzniks have been remarkably successful at surviving in the face of extraordinary odds. Though life was hard and work seemed unending in the early days, today kibbutz members enjoy a standard of living that is higher than that of most Israelis. The collective principle still holds; residents together own all property and means of production.

But the original dream of sexual and sex-role equality has faded and the division of labor on the kibbutz has reverted to the old ways. Lionel Tiger and Joseph Shepher (1975) studied some 16,000 women in two communes, and Martha Mednick (1975) interviewed a random sample of kibbutzniks from fifty-five settlements, 400 original settlers and 918 adults of the second generation. The women are in fact back at the service jobs in the kitchen, laundry, and schools, and those who do work in agriculture are concentrated in poultry raising and plant nurseries. Fewer occupations are open to women than to men, and the dream of a fifty-fifty share in the work of production has vanished. As the kibbutzim prospered and the population grew, the need for support services and the desire for physical amenities increased, and the women left the fields for the household.

It might seem that feeding an entire community and raising loyal members of the kibbutz are as important as driving a tractor or picking apples. But that is not how it is on the kibbutz. The jobs that produce income for the community, the jobs that men do, are held in higher esteem than the jobs women do. And when members rate their own status in the community, women rate themselves lower than men:

> Work is the central value of the kibbutz. Moreover, *productive* work, that which results in economic gain, is valued most highly. On the other hand, services, which include the kitchen, the laundry, the clothing factory, and the dining room, are regarded as necessary, but *nonproductive* and therefore less valued. (Mednick 1975, p. 88)

Men have the political power too, although there are no official barriers in the women's way. The kibbutz is a true participatory democracy. A general assembly of all members meets regularly to make major decisions, and each member has one vote. Yet women are not equal participants in this system. They rarely run for political office, although these positions rotate every few years; they show up in fewer numbers at the meetings; when they do attend they are less vocal than the men. Although almost half of all kibbutz members serve on community committees, women work on those connected with education, social welfare, and cultural activities, while men dominate on the economic committee—which determines economic goals and policies, controls the budget, and wields the real power (Mednick 1975). The second-generation women, said Mednick, seem quite content to leave political matters to men. So although there are no status differences based on class and wealth, the bane of Marxist theory, there *are* status differences based on work and political participation. And men have the prestige. In more recent studies, this has been shown to be still true (Safir 1983; Palgi et al. 1983).

The kibbutz, then, presents us with a puzzle. Kibbutz women are economically independent. They do not get status from their husbands' incomes or jobs. They have total job security no matter how many children they choose to have, and they are guaranteed high-quality care and education for their children. They do not have complicated housework to contend with and they do not have to feed their families or clean up after them. Yet kibbutz women lack political power, and they don't seem to want it. They do not work in the high-prestige occupations, and they don't seem to want to. The feminine mystique has returned with a vengeance.

an American experiment: the dual-career couple

In the 1970s there was much excited talk about the "dual-career couple" as a paradigm of sex-role equality in the future. A husband and wife, each equally committed to work and family, would represent a new integration of the two roles—for both sexes (Rapoport and Rapoport 1972). (It is not coincidental, we think, that this paradigm was of special interest to husband-and-wife social scientist teams.) But recent research suggests that in actual practice, the dual-career model is neither as egalitarian as it seems nor especially desirable for most couples.

Janet G. Hunt and Larry L. Hunt (1981) have argued that as careers become more legitimate for women, careers and families will become more *polarized*, not more *integrated*. The early studies of dual-career couples, they observed, found that most of them conformed to traditional sex roles. The wife had a nontraditional career, by definition, but within the family both spouses regarded the man as the primary provider, the woman primarily as wife and mother. Career wives felt privileged to be "allowed" to work; their husbands felt good about "letting" their wives work, while making virtually no concessions in their own careers or in their contributions to family tasks.

What has happened in recent years, wrote the Hunts, is not that men do more at home, but that women do less. The dual-career couple has become dual *career*, all right, but not dual career-plus-family. The system in the past assigned men to work roles that truncated their family lives; women were assigned to family roles that precluded satisfying work lives. Nowadays, say the Hunts, the commitment to career (by a man or woman) still demands an individual's full energies, causing family life to suffer. The contradiction is not between gender and work, but, in columnist Ellen Goodman's terms, between "family-first people and work-first people." "*Career and family involvement*," said the Hunts emphatically, " *have never been combined easily in the same person.*"

The Hunts have made a gloomy prognosis. People of either sex who are "work-first," they predict, will tend to remain childless (or, in careerist terms, "childfree"). Or such couples may avoid long commitments altogether. Those who are "family-first" may give priority to sex-role equality in the home, at the expense of career success. The result will be a widening discrepancy between childless couples and parents, which will enable the former to monopolize the highest-paying jobs and pool their resources to drive up the price of everything from houses to health care. In Sweden, they observe, this has already begun to happen: The most significant cause of a declining birthrate has been the lower living standard of families with children in contrast to childless couples.

Similarly, sociologist Harold Benenson (1981) asserted that the dual-career paradigm is not now, and can never be, a model for sex-role equality for everyone. He offered several reasons:

1. The careers of dual-career couples are elite and restricted (doctors, lawyers, professors). Married women who have such careers are numerically insignificant among all married women; in 1980 they constituted less than 0.6 percent of all wives.

2. The dual-career pattern retains traditional inequalities between husband and wife. Husbands still earn far more than their wives; in fact, among professional couples the wage gap is huge, far greater than that between middle- and working-class employed spouses! Further, the husband's job still takes priority, and the wives are still responsible for the homemaking role, with only occasional help from husbands.

3. In the last decade the largest numerical increase in employment for women occurred in clerical and service occupations; in spite of the apparent expansion of professional employment for women, the movement for job equality and integration actually lost steam and did not accelerate during this decade. (Indeed, said Benenson, 40 percent of all married women who work are concentrated in two job categories: elementary-school or kindergarten teaching and nursing.)

4. Women in elite professions and management positions are far more likely than comparable men to be single, married with no children (the Hunts' observation again), or divorced as a consequence of their career involvement.

"By channeling feminist concerns with sexual equality into an elite vision of family and career advancement," concluded Benenson, "the dual-career framework distorts the realities of social class constraint, occupational segregation and female subordination that shape the experience of close to ninety-nine percent of employed adult women." A model of sexual equality must apply to more than 1 percent of the population.

defining equality

As these case studies illustrate, many modern nations have made great strides in their efforts to unravel the work and family knot. To get women into the labor force, they have used a variety of approaches to enable women to combine "their" responsibilities of home and job. In one summary review, sociologist Constantina Safilios-Rothschild (1975) studied the male-female division of labor in twenty-three countries at all levels of economic development and noted four patterns:

1. *The Soviet Union, Poland, Hungary, Finland:* Women work, many in formerly male occupations, but men do not do women's work. State-supported nursery schools and day care and a national ideology that favors communal child rearing help women work but require no changes on the part of husbands.

2. *Scandinavian countries:* Fewer women work, though the ideology favors complete equality. Men are encouraged to split housework and child care equally, though there are many fewer househusbands than housewives.

3. *Argentina, Austria, Japan, Greece, Turkey:* About one-third of the women work, and an even smaller proportion of wives. None of these countries provides day-care centers or nursery schools, except a few understaffed ones for working-class women. Wealthy wives can combine work and family because maid service is cheap and available and the extended family still thrives. Grandmothers often do housework and babysit for their working daughters.

4. *The United States, Canada, and to some extent England, France, West Germany, and Australia:* In all these countries the cultural values are at odds with the realities. While many women work (in numbers ranging from one-third to two-thirds), the ideology is that child care is a full-time occupation and that children need their mothers. These nations provide no system-wide professional help or day care for working mothers, who are left to work out a solution on an individual basis. Partly because so many women in these countries must wait until their children are in school before they can work full time, women have not entered traditionally male occupations in significant numbers.

In most of these countries women are steadily (though in some, slowly) being absorbed into the work force, doing a great number of jobs. Some countries make it easier for women to work and raise families and some make it harder, but none has succeeded in getting men to share domestic work equally. And in no nation are women 50 percent of the key politicians and leaders.

National studies show too how complicated it is to define equality. The definition varies according to a country's particular needs, history, and economic and political system. Equality can mean getting women out of the home and into the work force, or assuring women of political power, or breaking down all personality and task differences, or changing archaic laws, or allowing both men and women sexual freedom. In some places efforts for equality are directed primarily at educated, affluent women and men; in others, the term implies equal opportunity at all levels. As a former New York State Education Commissioner once put it, "Equality is not when a female Einstein gets promoted to assistant professor; equality is when a female schlemiel moves ahead as fast as a male schlemiel."

Still, virtually all modern efforts have defined equality primarily in economic terms. When people speak of liberating women and ending discrimination, they are generally thinking of how to get women out of the home and into the work force; they are generally not thinking of how to get men to do more at home. Even countries that pride themselves on the equality achieved by their women usually mean that women now clean the streets, not that men now clean the house.

The apparent failure of the dual-career model in the United States, paternity programs in Sweden, egalitarianism on the kibbutz, and large-scale revolutions in the U.S.S.R. and China has caused some modern writers to conclude that men and women have built-in biological roles, after all, and that it won't do to muck around with nature's program. (They overlook the lessons of anthropology, as we showed in Chapter 8, that nature is expressed in hundreds of different cultural forms.) Each of the perspectives in this book offers reasons for the continuing status differences between the sexes; for the difficulty of getting men to do women's work; for the "flight to the family" that women take when equality fails. Let's review them.

the perspectives in perspective

The most talked-about perspective today is undoubtedly the biological one in its various guises (sociobiology, genes, hormones, brain structure). Hardly a week goes by without another "new" argument about the biological nature of man and woman,[3] of which Tiger and Shepher's analysis of the kibbutz (1975) is typical if not as recent. Tiger and Shepher asserted that the kibbutz is the perfect laboratory to test biological imperatives because there, if anywhere, every effort was made to create sexual equality in practice as well as in ideology. If the effort failed, they argued, it must be because equality goes against the grain that evolution has determined for us. They wrote, "There is at birth a basic diagram, a set of biologically determined dispositions which has been called a 'biogrammar.' . . . Culture (i.e., socialization) in its plasticity may go against those dispositions, but not for long and not for many people, without causing serious difficulties for both the individual and society" (Tiger and Shepher 1975). In other words, the kibbutz has reverted to the traditional ways because women have a universal need to be close to their children, care for their families, and leave the driving to men. Women by nature don't want to play politics or defend the group. All they want is a nest, a small, warm place to raise children. Women may tolerate the frustration of their basic needs in times of crisis, when their country needs pioneers, but as soon as conditions allow, Tiger and

---

[3]For example, popular writers Jo Durden-Smith and Diane De Simone argued, in *Sex and the Brain* (1983), that differences between the sexes—in sexual preferences and disorders, in pains and pleasures, in abilities and interests, in emotions and intellect—are etched into the brain and reflect different brain structures. From another direction, anthropologist Derek Freeman challenged the cultural arguments of Margaret Mead in his book *Margaret Mead and Samoa* (1983), arguing that her cultural bias obscured certain *biological* truths. Neither of these books presented novel, original, or creative interpretations, so what is interesting is the media attention they have received. When anthropologist Annette Weiner (see Chapter 8, p. 299) reanalyzed Malinowski's work on the Trobriand Islanders, showing the power and influence that Trobriand women in fact had, she didn't get a fraction of the attention Freeman did.

Shepher said, they inevitably "return to a pattern more typical of our species." This conclusion, which ignores the fact that there are many patterns typical of our species, has been applied to the egalitarian experiments of other nations and, of course, our own. When a modern American woman decides she doesn't want the "two jobs" of career and family, her action is taken as evidence of her "real" underlying needs. When a modern American man doesn't have time to care for his young children, this lack of involvement is taken as evidence of the male's "real" lack of paternal feeling.

Similarly, the psychoanalytic view predicts that no society can eradicate the unique components of feminine personality that are based on unconscious motives and anatomical differences. Women will continue to feel inferior to men, whether they get equal pay for equal work or not, because no government can issue them a penis. According to traditional Freudians, women will continue to bear children as a substitute for the missing organ, and efforts to avoid the Oedipus complex by raising children in communal systems are doomed because of the deeply rooted needs and driving forces of the unconscious. Some psychoanalytic writers, though, are modifying the theory to allow for changing psychodynamics. Unconscious dispositions are determined by the structure of the nuclear family, some maintain (Chodorow 1978), so if the structure changes, the content of unconscious fantasies and desires will change as well.

The learning perspective suggests that efforts at equality have failed so far because adults have not been able to overcome their own socialization histories. If the first generation of reformers cannot change their own deepest feelings about the place of women, they probably transmit those feelings to their children, professed egalitarian philosophies notwithstanding. Jessie Bernard (1976) cited a male kibbutznik's attitude toward women, unconsciously revealed while he was reminiscing with, of all people, Golda Meir. "He told Golda that though she herself was perhaps not sensitive to it, the men of her generation believed women to be weak and incompetent beings, and tried as best they could to keep them out of the way, at which point *he made the gesture one usually makes when brushing flies away.*"

The heat of a passionate ideology can blind people to the subtleties of socialization. Settlers on the kibbutz and revolutionaries in the Soviet Union seem to have assumed that by declaring the sexes equal and putting women to work, they had created equality. They did not worry about whether role changes would outlast crisis conditions. As Hilda Scott (1974) noted, if inequality is assumed to be merely a matter of the wrong economic system, then once you have changed the system there is no need to define equality, to see how men and women continue to treat each other, or to be concerned with whether women have overcome their low self-regard. "In other words, [there is] no need to unwrap people's minds and souls or air their misconceptions and prejudices. If patriarchal beliefs then continue to lie just below the surface in men and women, these are likely to determine the kind of equality that is set as the goal."

The socialization perspective suggests, therefore, that for children to be prepared for a changing future, they need to learn to balance *both* roles, work and family. Just as research shows that women with two sources of self-esteem—family and work—are healthier and happier than women with just one, the same is true for men. Now that women are discovering work, men are discovering that work isn't everything. Many contemporary writers are saying that modern life should not require total commitment to any one role, that people feel better when they have many roles to carry out. Those who put all their eggs in one basket may be in for depression and helplessness when the basket breaks. Women who get their whole sense of identity from motherhood, and men who get theirs from work, are more likely to suffer and turn sick when the children leave home or the job ends through retirement (or firing). Not much will have been achieved, some people argue, if women's liberation merely gets women out of the house and into jobs that turn them into achievement-mad competitors, or makes contented housewives feel dissatisfied, or creates a generation of depressed househusbands.

To avoid these alternatives, boys and girls would have to learn that both work and family are responsibilities, not duties divided by gender. Alice Baumgartner (1983), who identified the contempt that boys learn to feel about "girl's work" (see Chapter 6), observed that "the guiding developmental rule for boys appears to be 'Don't be female.' Every time we reinforce that rule, we teach boys to have contempt for females." She also pointed out:

> Boys learn at a very young age that their jobs are taking out the garbage and helping Dad wash the car—and they learn that washing anything else (dishes, laundry, and baby) is for girls. This early segregation of chores not only makes boys disdainful of "women's work," but also deprives them of the chance to learn some housekeeping skills—such as cooking dinner, ironing a shirt or sewing on buttons—that they will need as adults! (in Tavris with Baumgartner 1983, p. 94)

Baumgartner added that socialization changes thus far have largely been in the direction of "fixing" girls to be more like boys. "The solution to stereotyping," she said, "is not just for women to do more things. Women's work is devalued precisely because *women* do it; therefore we ought to be suggesting that males start doing a few 'female' things to balance the scales."

The socialization perspective argues that there is nothing mysterious about women's "flight to the family"; twenty years of instruction about the proper roles of male and female, and about the social consequences of stepping out of line, are enough to keep both sexes doing what feels most comfortable (even if what is most comfortable is least satisfying).

Like learning theorists, most sociologists and social psychologists resist the reduction of complex social issues to biological or psychoanalytic imperatives that are unchanging and unchangeable. Bernard (1976) attacked Tiger and Shepher's concept of "biologically determined dispositions," pointing out, for example, that "women of the nobility and upper classes have matter-of-factly and routinely turned their children over to the care of nurses and nannies for generations and that countless middle-class and working-class mothers would cheerfully do likewise if they could." Further, she observed, Tiger and Shepher occasionally bent their argument when it didn't fit the data. People who believe in an instinctive mother-child bond often argue that when mothers go off to work, the children invariably suffer. But Tiger and Shepher were in somewhat of a bind because kibbutz children grow into happy, healthy adults, physically and emotionally. So, Bernard observed, they must concede that " 'the biogrammatical rules . . . need not be followed precisely; the kibbutz example suggests that one can drastically alter the ways of being a mother' and still turn out a great product." Finally, while Tiger and Shepher explained the very high level of dissatisfaction among kibbutz women in terms of the women's thwarted maternal instinct, Bernard thinks a more plausible explanation is the low level of prestige and professionalism of their work.

Martha Mednick's (1975, 1983) explanation for the kibbutz's feminine backlash relies on events, not instincts. The return to family and home, she wrote, occurred because of these nonbiological factors:

1. The kibbutzim were founded in an atmosphere of economic and military crisis, in which "masculine" attributes and values were needed for survival and rewarded. The early emancipation of women came about as much out of need as ideology. (A similar argument can be made for the U.S.S.R. and China.)

2. Certain roles never changed. "Women had the *privilege* of working and fighting like men," she wrote, "but men did not have the obvious reciprocal privileges." The care and education of children always remained tasks for women only.

3. As the early hardships lessened, the need for children to sustain the kibbutz increased, and pronatalist values returned. More children meant more support services; at the same time the economic successes of the kibbutzim spurred demands for more amenities, a more comfortable life. At this point it seemed natural, wrote Mednick, for women to return to the traditional tasks and for men to continue in production; rationalizations about women's "true nature" followed this break from the original ideology of equality.

4. At present, the only female activity that is rewarded on the kibbutz and that brings self-esteem is having children. Women who have many children, though they may not get titles like Mother Heroine, are highly regarded for producing more members of the kibbutz.

Similarly, as developmental psychologist Michael Lamb (1982) observed, the "failure" of the paternity-leave program in Sweden cannot be attributed to the lack of a male nurturing instinct. Most fathers prefer to take their leave when their infants have been weaned, but there is a financial motive for not doing this—that is exactly when their paid reimbursement is at its lowest. Second, because women tend to have less prestigious occupations than their husbands and are less likely to be working in a career than their husbands are, some men feel that their wives can take maternity leave without causing major disruptions in their career line or in their places of employment. (This situation is the same in the United States, but of course it creates a vicious cycle: Women, knowing they will have to take time out to care for infants, do not seek the jobs that will prohibit such interruptions; once they have lower-status, lower-paying jobs, wives become the logical spouses to bow out for child-rearing years.) Lamb reported that nearly 10 percent of the major American corporations offer *unpaid* paternity leave, "but, not surprisingly, relatively few men have taken advantage of this costly option."

In the case of the Soviet Union, which began with an explicit ideology to expand women's economic and political participation, Gail Lapidus (1978) observed that the terms on which this expansion occurred actually "sustained and reinforced a pervasive asymmetry of male and female roles." The basic social structure remained intact, she found, perpetuating the "official perceptions, priorities, and institutional arrangements" that kept women in fact from achievements and that kept men from shared work in the domestic sphere. China likewise has maintained its basic asymmetry of sexual roles (Stacey 1983).

The sociological and anthropological perspectives alert us to the difference between ideology and equality, to the importance of watching what people *do* and not simply what they *say*. Sometimes the ideology has praised equality, which is far from achieved (as in the Soviet Union); sometimes the ideology has praised separation of roles, when in fact both sexes have changed (as in the United States). These perspectives show too that as economic conditions rise and fall, some of the most entrenched cultural values and customs can change as well.[4]

The sociological and anthropological perspectives suggest that if equality is to be reached, then woman's work must yield as many rewards from society as man's work: economic and psychological rewards, not empty words about the nobility of housework and motherhood. Both sexes must feel that women are producers rather than consumers, and the work that both sexes do must generate income for the family. Then people will be able to make decisions about what they want to do on the basis of ability and temperament, not gender, and neither sex will be at the economic mercy of the other. All occupations, from raising children to raising soybeans, will be valuable. Some people object to this kind of argument, saying it reflects the crass materialism of American life. But we base our observation on the data from Chapter 8, which show that every culture in human history has valued income-producing work more than domestic work and child rearing.

John Kenneth Galbraith (1973), the noted economist, argued that the conversion of American women into an unpaid servant class was "an economic accomplishment of the first importance. Menial employed servants were available only to a minority of the pre-industrial population; the servant-wife is available, democratically, to almost the entire present male population. . . . The servant role of women is critical for the expansion of consumption in the modern economy."

[4]The situation of women in contemporary Japan is particularly interesting. According to Robert Christopher (1983), a close observer of Japan since World War II, women's status is rapidly rising. Women are joining the work force in increasing numbers. That is partly because Japan has become a consumer society, like the United States; partly because more Japanese young women are becoming educated; and partly because a declining birthrate has created a shortage of new male entrants into the labor force (a familiar reason). These changes, in Japan and elsewhere, have repercussions in the home. "Since I sometimes can't get home in time to make dinner," one young working woman told Christopher. "I've been teaching my husband how to cook for himself. The idea shocks his mother, but he rather seems to enjoy it."

In other words, an economy that is based on spending and growth, as ours is, needs an "underclass" that does not cost employers anything and whose function is to spend what employees earn. The housewife role has been fundamental to the entire system, but its economic significance has been overlooked. As we move from an economy based on expansion to one based on containment (in a world that is slowly learning that resources are not infinite), the need for a class of consumers will diminish.

In short, if men and women are to be equal in opportunity, then work and the family must become more flexible, more integrated, and less sex-typed. According to these perspectives, there is nothing mysterious about the difficulties encountered by dual-career couples, and nothing instinctive about the fact that some women decide not to be superwomen by juggling a career, children, and household by themselves. The problem lies not in the biology or personality of the couples who try to combine career and family, but in the structure of occupations—which make it so very difficult for women *or* men to combine roles.

Thus we do not need to postulate all sorts of biological urges and surges to understand why the sexual division of labor persists. Of course, we must start with the fact that women bear and often nurse children, but these activities (in the modern United States) by no means occupy all of a woman's adult life, so there is no logical reason that they should keep the sexes unequal in status and opportunity. More useful answers, we think, come from economics, sociology, and psychology—not that any one level of explanation is sufficient; they intersect in fascinating ways. To illustrate, we want to look now at two current explanations for social change that demonstrate the connection between objective conditions and psychological attitudes.

sex ratios and social life

Consider two societies, each of which has the following attitudes about love, sex, marriage, and woman's place:

Society 1	Society 2
Adultery is morally wrong.	Adultery is acceptable.
Marriage is forever.	Marriage is temporary.
Woman's place is in the home.	Woman's place is at work.
Family life is essential.	Family life is optional.
Women should be prized and protected.	Women should be neither prized nor protected.

What causes the differences between societies 1 and 2? Social psychologists Marcia Guttentag and Paul Secord (1983) offered a provocative answer: the ratio of marriageable men to marriageable women. When this ratio is high (for example, 120 men for every 100 women in an age group), women are a scarce resource; therefore, men prize catching one and keeping her. Marital and sexual commitments are emphasized; male and female roles are complementary and segregated; women are valued as romantic love objects. But when men are in short supply, Guttentag and Secord argued (with perhaps only 70 or 80 men for every 100 women), men become the scarce resource. Now there are more unattached women who must rely on themselves, so more of them go to school, get jobs, become self-supporting and self-reliant, and organize social movements to improve their economic and political position. Societies that have fewer men than women in a marriageable cohort are characterized by family disruption (as measured by a high divorce rate, many single-parent families, illegitimate births, more singles and divorcees who don't marry or remarry).

Naturally, the simple ratio of marriageable men to women is not enough to determine all of a culture's sex and sex-role practices (see Chapter 8), but Guttentag and Secord have suggested that the basic differences between Society 1 and Society 2 are recognizable across time and culture. Ancient Athens (which had more men than women) differed from ancient Sparta (which had far fewer men than women) in the predicted ways, and Spartan women were relatively more educated and "liberated" than their cloistered Athenian sisters.

Perhaps you've already guessed it: In the United States, since World War II, the ratio of men to women has dropped significantly. The postwar baby boom produced a hugh cohort of women without enough men to go around. Why? Because most men marry women who are at least two years younger than they and women seek men at least two years older. So if you were a woman of the baby-boom years, there wouldn't be enough men in the cohort *older* than you to go around. (Those men would have plenty of women your age or younger to choose from, however.) Moreover, this numbers gap would last your whole life, as your age cohort matured.

This is why the decade 1960–1970 saw "a grave shortage of potential partners for young women," reported Guttentag and Secord. For example, most American women marry between the ages of 20 and 24. In 1960, for every 100 unmarried women in that age bracket there were 93 unmarried men aged 23 to 27—a ratio fairly close to even. But by 1970, for every 100 women in that age group there were only 67 men in the slightly older bracket.

The situation is even worse for black women. For every 100 black women aged 16 to 42 in 1970 there were only 73 black men aged 18 to 44—and this imbalance, Guttentag and Secord showed from demographic trends, will continue through 1990. It was racism, not "black matriarchy," that caused the lowered sex ratio, through the migration of black males (for work) and the high black male mortality rate. The authors demonstrated that the so-called consequences of "black matriarchy" and "lack of black family values"—high divorce rate, high illegitimacy rates, sexual promiscuity among males, and devaluation of women—are by no means specific to anything in black culture, but can be explained virtually entirely by the uneven black sex ratio. As the white sex ratio has shifted in the same direction, white family dissolution has increased correspondingly (but no one writes about "white matriarchy"). Conversely, when there was a high sex ratio among blacks, their sexual behavior and family values adhered to Guttentag and Secord's prediction.

This argument illustrates how human behavior, emotions, and sexual attitudes can derive from something at once profoundly fundamental—the simple ratio of one sex to the other—yet invisible in people's conscious thoughts. Guttentag and Secord proposed that demographic trends translate into people's lives through the psychological process described by social exchange theory: The sex that is relatively scarce holds the balance of emotional power in a relationship. In the contemporary United States, they argued, most men don't have to work at a relationship or even commit themselves to one, because they can always find another woman. Women, they said, must compromise or lose, with devastating effects on their self-esteem and happiness. Why, then, don't women behave like men when *women* are the scarce resource? Because, Guttentag and Secord answered, men hold the *structural* power in every society, even when they are outnumbered by women: Men control the laws, money, power, and politics.

Of course Guttentag and Secord did not claim that their theory explains every aspect of sexual inequities between men and women, only that they had identified one important factor.[5] If the theory is right, however, a powerful implication follows. They are saying that the rising rates of female education, employment, divorce, sexual activity, and even feminist protest are all a result of a low male-to-

[5]Obviously, their theory cannot account for everything; in the previous century, when the sex ratio in America was still 102 to 106 men for every 100 women, the women's movement for equal rights began and the industrial revolution required the services of women, as cheap labor, in the work force.

female sex ratio. It therefore follows, if they are right, that *a change in sex ratios in the opposite direction* may send women back to home and hearth, may cause men again to glorify the family and denigrate divorce, may produce movements for sexual and social conservatism. Such a future, their theory predicts, is inevitable unless the structural bases of male power are changed; unless women have become committed to work and education; unless men do not wish to return to the privileged burdens of the good-provider role. Keeping these "unlesses" in mind, take a look at Figure 7, which illustrates the sex ratios and marital opportunities for women through 1990. What do you think will happen?

the denial of disadvantage

Evils which are patiently endured when they seem inevitable become intolerable when once the idea of escape from them is suggested.

—*Alexis de Tocqueville*

Having just described an objective condition that seems to have a significant effect on people's behavior, we now want to say that objective conditions are not sufficient to understand behavior. Sociologists themselves, for example, know that an actual situation of economic deprivation, discrimination, or injustice is not enough to cause people to feel angry about such situations or motivated to change them. The Untouchables of India have accepted a caste of degradation for centuries (see Moore 1978); most women in purdah do not regard themselves as inferior to men; male circumcision in the United States and female circumcision in Egypt continue without significant protest. Hence sociologists predict that social movements for change arise under conditions not of *objective* deprivation ("I don't have much") but of *relative* deprivation ("My group doesn't have as much as their group")—when individuals compare themselves to others and feel deprived relative to what they have, what they want, and what they feel they deserve (Crosby 1982). Sociologists borrow psychological concepts—how people interpret a situation, how they compare themselves to others, how they feel about their conditions in life—to explain large-scale changes.

Psychologist Patricia Gurin (1982) has been studying group consciousness, "a specific set of attitudes that must develop before a disadvantaged group will organize to improve its lot." Group consciousness, she has suggested, consists of four elements: (1) group identification, a psychological feeling of belonging to that group; (2)

becoming discontented with the group's power and influence; (3) believing that the disparity between your group's power and that of other groups is unfair; and (4) approval of collective action to improve the status of your group. By these criteria, women are identified with their gender as a social group more than they used to be, and they are far more likely than they were to agree that women as a group are discriminated against economically. But although most women agree that sex discrimination is widespread, they deny that discrimination has happened to them personally. Social psychologist Faye Crosby (1982) offered several explanations for this paradox:

1. Women compare themselves as a group to other groups, but most individual women compare themselves not to men but to other women. Hence, at an individual level, each woman concludes she is treated no differently from anyone else. Anyone else who is a woman, that is.

2. Women compare their achievements not to those of men, but to their own earlier standards. A woman who is earning a steady paycheck is so happy that she is contributing to the family income or able to support herself that she doesn't complain that her paycheck is 60 percent of what a man would earn.

3. People think of discrimination in terms of villain and victim, not in terms of entrenched system-wide customs, so they resist thinking of themselves as being discriminated against—it would imply that someone in particular is doing the discriminating.

Gurin (1982) added another element: Most women don't want to compare themselves to men because they want to live with men:

> I think it's very hard for women to develop group consciousness, harder than for other subordinate groups such as blacks or old people. In order for women to become aware of the status and treatment of their group they must compare themselves to men. And this is very uncomfortable because women are, after all, the mothers, wives, lovers, sisters, and daughters of men. There is no other subordinate group that has such an intimate relationship with the dominant group. (pp. 4–5)

And what about men? To whom do they compare themselves? Writer Barbara Ehrenreich (1983) believes that men, like women, began rebelling against restrictive sex roles in the 1950s and 1960s, but that it was not a collective rebellion as the women's movement came to be. Men protested against the good-provider role in many ways, she observed: the beatniks, the Playboy generation, antiestablishment intellectuals, and eventually hippies all shared a disdain for

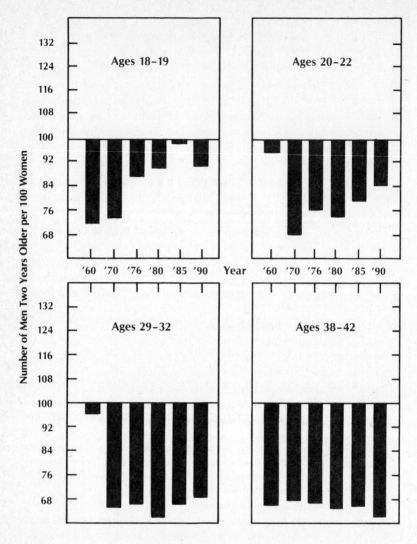

Marital Opportunities of Black Women

Figure 7: Marital opportunities for black women and white women, selected ages, between 1960 and 1990.
SOURCE: From Marcia Guttentag and Paul Secord, *Too Many Women?* Beverly Hills, Calif.: Sage Publications, © 1983. Figures 7.2, 8.3. Reprinted by permission of Sage Publications, Inc.

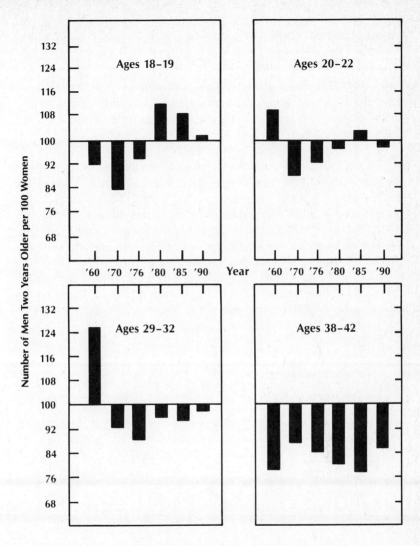

Marital Opportunities of White Women

the "trap" of marriage, for the heavy burdens of total financial responsibility for wife and children. In the 1970s some men argued that they were as oppressed by the rigidity of sex-role obligations as women were, with different but equally unhappy consequences (Nichols 1975; Pleck 1981). While acknowledging that objective conditions favored them, these men noted the psychological and medical disadvantages of the male role—the costs in intimacy, community, sustained friendships, even longevity.

Our point here is not to get into a "which sex is better off?" debate, but to point out that the actual requirements of sex-role standards do not in themselves produce anger or protest. As long as people regard those requirements as God's law or nature's way, they accept them—with varying degress of happiness, to be sure (Moore 1978; Crosby 1982; Tavris 1982). It is only, as de Tocqueville observed, when people see *alternatives* to their way of life, and believe they deserve those alternatives, that they go after them.

And so it seems today that many women and men regard each other's condition with a mixture of suspicion and envy. The grass is always greener on the other side of the fence, of course, but perhaps the time has come to tear down the fence.

the age of alliance

To go wrong on the fundamental problem of "man and woman," to deny the most abysmal antagonism between them and the necessity of an eternally hostile tension, to dream perhaps of equal rights, equal education, equal claims and obligations—that is a *typical* sign of shallowness.

—*Friedrich Nietzsche*

I've been married to a fascist and married to a Marxist, and neither one of them took out the garbage.

—*Attributed to a well-known actress*

We are persuaded that Nietzsche was wrong—that the sexes need not be antagonistic and that improvements in the status of women are continuing. But the actress has a point: Although increasing numbers of women are taking their place alongside men in the working world, men are not taking their place alongside women in the nursery and the kitchen. Until they do, the hand that rocks the cradle will be too tired to rule the world.

No one perspective is sufficient to explain all the riddles of male–female relations posed in this book. The lessons of an interdisciplinary approach cause us to anticipate the future with hope and with caution. If it is true that sustained improvements will depend on modifying or even transforming institutions and relationships, those who have power in their institutions and relationships will not look too kindly on these efforts. They will prefer explanations of male– female differences that are based on biology, because you can't tinker much with a gene or hormone; or explanations that are based on personality, because then people blame themselves for their failings ("It's my fear of success") and go into therapy instead of politics.

On the other hand, as economic conditions and social programs evolve, we have already seen rapid change: In what it means to be "masculine" and "feminine," in legal reforms, in attitudes about equal rights. (As recently as the early 1970s, you could not read a "Help Wanted" section of the newspaper: It was "Help Wanted— Female" and "Help Wanted—Male.") Some people overestimate what a society can accomplish in a few years, as disillusioned observers of the U.S.S.R., China, and the United States tend to do. ("We have been trying to educate and agitate around women's liberation for several years," wrote Marge Piercy in 1971, when the modern women's movement was in its infancy. "How come things are getting worse?") But others underestimate the speed of change, once conditions are right, and no century has witnessed faster changes than ours.

Change is certain, but how women and men will get along during the decades of transition is not. Change frightens some people, angers some, and exhilarates some. Some people may prefer, to paraphrase Hamlet, to bear the ills they have than fly to others they know not of. But we are optimistic that the alliance the sexes will forge on the far side of change will be stronger, and will make more people happier, than the uneasy compromises of the longest war.

References

Chapter 1
Introduction: The longest war

Aronoff, Joel, and Crano, William D. A re-examination of the cross-cultural principles of task segregation and sex role differentiation in the family. *American Sociological Review*, 1975, *40*, 12–20.

Bamberger, Joan. The myth of matriarchy. In Michelle Zimbalist Rosaldo and Louise Lamphere (eds.), *Woman, culture, and society*. Stanford, Calif.: Stanford University Press, 1974, 263–281.

Barnstone, Aliki, and Barnstone, Willis (eds.). *A book of women poets from antiquity to now*. New York: Schocken, 1980.

Barry, H.; Bacon, Margaret K.; and Child, I. I. A cross-cultural survey of some sex differences in socialization. *Journal of Abnormal and Social Psychology*, 1957, *55*, 327–332.

Beard, Mary. *Woman as force in history*. New York: Collier Books, 1973.

Blakely, Mary Kay. Who are the real man-haters? *Vogue*, April 1983, 136, 148.

Briere, John; Malamuth, Neil; and Ceniti, Joe. Self-assessed rape proclivity: Attitudinal and sexual correlates. Paper presented at the 90th annual convention of the American Psychological Association, Washington, D.C., 1981.

Broverman, Inge K.; Vogel, Susan R.; Broverman, Donald; Clarkson, Frank E.; and Rosenkrantz, Paul S. Sex-role stereotypes: A current appraisal. *Journal of Social Issues*, 1972, *28*, 59–79.

Brown, Judith K. Iroquois women: An ethnohistoric note. In Rayna R. Reiter (ed.), *Toward an anthropology of women*. New York and London: Monthly Review Press, 1975, 141–157.

Brownmiller, Susan. *Against our will: Men, women, and rape*. New York: Simon and Schuster, 1975.

Bullough, Vern L. *The subordinate sex*. Baltimore: Penguin, 1973.

Cole-Alexander, Lenora. Remarks at "Womenpower Reconsidered" conference, unpublished paper. New School for Social Research, New York, September 1982.

Cocks, Jay. How long till equality? *Time*, July 12, 1982, 20–29.

D'Andrade, Roy G. Sex differences and cultural institutions. In Eleanor Maccoby (ed.), *The development of sex differences*. Stanford, Calif.: Stanford University Press, 1966, 173–204.

Dwyer, Daisy Hilse. *Images and self-images: Male and female in Morocco*. New York: Columbia University Press, 1978.

Epstein, Cynthia Fuchs. The partnership push. *Savvy*, March 1980, 29–35.

Figes, Eva. *Patriarchal attitudes*. New York: Stein and Day, 1970.

Foner, Philip S. *Women and the American labor movement*. New York: The Free Press, 1979.

Friedan, Betty. *The second stage*. New York: Summit, 1981.

Friedl, Ernestine. *Women and men: An anthropologist's view*. New York: Holt, Rinehart and Winston, 1975.

Guttentag, Marcia, and Secord, Paul. *Too many women?* Beverly Hills: Sage, 1983.

Herlihy, David. The natural history of medieval women. *Natural History*, March 1978, *87*(3), 56–68.

Herzog, A. Regula, and Bachman, Jerald. *Sex role attitudes among high school seniors: Views about work and family roles*. Research reports. Ann Arbor, Mich.: Institute for Social Research, 1982.

Hunt, Morton. *The natural history of love*. Minerva Press, 1967.

Johnson, Allan G. On the prevalence of rape in the United States. *Signs*, Autumn 1980, *6*(1), 136–146.

Kagan, Susan. Camilla Urso: A nineteenth-century violinist's view. *Signs*, Spring 1977, *2*(3), 727–734.

Komarovsky, Mirra. College women and careers. *The New York Times*, January 23, 1981.

Lott, Bernice; Reilly, Mary Ellen; and Howard, Dale R. Sexual assault and harassment. *Signs*, Winter 1982, *8*(2), 296–319.

Malamuth, Neil M. Rape proclivity among males. *Journal of Social Issues*, December 1981, *37*(4), 138–157.

Mead, Margaret. *Sex and temperament in three primitive societies*. New York: Dell, 1963 (original printing 1935).

Mernissi, Fatima. *Beyond the veil: Male-female dynamics in a modern Muslim society*. New York: Wiley, 1975.

Murdock, George P., and Provost, Caterina. Factors in the division of labor by sex: A cross-cultural analysis. *Ethnology*, 1973, *12*, 203–225.

Myrdal, Gunnar. A parallel to the Negro problem (Appendix 5), in *An American dilemma*. New York: Harper and Row, 1944.

Nickles, Elizabeth, with Laura Ashcraft. *The coming matriarchy*. New York: Seaview, 1981.

Offir, Carole Wade. *Human sexuality*. New York: Harcourt Brace Jovanovich, 1982.

Pomeroy, Sarah B. *Goddesses, whores, wives and slaves—women in classical antiquity*. New York: Schocken, 1975.

Rosaldo, Michelle Z. Woman, culture, and society: A theoretical overview. In Michelle Z. Rosaldo and Louise Lamphere (eds.), *Woman, culture, and society*. Stanford, Calif.: Stanford University Press, 1974, 17–42.

Rubenstein, Carin. Real men don't earn less than their wives. *Psychology Today*, November 1982, *16*(6), 36–41.

Russell, Diana E. H. *Rape in marriage*. New York: Macmillan, 1982.

Russell, Diana E. H., and Howell, Nancy. The prevalence of rape in the United States revisited. *Signs*, 1983, *8*(4), 688–695.

Shields, Stephanie. Functionalism, Darwinism, and the psychology of women. *American Psychologist*, 1975, *30*, 739–754.

Shorter, Edward. *A history of women's bodies*. New York: Basic Books, 1982.

Steinem, Gloria. Losing a battle but winning the war? *Ms.*, January 1983, 35–36, 65–66.

Straus, Murray; Gelles, Richard; and Steinmetz, Suzanne. *Behind closed doors: Violence in the American family*. Garden City, N.Y.: Anchor/Doubleday, 1980.

Straus, Murray, and Hotaling, Gerald T. (eds.). *The social causes of husband-wife violence*. Minneapolis: University of Minnesota Press, 1980.

Tavris, Carol. The love/work questionnaire: Who will you be tomorrow? *Mademoiselle*, March 1982, 139–141, 235–236. (a)

Tavris, Carol. Were you born to work? *Mademoiselle*, October 1982, 180–181, 234. (b)

van Vuuren, Nancy. *The subversion of women*. Philadelphia: Westminster Press, 1973.

Wadley, Susan S. Women and the Hindu tradition. *Signs*, Autumn 1977, *3*(1), 113–125.

Webster, Paula. Matriarchy: A vision of power. In Rayna R. Reiter (ed.), *Toward an anthropology of women*. New York and London: Monthly Review Press, 1975, 141–157.

Whitley, Bernard E., Jr. Sex roles and psychotherapy: A current appraisal. *Psychological Bulletin*, 1979, *86*(6), 1309–1321.

Wikler, Norma. Myth in the making: The status of women in the 80's. Speech presented to the Detroit Bar Association, May 1982.

Chapter 2
Sex differences, real and imagined

Antill, John K., and Cunningham, John D. Sex differences in performance on ability tests as a function of masculinity, femininity, and androgyny. *Journal of Personality and Social Psychology*, 1982, *42*, 718–728.

Armstrong, Jane M. Achievement and participation of women in mathematics. Final report to the National Institute of Education, Washington, D.C., 1980.

Averill, James R. *Anger and aggression: An essay on emotion*. New York: Springer-Verlag, 1982.

Bardwick, Judith M. *Psychology of women: A study of bio-cultural conflicts*. New York: Harper and Row, 1971.

Bem, Sandra L. The measurement of psychological androgyny. *Journal of Consulting and Clinical Psychology*, 1974, *42*, 155–162.

Bem, Sandra Lipsitz. Androgyny vs. the tight little lives of fluffy women and chesty men. *Psychology Today*, September 1975, *9*(4), 58–59ff.

Benbow, Camilla Persson, and Stanley, Julian C. Sex differences in mathematical ability: Fact or artifact? *Science*, 1980, *210*, 1262–1264.

Berman, Phyllis W. Attraction to infants: Are sex differences innate and invariant? Paper presented at the 83rd annual convention of the American Psychological Association, Chicago, 1975.

Bernstein, R. C., and Jacklin, Carol N. The $3\frac{1}{2}$-month-old infant: Stability of behavior, sex differences, and longitudinal findings. Unpublished master's thesis, Stanford University, 1973.

Block, Jeanne H. Debatable conclusions about sex differences. *Contemporary Psychology*, 1976, *21*, 517–522.

Bok, Sissela. *Secrets: On the ethics of concealment and revelation*. New York: Pantheon, 1983.

Brehony, Kathleen; Augustine, Mark; Barachie, Dave; Miller, Beth; and Woodhouse, William. Psychological androgyny and social conformity. Paper presented at the 85th annual convention of the American Psychological Association, San Francisco, 1977.

Broverman, Donald M.; Klaiber, Edward L.; Kobayashi, Yutaka; and Vogel, William. Roles of activation and inhibition in sex differences in cognitive abilities. *Psychological Review*, 1968, *75*, 23–50.

Bryant, Kendall J. Personality correlates of sense of direction and geographical orientation. *Journal of Personality and Social Psychology*, 1982, *43*, 1318–1324.

Burnett, Sarah A., and Lane, David M. Effects of academic instruction on spatial
visualization. *Intelligence*, 1980, *4*, 233–242.

Cherulnik, Paul D. Sex differences in the expression of emotion in a structured social
encounter. *Sex Roles*, 1979, *5*, 413–424.

Connor, Jane Marantz; Schackman, Maxine; and Serbin, Lisa A. Sex-related differences in response to practice on a visual-spatial test and generalization to a related
test. *Child Development*, 1978, *49*, 24–29.

Crandall, Virginia J. Sex differences in expectancy of intellectual and academic reinforcement. In Charles P. Smith (ed.), *Achievement-related motives in children*. New
York: Russell Sage Foundation, 1969, 11–45.

Deaux, Kay. Ahhh, she was just lucky. *Psychology Today*, December 1976, *10*(7), 70ff.

Deaux, Kay; White, Leonard; and Farris, Elizabeth. Skill versus luck: Field and laboratory studies of male and female preferences. *Journal of Personality and Social
Psychology*, 1975, *32*, 629–636.

DiPietro, Janet A. Rough and tumble play: A function of gender. *Developmental
Psychology*, 1981, *17*, 50–58.

Dowling, Colette. *The Cinderella complex: Women's hidden fear of independence.*
New York: Summit, 1981.

Droege, Robert C. Sex differences in aptitude maturation during high school. *Journal of
Counseling Psychology*, 1967, *14*, 407–411.

Eagly, Alice H. Sex differences in influenceability. *Psychological Bulletin*, 1978, *85*,
86–116.

Eagly, Alice H. Gender and social influence: A social psychological analysis. *American Psychologist*, 1983, *38*, 971–981.

Eagly, Alice H., and Wood, Wendy. Inferred sex differences in status as a determinant of
gender stereotypes about social influence. *Journal of Personality and Social Psychology*, 1982, *43*, 915–928.

Eccles (Parsons), Jacquelynne. Sex differences in math achievement and course enrollment. Paper presented at the annual meeting of the American Educational
Research Association, New York, March 1982.

Edwards, Carolyn Pope, and Whiting, Beatrice. *Sex differences in children's social
interaction.* Unpublished report to Ford Foundation, 1977. (Cited in Maccoby 1980.)

Feldman, S. Shirley, and Nash, Sharon Churnin. Interest in babies during young
adulthood. *Child Development*, 1978, *49*, 617–622.

Feldman, S. Shirley; Nash, Sharon Churnin; and Cutrona, Carolyn. The influence of
age and sex on responsiveness to babies. *Developmental Psychology*, 1977, *13*,
675–676.

Fennema, Elizabeth, and Sherman, Julia. Sex related differences in mathematics
achievement, spatial visualization and affective factors. *American Educational Research Journal*, 1977, *14*, 51–71.

Feshbach, Seymour, and Feshbach, Norma. The young aggressors. *Psychology Today*,
April 1973, 6(11), 90–95.

Frieze, Irene Hanson. Women's expectations for and causal attributions of success and
failure. In Martha T. Shuch Mednick, Sandra Schwartz Tangri, and Lois Wladis
Hoffman (eds.), *Women and achievement: Social and motivational analyses.* New
York: Halsted, 1975, 158–171.

Frodi, Ann M., and Lamb, Michael E. Sex differences in responsiveness to infants: A
developmental study of psychophysiological and behavioral responses. *Child Development*, 1978, *49*, 1182–1188.

Frodi, Ann M.; Macaulay, Jacqueline; and Thome, Pauline Ropert. Are women always less aggressive than men? A review of the experimental literature. *Psychological Bulletin*, 1977, *84*, 634–660.

Garai, Josef E., and Scheinfeld, Amram. Sex differences in mental and behavioral traits. *Genetic Psychology Monographs*, 1968, *77*, 169–299.

Gilligan, Carol. *In a different voice: Psychological theory and women's development*. Cambridge, Mass.: Harvard University Press, 1982.

Goldberg, Herb. *The hazards of being male: Surviving the myth of masculine privilege*, New York: Nash, 1976.

Hall, Judith A. Gender effects in decoding nonverbal cues. *Psychological Bulletin*, 1978, *85*, 845–857.

Harlow, Harry F. *Learning to love*. San Francisco: Albion, 1971.

Haviland, John Beard. *Gossip, reputation, and knowledge in Zinacantan*. Chicago: University of Chicago Press, 1977.

Haynes, Suzanne, and Feinleib, Manning F. Women, work, and coronary heart disease: Prospective findings from the Framingham Heart Study. *American Journal of Public Health*, 1980, *70*(2), 133–141.

Hetherington, E. Mavis; Cox, Martha; and Cox, Roger. Divorced fathers. *The family coordinator*, 1976, *25*, 417–428.

Hoffman, Martin L. Sex differences in empathy and related behaviors. *Psychological Bulletin*, 1977, *84*, 712–722.

Hollander, Edwin P., and Marcia, James E. Parental determinants of peer-orientation and self-orientation among preadolescents. *Developmental Psychology*, 1970, *2*, 292–302.

Hyde, Janet S. How large are cognitive gender differences? A meta-analysis using ω^2 and d. *American Psychologist*, 1981, *36*, 892–901.

Jacklin, Carol Nagy; Snow, Margaret Ellis; and Maccoby, Eleanor E. Tactile sensitivity and muscle strength in newborn boys and girls. *Infant Behavior and Development*, 1981, *4*, 261–268.

Kagan, Jerome. Family experience and the child's development. *American Psychologist*, 1979, *34*, 886–891.

Karlen, Amy; Hagin, Rosa A.; and Beecher, Ronnie. Are boys really more vulnerable to learning disability than girls? Paper presented at the 90th annual convention of the American Psychological Association, Washington, D.C., 1981.

Kohlberg, Lawrence. Stage and sequence: The cognitive-development approach to socialization. In David A. Goslin (ed.), *Handbook of socialization theory and research*. Chicago: Rand McNally, 1969.

Kohlberg, Lawrence. Moral stages and moralization: The cognitive-developmental approach. In Thomas Lickona (ed.), *Moral development and behavior: Theory, research and social issues*. New York: Holt, Rinehart and Winston, 1976.

Layden, Mary Anne, and Ickes, William J. Self-esteem and sex differences in attributional style: Effect upon performance. Paper presented at the 85th annual convention of the American Psychological Association, San Francisco, 1977.

Lenney, Ellen. Women's self-confidence in achievement settings. *Psychological Bulletin*, 1977, *84*, 1–13.

Lenney, Ellen, and Gold, Joel. Sex differences in self-confidence: The effects of task completion and of comparison to competent others. *Personality and Social Psychology Bulletin*, 1982, *8*, 74–80.

Levy, Jerre. Yes, Virginia, there is a difference: Sex differences in human brain asymmetry and in psychology. *The L. S. B. Leakey Foundation News*, no. 20, Fall 1981.

Lewis, Michael; Kagan, Jerome; and Kalafat, John. Patterns of fixation in the young infant. *Child Development*, 1966, *37*, 331–341.

Maccoby, Eleanor E. *Social development: Psychological growth and the parent-child relationship*. New York: Harcourt Brace Jovanovich, 1980.

Maccoby, Eleanor Emmons, and Jacklin, Carol Nagy. *The psychology of sex differences*. Stanford, Calif.: Stanford University Press, 1974.

Maccoby, Eleanor E., and Jacklin, Carol Nagy. Waiting room behavior of fathers and 12-month-old infants. Working paper, Stanford Longitudinal Study, Stanford, Calif., 1979.

Mayo, Clara and Henley, Nancy M. Nonverbal behavior: Barrier or agent for sex role change? In Clara Mayo and Nancy M. Henley (eds.), *Gender and nonverbal behavior*. New York: Springer-Verlag, 1981.

Minton, Cheryl; Kagan, Jerome; and Levine, Janet A. Maternal control and obedience in the two-year-old. *Child Development*, 1971, *42*, 1873–1894.

Nash, Sharon C. The relationship among sex-role stereotyping, sex-role preference, and the sex difference in spatial visualization. *Sex Roles*, 1975, *1*, 15–32.

Nichols, Jack. *Men's liberation*. New York: Penguin, 1975.

Orbach, Susie, and Eichenbaum, Luise. *What do women want? Exploding the myth of dependency*. New York: Putnam, 1983.

Parke, Ross D. Perspectives on father-infant interaction. In Joy D. Osofsky (ed.), *Handbook of infancy*. New York: Wiley, 1978.

Parke, Ross D., and Sawin, Douglas B. The father's role in infancy: A reevaluation. *The family coordinator*, 1976, *25*, 365–371.

Parlee, Mary B. Comments on "Roles of activation and inhibition in sex differences in cognitive abilities" by Donald M. Broverman, Edward L. Klaiber, Yutaka Kobayashi, and William Vogel. *Psychological Review*, 1972, *79*, 180–184.

Parsons, Jacquelynne E. Attributional factors mediating female underachievement and low career aspirations. Paper presented at the 85th annual meeting of the American Psychological Association, San Francisco, 1977.

Rosenthal, Robert. *Experimenter effects in behavioral research*. New York: Appleton-Century-Crofts, 1966.

Rosenthal, Robert. Self-fulfilling prophecy. *Psychology Today*, September 1968, *2*(4), 44–51.

Rosenthal, Robert; Archer, Dane; DiMatteo, M. Robin; Koivumaki, Judith Hall; and Rogers, Peter L. Body talk and tone of voice: The language without words. *Psychology Today*, September 1974, *8*(4), 64–68.

Rosenthal, Robert; Hall, Judith A.; DiMatteo, M. Robin; Rogers, Peter L.; and Archer, Dane. *Sensitivity to nonverbal communication: The PONS test*. Baltimore: Johns Hopkins University Press, 1979.

Rosnow, Ralph L., and Fine, Gary A. *Rumor and gossip: The social psychology of hearsay*. New York: Elsevier, 1976.

Schachter, Frances Fuchs; Shore, Ellen; Hodapp, Robert; Chalfin, Susan; and Bundy, Carole. Do girls talk earlier? Mean length of utterance in toddlers. *Developmental Psychology*, 1978, *14*, 388–392.

Sells, Lucy W. Mathematics—a critical filter. *The Science Teacher*, February 1978, *45*(2), 28–29.

Sells, Lucy W. The mathematics filter and the education of women and minorities. In Lynn H. Fox, Linda Brody, and Dianne Tobin (eds.), *Women and the mathematical mystique*. Baltimore: Johns Hopkins Press, 1980, 66–75.

Sherif, Carolyn Wood. Bias in psychology. In Julia A. Sherman and Evelyn Torton Beck (eds.), *The prism of sex: Essays in the sociology of knowledge*. Madison: University of Wisconsin Press, 1979, 93–133.

Sherman, Julia. Problems of sex differences in space perception and aspects of intellectual functioning. *Psychological Review*, 1967, *74*, 290–299.

Sherman, Julia. *On the psychology of women: A survey of empirical studies*. Springfield, Ill.: Charles C. Thomas, 1971.

Simon, J. G., and Feather, N. T. Causal attributions for success and failure at university examinations. *Journal of Educational Psychology*, 1973, *64*, 46–56.

Smith, Peter K., and Daglish, Linda. Sex differences in parent and infant behavior in the home. *Child Development*, 1977, *48*, 1250–1254.

Spence, Janet T., and Helmreich, Robert L. *Masculinity & femininity: Their psychological dimensions, correlates, & antecedents*. Austin: University of Texas Press, 1978.

Stassinopoulos, Arianna. The natural woman. In *The female woman*, 1973. Quoted in Elaine Partnow (ed.), *The quotable woman 1800–on*. Garden City, N.Y.: Anchor/Doubleday, 1978.

Steinem, Gloria. Sisterhood. *Ms.*, Spring 1972, 46–49.

Tavris, Carol. *Anger: The misunderstood emotion*. New York: Simon and Schuster, 1982.

Tiger, Lionel. *Men in groups*. New York: Random House, 1969.

Tobias, Sheila. Math anxiety: Why is a smart girl like you counting on your fingers? *Ms.*, September 1976, *5*, 56–59ff.

Tobias, Sheila. *Overcoming math anxiety*. New York: Norton, 1978.

Tobias, Sheila. Sexist equations. *Psychology Today*, January 1982, *15*(8), 14, 16, 18.

Tooney, Nancy. The "math gene" and other symptoms of the biology backlash. *Ms.*, September 1981, *10*, 56, 59.

Unger, Rhoda K. Toward a redefinition of sex and gender. *American Psychologist*, 1979, *34*, 1085–1094.

Vandenberg, Steven G., and Kuse, Allan R. Spatial ability: A critical review of the sex-linked major gene hypothesis. In Michele Andrisin Wittig and Anne C. Petersen (eds.), *Sex-related differences in cognitive functioning*. New York: Academic Press, 1979, 67–95.

Wagman, Morton. Sex differences in types of daydreams. *Journal of Personality and Social Psychology*, 1967, *3*, 329–332.

Wechsler, David. *The measurement and appraisal of adult intelligence*, 4th ed. Baltimore: Williams and Wilkins, 1958.

Whiting, Beatrice, and Edwards, Carolyn Pope. A cross-cultural analysis of sex differences in the behavior of children aged three through 11. *Journal of Social Psychology*, 1973, *91*, 171–188.

Witkin, Herman A.; Birnbaum, Judith; Lomonaco, Salvatore; Lehr, Suzanne; and Herman, Judith L. Cognitive patterning in congenitally totally blind children. *Child Development*, 1968, *39*, 768–786.

Zimmerman, Don H., and West, Candace. Sex roles, interruptions, and silences in conversation. In Barrie Thorne and Nancy Henley (eds.), *Language and sex: Difference and dominance*. Rowley, Mass.: Newbury House, 1975.

Chapter 3
Sex and love

Addiego, Frank; Belzer, Edwin G., Jr.; Comolli, Jill; Moger, William; Perry, John D.; and Whipple, Beverly. Female ejaculation: A case study. *Journal of Sex Research*, 1981, *17*, 13–21.

Athanasiou, Robert; Shaver, Phillip; and Tavris, Carol. Sex. *Psychology Today*, July 1970, 4(2), 37–52.

Barbach, Lonnie G. *For yourself: The fulfillment of female sexuality.* Garden City, N.Y.: Doubleday, 1975.

Bardwick, Judith M. *Psychology of women: A study of bio-cultural conflicts.* New York: Harper and Row, 1971.

Bart, Pauline B. Male views of female sexuality: From Freud's phallacies to Fisher's inexact test. Paper presented at the 2nd national meeting of the special section of Psychosomatic Obstetrics and Gynecology, Key Biscayne, Fla., 1974.

Bell, Alan P., and Weinberg, Martin S. *Homosexualities: A study of diversity among men and women.* New York: Simon and Schuster, 1978.

Bell, Robert R. *Premarital sex in a changing society.* Englewood Cliffs, N. J.: Prentice-Hall, 1966.

Bergler, Edmund, and Kroger, William S. *Kinsey's myth of female sexuality.* New York: Grune and Stratton, 1954.

Berscheid, Ellen. Interpersonal attraction. In E. Aronson and G. Lindzey (eds.), *Handbook of social psychology*, 3rd ed. Reading, Mass.: Addison-Wesley, in press.

Brecher, Edward M. *The sex researchers.* Boston: Little, Brown, 1969.

Campbell, Bruce, and Berscheid, Ellen. The perceived importance of romantic love as a determinant of marital choice: Kephart revisited ten years later. Unpublished manuscript, 1976.

Christensen, Harold T., and Gregg, Christina F. Changing sex norms in America and Scandinavia. *Journal of Marriage and the Family*, 1970, *32*, 616–627.

Degler, Carl N. What ought to be and what was: Women's sexuality in the nineteenth century. *American Historical Review*, 1974, *79*, 1467–1490.

Deutsch, Helene. *The psychology of women: A psychoanalytic interpretation*, vol. II. New York: Grune and Stratton, 1945.

Dion, Kenneth L., and Dion, Karen K. Personality and behavioral correlates of romantic love. In Mark Cook and Glenn Wilson (eds.), *Love and attraction: An international conference.* Oxford: Pergamon Press, 1977, 213–220.

Doi, L. T. *The anatomy of dependence.* Tokyo: Kodansha, 1973.

Gebhard, Paul H. Factors in marital orgasm. *Journal of Social Issues*, 1966, *22*(2), 88–95.

Giarrusso, Roseann; Johnson, Paula; Goodchilds, Jacqueline; and Zellman, Gail. Adolescents' cues and signals: Sex and assault. Paper presented at the annual meeting of the Western Psychological Association, San Diego, 1979.

Gilligan, Carol. *In a different voice: Psychological theory and women's development.* Cambridge, Mass.: Harvard University Press, 1982.

Goldberg, Daniel C.; Whipple, Beverly; Fishkin, Ralph E.; Waxman, Howard; Fink, Paul J.; and Weisberg, Martin. The Grafenberg spot and female ejaculation: A review of initial hypotheses. *Journal of Sex and Marital Therapy*, 1983, *9*(1), 27–37.

Greenblat, Cathy Stein, and Baron, Larry. Are feminists less romantic? Paper presented at the annual meeting of the American Sociological Association, 1983.

Hall, Edward T. *The dance of life.* Garden City, N. Y.: Anchor/Doubleday, 1983.

Hariton, E. Barbara. The sexual fantasies of women. *Psychology Today*, March 1973, 6(10), 39–44.

Hatkoff, Terry Smith, and Lasswell, Thomas E. Male-female similarities and differences in conceptualizing love. In Mark Cook and Glenn Wilson (eds.), *Love and attraction: An international conference.* Oxford: Pergamon Press, 1977, 221–227.

Heiman, Julia R. The physiology of erotica: Women's sexual arousal. *Psychology Today*, April 1975, *8*(11), 90–94.

Hessellund, Hans. Masturbation and sexual fantasies in married couples. *Archives of Sexual Behavior*, 1976, *5*, 133–147.

Hill, Charles T.; Rubin, Zick; and Peplau, Lititia Anne. Breakups before marriage: The end of 103 affairs. *Journal of Social Issues*, 1976, *32*(1), 147–168.

Hite, Shere. *The Hite report: A nationwide study of female sexuality*. New York: Dell, 1976.

Hite, Shere. *The Hite report on male sexuality*. New York: Knopf, 1981.

Hochschild, Arlie Russell. The sociology of feeling and emotion. In Marcia Millman and Rosabeth M. Kanter (eds.), *Another voice*. Garden City, N. Y.: Anchor/ Doubleday, 1975, 280–308.

Hopkins, J. Roy. Sexual behavior in adolescence. *Journal of Social Issues*, 1977, *33*(2), 67–85.

Hunt, Morton. *Sexual behavior in the 1970s*. Chicago: Playboy Press, 1974.

Jessor, Richard; Costa, Frances; Jessor, Lee; and Donovan, John E. Time of first intercourse: A prospective study. *Journal of Personality and Social Psychology*, 1983, *44*(3), 608–626.

Jessor, Shirley, and Jessor, Richard. Transition from virginity to nonvirginity among youth: A social-psychological study over time. *Developmental Psychology*, 1975, *11*, 473–484.

Kantner, John F., and Zelnik, Melvin. Sexual experience of young unmarried women in the United States. *Family Planning Perspectives*, 1972, *4*(4), 9–18.

Kephart, William M. Some correlates of romantic love. *Journal of Marriage and the Family*, 1967, *29*, 470–474.

Kinget, G. Marion. The "many-splendored thing" in transition or "the agony and the ecstasy" revisited. In Mark Cook and Glenn Wilson (eds.), *Love and attraction: An international conference*. Oxford: Pergamon Press, 1977.

Kinsey, Alfred C.; Pomeroy, Wardell B.; and Martin, Clyde E. *Sexual behavior in the human male*. Philadelphia: Saunders, 1948.

Kinsey, Alfred C.; Pomeroy, Wardell B.; Martin, Clyde E.; and Gebhard, Paul H. *Sexual behavior in the human female*. Philadelphia: Saunders, 1953.

Lee, John Alan. The styles of loving. *Psychology Today*, October 1974, *8*(5), 43–51.

LoPiccolo, Joseph, and Heiman, Julia. Cultural values and the therapeutic definition of sexual function and dysfunction. *Journal of Social Issues*, 1977, *33*(2), 166–183.

Malamuth, Neil. Rape proclivity among males. *Journal of Social Issues*, December 1981, *37*(4), 138–157.

Masters, William H., and Johnson, Virginia E. *Human sexual response*. Boston: Little, Brown, 1966.

Masters, William H., and Johnson, Virginia E. *Human sexual inadequacy*. Boston: Little, Brown, 1970.

McCormick, Naomi B. Power strategies in sexual encounters. Paper presented at the 85th annual meeting of the American Psychological Association, San Francisco, 1977.

Moore, Burness E. Frigidity in women (panel report). *Journal of the American Psychoanalytic Association*, 1961, *9*, 571–584.

Mosher, Clelia D. *The Mosher survey: Sexual attitudes of 45 Victorian women*. (Edited by James MaHood and Kristine Wenburg.) New York: Arno Press, 1980.

Offir, Carole Wade. *Human sexuality*. New York: Harcourt Brace Jovanovich, 1982.

Payn, Nadine. *Beyond orgasm.* Unpublished Ph.D. dissertation, University of California, Berkeley, 1980.

Perry, John Delbert, and Whipple, Beverly. Pelvic muscle strength of female ejaculators: Evidence in support of a new theory of orgasm. *Journal of Sex Research,* 1981, *17,* 22–39.

Pollack, Susan, and Gilligan, Carol. Images of violence in Thematic Apperception Test stories. *Journal of Personality and Social Psychology,* 1982, *42*(1), 159–167.

Pomeroy, Wardell B. The male orgasm. *Cosmopolitan,* April 1976, *180,* 203–205ff.

Reiss, Ira L. *Premarital sexual standards in America.* Glencoe, Ill.: The Free Press, 1960.

Reiss, Ira L. Premarital sexual standards. In Carlfred B. Broderick and Jessie Bernard (eds.), *The individual, sex, and society.* Baltimore: Johns Hopkins Press, 1969, 109–118.

Robbins, Mina B., and Jensen, Gordon D. Multiple orgasm in males. In R. Gemme and C. C. Wheeler (eds.), *Progress in sexology.* New York: Plenum, 1977, 323–334.

Robinson, Paul. *The modernization of sex.* New York: Harper and Row, 1976.

Rubenstein, Carin. The modern art of courtly love. *Psychology Today,* July 1983, *17*(2), 40–41, 44–49.

Rubenstein, Carin, and Shaver, Phillip. *In search of intimacy.* New York: Delacorte, 1982.

Schmidt, Gunter, and Sigusch, Volkmar. Women's sexual arousal. In Joseph Zubin and John Money (eds.), *Contemporary sexual behavior: Critical issues in the 1970s.* Baltimore: Johns Hopkins Press, 1973, 117–143.

Scully, Diana, and Bart, Pauline. A funny thing happened on the way to the orifice: Women in gynecology textbooks. In Joan Huber (ed.), *Changing women in a changing society.* Chicago: University of Chicago Press, 1973, 283–288.

Seaman, Barbara. *Free and female.* Greenwich, Conn.: Fawcett, 1972.

Shorter, Edward. *The making of the modern family.* New York: Basic Books, 1975.

Singer, Jerome L., and Switzer, Ellen E. *Mind play: The creative uses of fantasy.* Englewood Cliffs, N.J.: Prentice-Hall, 1980.

Singer, Josephine, and Singer, Irving. Types of female orgasm. *Journal of Sex Research,* 1972, *8,* 255–267.

Steinem, Gloria. Erotica and pornography: A clear and present difference. *Ms.,* November 1978, *7*(5), 53–54, 75, 78.

Sue, D. Erotic fantasies of college students during coitus. *Journal of Sex Research,* 1979, *15,* 299–305.

Tavris, Carol. Who likes women's liberation and why: The case of the unliberated liberals. *Journal of Social Issues,* 1973, *29*(4), 175–194.

Tavris, Carol. *Anger: The misunderstood emotion.* New York: Simon and Schuster, 1982.

Tavris, Carol, and Sadd, Susan. *The Redbook report on female sexuality.* New York: Dell, 1977.

Vance, Ellen Belle, and Wagner, Nathaniel N. Written descriptions of orgasm: A study of sex differences. In Donn Byrne and Lois A. Byrne (eds.), *Exploring human sexuality.* New York: Thomas Y. Crowell, 1977, 201–212.

Veroff, Joseph; Douvan, Elizabeth; and Kulka, Richard A. *The inner American: A self-portrait from 1957 to 1976.* New York: Basic Books, 1981.

Waller, Willard. *The family: A dynamic interpretation.* New York: Dryden, 1938.

Wieder, Robert S. How to make love to a G spot. *This World (San Francisco Chronicle),* February 27, 1983.

Zellman, Gail L.; Johnson, Paula B.; Giarrusso, Roseann; and Goodchilds, Jacqueline D. Adolescent expectations for dating relationships: Consensus and conflict between the sexes. Paper presented at the 87th annual convention of the American Psychological Association, New York, 1979.

Zelnik, Melvin, and Kantner, John F. Sexual and contraceptive experience of young unmarried women in the United States, 1976 and 1971. *Family Planning Perspectives*, 1977, *9*(2), 55–71.

Zilbergeld, Bernie. *The shrinking of America: Myths of psychological change.* Boston: Little, Brown, 1983.

Zilbergeld, Bernie, and Evans, Michael. The inadequacy of Masters and Johnson. *Psychology Today*, August 1980, *14*(3), 29–43.

Chapter 4
Genes, hormones, and instincts: The biological perspective

Averill, James R. *Anger and aggression: An essay on emotion.* New York: Springer-Verlag, 1982.

Baack, J.; de Lacoste-Utamsing, C.; and Woodward, D. J. Sexual dimorphism in human fetal corpora callosa. *Society for Neuroscience Abstracts*, 1982, *8*(57), 213.

Barlow, George W., and Silverberg, James (eds.). *Sociobiology: Beyond nature/nurture? Reports, definitions and debate.* AAAS selected symposium no. 35. Boulder: Westview Press, 1980.

Baron, Robert A. *Human aggression.* New York: Plenum, 1977.

Bart, Pauline B. Depression in middle-aged women. In Vivian Gornick and Barbara K. Moran (eds.), *Woman in sexist society: Studies in power and powerlessness.* New York: New American Library, 1971, 163–186.

Benedek, Thérèse F., and Rubenstein, B. B. The correlations between ovarian activity and psychodynamic processes. I. The ovulative phrase. *Psychosomatic Medicine*, 1939, *1*, 245–270.(a)

Benedek, Thérèse F., and Rubenstein, B. B. The correlations between ovarian activity and psychodynamic processes. II. The menstrual phase. *Psychosomatic Medicine*, 1939, *1*, 461–485.(b)

Beumont, P. J. V.; Richards, D. H.; and Gelder, M. G. A study of minor psychiatric and physical symptoms during the menstrual cycle. *British Journal of Psychiatry*, 1975, *126*, 431–434.

Bock, R. D., and Kolakowski, D. Further evidence of sex-linked major-gene influence on human spatial visualizing ability. *American Journal of Human Genetics*, 1973, *25*, 1–14.

Bryden, M. P. Evidence for sex-related differences in cerebral organization. In Michele Andrisin Wittig and Anne C. Petersen (eds.), *Sex-related differences in cognitive functioning.* New York: Academic Press, 1979, 121–143.

Burke, Deborah; Burnett, Gayle; and Levenstein, Peggy. Menstrual symptoms: New data from a double-blind study. Paper presented at the annual meeting of the Western Psychological Association, San Francisco, 1978.

Cioffi, Joseph, and Kandel, Gillray L. Laterality of stereognostic accuracy of children for words, shapes and bigrams: A sex difference for bigrams. *Science*, 1979, *204*, 1432–1434.

Dalton, Katherina. Effect of menstruation on school girls' weekly work. *British Medical Journal*, 1960, *1*, 326–328.

Dalton, Katherina. *The premenstrual syndrome*. Springfield, Ill.: Charles C. Thomas, 1964.

DeFries, J. C.; Johnson, R. C.; Kuse A. R.; McClearn, G. E.; Polovina, J.; Vandenberg, S. G.; and Wilson, J. R. Familial resemblance for specific cognitive abilities. *Behavior Genetics*, 1979, *9*, 23–43.

de Lacoste-Utamsing, Christine, and Holloway, Ralph L. Sexual dimorphism in the human corpus callosum. *Science*, 1982, *216*, 1431–1432.

de Lacoste-Utamsing, C., and Woodward, D. J. Intra- and interhemispheric asymmetries in the human brain. *Society for Neuroscience Abstracts*, 1982, *8*(57), 212.

DeMause, Lloyd. Our forebears made childhood a nightmare. *Psychology Today*, April 1975, *8*(11), 85–88,

DeVore, I. Male dominance and mating behavior in baboons. In Frank A. Beach (ed.), *Sex and behavior*. New York: Wiley, 1965, 266–289.

Diamond, Marion C.; Johnson, Ruth E.; Young, Daniel; and Singh, S. Sukhwinder. Age related morphologic differences in the rat cerebral cortex and hypocampus: Male-female; right-left. *Experimental Neurology*, 1983, in press.

Divale, William Tulio, and Harris, Marvin. Population, warfare, and the male supremacist complex. *American Anthropologist*, 1976, *78*, 521–539.

Doering, Charles H.; Brodie, H. K. H.; Kraemer, H. C.; Becker, H. B.; and Hamburg, D. A. Plasma testosterone levels and psychologic measures in men over a 2-month period. In Richard C. Friedman, Ralph M. Richart, and Raymond L. Vande Wiele (eds.), *Sex differences in behavior*. New York: Wiley, 1974, 413–431.

Doering, Charles H.; Brodie, H. Keith H.; Kraemer, Helena C.; Moos, Rudolf H.; Becker, Heather B.; and Hamburg, David A. Negative affect and plasma testosterone: A longitudinal human study. *Psychosomatic Medicine*, 1975, *37*, 484–491.

Durden-Smith, Jo. Male and female—why? *Quest/80*, October 1980, 15–19, 93–98.

Ehrhardt, Anke A., and Baker, Susan W. Fetal androgens, human central nervous system differentiation, and behavior sex differences. In Richard C. Friedman, Ralph M. Richart, and Raymond L. Vande Wiele (eds.), *Sex differences in behavior*. New York: Wiley, 1974, 33–51.

Ehrhardt, Anke A., and Meyer-Bahlburg, Heino F. L. Effects of prenatal sex hormones on gender-related behavior. *Science*, 1981, *211*, 1312–1318.

Fisher, Alan E. Maternal and sexual behavior induced by intracranial chemical stimulation. *Science*, 1956, *124*, 228–229.

Fisher, Helen E. *The sex contract: The evolution of human behavior*. New York: Morrow, 1982.

Gardner, Lytt I., and Nieu, Richard L. Evidence linking an extra Y chromosome to sociopathic behavior. *Archives of General Psychiatry*, 1972, *26*, 220–222.

Ginsburg, Benson E. Coaction of genital and nongenital factors influencing sexual behavior. In Frank A. Beach (ed.), *Sex and behavior*. New York: Wiley, 1965, 53–75.

Golub, Sharon. The effect of premenstrual anxiety and depression on cognitive function. Paper presented at the 83rd annual convention of the American Psychological Association, Chicago, 1975.

Gorski, R. A.; Gordon, J. H.; Shryne, J. E.; and Southam, A. M. Evidence for a morphological sex difference within the medial preoptic area of the rat brain. *Brain Research*, 1978, *148*, 333–346.

Gorski, R. A.; Harlan, R. E.; Jacobson, C. D.; Shryne, J. E.; and Southam, A. M. Evidence for the existence of a sexually dimorphic nucleus in the preoptic area of the rat. *Journal of Comparative Neurology*, 1980, *193*, 529.

Gould, Stephen Jay. Sociobiology and the theory of natural selection. In George W. Barlow and James Silverberg (eds.), *Sociobiology: Beyond nature/nurture? Reports, definitions and debate*. AAAS selected symposium no. 35. Boulder: Westview Press, 1980.

Goy, Robert W. Organizing effects of androgen on the behavior of rhesus monkeys. In Richard P. Michael (ed.), *Endocrinology and human behavior*. London: Oxford University Press, 1968.

Goy, Robert W. and McEwen, Bruce S. (eds.). *Sexual differentiation of the brain*. Cambridge, Mass.: MIT Press, 1980.

Groth, A. Nicholas, and Burgess, Ann W. Rape: A sexual deviation. *American Journal of Orthopsychiatry*, 1977, *47*(3), 400–406.

Hackler, Tim. Is anatomy destiny? *Cosmopolitan*, March 1982, 219–221, 262–263, 267.

Hall, Elizabeth. A conversation with D. O. Hebb. *Psychology Today*, November 1969, *3*(6), 20–28.

Harlow, Harry F. The heterosexual affectional system in monkeys. *American Psychologist*, 1962, *17*, 1–9.

Harlow, Harry F. Sexual behavior in the rhesus monkey. In Frank A. Beach (ed.), *Sex and behavior*. New York: Wiley, 1965, 234–265.

Hausfater, Glenn. Long-term consistency of dominance relations in baboons *(Papio cynocephalus)*. Paper presented at the eighth International Congress of Primatology, Florence, Italy, July 1980. (Cited in Hrdy 1981.)

Hediger, H. Environmental factors influencing the reproduction of zoo animals. In Frank A. Beach (ed.), *Sex and behavior*. New York: Wiley, 1965, 319–354.

Hier, Daniel B., and Crowley, William F., Jr. Spatial ability in androgen-deficient men. *New England Journal of Medicine*, 1982, *306*(20), 1202–1205.

Hrdy, Sarah Blaffer. *The woman that never evolved*. Cambridge, Mass.: Harvard University Press, 1981.

Hyde, Janet S.; Rosenberg, B. G.; and Behrman, JoAnn. Tomboyism: Implications for theories of female development. Paper presented at the annual convention of the Western Psychological Association, San Francisco, 1974.

Imperato-McGinley, Julianne; Guerrero, Luis; Gautier, Teofilo; and Peterson, Ralph E. Steroid 5α-reductase deficiency in man: An inherited form of male pseudohermaphroditism. *Science*, 1974, *186*, 1213–1215.

Imperato-McGinley, Julianne; Peterson, Ralph E.; Gautier, Teofilo; and Sturla, Erasmo. Androgens and the evolution of male-gender identity among male pseudohermaphrodites with 5α-reductase deficiency. *New England Journal of Medicine*, 1979, *300*, 1233–1237.

Inglis, James, and Lawson, J. S. Sex differences in the effects of unilateral brain damage on intelligence. *Science*, 1981, *212*, 693–695.

Ivey, Melville E., and Bardwick, Judith M. Patterns of affective fluctuations in the menstrual cycle. *Psychosomatic Medicine*, 1968, *30*, 336–345.

Jarvik, Lissy F.; Klodin, Victor; and Matsuyama, Steven S. Human aggression and the extra Y chromosome. *American Psychologist*, 1973, *28*, 674–682.

Jolly, Alison. *The evolution of primate behavior*. New York: Macmillan, 1972.

Keen, Sam. Eros and Alley Oop (Interview with Donald Symons). *Psychology Today*, February 1981, 53–56, 59–61.

Konner, Melvin. She & he: The differences start in the genes, trigger the hormones, shape the brain, and direct behavior. *Science 82*, September 1982, *3*, 54–61.

Kreuz, Leo E., and Rose, Robert M. Assessment of aggressive behavior and plasma testosterone in a young criminal population. *Psychosomatic Medicine*, 1972, *34*, 321–332.

Lancaster, Jane Beckman. In praise of the achieving female monkey. *Psychology Today*, September 1973, *7*, 30ff.

Levine, Seymour. Sex differences in the brain. *Scientific American*, April 1966, *214*, 84–90.

Levy, Jerre. Yes, Virginia, there is a difference: Sex differences in human brain asymmetry and in psychology. *The L.S.B. Leakey Foundation News*, No. 20, Fall 1981.

Loehlin, John C.; Sharan, Shlomo; and Jacoby, Rivka. In pursuit of the "spatial gene": A family study. *Behavior Genetics*, 1978, *8*, 27–42.

Maccoby, Eleanor E. *Social development: Psychological growth and the parent-child relationship*. New York: Harcourt Brace Jovanovich, 1980.

Mandler, George. *Mind and body*. New York: Norton, 1984.

McEwen, Bruce S. Interactions between hormones and nerve tissue. *Scientific American*, 1976, *235*, 48–58.

McEwen, Bruce S. Estrogens: Influences on brain development and neuroendocrine function. *Banbury Report 11*, Cold Spring Harbor Laboratory, 1982.

McEwen, Bruce S. Gonadal steroid influences on brain development and sexual differentiation. In Roy O. Greep (ed.), *Reproductive physiology IV. International Review of Physiology*, vol. 27. Baltimore: University Park Press, 1983, 99–145.

McGlone, Jeannette. Sex differences in functional brain asymmetry. *Cortex*, 1978, *14*, 122–128.

McGlone, Jeannette. Sex differences in human brain asymmetry: A critical survey. *Behavioral and Brain Sciences*, 1980, *3*, 215–227.

Meyer-Bahlburg, Heino F. L.; Boon, Donald A.; Sharma, Minoti; and Edwards, John A. Aggressiveness and testosterone measures in man. *Psychosomatic Medicine*, 1974, *36*, 269–274.

Mitchell, Gary; Redican, William K.; and Gomber, Jody. Lesson from a primate: Males can raise babies. *Psychology Today*, April 1974, *7*(11), 63–68.

Money, John. Sex determination and sex stereotyping: Aristotle to H-Y antigen. Invited address delivered at the 58th annual meeting of the Western Psychological Association, San Francisco, 1978.

Money, John, and Ehrhardt, Anke A. *Man and woman, boy and girl*. Baltimore: Johns Hopkins Press, 1972.

Moyer, Kenneth E. Sex differences in aggression. In Richard C. Friedman, Ralph M. Richart, and Raymond L. Vande Wiele (eds.), *Sex differences in behavior*. New York: Wiley, 1974, 335–372.

Neugarten, Bernice L. A new look at menopause. *Psychology Today*, December 1967, *1*(7), 42–45ff.

Neugarten, Bernice L. Adult personality: Towards a psychology of the life cycle. In W. Sze (ed.), *Human life cycle*. New York: Aronson, 1975.

Nolen, William. *Healing: A doctor in search of a miracle*. New York: Random House, 1975.

Paige, Karen E. The effects of oral contraceptives on affective fluctuations associated with the menstrual cycle. *Psychosomatic Medicine*, 1971, *33*, 515–537.

Paige, Karen E. Women learn to sing the menstrual blues. *Psychology Today*, September 1973, *7*(4), 41–43ff.

Paige, Karen E., and Paige, Jeffery M. *Politics and reproductive rituals*. Berkeley: University of California Press, 1981.

Pappas, C. T. E.; Diamond, M. C.; and Johnson, R. E. Effects of ovariectomy and differential experience on rat cerebral cortical morphology. *Brain Research*, 1978, *154*, 53.

Parlee, Mary Brown. The premenstrual syndrome. *Psychological Bulletin*, 1973, *80*, 454–465.

Parlee, Mary Brown. Changes in moods and activation levels during the menstrual cycle in experimentally naive subjects. *Psychology of Women Quarterly*, 1982, *7*(2), 119–131.

Parsons, Jacquelynne E. Psychosexual neutrality: Is anatomy destiny? In Jacquelynne E. Parsons (ed.), *The psychobiology of sex differences and sex roles*. Washington: Hemisphere Publishing, 1980.

Perlmutter, Johanna F. A gynecological approach to menopause. In Malkah T. Notman and Carol C. Nadelson (eds.), *The woman patient: Medical and psychological interfaces*. Vol. 1 of *Sexual and reproductive aspects of women's health care*. New York: Plenum, 1978.

Persky, Harold. Reproductive hormones, moods, and the menstrual cycle. In Richard C. Friedman, Ralph M. Richart, and Raymond L. Vande Wiele (eds.), *Sex differences in behavior*. New York: Wiley, 1974, 455–466.

Persky, Harold; Smith, Keith D.; and Basu, Gopal K. Relation of psychologic measures of aggression and hostility to testosterone production in man. *Psychosomatic Medicine*, 1971, *33*, 265–277.

Petersen, Anne C. Physical androgyny and cognitive functioning in adolescents. *Developmental Psychology*, 1976, *12*, 524–533.

Petersen, Anne C. Biopsychosocial processes in the development of sex-related differences. In Jacquelynne E. Parsons (ed.), *The psychobiology of sex differences and sex roles*. Washington: Hemisphere Publishing, 1980, 31–55.

Phoenix, Charles; Goy, Robert; and Resko, J. A. Psychosexual differentiation as a function of androgenic stimulation. In M. Diamond (ed.), *Reproduction and sexual behavior*. Bloomington, Ind.: Indiana University Press, 1968, 33–49.

Powledge, Tabitha M. Just-so stories. *The Nation*, May 29, 1982, 658–660.

Raisman, Geoffrey, and Field, Pauline M. Sexual dimorphism in the neuropil of the preoptic area of the rat and its dependence on neonatal androgen. *Brain Research*, 1973, *54*, 1–29.

Reuben, David. *Everything you always wanted to know about sex (but were afraid to ask)*. New York: D. McKay, 1969.

Rose, Robert M.; Gordon, Thomas P.; and Bernstein, Irwin S. Plasma testosterone levels in the male rhesus: Influences of sexual and social stimuli. *Science*, 1972, *178*, 643–645.

Rose, Robert M.; Holaday, John W.; and Bernstein, Irwin S. Plasma testosterone, dominance rank, and aggressive behavior in male rhesus monkeys. *Nature*, 1971, *231*, 366–368.

Rosenblatt, Jay S. Nonhormonal basis of maternal behavior in the rat. *Science*, 1967, *156*, 1512–1514.

Rosenblatt, Jay S. The development of maternal responsiveness in the rat. *American Journal of Orthopsychiatry*, 1969, *39*, 36–56.

Rubin, Robert T.; Reinisch, June M.; and Haskett, Roger F. Postnatal gonadal steroid effects on human behavior. *Science*, 1981, *211*, 1318–1324.

Ruble, Diane N. Premenstrual symptoms: A reinterpretation. *Science*, 1977, *197*, 291–292.

Ruble, Diane N.; Brooks-Gunn, Jeanne; and Clarke, Anne. Research on menstrual-related psychological changes: Alternative perspectives. In Jacquelynne E. Parsons (ed.), *The psychobiology of sex differences and sex roles*. Washington: Hemisphere Publishing, 1980, 227–243.

Seaman, Barbara. *Free and female*. Greenwich, Conn.: Fawcett Publications, 1972.

Sherfey, Mary Jane. *The nature and evolution of female sexuality*. New York: Vintage, 1973.

Sherif, Carolyn Wood. Bias in psychology. In Julia A. Sherman and Evelyn Torton Beck (eds.), *The prism of sex: Essays in the sociology of knowledge*. Madison: University of Wisconsin Press, 1979, 93–133.

Sherman, Julia. *On the psychology of women: A survey of empirical studies*. Springfield, Ill.: Charles C. Thomas, 1971.

Shields, Stephanie. Functionalism, Darwinism, and the psychology of women. *American Psychologist*, 1975, *30*, 739–754.

Silverberg, James. Sociobiology, the new synthesis? An anthropologist's perspective. In George W. Barlow and James Silverberg (eds.), *Sociobiology: Beyond nature/ nurture? Reports, definitions and debate*. AAAS selected symposium. Boulder: Westview Press, 1980, 25–74.

Stannard, Una. Adam's rib, or the woman within. *Trans-action*, 1970, *8*(1), 24–25.

Strum, Shirley C. Life with the "Pumphouse Gang." *National Geographic*, 1975, *147*, 673–691.

Symons, Donald. *The evolution of human sexuality*. New York: Oxford University Press, 1979.

Tampax, Inc. *The Tampax report*. (Conducted by Research & Forecasts, Inc.) Lake Success, N. Y., 1981.

Tavris, Carol. Who likes women's liberation and why: The case of the unliberated liberals. *Journal of Social Issues*, 1973, *29*(4), 175–194.

Thornhill, Randy. Rape in *Panorpa* scorpionflies and a general rape hypothesis. *Animal behavior*, 1980, *28*, 52–59.

Tiger, Lionel. Male dominance? Yes, alas. A sexist plot? No. *New York Times Magazine*, October 25, 1970, 35–37ff.

Toran-Allerand, C. D. Sex steroids and the development of the newborn mouse hypothalamus and preoptic area *in vitro*: Implications for sexual differentiation. *Brain Research*, 1976, *106*, 407–412.

Toran-Allerand, C. D. Gonadal hormones and brain development: Cellular aspects of sexual differentiation. *American Zoologist*, 1978, *18*, 553.

Toran-Allerand, C. D. Sex steroids and the development of the newborn mouse hypothalamus and preoptic area *in vitro*: Implications for sexual differentiation. *Brain Research*, 1976, *106*, 407–412.

Weisstein, Naomi. Tired of arguing about biological inferiority? *Ms.*, November 1982, 41–42, 45–46, 85.

Wilcoxon, Linda A.; Schrader, Susan L.; and Sherif, Carolyn W. Daily self-reports on activities, life events, moods and somatic changes during the menstrual cycle. *Psychosomatic Medicine*, 1976, *38*, 399–417.

Wilson, Edward O. *Sociobiology: The new synthesis*. Cambridge, Mass.: Belknap/ Harvard University Press, 1975.

Wilson, Edward O. *On human nature*. Cambridge, Mass.: Harvard University Press, 1978.

Wispé, Lauren G., and Thompson, James N., Jr. The war between the words: Biological versus social evolution and some related issues. *American Psychologist*, 1976, *31*, 341–347.

Witelson, Sandra F. Sex and the single hemisphere: Specialization of the right hemisphere for spatial processing. *Science*, 1976, *193*, 425–427.

Witkin, Herman A.; Mednick, Sarnoff A.; Schulsinger, Fini; Bakkestrom, Eskild; Christiansen, Karl O.; Goodenough, Donald R.; Hirschhorn, Kurt; Lundsteen, Claes; Owen, David R.; Philip, John; Rubin, Donald B.; and Stocking, Martha. Criminality in XYY and XXY men. *Science*, 1976, *193*, 547–555.

Yen, Wendy M. Sex-linked major-gene influences on human spatial abilities. Unpublished doctoral dissertation, University of California, Berkeley, 1973.

Young, William C.; Goy, Robert W.; and Phoenix, Charles H. Hormones and sexual behavior. *Science*, 1964, *143*, 212–218.

Chapter 5
Freud, fantasy, and the fear of woman:
The psychoanalytic perspective

Bettelheim, Bruno. *Symbolic wounds*. New York: Collier, 1962.

Blum, H. P. (ed.). *Female psychology: Contemporary psychoanalytic views*. New York: International Universities Press, 1977.

Burton, Roger V., and Whiting, John W. M. The absent father and cross-sex identity. *Merrill-Palmer Quarterly*, 1961, *7*, 85–95.

Chodorow, Nancy. *The reproduction of mothering: Psychoanalysis and the sociology of gender*. Berkeley: University of California Press, 1978.

Drucker, Peter F. What Freud forgot. *Human Nature*, March 1979, *2*(3), 40–50.

Figes, Eva. *Patriarchal attitudes*. New York: Stein and Day, 1970.

Finkelhor, David. *Sexually victimized children*. New York: Free Press, 1979.

Finkelhor, David. Child sexual abuse in a sample of Boston families. Paper presented at the National Conference on Child Sexual Abuse, Washington, D.C., May 1982. (a)

Finkelhor, David. Public knowledge and attitudes about child sexual abuse. Paper presented at the National Conference on Child Sexual Abuse, Washington, D.C., May 1982, (b)

Freud, Sigmund. Fragment of an analysis of a case of hysteria (the case of Dora). In James Strachey (ed.), *The Standard edition of the complete psychological works of Sigmund Freud*, vol. IX. London: The Hogarth Press and the Institute of Psycho-Analysis (1964 edition), 1905a.

Freud, Sigmund. Three essays on the theory of sexuality. In *Standard edition*, vol. VII, 1905b.

Freud, Sigmund. Civilized sexual morality and modern nervousness. In *Standard edition*, vol. IX, 1908.

Freud, Sigmund. The taboo of virginity. In *Standard edition*, vol. XI, 1918.

Freud, Sigmund. The dissolution of the Oedipus complex. In *Standard edition*, vol. XIX, 1924a.

Freud, Sigmund. Some psychical consequences of the anatomical distinction between the sexes. In *Standard edition*, vol. XIX, 1924b.

Freud, Sigmund. Femininity. In *Standard edition*, vol. XXII, 1933.

Freud, Sigmund. *A general introduction to psychoanalysis*, Joan Riviere (tr.). New York: Washington Square Press, 1960.

Freud, Sigmund. *Letters of Sigmund Freud, 1873–1939*. Ernst L. Freud (ed.). London: Hogarth Press, 1961.

Horney, Karen. *Feminine psychology*. New York: Norton, 1967.

Horney, Karen. On the genesis of the castration complex in women. In Jean B. Miller (ed.), *Psychoanalysis and women*. New York: Brunner/Mazel, 1973.

Lederer, Wolfgang. *The fear of women*. New York: Harcourt Brace Jovanovich, 1968.

Mahl, George F. *Psychological conflict and defense*. New York: Harcourt Brace Jovanovich, 1971.

Mead, Margaret. *Sex and temperament*. New York: Dell (Laurel edition), 1963.

Mead, Margaret. *Male and female*. New York: Dell (Laurel edition), 1968.

Medawar, Peter B. Victims of psychiatry. *New York Review of Books*, January 23, 1975.

Miller, Jean Baker (ed.). *Psychoanalysis and women*. New York: Brunner/Mazel, 1973.

Miller, Jean Baker. *Toward a new psychology of women*. Boston: Beacon, 1976.

Mitchell, Juliet. *Psychoanalysis and feminism*. New York: Pantheon, 1974.

Parker, Seymour; Smith, Janet; and Ginat, Joseph. Father absence and cross-sex identity: The puberty rites controversy revisited. *American Ethnologist*, 1975, *2*, 687–707.

Rush, Florence. *The best kept secret: Sexual abuse of children*. Englewood Cliffs, N.J.: Prentice-Hall, 1980.

Sanday, Peggy Reeves. *Female power and male dominance*. Cambridge: Cambridge University Press, 1981.

Story, Marilyn, and Story, Norman. Preliminary summary of results from factors affecting the incidence of incest among university students. Unpublished paper presented at the Society for the Scientific Study of Sex, 1982.

Sulloway, Frank J. *Freud, biologist of the mind*. New York: Basic Books, 1979.

Chapter 6
Getting the message:
The learning perspective

Atkinson, John W. (ed.) *Motives in fantasy, action, and society: A method of assessment and study*. Princeton, N.J.: Van Nostrand, 1958.

Bandura, Albert. Social-learning theory of identificatory processes. In David A. Goslin (ed.), *Handbook of socialization theory and research*. Chicago: Rand McNally, 1969, 213–262.

Bandura, Albert, and Huston, Aletha C. Identification as a process of incidental learning. *Journal of Abnormal and Social Psychology*, 1961, *63*, 311–318.

Bandura, Albert; Ross, Dorothea; and Ross, Sheila A. A comparative test of the status envy, social power, and secondary reinforcement theories of identificatory learning. *Journal of Abnormal and Social Psychology*, 1963, *67*, 527–534.

Bandura, Albert, and Walters, Richard H. *Social learning and personality development*. New York: Holt, Rinehart and Winston, 1963.

Baumgartner, Alice. "My daddy might have loved me": Student perceptions of differences between being male and being female. Paper published by the Institute for Equality in Education, Denver, 1983.

Baumrind, Diana. New directions in socialization research. *American Psychologist*, 1980, *35*, 639–652.

Beauvoir, Simone de. The second sex (H. M. Parshley, tr. and ed.). New York: Knopf, 1953.

Bem, Sandra L. The measurement of psychological androgyny. *Journal of Consulting and Clinical Psychology*, 1974, *42*, 155–162.

Bem, Sandra Lipsitz. Androgyny vs. the tight little lives of fluffy women and chesty men. *Psychology Today,* September 1975, *9*(4), 58–59ff.

Bem, Sandra L. Beyond androgyny: Some presumptuous prescriptions for a liberated sexual identity. In Julia Sherman and Florence Denmark (eds.), *The Future of women: Issues in psychology.* New York: Psychological Dimensions, 1978.

Bem, Sandra Lipsitz. Gender schema theory: A cognitive account of sex typing. *Psychological Review,* 1981, *88,* 354–364.

Bem, Sandra Lipsitz. Gender schema theory and its implications for child development: Raising gender-aschematic children in a gender-schematic society. *Signs,* Summer 1983, *8*(4), 598–616.

Bem, Sandra L., and Bem, Daryl J. Case study of a nonconscious ideology: Training the woman to know her place. In Sue Cox (ed.), *Female psychology: The emerging self.* Chicago: Science Research Associates, 1976, 180–190.

Bernard, Jessie. *Women, wives, mothers: Values and options.* Chicago: Aldine, 1975.

Brown, Roger, and Ford, Marguerite. Address in American English. *Journal of Abnormal and Social Psychology,* 1961, *62,* 375–385.

Brown, Roger, and Gilman, Albert. The pronouns of power and solidarity. In Thomas A. Sebeok (ed.), *Style in language.* Cambridge, Mass.: MIT Press, 1960.

Burr, Elizabeth; Dunn, Susan; and Farquhar, Norma. Women and the language of inequality. *Social Education,* 1972, *36,* 841–845.

Casserly, P. L. The advanced placement teacher as the critical factor in high school women's decisions to persist in the study of mathematics. Paper presented at the annual meeting of the American Educational Research Association, San Francisco, 1979.

Chodorow, Nancy. *The reproduction of mothering: Psychoanalysis and the sociology of gender.* Berkeley and Los Angeles: University of California Press, 1978.

Condry, John, and Condry, Sandra. Sex differences: A study of the eye of the beholder. *Child Development,* 1976, *47,* 812–819.

Condry, John, and Dyer, Sharon. Fear of success: Attribution of the cause to the victim. *Journal of Social Issues,* 1976, *32*(3), 63–83.

Connor, Jane M., and Serbin, Lisa A. Behaviorally based masculine- and feminine-activity-preference scales for preschoolers: Correlates with other classroom behaviors and cognitive tests. *Child Development,* 1977, *48,* 1411–1416.

Constantinople, Anne. Masculinity-femininity: An exception to a famous dictum? *Psychological Bulletin,* 1973, *80,* 389–407.

Crosby, Faye, and Nyquist, Linda. Androgyny and its assumptions. Unpublished paper, Yale University, 1978.

Damon, William. *The social world of the child.* San Francisco: Jossey-Bass, 1977.

Dinnerstein, Dorothy. *The mermaid and the minotaur: Sexual arrangements and human malaise.* New York: Harper and Row, 1977.

Eccles (Parsons), Jacquelynne. Sex differences in math achievement and course enrollment. Paper presented at the annual meeting of the American Educational Research Association, New York, March 1982.

Fishman, Pamela M. Interaction: The work women do. *Social Problems,* 1978, *25,* 397–406.

Fox, Lynn H. The effects of sex-role socialization on mathematics participation and achievement. *Women and mathematics: Research perspectives for change.* NIE Papers in Education and Work no. 8, 1977.

Francis, Susan J. Sex differences in nonverbal behavior. *Sex Roles,* 1979, *5,* 519–535.

Gagnon, John H., and Simon, William. They're going to learn in the streets anyway. *Psychology Today*, July 1969, *3*(2), 46–47ff.

Gagnon, John H., and Simon, William. *Sexual conduct: The social sources of human sexuality*. Chicago: Aldine, 1973.

Garnets, Linda, and Pleck, Joseph. Sex role identity, androgyny, and sex role transcendence: A sex role strain analysis. Paper presented at the 86th annual convention of the American Psychological Association, Toronto, 1978.

Gerbner, George, and Gross, Larry. The scary world of TV's heavy viewer. *Psychology Today*, April 1976, *9*(11), 41–45ff.

Gerbner, George; Gross, Larry; Morgan, Michael; and Signorielli, Nancy. Media and the family: Images and impact. Paper presented at the National Research Forum on Family Issues, White House Conference on Families, Washington, D.C., April 1980.

Gerbner, George, and Signorielli, Nancy. Women and minorities in television drama 1969–1978. The Annenberg School of Communications, University of Pennsylvania, 1979.

Gilligan, Carol. *In a different voice: Psychological theory and women's development*. Cambridge, Mass.: Harvard University Press, 1982.

Hacker, Helen Mayer. Women as a minority group. *Social Forces*, October 1951, *30*, 60–69.

Henley, Nancy. The politics of touch. Paper presented at the 78th annual meeting of the American Psychological Association, Miami Beach, 1970.

Henley, Nancy, and Freeman, Jo. The sexual politics of interpersonal behavior. In Sue Cox (ed.), *Female psychology: The emerging self*. Chicago: Science Research Associates, 1976, 171–179.

Hoffman, Lois Wladis. Early childhood experiences and women's achievement motives. *Journal of Social Issues*, 1972, *28*(2), 129–155.

Hoffman, Lois Wladis. Fear of success in males and females: 1965 and 1971. *Journal of Consulting and Clinical Psychology*, 1974, *42*, 353–358.

Hoffman, Lois Wladis. Fear of success in 1965 and 1974: A follow-up study. *Journal of Consulting and Clinical Psychology*, 1977, *45*, 310–321.

Horner, Matina S. Fail: bright women. *Psychology Today*, November 1969, *3*(6), 36–38ff.

Hyde, Janet Shibley. Children's understanding of sexist language. *Developmental Psychology*, 1984 (in press).

Joffe, Carole. Sex role socialization and the nursery school: As the twig is bent. *Journal of Marriage and the Family*, 1971, *33*, 467–475.

Kelly, Jeffrey A., and Worell, Judith. New formulations of sex roles and androgyny: A critical review. *Journal of Consulting and Clinical Psychology*, 1977, *45*, 1101–1115.

Kohlberg, Lawrence. A cognitive-developmental analysis of children's sex-role concepts and attitudes. In Eleanor E. Maccoby (ed.), *The development of sex differences*. Stanford, Calif.: Stanford University Press, 1966, 82–173.

Kohlberg, Lawrence. Stage and sequence: The cognitive-developmental approach to socialization. In David A. Goslin (ed.), *Handbook of socialization theory and research*. Chicago: Rand McNally, 1969, 347–480.

Kohlberg, Lawrence, and Zigler, Edward. The impact of cognitive maturity on the development of sex-role attitudes in the years 4 to 8. *Genetic Psychology Monographs*, 1967, *75*, 89–165.

Lakoff, Robin. *Language and woman's place*. New York: Colophon/Harper and Row, 1975.

Langlois, Judith H., and Downs, A. Chris. *Mothers and peers as socialization agents of sex-typed play behaviors in young children.* Unpublished paper, Psychology Department, University of Texas, Austin, Texas, 1979.

Lever, Janet. Sex differences in the games children play. *Social Problems,* 1976, *23*(4), 478–487.

Lever, Janet. Sex differences in the complexity of children's play and games. *American Sociological Review,* 1978, *43,* 471–483.

Lubinski, David; Tellegen, Auke; and Butcher, James N. Masculinity, femininity, and androgyny viewed and assessed as distinct concepts. *Journal of Personality and Social Psychology,* 1983, *44,* 428–439.

Lynn, David B. The process of learning parental and sex-role identification. *Journal of Marriage and the Family,* 1966, *28,* 466–470.

Maccoby, Eleanor E. *Social development: Psychological growth and the parent-child relationship.* New York: Harcourt Brace Jovanovich, 1980.

Maccoby, Eleanor Emmons, and Jacklin, Carol Nagy. *The psychology of sex differences.* Stanford, Calif.: Stanford University Press, 1974.

MacKay, Donald G., and Konishi, Toshi. Pronouns, attitudes, personification, and sexism in language. Paper presented at the 90th annual meeting of the American Psychological Association, Washington, D.C., August 1982.

Martyna, Wendy. Comprehension of the generic masculine: Inferring "she" from "he." Paper presented at the 85th annual meeting of the American Psychological Association, San Francisco, August 1977.

Mayo, Clara, and Henley, Nancy M. (eds.). *Gender and nonverbal behavior.* New York: Springer-Verlag, 1981.

McArthur, Leslie Zebrowitz. Television and sex role stereotyping: Are children being programmed? *The Brandeis Quarterly,* January 1982, *2,* 12–13.

Mischel, Walter. A social-learning view of sex differences in behavior. In Eleanor E. Maccoby (ed.), *The development of sex differences.* Stanford, Calif.: Stanford University Press, 1966, 56–81.

Mischel, Walter. Sex-typing and socialization. In Paul H. Mussen (ed.), *Carmichael's manual of child psychology,* vol. 2. New York: Wiley, 1970, 3–72.

Mischel, Walter, and Grusec, Joan. Determinants of the rehearsal and transmission of neutral and aversive behaviors. *Journal of Personality and Social Psychology,* 1966, *3,* 197–205.

Morgan, Michael. Television and adolescents' sex role stereotypes: A longitudinal study. *Journal of Personality and Social Psychology,* 1982, *43,* 947–955.

Motowidlo, Stephan J. Sex role orientation and behavior in a work setting. *Journal of Personality and Social Psychology,* 1982, *42,* 935–945.

Mussen, Paul H. Long-term consequents of masculinity of interests in adolescence. *Journal of Consulting Psychology,* 1962, *26,* 435–440.

Parlee, Mary Brown. Conversational politics. *Psychology Today,* May 1979, *12*(12), 48–49, 51–52, 55–56.

Pleck, Joseph H. *The myth of masculinity.* Cambridge, Mass.: MIT Press, 1981.

Rebecca, Meda; Hefner, Robert; and Oleshansky, Barbara. A model of sex-role transcendence. *Journal of Social Issues,* 1976, *32*(3), 197–206.

Robbins, Lillian, and Robbins, Edwin. Comment on "Toward an understanding of achievement-related conflicts in women." *Journal of Social Issues,* 1973, *29*(1), 133–137.

Rubin, Jeffrey Z.; Provenzano, Frank J.; and Luria, Zella. The eye of the beholder: Parents' views on sex of newborns. *American Journal of Orthopsychiatry,* 1974, *44,* 512–519.

Sears, Robert R. Sex-typing, object choice, and child rearing. In Herant A. Katchadourian (ed.), *Human sexuality: A comparative and developmental perspective*. Berkeley and Los Angeles: University of California Press, 1979, 204–222.

Serbin, Lisa A., and Connor, Jane M. Environmental control of sex related behaviors in the preschool. Paper presented to the Society for Research in Child Development, San Francisco, March 1979.(a)

Serbin, Lisa A., and Connor, Jane M. Sex-typing of children's play preferences and patterns of cognitive performance. *Journal of Genetic Psychology*, 1979, *134*, 315–316.(b)

Serbin, Lisa A., and O'Leary, K. Daniel. How nursery schools teach girls to shut up. *Psychology Today*, December 1975, 9(7), 56–58ff.

Shaver, Phillip. Questions concerning fear of success and its conceptual relatives. *Sex Roles*, 1976, *2*, 305–320.

Simon, William, and Gagnon, John H. Psychosexual development. *Trans-action*, March 1969, 6, 9–18.

Smith, Peter K., and Daglish, Linda. Sex differences in parent and infant behavior in the home. *Child Development*, 1977, *48*, 1250–1254.

Spence, Janet T. Comment on Lubinski, Tellegen, and Butcher's "Masculinity, femininity, and androgyny viewed and assessed as distinct concepts." *Journal of Personality and Social Psychology*, 1983, *44*, 440–446.

Spence, Janet T., and Helmreich, Robert L. *Masculinity & femininity: Their psychological dimensions, correlates, and antecedents*. Austin: University of Texas Press, 1978.

Spence, Janet T.; Helmreich, Robert L.; and Stapp, Joy. Ratings of self and peers on sex role attributes and their relation to self-esteem and conceptions of masculinity and femininity. *Journal of Personality and Social Psychology*, 1975, *32*, 29–39.

St. Peter, Shirley. Jack went up the hill . . . but where was Jill? *Psychology of Women Quarterly*, 1979, *4*, 256–260.

Sternglanz, Sarah H., and Serbin, Lisa A. Sex role stereotyping in children's television programs. *Developmental Psychology*, 1974, *10*, 710–715.

Thorne, Barrie, and Henley, Nancy M. (eds.). *Language and sex: Difference and dominance*. Rowley, Mass.: Newbury House, 1975.

Tresemer, David. Fear of success: Popular but unproven. *Psychology Today*, March 1974, 7(10), 82–85.

U'Ren, Marjorie B. The image of women in textbooks. In Vivian Gornick and Barbara K. Moran (eds.), *Woman in sexist society: Studies in power and powerlessness*. New York: New American Library, 1971, 318–346.

Walkup, Hugh, and Abbott, Robert D. Cross-validation of item selection on the Bem Sex Role Inventory. *Applied Psychological Measurement*, 1978, *2*(1), 63–71.

Weitzman, Lenore J.; Eifler, Deborah; Hokada, Elizabeth; and Ross, Catherine. Sex role socialization in picture books for pre-school children. *American Journal of Sociology*, 1972, *77*, 1125–1150.

Will, Jerrie; Self, Patricia; and Datan, Nancy. Paper presented at the 82nd annual convention of the American Psychological Association, 1974.

Women on Words and Images. *Dick and Jane as victims: Sex stereotyping in children's readers*. Expanded edition. Princeton, N.J., 1975. (a)

Women on Words and Images. Channeling children: Sex stereotyping on prime TV. Princeton, N.J., 1975. (b)

Zimmerman, Don H., and West, Candace. Sex roles, interruptions, and silences in conversation. In Barrie Thorne and Nancy Henley (eds.), *Language and sex: Difference and dominance*. Rowley, Mass.: Newbury House, 1975.

Chapter 7
Earning the bread versus baking it: The sociological perspective

Bart, Pauline. Depression in middle-aged women. In Vivian Gornick and Barbara K. Moran (eds.), *Woman in sexist society*. New York: New American Library, 1971, 163–186.

Baucom, Donald H. Sex role identity and the decision to regain control among women: A learned helplessness investigation. *Journal of Personality and Social Psychology*, February 1983, *44*(2), 334–343.

Becker, Gary. *Human capital*. New York: Columbia University Press, 1964.

Bernard, Jessie. *The future of marriage*. New York: Bantam, 1972.

Bernard, Jessie. The good-provider role: Its rise and fall. *American Psychologist*, January 1981, *36*(1), 1–12.

Birnbaum, Judith A. Life patterns and self-esteem in gifted family-oriented and career-committed women. In Martha Mednick, Sandra Tangri, and Lois Hoffman (eds.), *Women and achievement*. New York: Halsted, 1975, 396–419.

Blumstein, Philip, and Schwartz, Pepper. *American couples*. New York: Morrow, 1983.

Brim, Orville, and Kagan, Jerome. Constancy and change: A view of the issues. In Orville G. Brim, Jr., and Jerome Kagan (eds.), *Constancy and change in human development*. Cambridge, Mass.: Harvard University Press, 1980, 1–25.

Brown, George W., and Harris, Tirril. *Social origins of depression*. Riverside, N.J.: Free Press, 1978.

Bunker, Barbara Benedict. Women in groups. Unpublished ms., 1976.

Campbell, Angus. The American way of mating: Marriage sí, children only maybe. *Psychology Today*, May 1975, *8*(12), 37–43.

Clancy, Kevin, and Gove, Walter. Sex differences in mental illness: An analysis of response bias in self-reports. *American Journal of Sociology*, 1975, *80*, 205–215.

Corcoran, Mary; Duncan, Greg J.; and Hill, Martha S. The economic fortunes of women and children—lessons from the panel study of income dynamics. Paper presented at the 90th annual convention of the American Psychological Association, Washington, D.C., 1982.

Coser, Rose L., and Rokoff, Gerald. Women in the occupational world: Social disruption and conflict. *Social Problems*, 1971, *18*, 535–554.

Crosby, Faye. Roles and their role in everyday awareness. Unpublished paper, Yale University, August 1981.

Crosby, Faye. *Relative deprivation and working women*. New York: Oxford, 1982.

Crowley, Joan E. Longitudinal and cross-cohort employment patterns of women. Paper presented at the 90th annual convention of the American Psychological Association, Washington, D.C., 1982.

Crowley, Joan E.; Levitin, Teresa E.; and Quinn, Robert P. Seven deadly half-truths about women. *Psychology Today*, March 1973, *6*(10), 94–96.

Davis, Nancy J. Childless and single-childed women in early twentieth-century America. *Journal of Family Issues*, December 1982, *3*(4), 431–458.

Donnell, Susan, and Hall, Jay. Men and women as managers: A significant case of no significant differences. In John A. Shtogren (ed.), *Models for management: The structure of competence*. The Woodlands, Tex.: Teleometrics International, 1980, 467–486.

Ehrenreich, Barbara. *The hearts of men*. Garden City, N.Y.: Anchor/Doubleday, 1983.

Epstein, Cynthia Fuchs. *Woman's place*. Berkeley and Los Angeles: University of California Press, 1970.

Epstein, Cynthia Fuchs. Separate and unequal. *Social Policy*, March/April 1976, 6(5), 17–23.

Epstein, Cynthia Fuchs. *Women in law*. New York: Basic, 1981.

Epstein, Cynthia Fuchs. The new total woman. *Working Woman*, April 1983, 100–103.

Ferber, M.; Huber, J.; and Spitze, G. Preference for men as bosses and professionals. *Social Forces*, December 1979, 58(2), 466.

Ferree, Myra Marx. The confused American housewife. *Psychology Today*, September 1976, 10(4), 76–80.

Fidell, Linda S., and Prather, Jane E. The housewife syndrome: Fact or fiction? Unpublished paper, 1976.

Gillespie, Dair L. Who has the power? the marital struggle. In Sue Cox (ed.), *Female psychology: The emerging self*. Chicago: Science Research Associates, 1976, 192–211.

Gore, Susan, and Mangione, Thomas W. Social roles, sex roles and psychological distress. *Journal of Health and Social Behavior*, in press, 1984.

Gove, Walter. The relationship between sex roles, mental illness, and marital status. *Social Forces*, 1972, 51, 34–44.

Gove, Walter R., and Tudor, Jeannette F. Adult sex roles and mental illness. *American Journal of Sociology*, 1973, 78, 812–832.

Hacker, Helen Mayer. Women as a minority group. *Social Forces*, 1951, 30, 60–69.

Heilman, Madeline E. Male and female reactions to altered sex ratios in male-dominated occupations. Paper presented at the 86th annual convention of the American Psychological Association, Toronto, 1978.

Heilman, Madeline E., and Kram, Kathy E. Self-derogating behavior in women—fixed or flexible: The effects of co-workers' sex. *Organizational Behavior and Human Performance*, December 1978, 22(3), 497–507.

Heller, Trudy. *Women and men as leaders*. New York: Praeger/J. F. Bergin, 1982.

Hennig, Margaret, and Jardim, Anne. *The managerial woman*. New York: Doubleday, 1977.

Hochschild, Arlie Russell. The sociology of feeling and emotion. In Marcia Millman and Rosabeth M. Kanter (eds.), *Another voice*. Garden City, N.Y.: Anchor/Doubleday, 1975, 380–308.

Howell, Elizabeth, and Bayes, Marjorie (eds.). *Women and mental health*. New York: Basic Books, 1981.

Hughes, Everett C. *Men and their work*. Glencoe, Ill.: Free Press, 1958.

Instone, Debra; Major, Brenda; and Bunker, Barbara B. Gender, self-confidence, and social influence strategies: An organizational simulation. *Journal of Personality and Social Psychology*, February 1983, 44(2), 322–333.

Johnson, Colleen L., and Johnson, Frank A. Attitudes toward parenting in dual-career families. In Elizabeth Howell and Marjorie Bayes (eds.), *Women and mental health*. New York: Basic Books, 1981, 347–356.

Kanter, Rosabeth Moss. Women and the structure of organizations: Explorations in theory and behavior. In Marcia Millman and Rosabeth M. Kanter (eds.), *Another voice*. Garden City, N.Y.: Anchor/Doubleday, 1975, 34–75.

Kanter, Rosabeth Moss. Why bosses turn bitchy. *Psychology Today*, May 1976, 9(12), 56–59. (a)

Kanter, Rosabeth Moss. Women in organizations: Sex roles, group dynamics, and change strategies. In Alice Sargent (ed.), *Beyond sex roles*. St. Paul, Minn.: West, 1976, 371–387. (b)

Kent, David. A man in no-man's-land. *Esquire*, October 1980, 87–90.

Kimble, Charles E.; Yoshikawa, Joyce C.; and Zehr, H. David. Vocal and verbal assertiveness in same-sex and mixed-sex groups. *Journal of Personality and Social Psychology*, 1981, *40*(6), 1047–1054.

Kohn, Melvin L., and Schooler, Carmi. Occupational experience and psychological functioning: An assessment of reciprocal effects. *American Sociological Review*, February 1973, *38*, 97–118.

Kohn, Melvin L., and Schooler, Carmi. The reciprocal effects of the substantive complexity of work and intellectual flexibility: A longitudinal assessment. *American Journal of Sociology*, July 1978, *84*, 24–52.

Kulka, Richard and Colten, Mary Ellen. Secondary analysis of a longitudinal survey of educated women: A social psychological perspective. *Journal of Social Issues*, Spring 1982, *38*(1), 73–87.

Lieberman, Seymour. The effects of changes in roles on the attitudes of role occupants. In H. Proshansky and B. Seidenberg (eds.), *Basic studies in social psychology*. New York: Holt, Rinehart and Winston, 1965, 485–494.

Lorber, Judith. Women and medical sociology: Invisible professionals and ubiquitous patients. In Marcia Millman and Rosabeth Moss Kanter (eds.), *Another voice*. Garden City, N.Y.: Anchor/Doubleday, 1975, 75–106.

Lykes, M. Brinton, and Stewart, Abigail. Studying the effects of early experiences on women's career achievement. Paper presented at the 90th annual convention of the American Psychological Association, Washington, D.C., 1982.

McElfresh, Stephen B. Conjugal power and legitimating norms: A new perspective on resource theory. Paper presented at the 90th annual convention of the American Psychological Association, Washington, D.C., 1982.

Milgram, Stanley. The frozen world of the familiar stranger. A conversation with Stanley Milgram, by Carol Tavris. *Psychology Today*, June 1974, *8*(1), 70–80.

Miller, Joanne; Schooler, Carmi; Kohn, Melvin L.; and Miller, Karen A. Women and work: The psychological effects of occupational conditions. *American Journal of Sociology*, July 1979, *85*, 66–94.

Mueller, Marnie W. Applying human capital theory to women's changing work patterns. *Journal of Social Issues*, Spring 1982, *38*(1), 89–95.

Myrdal, Gunnar. A parallel to the Negro problem (appendix 5), in *An American dilemma*. New York: Harper and Row, 1944.

Oakley, Ann. *Woman's work: The housewife, past and present*. New York: Pantheon, 1974.

Oppenheimer, Valerie Kincade. *The female labor force in the United States*. Population Monograph Series no. 5. Berkeley: University of California Press, 1970.

Oppenheimer, Valerie Kincade. The sex-labeling of jobs. In Mednick et al. (eds.), *Women and achievement*. New York: Halsted, 1975, 307–325.

Osmond, Marie W., and Martin, Patricia Y. Sex and sexism: A comparison of male and female sex-role attitudes. *Journal of Marriage and the Family*, 1975, *37*, 744–758.

Paige, Karen E. Indicators of sex differences in socioeconomic achievement. Unpublished paper, University of California at Davis, 1976.

Pleck, Joseph H. *The myth of masculinity*. Cambridge, Mass.: MIT Press, 1981.

Pleck, Joseph H., and Lang, Linda. Men's family role: Its nature and consequences. Unpublished paper, Wellesley College, 1978.

Poloma, Margaret M. Role conflict and the married professional woman. In Constantina Safilios-Rothschild (ed.), *Toward a sociology of women*. Lexington, Mass.: Xerox College Publishing, 1972, 187–199.

Reskin, Barbara. Scientific productivity, sex, and the location in the institution of science. *American Journal of Sociology*, March 1978, *83*(5), 1235.

Robertson, Wyndham. The ten highest-ranking women in big business. *Fortune*, April 1973, 81–89.

Robinson, Nancy H., and Robinson, John P. Sex role and the territoriality of everyday behavior. Unpublished paper, University of Michigan Survey Research Center, Ann Arbor, 1975.

Rubenstein, Carin. Wellness is all. *Psychology Today*, October 1982, *16*(5), 28–38.

Rubenstein, Carin, and Shaver, Phillip. *In search of intimacy*. New York: Delacorte, 1982.

Ruble, Diane N. and Higgins, E. Tory. Effects of group sex composition on self-presentation and sex-typing. *Journal of Social Issues*, 1976, *32*, 725–731.

Russo, Nancy F., and Olmedo, Esteban. Women's utilization of outpatient psychiatric services. *Rehabilitation Psychology*, 1983, *28*(3), 141–155.

Russo, Nancy F., and Sobel, Suzanne B. Sex differences in the utilization of mental health facilities. *Professional Psychology*, February 1981, *12*(1), 7–19.

Shaver, Phillip, and Freedman, Jonathan. Your pursuit of happiness. *Psychology Today*, August 1976, *10*(3), 26–32.

Staines, Graham; Tavris, Carol; and Jayaratne, Toby E. The queen bee syndrome. *Psychology Today*, January 1974, *7*(8), 55–60.

Steinem, Gloria. John Kenneth Galbraith: The economics of housework. *Ms.*, April 1983, 27–31.

Stewart, Abigail, and Salt, Patricia. Life stress, life-styles, depression, and illness in adult women. *Journal of Personality and Social Psychology*, 1981, *40(6), 1063–1069*.

Stone, Philip J. Child care in twelve countries. In Alexander Szalai (ed.), *The use of time*. The Hague, Netherlands: Mouton, 1972, 249–264.

Strasser, Susan. *Never done: A history of American housework*. New York: Pantheon, 1982.

Straus, Murray; Gelles, Richard; and Steinmetz, Suzanne. *Behind closed doors: Violence in the American family*. Garden City, N.Y.: Anchor/Doubleday, 1980.

Szalai, Alexander (ed.). *The use of time*. The Hague, Netherlands: Mouton, 1972.

Treiman, Donald, and Hartmann, Heidi (eds.). *Women, work, and wages*. Washington, D.C.: National Academy of Sciences Press, 1981.

Treiman, Donald, and Terrell, Kermit. Sex and the process of status attainment: A comparison of working women and men. *American Sociological Review*, 1975, *40*, 174–200.

Tsui, Anne S., and Gutek, Barbara A. A Field investigation of performance between male and female managers. Paper presented at the 90th annual convention of the American Psychological Association, Washington, D.C., 1982.

United States Department of Health, Education, and Welfare. *Selected symptoms of psychological distress*. Series 11, no. 37. Washington, D.C.: National Center for Health Statistics, 1970.

United States Department of Labor. *Monthly Labor Review*, April 1974.

Van Dusen, Roxann A., and Sheldon, Eleanor. The changing status of American women: A life cycle perspective. *American Psychologist*, 1976, *31*, 106–117.

Vanek, Joann. Time spent in housework. *Scientific American*, November 1974, *231*, 14, 116–120.

Veroff, Joseph; Douvan, Elizabeth; and Kulka, Richard. *The inner American: A self-portrait from 1957 to 1976*. New York: Basic Books, 1981.

Waldron, Ingrid. Relationships between labor force participation and women's health. Paper presented at the 90th annual convention of the American Psychological Association, Washington, D.C., 1982.

Walshok, Mary. *Blue collar women*. New York: Random House, 1981.

Weissman, Myrna M., and Klerman, Gerald L. Sex differences and the epidemiology of depression. In Elizabeth Howell and Marjorie Bayes (eds.), *Women and mental health*. New York: Basic Books, 1981, 160–195.

Wolman, Carol, and Frank, Hal. The solo woman in a professional peer group. *American Journal of Orthopsychiatry*, 1975, 45, 164–171.

Yllo, Kersti. Sexual inequality and domestic violence in American states. *Journal of Comparative Family Studies*, January 1983.

Yllo, Kersti, and Straus, Murray. Patriarchy and violence against wives: The impact of structural and normative factors. Unpublished paper, Family Research Laboratory, University of New Hampshire, 1981.

Chapter 8
The origins of roles and rituals:
The anthropological perspective

Abu-Lughod, R. Lila. A community of secrets: The separate world of Bedouin women. Paper presented at the Conference on Communities of Women, sponsored by *Signs*, Stanford University, 1983.

Atkinson, Jane M. Review essay: Anthropology. *Signs*, Winter 1982, 8(2), 236–258.

Benería, Lourdes, and Sen, Gita. Accumulation, reproduction, and women's role in economic development: Boserup revisited. *Signs*, Winter 1981, 7(2), 279–298.

Bohannan, Laura, and Bohannan, Paul. *The Tiv of central Nigeria*. Ethnographic Survey of Africa: Western Africa, part 7. London: International African Institute, 1953.

Boserup, Ester. *Woman's role in economic development*. New York: St. Martin's Press, 1970.

Brown, Judith K. Economic organization and the position of women among the Iroquois. *Ethnohistory*, 1970, 17, 151–167.

Brown, Judith K. Iroquois women: An ethnohistoric note. In Rayna R. Reiter (ed.), *Toward an anthropology of women*. New York and London: Monthly Review Press, 1975, 235–251.

Collier, Jane F., and Rosaldo, Michelle Z. Politics and gender in simple societies. In Sherry B. Ortner and Harriet Whitehead (eds.), *Sexual meanings: The cultural construction of gender and sexuality*. Cambridge: Cambridge University Press, 1981, 275–330.

Dahlberg, Frances (ed.). *Woman the gatherer*. New Haven: Yale University Press, 1981.

Deaver, Sherri. The contemporary Saudi woman. In Erike Bourguigon (ed.), *A world of women*. New York: Praeger/Bergin, 1980.

Divale, William T., and Harris, Marvin. Population, warfare, and the male supremacist complex. *American Anthropologist*, 1976, 78, 521–539.

Draper, Patricia. !Kung women: Contrasts in sexual egalitarianism in foraging and sedentary contexts. In Rayna R. Reiter (ed.), *Toward an anthropology of women*. New York and London: Monthly Review Press, 1975, 77–110.

El Guindi, Fadwa. Veiling *Infitah* with Muslim ethic: Egypt's contemporary Islamic movement. *Social Problems*, April 1981, 28(4), 465–485.

Engels, Friedrich. *The origin of the family, private property and the state*, Eleanor Leacock (ed.). New York: International Publishers, 1973.

Etienne, Mona, and Leacock, Eleanor (eds.). *Women and colonization*. New York: Praeger/Bergin, 1980.

Fazel, G. Reza. Social and political status of women among pastoral nomads: The Boyr Ahmad of southwest Iran. *Anthropological Quarterly*, 1977, *50*(2), 77–88.

Fernea, Elizabeth, and Fernea, Robert. A look behind the veil. *Human Nature*, January 1979, *2*(1), 69–80.

Friedl, Ernestine. *Women and men: An anthropologist's view*. New York: Holt, Rinehart and Winston, 1975.

Gmelch, Sharon B. Economic and power relations among urban Tinkers: The role of women. *Urban Anthropology*, Fall 1977, *6*(3), 237–247.

Gouldner, Alvin W. *The coming crisis of Western sociology*. New York and London: Basic Books, 1970.

Guttentag, Marcia, and Secord, Paul. *Too many women?* Beverly Hills: Sage, 1983.

Harris, Marvin. *Cows, pigs, wars, and witches: The riddles of culture*. New York: Random House, 1974.

Hayes, Rose O. Female genital mutilation, fertility control, women's roles, and the patrilineage in modern Sudan: A functional analysis. *American Ethnologist*, 1975, *2*, 617–634.

Johnson, Orna R., and Johnson, Allen. Male/female relations and the organization of work in a Machiguenga community. *American Ethnologist*, 1975, *2*, 634–648.

Kessler, Suzanne K., and McKenna, Wendy. *Gender: An ethnomethodological approach*. New York: Wiley, 1978.

Lamphere, Louise. Strategies, cooperation, and conflict among women in domestic groups. In Michelle Zimbalist Rosaldo and Louise Lamphere (eds.), *Woman, culture, and society*. Stanford, Calif.: Stanford University Press, 1974, 97–113.

Lancaster, C. S. Women, horticulture, and society in sub-Saharan Africa. *American Anthropologist*, 1976, *78*, 539–565.

Leis, Nancy B. Women in groups: Ijaw women's associations. In Michelle Zimbalist Rosaldo and Louise Lamphere (eds.), *Woman, culture, and society*. Stanford, Calif.: Stanford University Press, 1974, 223–243.

MacCormack, Carol P. Biological events and cultural control. *Signs*, Autumn 1977, *3*(1), 93–100.

MacCormack, Carol P., and Strathern, Marilyn (eds.). *Nature, culture and gender*. Cambridge: Cambridge University Press, 1980.

Martin, M. Kay, and Voorhies, Barbara. *Female of the species*. New York and London: Columbia University Press, 1975.

Marx, Karl. *Selected writings in sociology and social philosophy*, T. B. Bottomore (tr.). New York: McGraw-Hill, 1964.

Meigs, Anna S. Male pregnancy and the reduction of sexual opposition in a New Guinea highlands society. *Ethnology*, October 1976, *15*(4), 393–407.

Mernissi, Fatima. *Beyond the veil: Male-female dynamics in a modern Muslim society*. New York: Wiley, 1975.

Nardi, Bonnie A. Review of *Female power and male dominance*, by Peggy Sanday. *Sex Roles*, 1982, *8*(11), 1157–1160.

O'Brien, Denise. Female husbands in southern Bantu societies. In Alice Schlegel (ed.), *Sexual stratification: A cross-cultural view*. New York: Columbia University Press, 1977.

Ortner, Sherry B. Is female to male as nature is to culture? In Michelle Z. Rosaldo and Louise Lamphere (eds.), *Woman, culture, and society.* Stanford Calif.: Stanford University Press, 1974, 67–87.

Ortner, Sherry B. The virgin and the state. *Feminist Studies,* October 1978, *4*(3), 19–35.

Paige, Karen E. Sexual pollution: Reproductive sex taboos in American society. *Journal of Social Issues,* 1977, *33*(2), 144–165.

Paige, Karen E. The ritual of circumcision. *Human Nature,* May 1978, *1*(5), 40–50.

Paige, Karen E. Virginity rituals and chastity control during puberty: Cross-cultural patterns. In Sharon Golub (ed.), *Menarche.* Lexington, Mass.: Lexington Books, 1983, 155–174.

Paige, Karen E. Excision rationales in Egypt. In M. J. Good et al. (eds.), *Self and affect in the Middle East,* in press.

Paige, Karen E., and Paige, Jeffery. *The politics of reproductive ritual.* Berkeley: University of California Press, 1981.

Papanek, Hanna. Purdah: Separate worlds and symbolic shelter. *Comparative Studies in Society and History,* June 1973, *15*(3), 289–325.

Poewe, Karla O. Universal male dominance: An ethnological illusion. *Dialectical Anthropology,* 1980, *5*, 111–125.

Rapp, Rayna. Review essay: Anthropology. *Signs,* Spring 1979, *4*(3), 497–513.

Reed, Evelyn. *Women's evolution.* New York: Pathfinder, 1975.

Reiter, Rayna R. (ed.). *Toward an anthropology of women.* New York and London: Monthly Review Press, 1975.

Rogers, Susan Carol. Female forms of power and the myth of male dominance: A model of female/male interaction in peasant society. *American Ethnologist,* 1975, *2*, 727–755.

Rosaldo, Michelle Z. Woman, culture, and society: A theoretical overview. In Michelle Rosaldo and Louise Lamphere (eds.), *Woman, culture, and society.* Stanford, Calif.: Stanford University Press, 1974, 17–43.

Rosaldo, Michelle Z. The use and abuse of anthropology: Reflections on feminism and cross-cultural understanding. *Signs,* Spring 1980, *5*(3), 389–417.

Rubin, Gayle. The traffic in women. In Rayna R. Reiter (ed.), *Toward an anthropology of women.* New York and London: Monthly Review Press, 1975, 157–211.

Sacks, Karen. State bias and women's status. *American Anthropologist,* 1976, *78*(3), 565–569.

Sacks, Karen. *Sisters and wives: The past and future of sexual inequality.* Westport, Conn.: Greenwood Press, 1979.

Sanday, Peggy R. *Female power and male dominance: On the origins of sexual inequality.* Cambridge: Cambridge University Press, 1981.

Sanday, Peggy R. Female status in the public domain. In Michelle Rosaldo and Louise Lamphere (eds.), *Woman, culture, and society.* Stanford, Calif.: Stanford University Press, 1974, 189–207.

Schlegel, Alice (ed.). *Sexual stratification: A cross-cultural view.* New York: Columbia University Press, 1977.

Schneider, Jane. Of vigilance and virgins: Honor, shame, and access to resources in Mediterranean societies. *Ethnology,* 1971, *10*, 1–24.

Sharma, Ursula. Women and their affines: The veil as a symbol of separation. *Man,* 1978, *13*, 218–233.

Sherfey, Mary Jane. *The nature and evolution of female sexuality.* New York: Vintage, 1973.

Stewart, Abigail J., and Winter, David G. The nature and causes of female suppression. *Signs*, Spring 1977, *2*(3), 531–553.

Sweet, Louise E. In reality: Some Middle Eastern women. In Carolyn J. Matthiasson (ed.), *Many sisters: Women in cross-cultural perspective*. New York: Free Press, 1974, 379–397.

Tanner, Nancy, and Zihlman, Adrienne. Woman in evolution. I. Innovation and selection in human origins. *Signs*, Spring 1976, *1*(3), 389–303.

Tilly, Louise. Paths of proletarianization: Organzation of production, sexual division of labor, and women's collective action. *Signs*, Winter 1981, *7*(2), 400–417.

Turner, Victor W. Three symbols of passage in Ndembu circumcision ritual: An interpretation. In Max Gluckman (ed.), *Essays on the ritual of social relations*. Manchester, England: Manchester University Press, 1962, 124–173.

Weiner, Annette. *Women of value, men of renown: New perspectives on Trobriand exchange*. Austin: University of Texas Press, 1976.

Whitehead, Harriet. The bow and the burden strap: A new look at institutionalized homosexuality in native North America. In Sherry Ortner and Harriet Whitehead (eds.), *Sexual meanings*. Cambridge: Cambridge University Press, 1981, 80–115.

Whiting, John W.; Kluckhohn, Richard; and Anthony, Albert. The function of male initiation ceremonies at puberty. In Eleanor E. Maccoby, Theodore Newcomb, and E. L. Hartley (eds.), *Readings in social psychology*. New York: Holt, 1958, 359–370.

Youssef, Nadia. Cultural ideals, feminine behavior and family control. *Comparative Studies in Society and History*, June 1973, *15*(3), 326–347.

Chapter 9
Conclusion: The age of alliance?

Baumgartner, Alice. "My daddy might have loved me": Student perceptions of differences between being male and being female. Paper published by the Institute of Equality in Education, Denver, 1983.

Benenson, Harold. Family success and sexual equality: The limits of the dual-career family model. Paper presented at the American Sociological Association, August 1981.

Bernard, Jessie. Maternal deprivation: A new twist. *Contemporary Psychology*, 1976, 21, 172–174.

Campbell, Colin. What happens when we get the manchild pill? *Psychology Today*, August 1976, *10*(3), 86–91.

Chodorow, Nancy. *The reproduction of mothering: Psychoanalysis and the sociology of gender*. Berkeley: University of California Press, 1978.

Christopher, Robert C. Changing face of Japan. *New York Times Magazine*, March 27, 1983, 40–41, 81ff.

Crosby, Faye. *Relative deprivation and working women*. New York: Oxford University Press, 1982.

Curtin, Katie. *Women in China*. New York and Toronto: Pathfinder, 1975.

Diamond, Norma. Collectivization, kinship, and status of women in rural China. In Rayna R. Reiter (ed.), *Toward an anthropology of women*. New York and London: Monthly Review Press, 1975, 372–396.

Dodge, Norton T. *Women in the Soviet economy: Their role in economic, scientific, and technical development*. Baltimore: Johns Hopkins Press, 1966.

Ehrenreich, Barbara. *The hearts of men*. Garden City, N.Y.: Anchor/Doubleday, 1983.

Engels, Friedrich. *The origin of the family, private property and the state*, Eleanor Leacock (ed.). New York: International Publishers, 1973.

Field, Mark G., and Flynn, Karin I. Worker, mother, housewife: Soviet woman today. In Georgene H. Seward and Robert C. Williamson (eds.), *Sex roles in changing society*. New York: Random House, 1970, 257–284.

Friedan, Betty. *The feminine mystique*. New York: Norton, 1963.

Galbraith, John Kenneth. The economics of the American housewife. *Atlantic Monthly*, August 1973, 78–83.

Gurin, Patricia. Group consciousness. Report in the *Institute for Social Research Newsletter*, Institute for Social Research, University of Michigan, Spring/Summer 1982, 4–5.

Guttentag, Marcia, and Secord, Paul. *Too many women?* Beverly Hills: Sage, 1983.

Haavio-Mannila, Elina. Convergences between east and west: Tradition and modernity in sex roles in Sweden, Finland, and the Soviet Union. In Martha Mednick, Sandra Tangri, and Lois Hoffman (eds.), *Women and achievement*. New York: Halsted, 1975, 71–84.

Harris, Marvin. Male supremacy is on the way out; it was just a phase in the evolution of culture. A conversation by Carol Tavris. *Psychology Today*, January 1975, 8(8), 61–69.

Hunt, Janet G., and Hunt, Larry L. The dualities of careers and families: New integrations or new polarizations? Paper presented at the American Sociological Association, August 1981.

Knaus, William. *Inside Russian medicine*. New York: Everest House, 1981.

Lamb, Michael. Why Swedish fathers aren't liberated. *Psychology Today*, October 1982, 16(5), 74–77.

Lapidus, Gail W. *Women in Soviet society*. Berkeley: University of California Press, 1978.

Leacock, Eleanor. History, development, and the division of labor by sex: Implications for organization. *Signs*, Winter 1981, 7(2), 474–491.

Mandel, William M. *Soviet women*. Garden City, N.Y.: Anchor/Doubleday, 1975.

Martin, M. Kay, and Voorhies, Barbara. *Female of the species*. New York and London: Columbia University Press, 1975.

Marx, Karl. *Selected writings in sociology and social philosophy*, T. B. Bottomore. (tr.). New York: McGraw-Hill, 1964.

Mednick, Martha T. Shuch. Social change and sex-role inertia: The case of the kibbutz. In Martha Mednick, Sandra Tangri, and Lois Hoffman (eds.), *Women and achievement*. New York: Halsted, 1975, 85–103. (Reprinted in Palgi et al. 1983)

Moore, Barrington, Jr. *Injustice: The social bases of obedience and revolt*. White Plains, N.Y.: M. E. Sharpe, 1978.

Morgan, Robin. The first feminist exiles from the U.S.S.R. *Ms.*, November 1980, 49–56, 80ff.

Myrdal, Alva, and Klein, Viola. *Women's two roles: Home and work*. London: Routledge and Kegan Paul, 1956.

Nichols, Jack. *Men's liberation*. New York: Penguin Books, 1975.

Palgi, Michal; Blasi, Joseph; Rosner, Menachem; and Safir, Marilyn (eds.). *Sexual equality: The Israeli kibbutz tests the theories*. Norwood, Pa.: Norwood Editions, Vol. VI, 1983.

Pleck, Joseph H. *The myth of masculinity*. Cambridge, Mass.: MIT Press, 1981.

Rapoport, Rhona, and Rapoport, Robert N. The dual-career family: A variant pattern and social change. In Constantina Safilios-Rothschild (ed.), *Toward a sociology of women*. Lexington, Mass.: Xerox College Publishing, 216–245.

Safilios-Rothschild, Constantina. A cross-cultural examination of women's marital, educational, and occupational options. In Martha Mednick, Sandra Tangri, and Lois Hoffman (eds.), *Women and achievement*. New York: Halsted, 1975, 48–70.

Safir, Marilyn. The kibbutz: An experiment in social and sexual equality? An historical perspective. In Michal Palgi et al. (eds.), *Sexual equality: The Israeli kibbutz tests the question*. Norwood, Pa.: Norwood Editions, 1983, 100–129.

Scott, Hilda. *Does socialism liberate women? Experiences from eastern Europe*. Boston: Beacon Press, 1974.

Stacey, Judith. *Patriarchy and socialist revolution in China*. Berkeley: University of California Press, 1983.

Tavris, Carol. Women in China: The speak-bitterness revolution. *Psychology Today*, May 1974, 7, 43–47ff.

Tavris, Carol. *Anger: The misunderstood emotion*. New York: Simon and Schuster, 1982. Touchstone edition, 1984.

Tavris, Carol, with Alice Baumgartner. How would your life be different if you'd been born a boy? *Redbook*, February 1983, 92–95.

Tiger, Lionel, and Shepher, Joseph. *Women in the kibbutz*. New York: Harcourt Brace Jovanovich, 1975.

Trotsky, Leon. *Women and the family*. Introduction by Caroline Lund. New York: Pathfinder Press, 1970.

Copyrights and Acknowledgments

SIMON & SCHUSTER, INC.   For excerpt from *Anger: The Misunderstood Emotion* by Carol Tavris, copyright © 1983 by Carol Tavris; reprinted by permission of Simon & Schuster, Inc.

STANFORD UNIVERSITY PRESS   For Table 10, adapted from *Woman, Culture and Society*, edited by Michelle Zimbalist Rosaldo and Louise Lamphere, with the permission of the publishers, Stanford University Press, © 1974 by the Board of Trustees of the Leland Stanford Junior University.

UNIVERSITY OF CALIFORNIA PRESS   For Table 9, from *The Politics of Reproductive Ritual* by Karen E. Paige and Jeffery Paige (Berkeley: University of California Press, 1981). Reprinted by permission of the publisher.

Illustration Credits

FIGURE 1   From W. D. Ellis, ed., *A Source Book of Gestalt Psychology*. Reprinted by permission of Humanities Press, Inc., Atlantic Highlands, N.J., and Routledge & Kegan Paul, London.

FIGURE 2   From *Personality Through Perception: An Experimental and Clinical Study*, by H. A. Witkin et al. Harper & Row, 1954. Drawn from photo of Rod and Frame Test.

FIGURE 3   From J. Roy Hopkins, "Sexual behavior in adolescence," *Journal of Social Issues*, 33(2), 1977, 67–85.

FIGURE 4   Adapted from William D. Odell and Dean L. Moyer, *Physiology of Reproduction*. The C. V. Mosby Company, St. Louis, 1971.

FIGURE 5   From Kersti Yllo, "Sexual Inequality and Domestic Violence in American States," *Journal of Comparative Family Studies*, January 1983.

FIGURE 6   Adapted from *Woman, Culture, and Society*, edited by Michelle Zimbalist Rosaldo and Louise Lamphere, with permission of the publishers, Stanford University Press. © 1974 by the Board of Trustees of the Leland Stanford Junior University.

Index

Abbott, Robert D., 241
Abélard, Pierre, 2
ability, sex differences in, 46–57
abortion, 9, 339, 341, 344
Abu-Lughod, Lila, 316
achievement motivation, 244–48, 256–57, 267
activity levels, 45
Acton, William: *Functions and Disorders of the Reproductive Organs*, 83
Adam and Eve, 6, 14
Addiego, Frank, 97
adrenal glands, 139, 154
adrenogenital syndrome, 139, 141, 143
adultery. *See* sex, extramarital
Age of Enlightenment, 14
aggressiveness, 62, 71–73; socialization of, 223–24, 225–26; testosterone and, 157–58; and Y chromosome, 136
aging, 156; and menopause, 155–57
Alternate Uses Test, 52, 53
altruism, 69, 130
"amaeru" (dependence), 118
Amazons, 2
Andreas-Salome, Lou, 175
androgen, 137, 138, 139, 142, 143; levels of, 143
androgen-insensitivity syndrome, 140
androgyny, 74–75, 184, 240–42; alternatives to, 242–43
anger, 62, 72
Anthony, Albert, 306
anthropological perspective, 34, 296–334; evaluation of, 331–34, 358
Antill, John K., 75
Antonucci, Toni, 278
Antony, Mark, 2, 6
anxiety: castration, 180, 181, 187, 201, 304; male, 8; math, 50–51, 226; during menopause, 155; and menstruation, 145–46, 150, 152; premenstrual, 152; sexual, 8. *See also* castration complex
Arapesh, 190

Ardrey, Robert, 132
Aristotle, 10
Armstrong, Jane M., 51
Aronoff, Joel, 16
Ashanti, 320
assertiveness, 73
Athanasiou, Robert, 109, 111
Athens, 3, 22, 360
Atkinson, Jane, 301, 321
Atkinson, John W., 245
Australia, aborigines of, 7
Averill, James R., 62, 168
Aymara, 328–29
Azande, 328–29
Aztecs, 193

Baack, J., 164
Bachman, Jerald, 31
Bachofen, Johann Jakob: *Das Mutterrecht*, 21
Bacon, Margaret, 20
Baker, Susan W., 142n.
Bamberger, Joan, 21
Bandura, Albert, 214, 215, 220
Bantu, 302
Barbach, Lonnie G., 103
barbiturates, 276
Bardwick, Judith M., 58, 110, 111, 146, 147, 152
Barlow, George W., 128
Barnett, Rosalind, 287
Barnstone, Aliki, 17
Barnstone, William, 17
Baron, Larry, 117n.
Baron, Robert A., 137
Barrett, Elizabeth, 2
Barry, H., 20
Bart, Pauline B., 85, 86, 157, 276
Baruch, Grace, 287
Baucom, Donald, 279
Baumgartner, Alice, 208, 226, 229, 239, 355
Baumrind, Diana, 219

Bayes, Marjorie, 275
Beatrice, 2
Beauvoir, Simone de, 203, 233
Becker, Gary, 271
Bedouins, 316, 330
Beecher, Ronnie, 48
Beguines, 18
Behrman, JoAnn, 142n.
Bell, Alan P., 109, 110
Bell, Robert R., 104
Bem, Daryl J., 242, 244, 248
Bem, Sandra L., 60, 74, 240, 241, 242, 243, 248
Benbow, Camilla P., 50
Benedek, Thérèse F., 146, 152
Benenson, Harold, 350, 351
Benería, Lourdes, 313
berdache, 302
Bergler, Edmund: Kinsey's Myth of Female Sexuality (with Kroger), 93n.
Berman, Edgar F.: Compleat Chauvinist, The, 124
Berman, Phyllis, W., 70
Bernard, Jessie, 249, 289, 291, 354, 356; Future of Marriage, The, 274, 275, 276
Bernays, Martha, 175
Bernstein, Irwin S., 158
Bernstein, R. C., 58
Berscheid, Ellen, 117
Bettelheim, Bruno, 189, 190, 191, 192, 194; Symbolic Wounds, 188
Beumont, P. J. V., 149
biological perspective, 33, 124–70, 353–54; evaluation of, 168–70, 353–54, 359. See also genetics; hormones
Birnbaum, Judith, 279, 281, 288
birth-control pill, 150, 293; and menstrual anxiety, 150
birth practices in tribal societies, 309
birthrate, declining, cause of, 293, 350
birth rituals, as claims to offspring, 308–10
"black matriarchy," 361
blacks, tokenism and, 262, 265
Blackwell, Antoinette Brown, 38
Blackwell, Elizabeth, 38
Blakely, Mary Kay, 5
Blanche of Castile, 17
Block, Jeanne H., 41
Blum, H. P., 203
Blumstein, Philip, 287
Bock, R. D., 136
Bohannan, Laura, 312, 313
Bohannan, Paul, 313
Bok, Sissela, 47

Book of Proverbs, 10
Boserup, Ester, 312, 334
boys: abilities of, 47–51; and dating, 113–14; and identification process, 218–19; learning about sex, 237; and Oedipus complex, 179, 180–81; and reading problems, 48; training of, 20
brain: and hormones, 164; lateralization of, 165–67; and sex differences, 163–68; and theory of inferiority of women, 15, 15n., 16
Brecher, Edward M.: Sex Researchers, The, 84
Brehony, Kathleen, 75
Briere, John, 29
Brim, Orville, 292
Brooks-Gunn, Jeanne, 148
Broverman, Donald M., 53, 54
Broverman, Inge K., 30
Brown, George, 279
Brown, Judith, 21, 298, 327
Brown, Roger, 234
Browning, Robert, 2
Brownmiller, Susan: Against Our Will, 10, 29
Brunswick, Ruth, 175
Bryant, Kendall J., 52n.
Bryden, M. P., 165
Bullough, Vern L., 6, 7, 8, 11
Bunker, Barbara, 260, 261
Burgess, Ann W., 133
Burke, Deborah, 149, 154
Burnett, Gayle, 149, 154
Burnett, Sarah A., 51
Burr, Elizabeth, 234
Burton, Roger V., 191
Butcher, James N., 241, 242n.

Campbell, Angus, 275
Campbell, Bruce, 117
cancer: fear of, 156; synthetic estrogen and, 155n.
Casanova, 112
Casserly, P. L., 226
castration complex, 180, 181, 185, 187, 201, 304
castration fantasies, 200
Cato, 12
celibacy, 7, 332
Ceniti, Joe, 29
Cherulnik, Paul D., 62
Child, I. I., 20
childbirth. See birth rituals; couvade
China, ancient, 10, 20
China, People's Republic of, 46, 339,

342–44; equality experiments in, 342–44
chivalry, 10
Chodorow, Nancy, 175, 202, 219, 354
Christensen, Harold T., 111
Christian church, attitudes to women, 7, 8
Christopher, Robert, 358n.
Cioffi, Joseph, 165
circumcision, 188–89, 303, 304–07; and castration anxiety, 304; female, 362; loyalty function of, 305, 307; male, 307n., 362; as rite of passage, 306
Clarke, Anne, 148
Cleopatra, 2, 6, 17
clitoris: during arousal, 91; effective stimulation of, 92; and masturbation, 102; and orgasm, 95, 96, 96n.
Cocks, Jay, 26, 27
cognitive-developmental theory, 215–17
cognitive style, 53–56, 167
Cole-Alexander, Lenora, 24
Coleman, Lerita, 278
Collier, Jane F., 320, 321
colonization, 331
color blindness, 136
Colten, Mary Ellen, 266
communication, nonverbal, 233–36
Comnena, Anna, 4
comparable worth laws, 272n.
competition, 266
Condry, John, 221, 222, 246, 247
Condry, Sandra, 221, 222
Connor, Jane M., 52, 217, 226, 227
Constantinople, Anne, 240
contraceptives: in Israeli kibbutz, 346–49; in People's Republic of China, 342–44; in Scandinavia, 344–46; scarcity of, in Russia, 341
cooptation, 265–66
Corcoran, Mary, 271
Coser, Rose, 282, 284
courtship, 112–15
couvade, 189–90, 303, 307–10
Cox, Martha, 65
Cox, Roger, 65
Crandall, Virginia J., 67
Crano, William D., 16
creativity, 52–53
crime: men and, 72; women and, 151–53
Crosby, Faye, 241, 242, 268, 280, 284, 362, 363, 366; on "role strain," 281
Crow, 302
Crowley, Joan E., 256, 272
Crowley, William F., Jr., 159
cultural consistencies, 20–22

Cunningham, John D., 75
Curie, Marie, 46, 229
Curtin, Katie, 34e
customs: circumcision, 304–07; couvade, 307–10; polyandry, 312–13; polygyny, 312–13; and population control, 311–12; purdah, 313–18; sexual, 310–11; in social context, 304–18
Cutrona, Carolyn, 70

Daglish, Linda, 65, 214
Dahlberg, Frances, 299
Dahomeans, 320
Dalton, Katherina, 152, 153
Damon, William, 216
D'Andrade, Roy G., 20
Dante, 2
Darwin, Charles: *On the Origin of Species*, 126
Datan, Nancy, 222
date rape, 29, 113
Davis, Nancy J., 293
Deaux, Kay, 67, 68
Deaver, Sherri, 316
decontextualization, 54
DeFries, J. C., 136
Degler, Carl N., 84
de Lacoste-Utamsing, Christine, 164
DeMause, Lloyd, 162, 163
dependence, 63–65, 118
de Pizan, Christine, 4
depression, 275, 279, 345; menopause and, 156; premenstrual, 152. *See also* housewife syndrome
De Simone, Diane, 353n.
de Troyes, Chrétien, 10
Deutsch, Helene, 95, 175
DeVore, I., 130
Diamond, Marion C., 165, 167
Diamond, Norma, 344
Dictionary of Occupational Titles, 23
Die Frauenbewegung, 18
Dinnerstein, Dorothy, 219
Dion, Karen K., 118
Dion, Kenneth L., 118
DiPietro, Janet A., 45
Disraeli, Benjamin, 274
Divale, William T., 133n., 310n.
divorce, 343, 344, 360, 361
Dodge, Norton T., 340
Doering, Charles H., 159
Doi, L. T., 118
Donnell, Susan, 260
double standard, 83–86, 127
Douvan, Elizabeth, 118, 287, 291

dowager's hump, 155
Dowling, Colette: *Cinderella Complex, The*, 63
Downs, A. Chris, 223
Draper, Patricia, 326
dress for women, regulations for, 8–9
Droege, Robert C., 48
Drucker, Peter F., 179n.
dual-career couple, 349–51
Duncan, Greg J., 271
Durden-Smith, Jo, 167
Dwyer, Daisy Hilse, 5
Dyer, Sharon, 246, 247
Dysmenorrhea, 146

Eagly, Alice H., 66, 74
earnings, median weekly for men and women, 25. *See also* wage difference
Eccles, Jacquelynne, 49, 50, 51, 226. *See also* Parsons, Jacquelynne
education, of women, 11–12, 16
Edwards, Carolyn Pope, 69
egalitarianism in society, 300–01
ego, 177
Ehrenreich, Barbara, 291, 345, 363
Ehrhardt, Anke A., 137, 141–43, 142n.
Eichenbaum, Luise, 64
El Guindi, Fadwa, 317
Ellis, Havelock, 13, 195; *Studies in the Psychology of Sex*, 84
embedded-figures test, 54–56
emotionality, 61–62; during menstruation, 145–52
empathy, 59–61
Enga, 321
Engels, Friedrich, 21, 320, 339, 340; *Origin of the Family, The*, 319
Enheduanna, 17
Enkidu, 5, 6
envy, 181, 239. *See also* penis envy
Epstein, Cynthia Fuchs, 23, 256, 257, 262, 268, 284
Equal Employment Opportunity Commission, 24
equality: definition of, 351–53; ERA, 26; experiments in, 339–53; and feminist movement, 12–13; job, 24; sex-role, 349; in Soviet Union, 339–42
Equal Rights act (Switzerland), 338
Equal Rights Amendment (ERA), 26
erotica, responses to, 100–01
erotogenic stages: anal, 179; oral, 179; phallic, 179
erotogenic zones, 179
estrogen, 137, 143, 145, 146, 147, 154–55.

See also menopause; menstruation
Etienne, Mona, 301, 331
Evans, Michael, 89

family: dual-career couple, 349–51; and female sex drive, 128, 310; and health, 274–80; in the kibbutz, 346–48; and subjugation of women, 319. *See also* housework; "role strain"
Farris, Elizabeth, 68
fathers: and child care, 286–87, 291, 355; and circumcision of sons, 305–07; in kibbutzim, 347; nurturance of, 70; primate, 161–62; as role models, 218–20; and sex-typing, 223; in Sweden, 345–46
father-son rivalry, 304
Fazel, G. Reza, 321
fear of success, 245–48
Feather, N. T., 68
Feinleib, Manning F., 45
Feldman, S. Shirley, 70
female "otherness," 31–34
female paradox: attitudes vs. reality, 16–31
females. *See* women
femininity, 74, 182, 184, 192, 194, 240, 241, 242, 349. *See also* androgyny
feminist movement, 367; beginnings of, 12–13, 18
feminists, 18, 101n., 117n., 125, 174, 175, 233, 300–01
feminization of poverty, 27, 28
Fénelon, François de La Mothe, 11
Fennema, Elizabeth, 49
Ferber, M., 259
Fernea, Elizabeth, 298, 314
Fernea, Robert, 298, 314
Ferree, Myra Marx, 277, 281
fertility, female ownership of, 9
Feshbach, Norma, 72
Feshbach, Seymour, 72
Fidell, Linda S., 276
Field, Mark G., 341, 342
Field, Pauline M., 164
field independence, 54–56
Figes, Eva, 6, 11, 174
Fine, Gary A., 47
Finkelhor, David, 197
Fisher, Alan E., 161
Fisher, Helen E., 127
Fishman, Pamela, 235
Fiske, Susan, 263
Fliess, Wilhelm, 179n.
Flynn, Karin, 341, 342

Foner, Philip S., 18
foot-binding, 314
Ford, Betty, 104
Ford, Marguerite, 234
Fowler, Orson: *Amativeness, or Evils and Remedies of Excessive and Perverted Sexuality, Including Warnings and Advice to the Married and Single*, 84
Fox, Lynn H., 226
Fox, Robin: *Imperial Animal, The* (with Tiger), 132
Francis, Susan J., 235, 236
Frank, Hal, 264, 266
Freedman, Jonathan, 276, 277, 288
Freeman, Derek: *Margaret Mead and Samoa*, 353n.
Freeman, Jo, 234, 235
Freud, Sigmund, 174–205, 346; criticisms of, 174, 195–203; on homosexuality, 184; and masturbation, 102; and men's fear of women, 192–95; and Oedipus complex, 180–81; and orgasm, 95; and penis envy, 181–82, 185–95; and psychosexual development, theory of, 179–85, 183, 218; and seduction theory of neurosis, 196–98; and the unconscious, 176–79
Friedan, Betty: *Feminine Mystique, The*, 273, 345; *Second Stage, The*, 24
Friedl, Ernestine, 17, 311, 312, 313, 325, 326, 331
Frieze, Irene H., 68
Frodi, Ann M., 70, 72
Fulfilled Woman, The, 5
Furtseva, Yekaterina A., 340

Gagnon, John, 237, 238
Galbraith, John Kenneth, 358
Gandhi, Indira, 17, 294
Garai, Josef E., 40, 41, 44, 48, 52, 58
Gardner, Lytt I., 136
Garnets, Linda, 243
Gebhard, Paul H., 87, 92
Geddes, P., 15
Gelder, M. G., 149
Gelles, Richard, 288
gender, psychological, 74, 301–02
gender change, 302
gender schema, 243, 244
genetics: and aggression, 136–37; determination of anatomical sex, 137–43; and math ability, 51; and psychological traits, 129–30; and spatial ability, 136
genital mutilation, 320, 333

Gerbner, George, 230, 231
Giarrusso, Roseann, 113
Gilder, George, 300
Gilgamesh epic, 5
Gillespie, Dair, 280
Gilligan, Carol, 59, 76, 77, 78, 118, 228
Gilman, Albert, 234
Ginat, Joseph, 191
Ginsberg, Dorothy, 60
Ginsburg, Benson E., 161
girls: abilities of, 47–51; attitudes toward male role, 210–11; and dating, 113–14; and learning about sex, 237; and Oedipus complex, 179–81, 183; physical abuse of, 28; and tomboyism, 142; training of, 20
Gmelch, Sharon B., 321
Gold, Joel, 67
Goldberg, Daniel C., 97, 98
Goldberg, Herb, 59
Golub, Sharon, 152
Goodman, Ellen, 350
"good-provider" role, 289–91
Gordon, Thomas P., 158
Gore, Susan, 279
Gorski, R. A., 165
Gould, Stephen Jay, 129
Gouldner, Alvin, 332
Gove, Walter, 275
Goy, Robert W., 138, 164
Grafenberg spot, 97, 98
Great Depression, 293, 345
Greece, 22
Greenblat, Cathy S., 117n.
Gregg, Christina F., 111
Gross, Larry, 230
Groth, A. Nicholas, 133
group consciousness, 362–63
Grusec, Joan, 214
Guitton, Jean, 22
Gurin, Patricia, 362, 363
Gutek, Barbara A., 266
Guttentag, Marcia, 4, 18, 331, 360, 361, 364–65
gym gap, 44
gynecology textbooks, 85–86

Haavio-Mannila, Elina, 345, 346
Hacker, Helen Mayer, 239, 262
Hackler, Tim, 167
Hagin, Rosa A., 48
Hall, Edward T., 118
Hall, Elizabeth, 132
Hall, Jay, 260
Hall, Judith A., 60

Hariton, E. Barbara, 99, 100
Harlow, Harry F., 69, 131, 161
Harris, Marvin, 133*n*., 310*n*., 324, 331, 332, 333, 338
Harris, Tirril, 279
Hartmann, Heidi, 268
Haskett, Roger F., 141
Hatkoff, Terry S., 111, 112, 115, 116
Hatshepsut, 17
Hausfater, Glenn, 134
Haviland, John Beard, 47
Hayes, Rose, 303
Haynes, Suzanne, 45
Headstart, 230
health, 44–45; and happiness of housewives, married professionals, and single professionals, 281; and women, 274–84
heart disease, 155
Hebb, D. O., 132
Hediger, H., 161
Hefner, Robert, 243
Heilman, Madeline E., 267*n*., 270
Heiman, Julia R., 85, 101
Heller, Trudy, 259
Helmreich, Robert L., 75, 240
Héloïse, 2
hemophilia, 136
Henley, Nancy M., 61, 74, 233, 234, 235
Hennig, Margaret, 265
Herlihy, David, 17
hermaphrodites, 139–43
hermaphroditism, progestin-induced, 139
Herzog, A. Regula, 31
Hessellund, Hans, 99
Hetherington, E. Mavis, 65
Hier, Daniel B., 159
Higgins, E. Tory, 254
Hill, Charles T., 115, 116
Hill, Martha S., 271
Hindu ideology, 7, 9
Hite, Shere, 88
Hochschild, Arlie R., 116, 288
Hoffman, Lois W., 219, 246, 247
Hoffman, Martin L., 60
Hollander, Edwin P., 65
Holloway, Ralph L., 164, 167
homosexuality, 108–10, 184, 199
homunculus theory of sperm, 189
Hopi, 320
Hopkins, J. Roy, 105
hormone levels: and emotional states, relation between, 146; during menstrual cycle, 147
hormones: in adults, 143–63; and the brain, 138, 164; and cognitive style, 54; and embryonic development, 137–38; influence on maternal behavior, 160; and motherhood, 15; prenatal, 137–43. *See also* androgen; estrogen; progesterone; testosterone
Horner, Matina S., 245, 246, 247
Horney, Karen, 175, 185, 186, 187, 200, 205
housewife syndrome, 276–91
housework: history of, 17, 277–78; husbands and, 284–87, 350; in Japan, 358*n*.; on kibbutz, 346–49; in Scandinavia, 344–46; in U.S.S.R., 341–42; wives and, 276–91
Howard, Dale R., 28
Howell, Elizabeth, 275
Hrdy, Sarah Blaffer, 134
Huber, J., 259
Hughes, Everett, 265
human capital theory, 271
Hunt, Jane G., 349, 350, 351
Hunt, Larry L., 349, 350, 351
Hunt, Morton, 4, 8, 10, 88, 99, 102, 104, 106, 107, 109
Huston, Aletha C., 214
Hyde, Janet S., 56, 57, 142*n*., 234

Ibos, 302
Ickes, William J., 68
id, 177
identification theories of sex-typing, 218–21
identity, masculine vs. feminine, 203–04, 219
Imperato-McGinley, Julianne, 140
incest, 196–98
incest taboo, 180
infanticide, 132, 133*n*., 162–63, 344*n*.
inferior status, justifying, 4, 13–16
infibulation, 303
influence: vs. power, 258, 321; susceptibility to, 65–66
Inglis, James, 166
Institute for Equality in Education, 208
Instone, Debra, 261
intelligence, 46–47
Iroquois, 21, 298, 320, 328
Israeli kibbutz. *See* kibbutz
Ivey, Melville E., 146, 147

Jacklin, Carol N., 40–41n 44, 46, 48–49, 51, 53, 55, 56, 58, 59, 63, 65, 67, 71, 214, 220, 223, 225; *Psychology of Sex Differences, The* (with Maccoby), 40

Jacoby, Rivka, 136
Japan, 118, 351, 358n.
Jardim, Anne, 265
Jarvik, Lissy F., 136
Jayaratne, Toby E., 265
Jensen, Gordon D., 94
Jessor, Richard, 105, 106, 111
Jessor, Shirley, 106
Joffe, Carole, 227
Johnson, Allan G., 28
Johnson, Allen, 329
Johnson, Colleen, 283
Johnson, Frank, 283
Johnson, Orna, 329
Johnson, Ruth E., 165
Johnson, Virginia E., 88, 89, 90, 91, 93, 95, 96, 119, 182, 310; *Human Sexual Inadequacy* (with Masters), 89; *Human Sexual Response* (with Masters), 89
Jolly, Alison, 134
Juvenal, 11

Kagan, Jerome, 63, 65, 292
Kagan, Susan, 18
Kandel, Gillray L., 165
Kanter, Rosabeth, 256, 259, 260–63, 265, 267
Kantner, John F., 105–07
Karlen, Amy, 48
Kazak, 305
Keen, Sam, 169
Kelly, Jeffrey A., 241
Kent, David, 263, 266
Kephart, William M., 117
Kessler, Suzanne K., 301
kibbutz, Israeli, 346–49, 353–54, 356–57
Kimble, Charles E., 254
Kinget, G. Marion, 117
Kinsey, Alfred C., 86, 87, 91, 95, 98, 99, 100, 103, 104, 106, 107, 108
Klein, Viola: *Women's Two Roles: Home and Work* (with Myrdal), 345
Klerman, Gerald L., 275
Klodin, Victor, 136
Kluckhohn, Richard, 306
Knaus, William, 341
Kohlberg, Lawrence, 76, 77, 215, 216, 217
Kohn, Melvin, 254, 261
Kolakowski, D., 136
Komarovsky, Mirra, 31
Konishi, Toshi, 243
Konner, Melvin, 167
Koran, 7
Kram, Kathy E., 267n.

Kramer, Heinrich: *Malleus Maleficarum* (with Sprenger), 8
Kreuz, Leo E., 158
Kroger, William S.: *Kinsey's Myth of Female Sexuality* (with Bergler), 93n.
Kulka, Richard A., 118, 266, 287, 291
!Kung-san, 325
Kuse, Allan R., 51

labor, sexual division of, 17, 20–21, 323–24, 359. *See also* family; housework; work, sexual segregation in
Ladies Home Journal survey, 87
Lakoff, Robin, 233
Lamb, Michael E., 70, 345, 357
Lamphere, Louise, 313
Lampl-de Groot, Jeanne, 175
Lancaster, C. S., 326
Lancaster, Jane Beckman, 134
Lane, David M., 51
Lane, Elizabeth, 24
Lang, Linda, 287
Langlois, Judith H., 223
language, sex-typing and, 233–36
Lapidus, Gail W., 340, 341, 357
Lasswell, Thomas E., 111, 112, 115, 116
lateralization, 166, 167
Lawson, J. S., 166
Layden, Mary Anne, 68
Leacock, Eleanor, 301, 331, 339
learning perspective, 33, 208–49; evaluation of, 244–49, 354–56. *See also* socialization
Lederer, Wolfgang, 192, 193, 194, 195, 200; *Fear of Women, The*, 188
Lee, John Alan, 111
Leis, Nancy B., 313
Lenin, Nikolai, 342
Lenney, Ellen, 67
lesbianism, 109–10
Levenstein, Peggy, 149, 154
Lever, Janet, 227
Levine, Janet A., 65
Levine, Seymour, 138n.
Levitin, Teresa E., 256
Levy, Jerre, 55, 166, 167, 169
Lewin, Kurt, 239n.
Lewis, Michael, 58
libido, 176
Lieberman, Seymour, 255
Lilith, 6
Livy, 10, 12
locus of control: external, 68; internal, 67
Loehlin, John C., 136
LoPiccolo, Joseph, 85

Lorber, Judith, 262
Lorenz, Konrad, 132
Los Angeles Times, 230, 318
Lott, Bernice, 28
love, 2–3, 111, 112, 205, 237–38; and economics, 116–17; sex differences in, 115–18, 288
Lubinski, David, 241, 242n.
Luria, Zella, 221
Lykes, M. Brinton, 292
Lynn, David B., 219

McArthur, Leslie Z., 231, 232n.
Macauley, Jacqueline, 72
Maccoby, Eleanor E., 40, 41, 44–59, 63, 65, 67, 71, 166, 214, 217, 220, 223, 223n., 225; *Psychology of Sex Differences, The* (with Jacklin), 40
MacCormack, Carol P., 321
McCormick, Naomi B., 113
McElfresh, Stephen, 288
McEwen, Bruce S., 164
McGlone, Jeannette, 166
MacKay, Donald G., 243
McKenna, Wendy, 301
Machiguenga, 302, 329
Mahl, George F., 202
Mailer, Norman, 203
Maine, Henry Sumner: *Ancient Law*, 21
Major, Brenda, 261
Malamuth, Neil, 29, 101n.
male-bonding, 191
male dominance, 22, 127, 319–21; conditions of, 330–31
male fantasies, 11
Malinowski, Bronislaw, 299
Mandel, William M., 342n.
Mandler, George, 168
Mangione, Thomas W., 279
manual dexterity, 45–46
Manu code of India, 6, 10
Marcia, James E., 65
market factors at work, 269–70
marriage, 12, 27, 31, 273–91, 349, 350. *See also* family; housework.
married women holding jobs, percentage, 269
Martin, Clyde E., 87
Martin, M. Kay, 341
Martin, Patricia Y., 286
Martyna, Wendy, 60, 234
Marx, Karl, 301, 319, 320, 339, 346
masculinity, 31, 74–75, 192, 203–04, 218–19, 239–42, 292. *See also* androgyny

masochism, 182, 186
Masters, William H., 88, 89, 90, 91, 93, 95, 96, 119, 182, 310; criticism of, 89; *Human Sexual Inadequacy* (with Johnson), 89; *Human Sexual Response* (with Johnson), 89
masturbation, 84, 92–93, 99, 102–04, 180, 182; role of, in sexual development, 102–03, 237; in sex therapy, 103–04
maternal behavior, 127
maternal instinct, 159–63
mathematical ability. *See* quantitative ability
matriarchy: "black" and "white," 361; myths of, 21
Matsuyama, Steven S., 136
Mayo, Clara, 61, 74, 233
Mbuti, 303
Mead, Margaret, 20, 46, 190, 203, 302
Medawar, Peter, 174
media, sex-typing in, 228–33
Mednick, Martha, 348, 356
Meigs, Anna S., 302
Meir, Golda, 17, 291, 354
Melissa of Epidaurus, 2
men: attitude toward women, 4; envy and fear of women, 186–88; as hunters, reasons for, 324–27; in private clubs, 262; women's attitude toward, 4. *See also* boys; fathers; "good-provider" role; masculinity; work
menarche, 143
menopause: and mood, 154–57; symptoms, 154–55
menstruation: and antisocial behavior, 152–54; anxiety during, 150; attitudes toward, 6–7, 144–45, 192; biology of, 145–46; and intellectual performance, 152; and mood, 146–54; names for, 144; onset of, 143
Mernissi, Fatima, 5, 314
Mesopotamia, 22
Meyer-Bahlburg, Heino F. L., 142, 158
Middle Ages, 7
mikvah, 7
Milgram, Stanley, 253, 303
Mill, John Stuart, 12
Miller, Jean Baker, 175, 185
Miller, Joanne, 255
Minton, Cheryl, 65
misandry, 2
Mischel, Walter, 213, 214, 215, 217, 244
misogynistic attitudes, 19
misogynistic religions, 194

misogyny, 2, 183; themes of, 5–16
Mitchell, Gary, 161, 162
Mitchell, Juliet, 174, 175
Mitchell, Margaret: *Gone With the Wind*, 18
Moebius, Paul, 183
Moll, Albert, 179*n.*
Money, John, 137, 141, 142*n.*, 143
Moore, Barrington, Jr., 362, 366
Moore, Burness E., 95
moral perceptions, 75–78
Morgan, Lewis Henry, 21
Morgan, Michael, 232
Morgan, Robin, 341
Morris, Desmond, 132
Moses, 307
Mosher, Clelia D., 84
mothers: maternal "instinct" of, 159–63; nurturance by, 68–71
Motowidlo, Stephan J., 242*n.*
Moyer, Kenneth E., 145, 157
Mueller, Marnie W., 271
Muhlenberg, Adeline T., 18
Müllerian ducts, 137
Mundurucú, 302, 329
Murasaki Shikibu: *Tale of Genji, The*, 17
Murdock, George P., 20
Mussen, Paul H., 248, 249
myotonia, 90
Myrdal, Alva: *Woman's Two Roles: Home and Work* (with Klein), 345
Myrdal, Gunnar, 12, 262

Napoleon, 183
narcissism, 185
Nardi, Bonnie A., 300
Nash, Sharon C., 70, 75
National Women's Party, 26
Ndembu, 307
Nee Lu, 17
Neugarten, Bernice, 156
neuroanatomists, and female inferiority, 15
neurosis, 177, 196–98
neurotransmitters, production of, 164
Newsweek, 50
New York Times, 230, 340, 344*n.*
Nichols, Jack, 59, 366
Nietzsche, Friedrich, 13, 366
Nieu, Richard L., 136
Nolen, William, 153
nurturance, 68–71
Nyquist, Linda, 241, 242

Oakley, Ann, 279, 285
occupational titles, 23–24

occupations. *See* wage difference; work
O'Connor, Sandra Day, 23*n.*, 26
Oedipus complex, 179–81, 182, 183, 197, 199, 202, 203, 346
Offir, Carole Wade, 29, 88, 105, 106
Old Testament, 7, 268*n.*, 307
O'Leary, K. Daniel, 224, 225, 226, 227
Oleshansky, Barbara, 243
Olmedo, Esteban, 275
Oppenheimer, Valerie, 269
Oppian Law, 12
opposite sex, schoolchildren's perception of life as, 210–11
Orbach, Susie, 64
orgasm, 85, 88–91; blended, 97; clitoral, 95, 96; female, 91–92; male, 91; and male ejaculation, 94; first experience of, 103; in masturbation, 92, 97–98, 102, 103, 103*n.*; multiple female, 93–94; multiple male, 94–95; physiological responses in, 89–93; types of, 95–97
Ortner, Sherry, 315, 320
Osmond, Marie, 286
ovulation, 145, 146

Paige, Jeffery M., 151, 304–07, 307*n.*, 308, 310, 315, 316
Paige, Karen E., 144, 148, 150–51, 156, 270, 304–07, 307*n.*, 315, 333
Palgi, Michal, 347
Pan Chao, 4
Papanek, Hanna, 313, 314, 316, 317
Pappas, C. T. E., 165
Pappenheim, Bertha, 176
paradigm shift, 241
parents, and sex-typing, 214–15, 218–24
Parke, Ross D., 70
Parker, Seymour, 191
Parkinson's Law, 285
Parlee, Mary Brown, 54*n.*, 148, 150, 233
Parsons, Jacquelynne Eccles, 67, 168. *See also* Eccles, Jacquelynne
Paul, Alice, 26, 27
Payn, Nadine, 104
pedestal-gutter syndrome, 3, 116, 234
penis, 181; during arousal and orgasm, 90–91
penis envy, 176, 199, 200, 201, 202; attacks on, 185–95; consequences of, 181; symbolic interpretation of, 201
Peplau, Letitia Anne, 115, 116
Perlmutter, Johanna F., 156
Perry, John D., 97
Persky, Harold, 148, 154, 158

personality, and power, 248–49
personality differences, 57–75;
    elusiveness of, 73–75; and status, 74
personality traits, instability of, 73–74
Petersen, Anne C., 136, 159, 166
philosophes, 11
Phoenix, Charles, 138
photoplethysmograph, 101
physical strength, 43–44
Piaget, Jean, 215
Piercy, Marge, 367
Pilagá, 189
Plato, 11, 13, 15
Playboy survey, 87–88, 102, 106. *See also*
    Hunt, Morton
Pleck, Joseph H., 218, 219, 223, 238, 239,
    240, 243, 287, 291, 366
Pliny, 7
Plutarch, 4
Poewe, Karla, 300, 301, 330
political systems, equality experiments in,
    339–53
politics, women in, 26, 294
Pollack, Susan, 118
Poloma, Margaret, 283
polyandry, 19, 310, 312–13
polygyny, 19, 310, 312–13; economics of,
    312
Pomeroy, Sarah B., 3, 8, 12, 14, 21
Pomeroy, Wardell B., 87, 94
population control, sexual customs and,
    311–12, 344n.
pornography, 100, 101
poverty, feminization of, 27–28
power, 61, 185, 193; in marriage, 280; in
    men and women, 258–62; sexual dif-
    ferences, 185. *See also* influence; status
Power of the Positive Woman, The, 5
Powledge, Tabitha M., 129
pragmatic love, 116
Prather, Jane E., 276
premenstrual syndrome (PMS), 146, 147,
    148, 149, 150, 153
Priesand, Sally, 23
primate behavior, 130–35, 161–62
Profile of Nonverbal Sensitivity (PONS),
    60, 61
progesterone, 137, 145, 146, 148, 154;
    and estrogen, balance between, 160
prolactin, 160
prostaglandins, 148
protégé system, 262
Provenzano, Frank J., 221
Provost, Caterina, 20
pseudohermaphrodites, 139

psychoanalysis, 174–205; evaluation of,
    195–205; and existential identity,
    203–05; experimental evidence on,
    201–03; objections to, 196
psychoanalytic perspective, 33, 85,
    174–205; evaluation of, 195–205, 354.
    See also Freud, Sigmund
Psychology Today survey, 109, 110, 276
psychosexual stages of development,
    179–85
purdah, 298, 313–18, 362; as chastity
    control, 316; expressed purpose of,
    314; honor and shame and, 314; two
    aspects of, 314; women's defense of,
    316–17

quantitative ability, 48–51; and
    sex-typing, 226
Queen Bee, 265–66
Quinn, Robert P., 256

Raisman, Geoffrey, 164
rape, 10, 28–29, 113, 133; marital, 29
Rapoport, Rhona, 349
Rapoport, Robert, 349
Rapp, Rayna, 302, 321
Rebecca, Meda, 243
Redbook survey, 87, 108
Reed, Evelyn, 324
refractory period, 93, 95
Reilly, Mary Ellen, 28
Reinecke, William, 28
Reinisch, June M., 141
Reiss, Ira L., 104
relative deprivation, 362–63, 366
religions, attitudes to women, 6–8,
    192–94
Remote Associates Test, 53
research, biased assumptions in, 38–39,
    133–34, 142, 147, 169–70
Resko, J. A., 138
Reuben, David, 155, 156, 157
Richards, D. H., 149
Ride, Sally, 23
rituals, 304–07
Robbins, Edwin, 246
Robbins, Lillian, 246
Robbins, Mina B., 94
Robertson, Wyndham, 262
Robinson, John, 286
Robinson, Nancy, 286
Robinson, Paul, 89
rod-and-frame test, 54
Rogers, Susan Carol, 301
Rokoff, Gerald, 282, 284

roles and rituals, origins of, 296–334
"role strain," 281–84
romance vs. intimacy, 115–19. *See also*
    love
Roman Empire, 22
Rorschach Ink Blot Test, 201
Rosaldo, Michelle, 21, 300, 320, 321
Rose, Robert M., 158
Rosenberg, B. G., 142n.
Rosenblatt, Jay S., 160, 161
Rosenthal, Robert, 38, 39, 60
Rosnow, Ralph L., 47
Ross, Dorothea, 214
Ross, Sheila A., 214
Rousseau, Jean Jacques: *Emile*, 12; *Social
    Contract, The*, 11
Rubenstein, B. B., 146
Rubenstein, Carin, 31, 107, 112, 118, 275,
    277, 288
Rubin, Gayle, 312, 319
Rubin, Jeffrey Z., 221
Rubin, Robert T., 141
Rubin, Zick, 115, 116
Ruble, Diane N., 148, 149, 254
Rush, Florence, 196, 198
Russell, Diana, 28, 29
Russo, Nancy F., 275
Rwala, 328

Sacks, Karen, 301
Sadd, Susan, 104, 106, 108
Safilios-Rothschild, Constantina, 340, 351
St. Peter, Shirley, 229
Salimbene, 7
Salt, Patricia, 280
Samson and Delilah, 6, 187
Sanday, Peggy R., 298, 301, 320, 321,
    327, 328, 330, 331
Sawin, Douglas B., 70
Scandinavian countries, equality
    experiments in, 344–46
Schachter, Francis F., 47
Schackman, Maxine, 52
Scheinfeld, Amram, 40, 41, 44, 48, 52, 58
Schlafly, Phyllis, 5
Schlegel, Alice, 301, 330
Schmidt, Gunter, 100
Schneider, Jane, 315
Schooler, Carmi, 254, 261
Schrader, Susan L., 154
Schwartz, Pepper, 287
Scott, Hilda, 340, 354
Scully, Diana, 85, 86
Seaman, Barbara, 96, 97, 156, 157; *Free
    and Female*, 155

Sears, Robert R., 236
Secord, Paul, 4, 18, 331, 360, 361,
    364–65
seduction, 8
seduction theory of neurosis, 196–98
Self, Patricia, 222
self-confidence, 66–68, 261
self-esteem, 66–68, 248–49; in marriage,
    277–81
Sells, Lucy W., 49
Semonides of Amorgos, 3, 14
Sen, Gita, 313
separation, in initiation rites, 191
Serbin, Lisa A., 52, 217, 224, 225, 226,
    227, 231
sex: and courtship, 112–15; double
    standard in, 83–86, 127–28;
    extramarital, 107–08, 127; fantasies,
    99–100; learning about, 236–38;
    motives for having, 110–12; and
    perceptions of love, 110–19; premarital,
    83, 104–07, 111; scientific study of,
    86–89; sex differences in behavior,
    98–110, 236–38; Victorian attitudes
    toward, 13, 83–86. *See also*
    homosexuality; masturbation
sex characteristics, secondary, 143
sex differences, 31, 38–78; in ability,
    47–57; in activity level, 45; in
    aggressiveness, 71–73; biological
    influences on, 168–70; in cognitive
    style, 53–57; in creativity, 52–53; in
    dependence, 63–65; in emotionality,
    61–62; in empathy, 59–61; in general
    intelligence, 46–47; in health, 44–45;
    in manual dexterity, 45–46; in moral
    perceptions, 75–78; in nurturance,
    68–71; overlap in, 41; in personality,
    57–75; in physical attributes, 43–46; in
    physical strength, 43–44; in
    quantitative ability, 48–50; in
    self-esteem and confidence, 66–68;
    and similarities, 42–13; in sociability,
    57–59; in spatial-visual ability, 51–52;
    summary table of, 42–43; in
    susceptibility to influence, 65–66; in
    verbal ability, 47–48
sex drive, female, 310–11
sexes, segregation of, 3, 298, 301–02,
    320, 323–24. *See also* purdah
sex hormones. *See* hormones
sex ratios, 331, 359–62
sex-role identification, 179, 218–21
sex taboo, 7, 9, 311–12
sex therapy, 103

sex-typing: in books, 228–30; in the media, 228–33; negative consequences of, 238–40; by parents, 218–24; and play activities, 227–28; by teachers, 224–27; on television, 230–33; and verbal and nonverbal communication, 233–36
sexual arousal: by erotica, 101; physiology of, 90–91
sexual behavior surveys, 87–88
sexual dimorphism, 130–31
sexual fantasies, 99–100
sexual hostilities, 2–3, 11, 28–30, 204, 311, 346
sexual molestation, 196–98
sexual response cycle, 89–93
sexual segregation. *See* sexes, segregation of
Sharan, Shlomo, 136
Sharma, Ursula, 314
Shaver, Phillip, 109, 111, 118, 246, 276, 277, 288
Shaw, George Bernard, 12, 13
Sheldon, Eleanor, 270
Shepher, Joseph, 348, 353, 356
Sherfey, Mary Jane, 135, 310, 311
Sherif, Carolyn W., 73, 132, 154
Sherman, Julia, 49, 55, 56, 58, 152
Shields, Stephanie, 15, 16, 160
Shorter, Edward, 9, 84
Signorielli, Nancy, 230
Sigusch, Volkmar, 100
Silverberg, James, 128, 130
Simbiti, 302
Simon, J. G., 68
Simon, William, 237, 238
Simonton, Archie, 28
Singer, Irving, 97
Singer, Jerome L., 100
Singer, Josephine, 97
Sipila, Helvi, 17n.
Smith, Janet, 191
Smith, Peter K., 65, 214
Snake Woman, 193
Snow, Margaret E., 44
Sobel, Suzanne B., 275
sociability, 57–59
socialization, sex-role: by children's books, 228–30; by media messages, 228; negative consequences of, 238–40; by parents, 221–24; sex-typing as child's play, 227–28; sources of, 221–23; subliminal communication, 233–36; teachers, 224–27; television, 230

socialization theories, 213–21; cognitive-developmental theory, 215–17; identification theories, 218–22; social-learning theory, 213–15
social-learning theory, 213–15
sociobiology: evaluation of, 128–35; primate behavior and, 130–35; theories of, 126–29
sociological perspective, 33, 252–94, 355–56; evaluation of, 291–94, 356–59; and marriage, 284–91; and work, 254–73
Somali, 328
Soviet Union, 353, 354, 357–58; equality experiments in, 339–42
Sparta, 22, 360
spatial-visual ability, 51–52, 55, 56, 75; children's play and, 227
Spence, Janet T., 75, 240, 242
Spitze, G., 259
Sprenger, Jacob: *Malleus Malificarum* (with Kramer), 8
Stacey, Judith, 344
Staines, Graham, 265
Stanley, Julian C., 50
Stannard, Una, 163n.
Stapp, Joy, 240
Stassinopoulos, Arianna, 38
status, 328–29, 334; effects on behavior, 74, 222, 249, 280; and violence, 289–90
Steinem, Gloria, 26, 38, 101n., 286n.
Steinmetz, Suzanne, 288
stereotypes, 30, 40–41, 47, 52, 58–59, 61, 65, 70, 78, 208–11, 227–33, 242
Sternglanz, Sarah H., 231
Stewart, Abigail, 280, 292, 331
Stone, Philip, 287
Story, Marilyn, 197
Story, Norman, 197
strain gauge, 101
Strasser, Susan, 277, 286
Strathern, Marilyn, 321
Straus, Murray, 288, 289
Strum, Shirley, 134
subincision, 189
"Subjection of Women, The," 12
sublimation, sexual, 178
subsistence contributed by females, percentage of 17, 323–24, 329
Sue, D., 99
suggestibility, 65–66
Sulloway, Frank J., 176, 179n., 195, 197
superego, 177, 181
superincision, 303

Sweet, Louise, 317
Switzer, Ellen E., 100
Symons, Donald, 127, 169
Szalai, Alexander, 285, 287

Tampax survey, 144, 145
Tanner, Nancy, 299
Tavris, Carol, 31, 62, 104, 106, 108–09,
    111, 113, 125, 265, 343, 366
Taylor, Shelley, 263
teachers, and sex-typing, 224–27
television, sex-typing in, 230–33
Tellegen, Auke, 241, 242n.
Terrell, Kermit, 271
testes, during arousal and orgasm, 90, 91
testosterone, 137, 138, 140, 141, 157, 158,
    159; and aggressiveness, 157–58; levels
    of, 143, 156; and maternal behavior,
    161; in mice, 165; prenatal, 141;
    in rats, 164; and studies of behavior,
    157–59
textbook regulations on sexual
    stereotyping, 230
Thatcher, Margaret, 124, 294
Thematic Apperception Test (TAT), 201
Thome, Pauline R., 72
Thompson, Clara, 175, 185
Thompson, James N., Jr., 129
Thomson, J. A., 16
Thonga, 306
Thorne, Barrie, 233
Thornhill, Randy, 133
Tiger, Lionel, 152, 348, 353, 356; Imperial
    Animal, The (with Fox), 132; Men in
    Groups, 59, 132
Tikopia, 328, 330
Tilly, Louise, 331
Time, 50
Tinkers, 321
Tiv, 305, 306, 312
Tobias, Sheila, 49, 50, 51
Toda, 328
tokenism, 262–67
Tooney, Nancy, 50
Toran-Allerand, C. D., 165
Total Woman, The, 5
toxic shock syndrome, 144
tranquilizers, 276
transvestism, 190–91
Treiman, Donald, 268, 271, 273
Tresemer, David, 246, 247
Tsui, Anne S., 266
Tudor, Jeannette, 275
Turner, Victor, 307
Turner's syndrome, 138

Unger, Rhoda K., 74
United Nations General Assembly, 338
untouchables, 362
U'Ren, Marjorie B., 229
Urso, Camilla, 18
uterus, during arousal and orgasm, 91

vagina, 91, 95, 155
Vance, Ellen B., 89, 90
Vandenberg, Steven G., 51
Van Dusen, Roxann A., 270
Vanek, Joann, 285
van Vuuren, Nancy, 8
vasocongestion, 90
veiling. See purdah
verbal ability, 47–48
Veroff, Joseph, 118, 287, 291
Victorian attitudes, 13, 83–86, 102
Voorhies, Barbara, 341

wage difference, sex based, 24–25,
    270–72, 350; in China, 333–34; on
    kibbutz, 348; in U.S.S.R., 340
Wagman, Morton, 59
Wagner, Nathaniel N., 89, 90
Waldron, Ingrid, 279
Walkup, Hugh, 241
Waller, Willard, 117
Walshok, Mary, 257
Walters, Richard H., 215
"wandering uterus" syndrome, 14
Warlpiri, 321
Watson, John, 160
Webster, Paula, 21
Wechsler, David, 53
Weinberg, Martin S., 109, 110
Weiner, Annette, 299, 353n.
Weissman, Myrna, 275
Weisstein, Naomi, 133, 135
Weitzman, Lenore J., 229
West, Candace, 74, 235
Whipple, Beverly, 97
White, Leonard, 68
Whitehead, Harriet, 302, 327
Whiting, Beatrice, 69
Whiting, John W., 191, 306
Whitley, Bernard E., Jr., 30
Wieder, Robert S., 98
Wikler, Norma, 24, 27
Wilcoxon, Linda A., 154
Will, Jerrie, 222
Wilson, Bob, 29
Wilson, Edward O., 127
Windsor, Duke and Duchess of, 2
Winter, David G., 331

Wispé, Lauren G., 129
witchcraft, 8
Witelson, Sandra F., 165
Witkin, Herman A., 56, 137
Wolman, Carol, 264, 266
womb envy, 186, 188–90
women: attitudes toward, 30; attitude
  toward men, 4; as controllers of
  economic resources, 327–31;
  education of, 11; equality and, 26;
  fertility, ownership of, 9; first, 22–23; as
  gatherers, reasons for, 324–27; hostility
  to, 320; as incompetent sex, 17;
  justifying, 13–16; keeping in place,
  9–13; and labor movement, 18–19; as
  lifegivers, 320; majority in certain job
  categories, 23; and math, 49; men's
  attitude toward, 4; men's fear of,
  192–95; as obedient sex, 18; and
  physical abuse, 28–30; in politics, 26;
  power of, 193; protest by, 12; religion
  and, 6; restrictions on occupations, 24;
  salary limitations, 24; seductiveness of,
  6; sexuality, control of, 4, 5–9; sexual
  suppression of, 310–11; status of, 32,
  290; stereotypes, 40, 52; value of, 10,
  334; as weaker sex, 17
Women on Words and Images (WWI),
  228–30, 232n.
Wood, Wendy, 74

Woodward, D. J., 164
Worell, Judith, 241
work, 254–73; effects on personality of,
  254–55, 279–81; health benefits of,
  278–80; market forces on, 267–73;
  opportunities in, 256–57; power and,
  258–62; sexual segregation in, 3–4, 20,
  24, 268–70, 329–30. See also "role
  strain"
working-wife syndrome, 280–84
Wylie, Philip: Generation of Vipers, 276

Yen, Wendy M., 136
Yllo, Kersti, 289, 290
Yoruba, 328
Yoshikawa, Joyce C., 254
Young, Daniel, 165
Young, William C., 138
Yourcenar, Marguerite, 22

Zehr, H. David, 254
Zellman, Gail L., 113
Zelnik, Melvin, 105, 106, 107
Zigler, Edward, 217
Zihlman, Adrienne, 299
Zilbergeld, Bernie, 89
Zimmerman, Don H., 74, 235
Zipporah, 307
Zoroaster, 7

A 3
B 4
C 5
D 6
E 7
F 8
G 9
H 0
I 1
J 2